STOP!

You are going the *wrong way!*

Manga is a *completely* different type of reading experience.

To start at the *BEGINNING*, go to the *END!*

That's right! Authentic manga is read the traditional Japanese way–from right to left, exactly the opposite of how American books are read. It's easy to follow: just go to the other end of the book, and read each page–and each panel–from the right side to the left side, starting at the top right. Now you're experiencing manga as it was meant to be.

A Kodansha Comics Trade Paperback Original
Attack on Titan: Before the Fall volume 6 copyright © 2015 Hajime Isayama/
Ryo Suzukaze/Satoshi Shiki
English translation copyright © 2015 Hajime Isayama/Ryo Suzukaze/Satoshi Shiki

Published in the United States by Kodansha Comics, an imprint of
Kodansha USA Publishing, LLC, New York.

Publication rights for this English edition arranged through
Kodansha Ltd, Tokyo.

First published in Japan in 2015 by Kodansha Ltd., Tokyo
as *Shingeki no kyojin Before the fall*, volume 6.

ISBN 978-1-63236-224-7

Character designs by Thores Shibamoto
Original cover design by Takashi Shimoyama (Red Rooster)

Printed in the United States of America.

www.kodanshacomics.com

9 8 7 6 5 4 3 2 1
Translation: Stephen Paul
Lettering: Steve Wands
Editing: Haruko Hashimoto & Ben Applegate
Kodansha Comics edition cover design by Phil Balsman

a Silent Voice

KODANSHA COMICS

"The word heartwarming was made for manga like this." –Manga Bookshelf

"A harsh and biting social commentary... delivers in its depth of character and emotional strength." -Comics Bulletin

"A very powerful story about being different and the consequences of childhood bullying... Read it." –Anime News Network

Shoya is a bully. When Shoko, a girl who can't hear, enters his elementary school class, she becomes their favorite target, and Shoya and his friends goad each other into devising new tortures for her. But the children's cruelty goes too far. Shoko is forced to leave the school, and Shoya ends up shouldering all the blame. Six years later, the two meet again. Can Shoya make up for his past mistakes, or is it too late?

Available now in print and digitally!

INUYASHIKI

A superhero like none you've ever seen, from the creator of "Gantz"!

ICHIRO INUYASHIKI IS DOWN ON HIS LUCK. HE LOOKS MUCH OLDER THAN HIS 58 YEARS, HIS CHILDREN DESPISE HIM, AND HIS WIFE THINKS HE'S A USELESS COWARD. SO WHEN HE'S DIAGNOSED WITH STOMACH CANCER AND GIVEN THREE MONTHS TO LIVE, IT SEEMS THE ONLY ONE WHO'LL MISS HIM IS HIS DOG.

THEN A BLINDING LIGHT FILLS THE SKY, AND THE OLD MAN IS KILLED... ONLY TO WAKE UP LATER IN A BODY HE ALMOST RECOGNIZES AS HIS OWN. CAN IT BE THAT ICHIRO INUYASHIKI IS NO LONGER HUMAN?

COMES IN EXTRA-LARGE EDITIONS WITH COLOR PAGES!

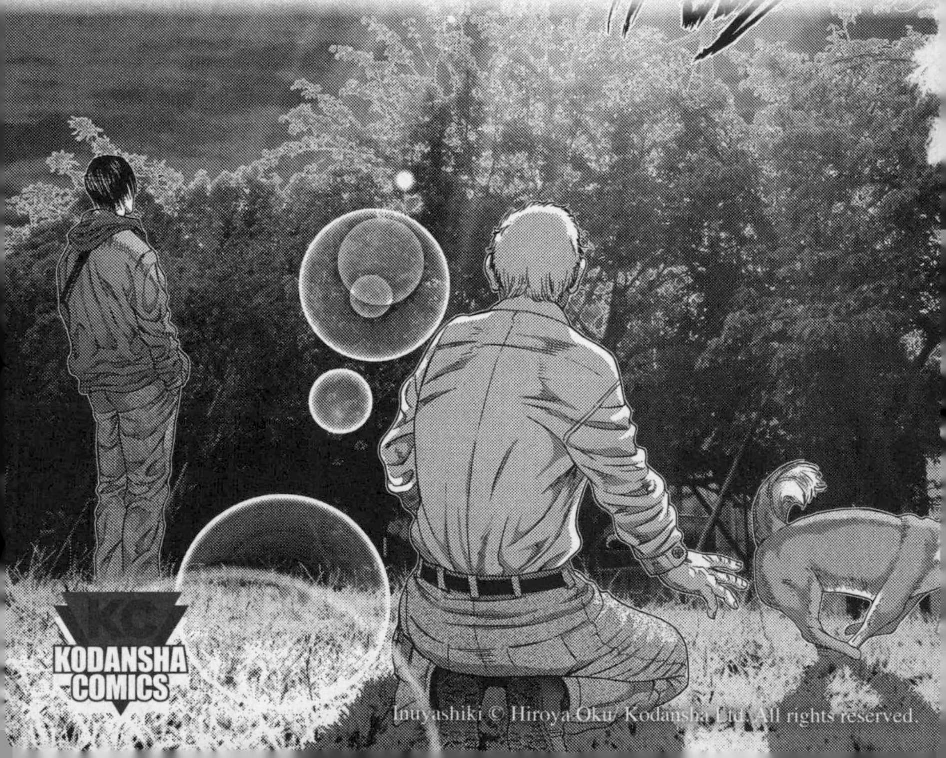

KODANSHA COMICS

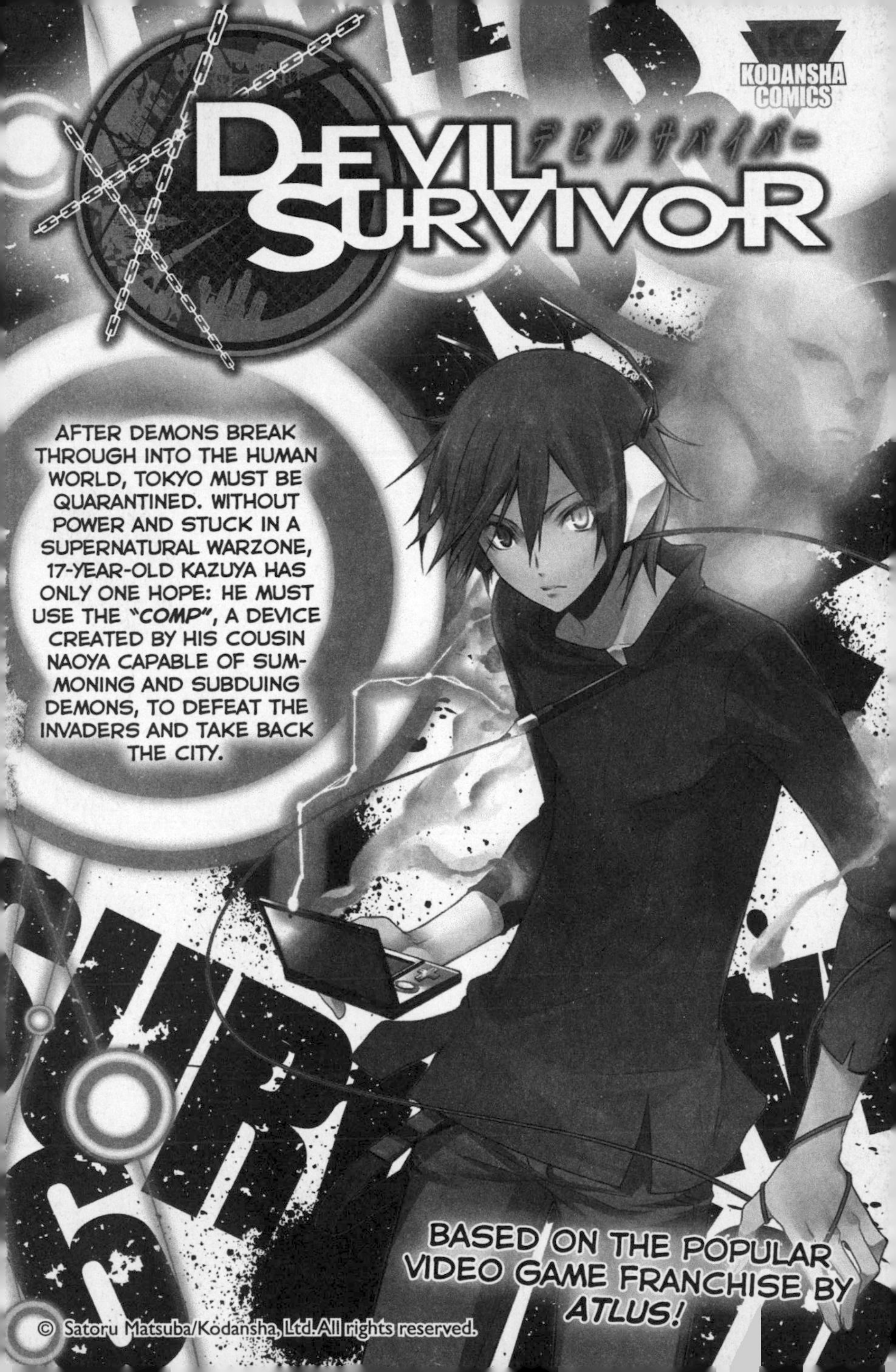
KODANSHA COMICS
DEVIL SURVIVOR
デビルサバイバー
AFTER DEMONS BREAK THROUGH INTO THE HUMAN WORLD, TOKYO MUST BE QUARANTINED. WITHOUT POWER AND STUCK IN A SUPERNATURAL WARZONE, 17-YEAR-OLD KAZUYA HAS ONLY ONE HOPE: HE MUST USE THE "COMP", A DEVICE CREATED BY HIS COUSIN NAOYA CAPABLE OF SUMMONING AND SUBDUING DEMONS, TO DEFEAT THE INVADERS AND TAKE BACK THE CITY.
BASED ON THE POPULAR VIDEO GAME FRANCHISE BY ATLUS!
© Satoru Matsuba/Kodansha, Ltd. All rights reserved.

KC
KODANSHA
COMICS

Fairy Tail takes place in a world filled with magic. 17-year-old Lucy is a wizard-in-training who wants to join a magic guild so that she can become a full-fledged wizard. She dreams of joining the most famous guild, known as Fairy Tail. One day she meets Natsu, a boy raised by a dragon which vanished when he was young. Natsu has devoted his life to finding his dragon father. When Natsu helps Lucy out of a tricky situation, she discovers that he is a member of Fairy Tail, and our heroes' adventure together begins.

FAIRY TAIL

MASTER'S EDITION

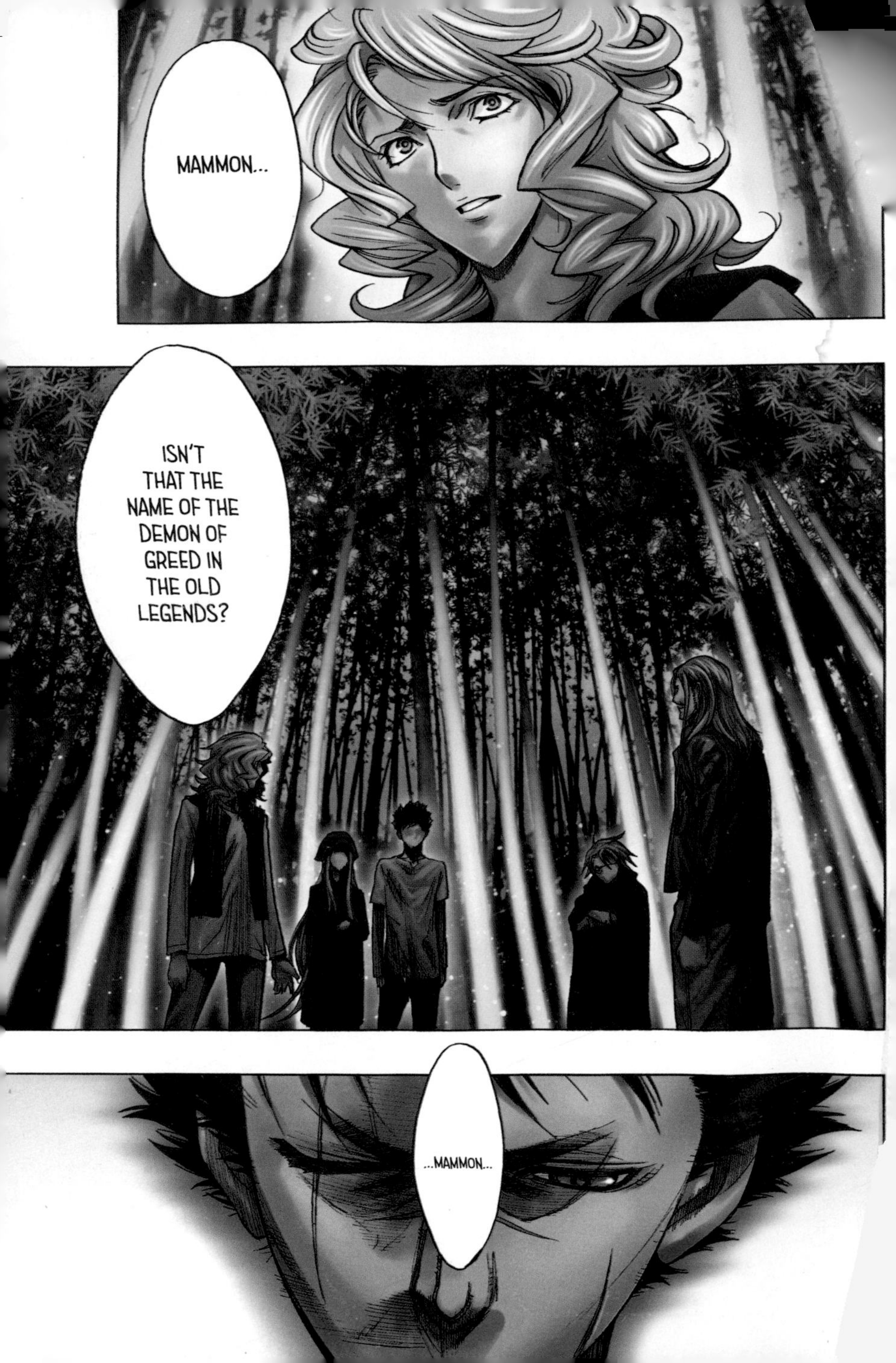
MAMMON...
ISN'T THAT THE NAME OF THE DEMON OF GREED IN THE OLD LEGENDS?
...MAMMON...

Based on "Attack on Titan"
created by Hajime Isayama
Story by: Ryo Suzukaze
Art by: Satoshi Shiki
Character designs by: Thores Shibamoto

Contents:

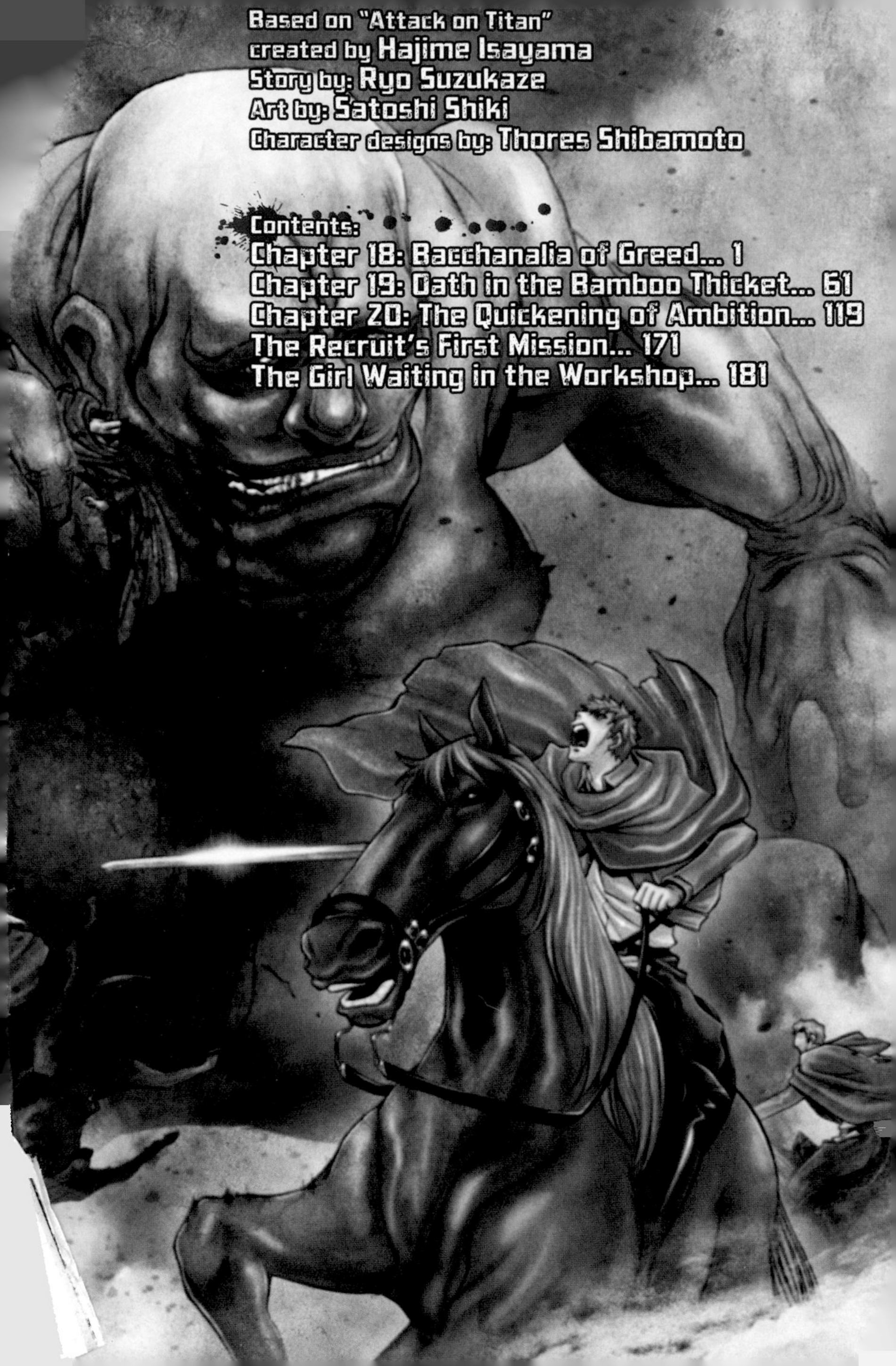

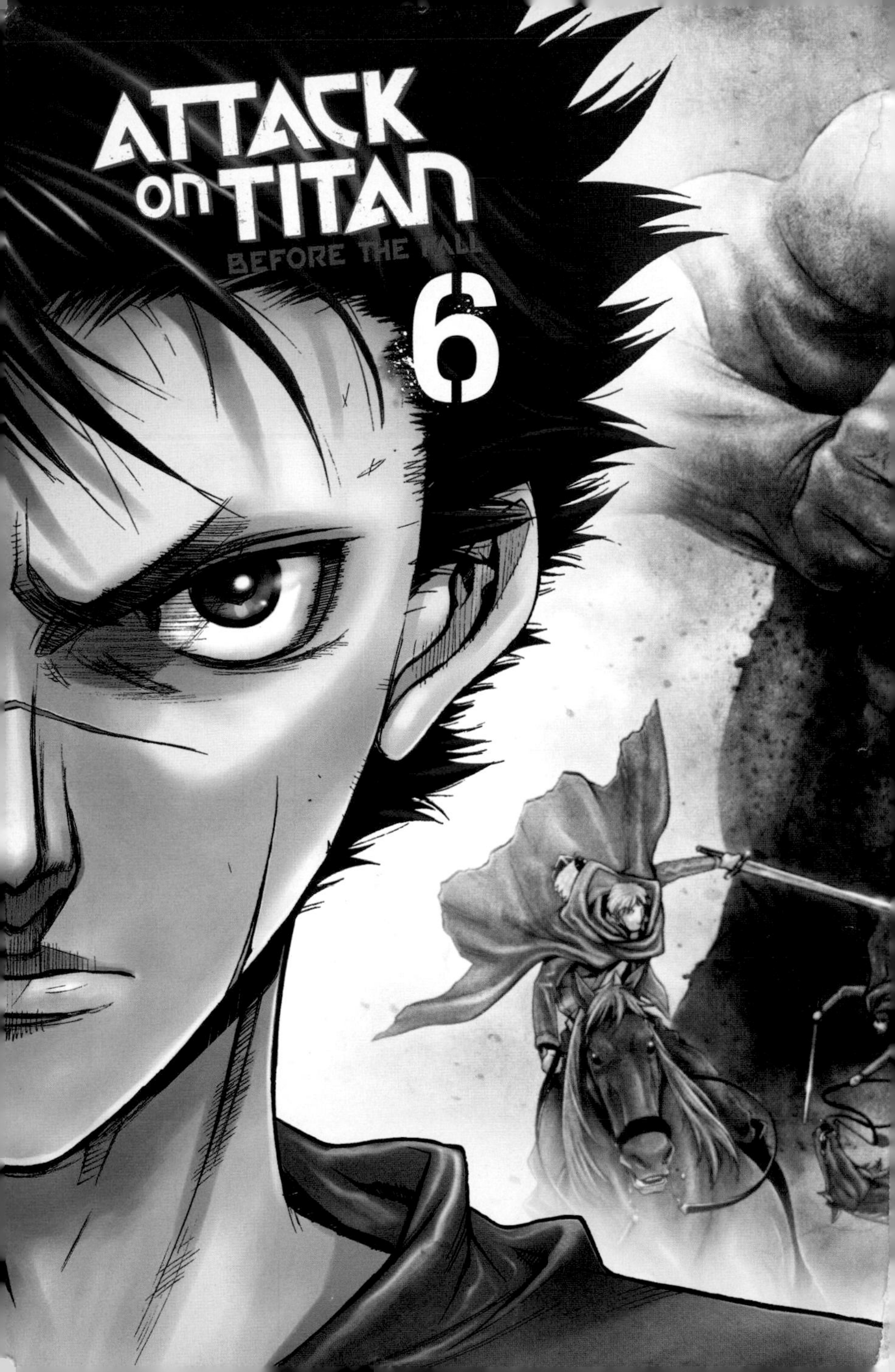
ATTACK on TITAN
BEFORE THE FALL
6

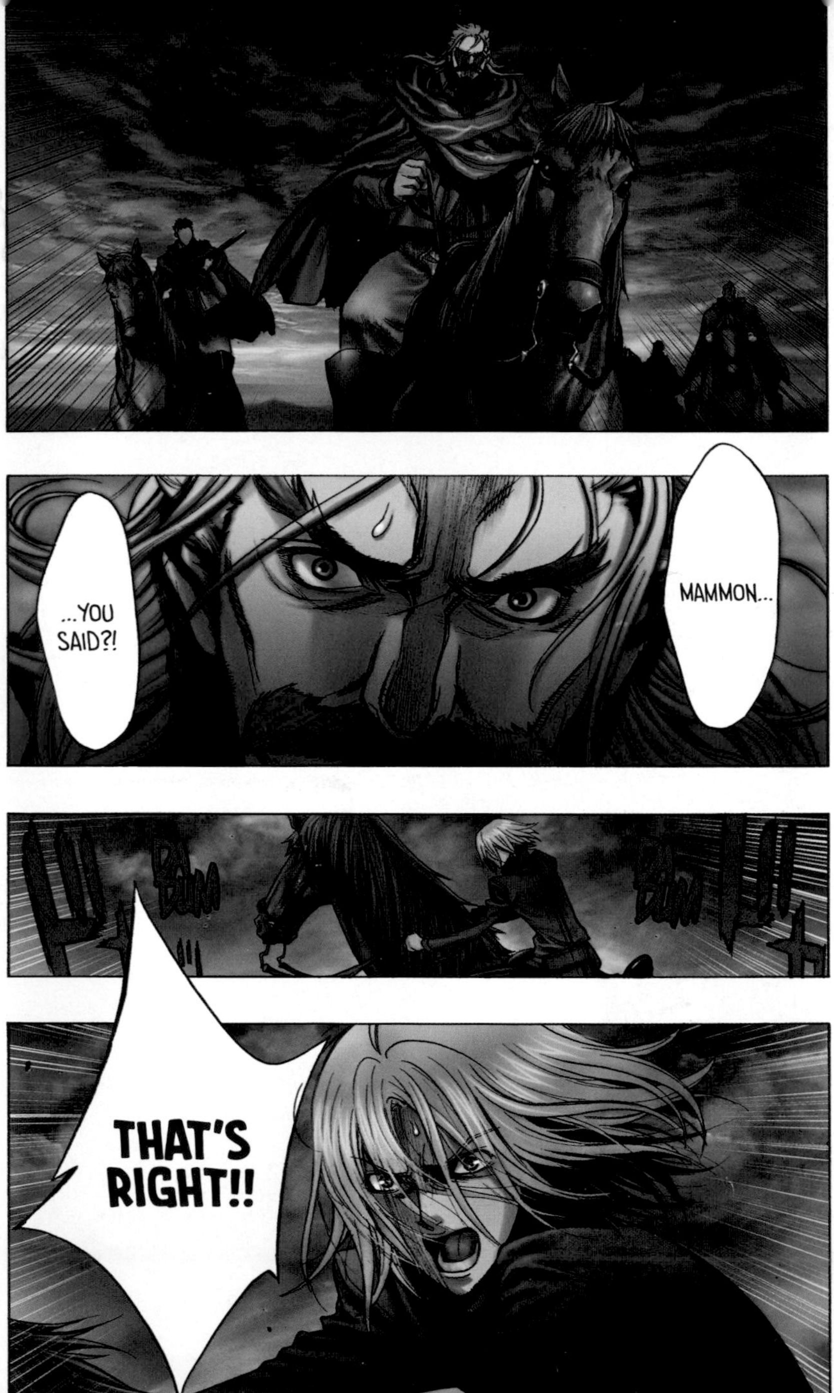
MAMMON...
...YOU SAID?!
BA DUM
BA DUM
THAT'S RIGHT!!

Character Profiles

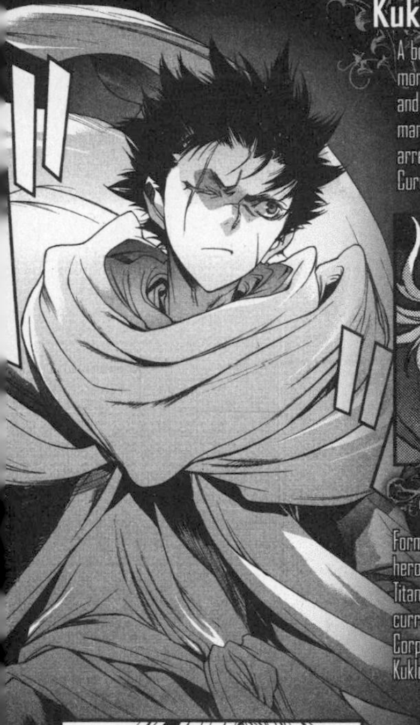

Kuklo

A boy born from a dead body packed into the vomit of a Titan, which earned him the moniker, "Titan's Son." His father was Heath Mansel, squad leader in the Survey Corps, and his mother was Elena, who let a Titan inside the Wall. He escaped the Inocencio mansion with Sharle when it was attacked by Titan-worshipers. After that, he was arrested by the MPs for a crime he did not commit, and sentenced to exile.
Currently 15 years old.

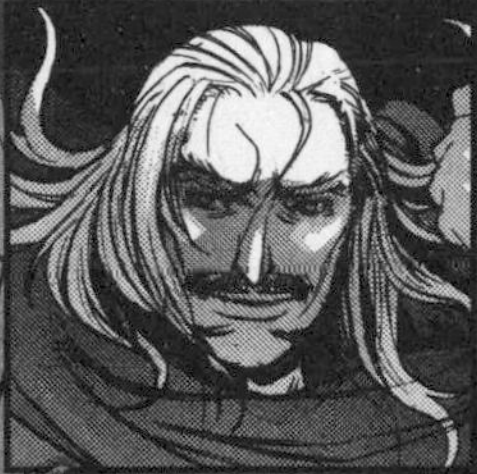

Jorge Pikale

Former captain of the Survey Corps, a hero who was the first human to defeat a Titan in battle, and father to Carlo. He is currently an instructor for the Training Corps. At Carlo's request, he saved Kuklo's life.

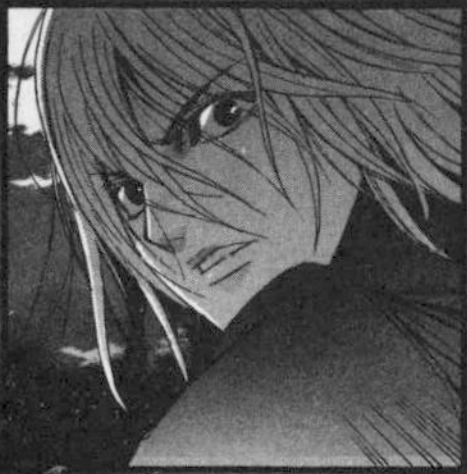

Angel Aaltonen

A brilliant young innovator who served as an advisor during the first expedition against the Titans 15 years ago. Afterwards, he went on to create "The Device." He lost his assistant Corina to a Titan.

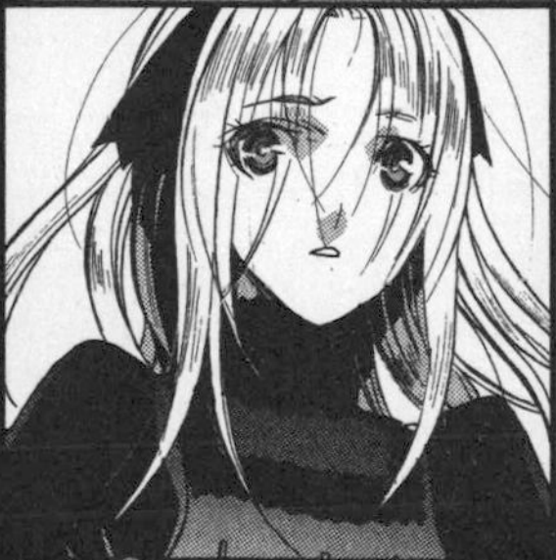

Sharle Inocencio

First daughter of the Inocencio family. She attempted to kill Kuklo after he was brought to the mansion, but became his only friend and taught him how to read, speak, and write when she realized that he was just a boy, not a monster. When Titan-worshipers invaded her home, she left with Kuklo and had a falling out with her brother Xavi. Since Kuklo's capture by the MPs, she's been hiding out in the Industrial City. Currently 15 years old.

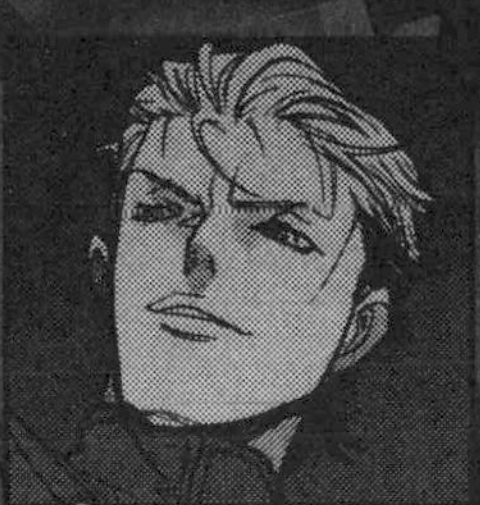

Xavi Inocencio

Sharle's brother, firstborn of the Inocencio children. His father Dario raised him to lead the military. He believes that Kuklo brought the Titan-worshipers into his home, and took the boy's right eye with his blade. As a member of the Training Corps, he exhibits his superiority in every facet.

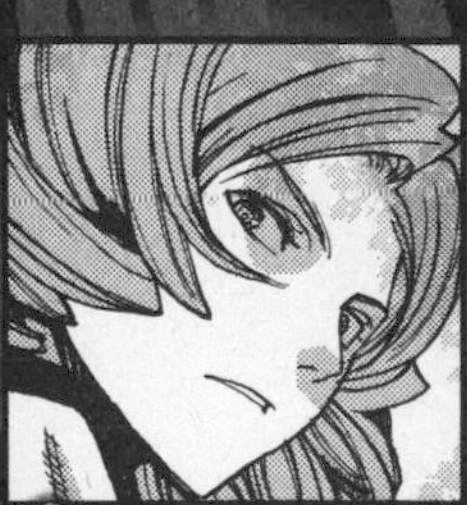

Cardina Baumeister

Son of the Baumeister family, one of the most prominent conservatives. He was thrown into prison as a result of his father's political schemes, but was rescued along with Kuklo by Jorge. Formerly Sharle's betrothed.

The Story So Far

When a Titan terrorized Shiganshina District and left behind a pile of vomit, a baby boy was miraculously born of a pregnant corpse. This boy was named Kuklo, the "Titan's Son," and was treated as a sideshow freak. Eventually the wealthy merchant Dario Inocencio bought Kuklo to serve as a punching bag for his son, Xavi. Meanwhile, Xavi's sister Sharle decided to teach him the language and knowledge of humanity instead. Kuklo put together an escape plan over two long years, but on the day of the escape, a group of Titan-worshipers invaded the mansion to take back the Titan's Son, and murdered Dario in the process. Kuklo narrowly managed to save Sharle, but Xavi accused him of being in league with the attackers. Kuklo took Sharle and escaped from Wall Sheena.

In Shiganshina District, the Survey Corps was preparing for its first expedition outside of the Walls in fifteen years. Kuklo wanted to see a Titan to confirm that he was indeed a human being. He left Sharle behind and snuck into the expedition's cargo wagon. As he had hoped, the Survey Corps ran across a Titan, but it was far worse of a monster than he expected. The group suffered grievous losses, but thanks to Captain Carlo and Kuklo's quick thinking, they eventually retreated safely behind Wall Maria. Kuklo helped the Survey Corps survive, but inside the walls he was greeted by the Military Police, who wanted the "Titan's Son" on charges of murdering Dario. In prison, he met Cardina, a young man jailed over political squabbles. They hoped to escape to safety when exiled beyond the Wall, but found themselves surrounded by a pack of Titans. Jorge, former Survey Corps captain and first human to defeat a Titan, helped the two boys escape with their lives. The equipment that Jorge used was the very "device" that was the key to defeating the Titan those fifteen years ago.

Kuklo and Cardina escaped the notice of the MPs by hiding in the Industrial City, where they found Sharle. It was there that the three youngsters learned the truth of the ill-fated Titan-capturing expedition fifteen years earlier, and the birth of the Device.

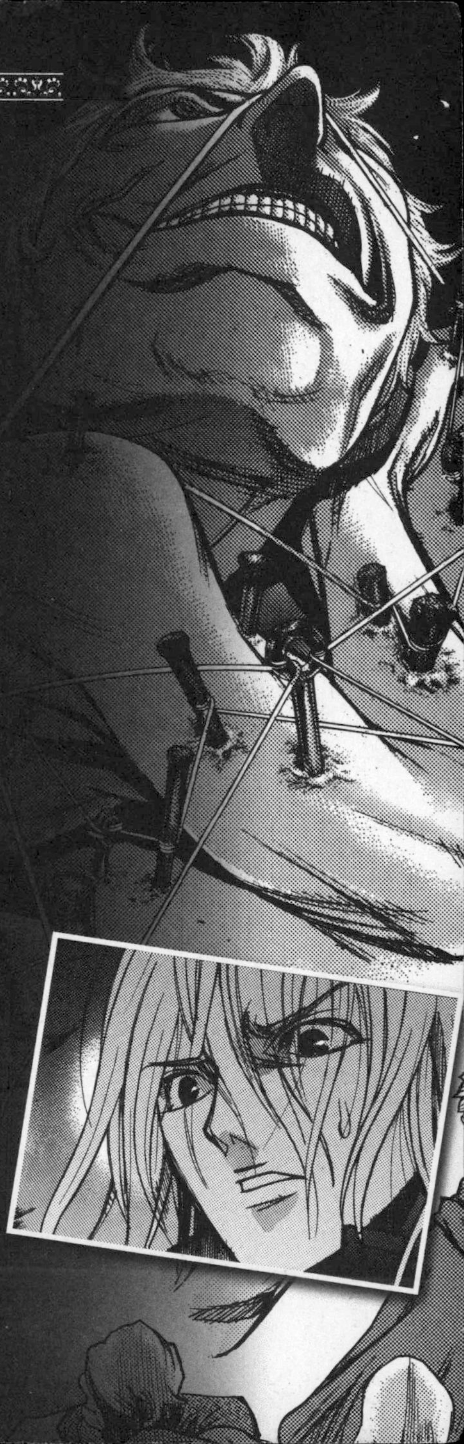

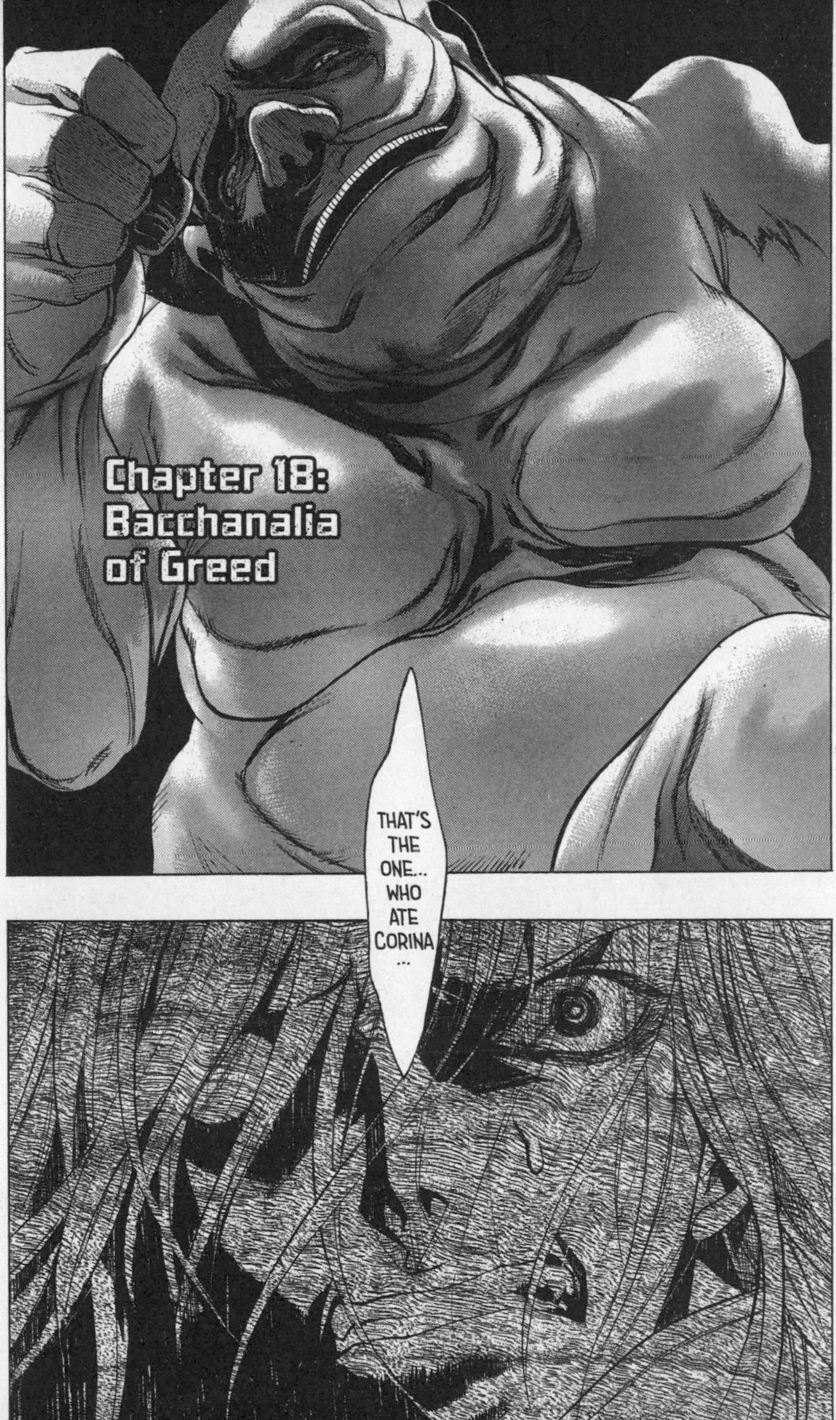
Chapter 18: Bacchanalia of Greed
THAT'S THE ONE... WHO ATE CORINA ...

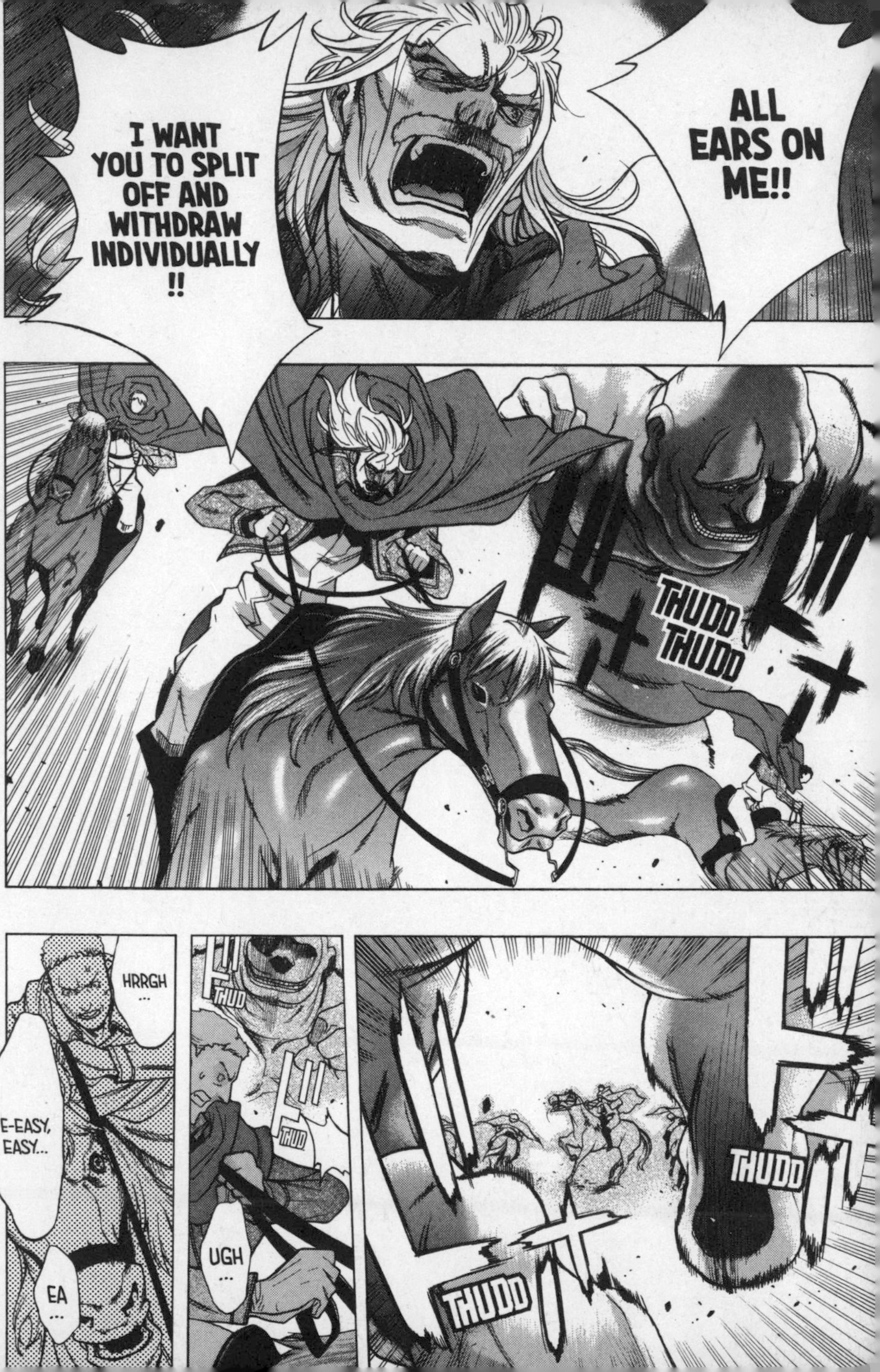
ALL EARS ON ME!!
I WANT YOU TO SPLIT OFF AND WITHDRAW INDIVIDUALLY!!
THUDD THUDD
THUDD
THUDD
THUD
THUD
UGH...
HRRGH...
E-EASY, EASY...
EA...

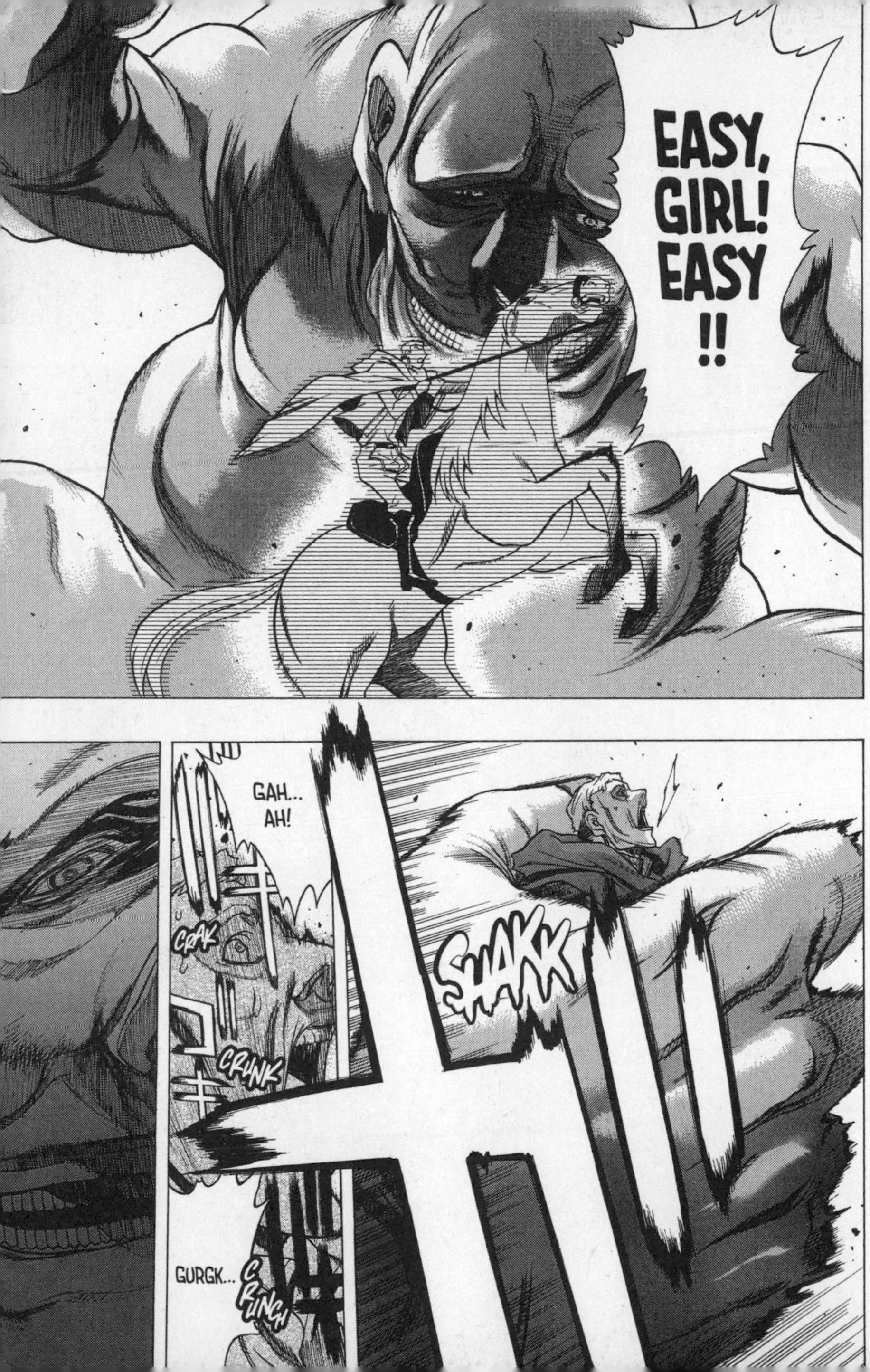
EASY, GIRL! EASY !!
SHAKK
GAH... AH!
CRAK
CRUNK
GURGK...
CRUNCH

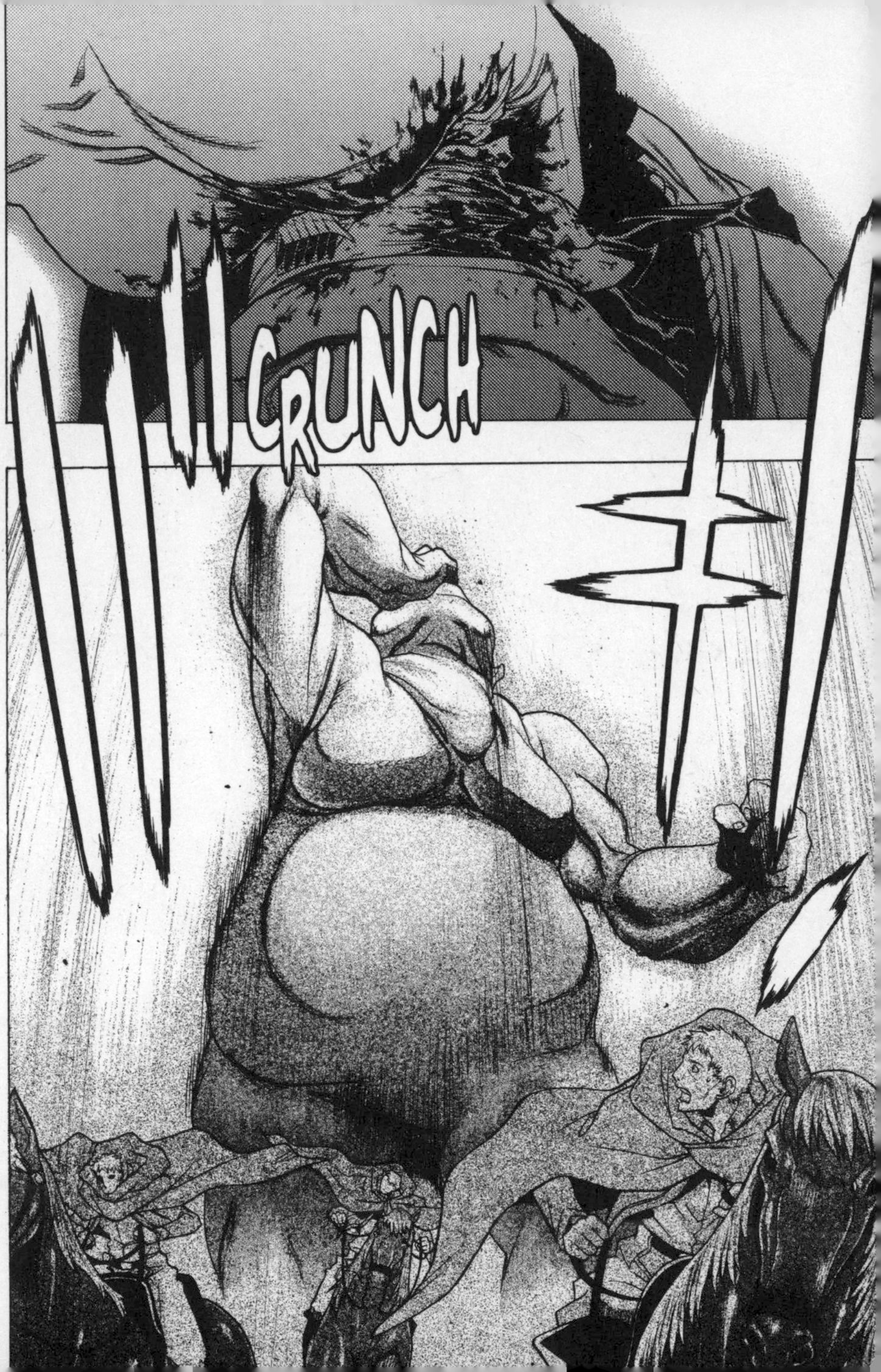
CRUNCH

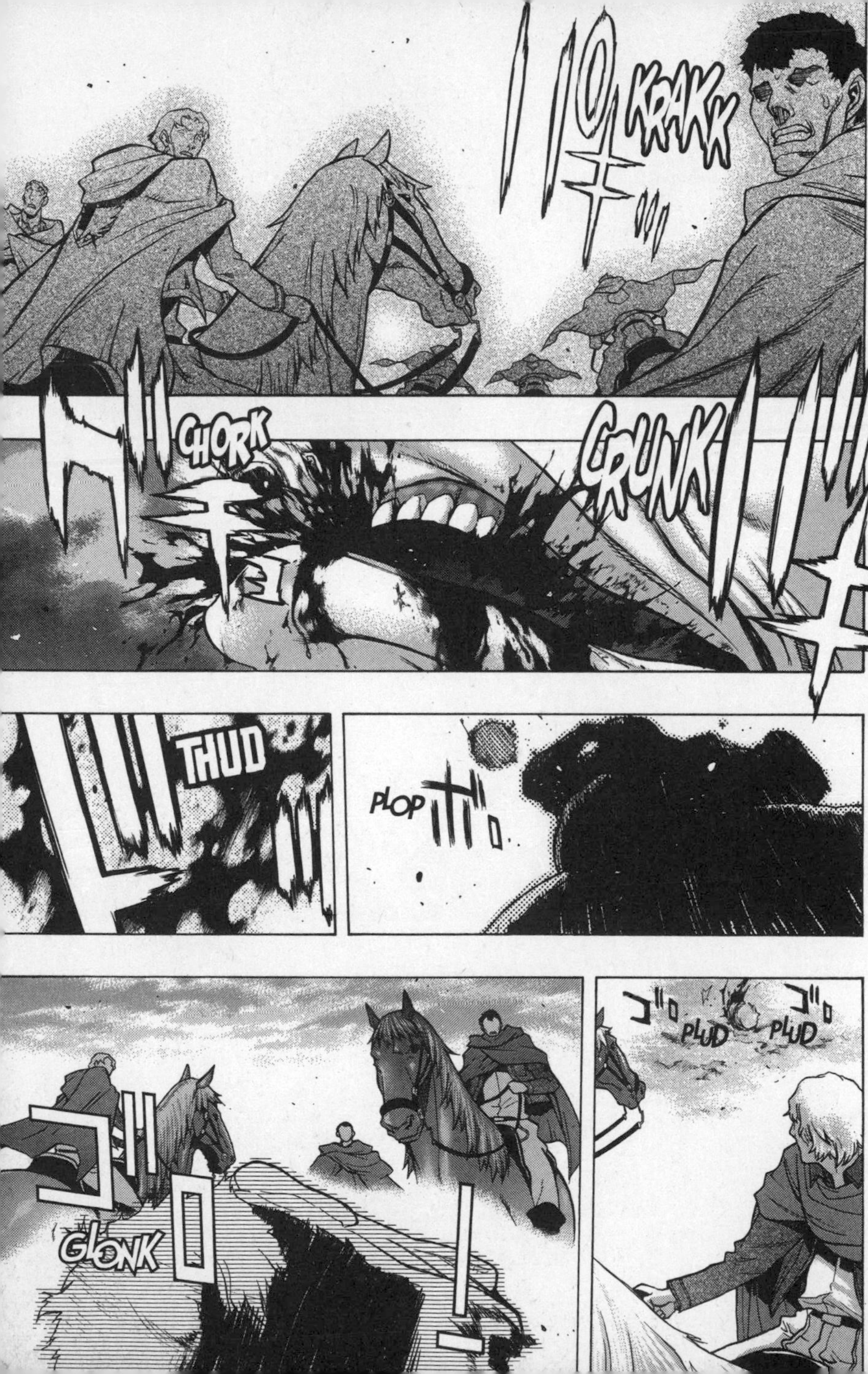
KRAKK
CRUNK
CHORK
PLOP
THUD
PLUD
PLUD
GLONK

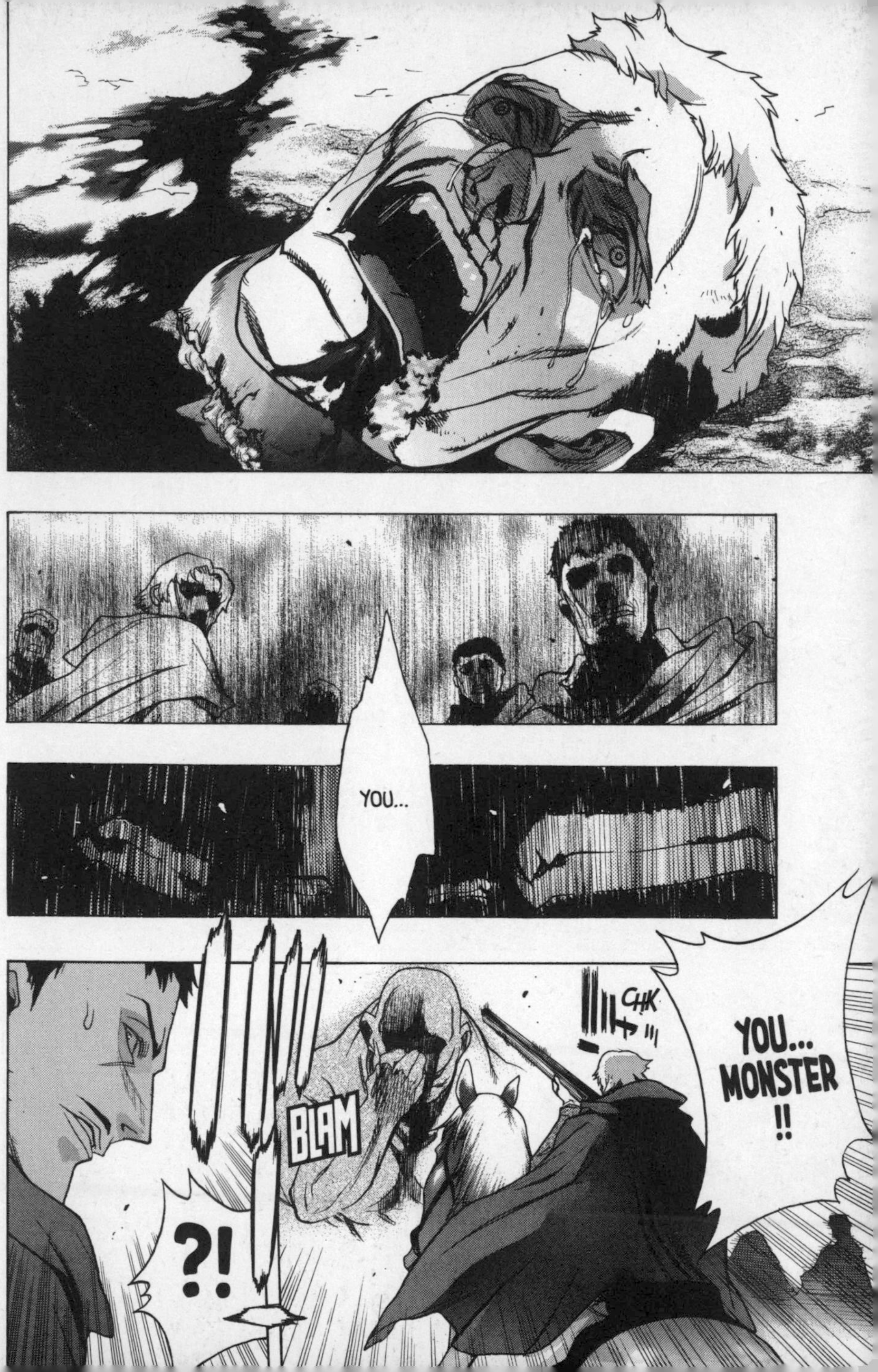
YOU...
CHK
YOU... MONSTER !!
BLAM
?!

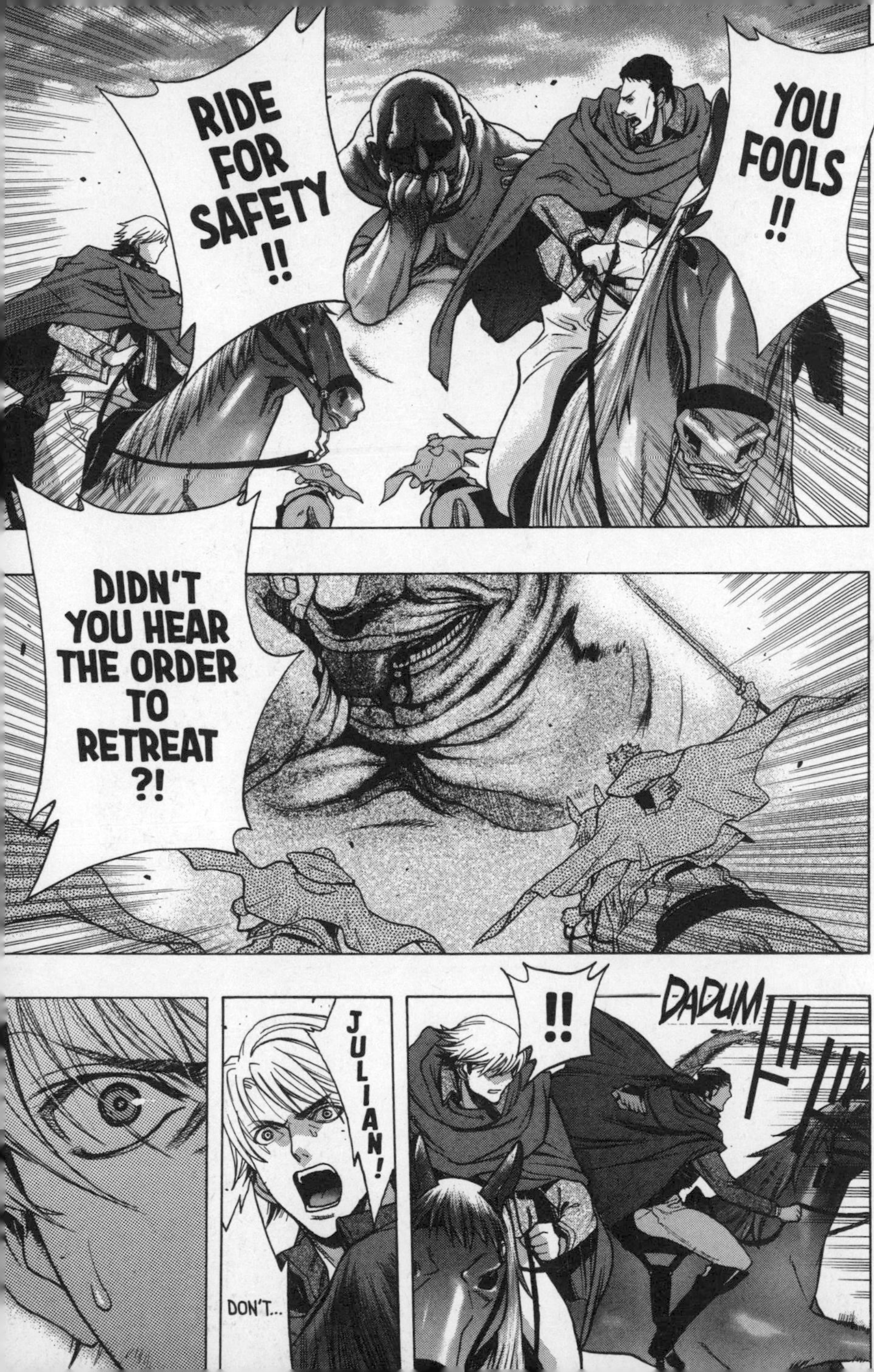
YOU FOOLS!!
RIDE FOR SAFETY!!
DIDN'T YOU HEAR THE ORDER TO RETREAT?!
!!
DADUM
JULIAN!
DON'T...

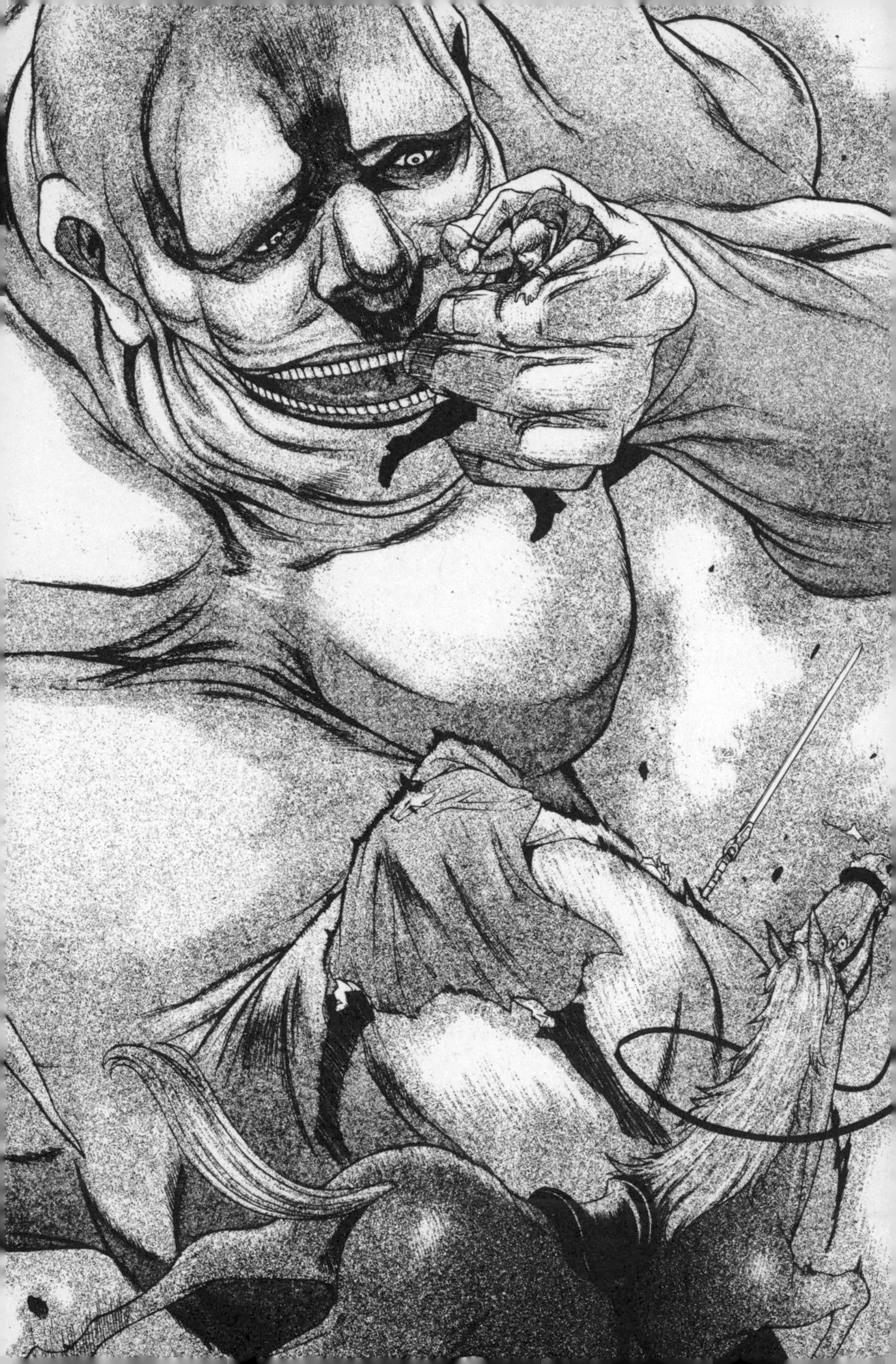

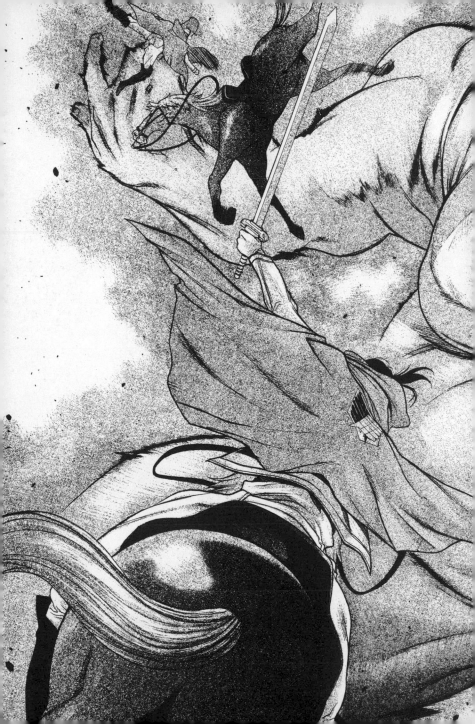

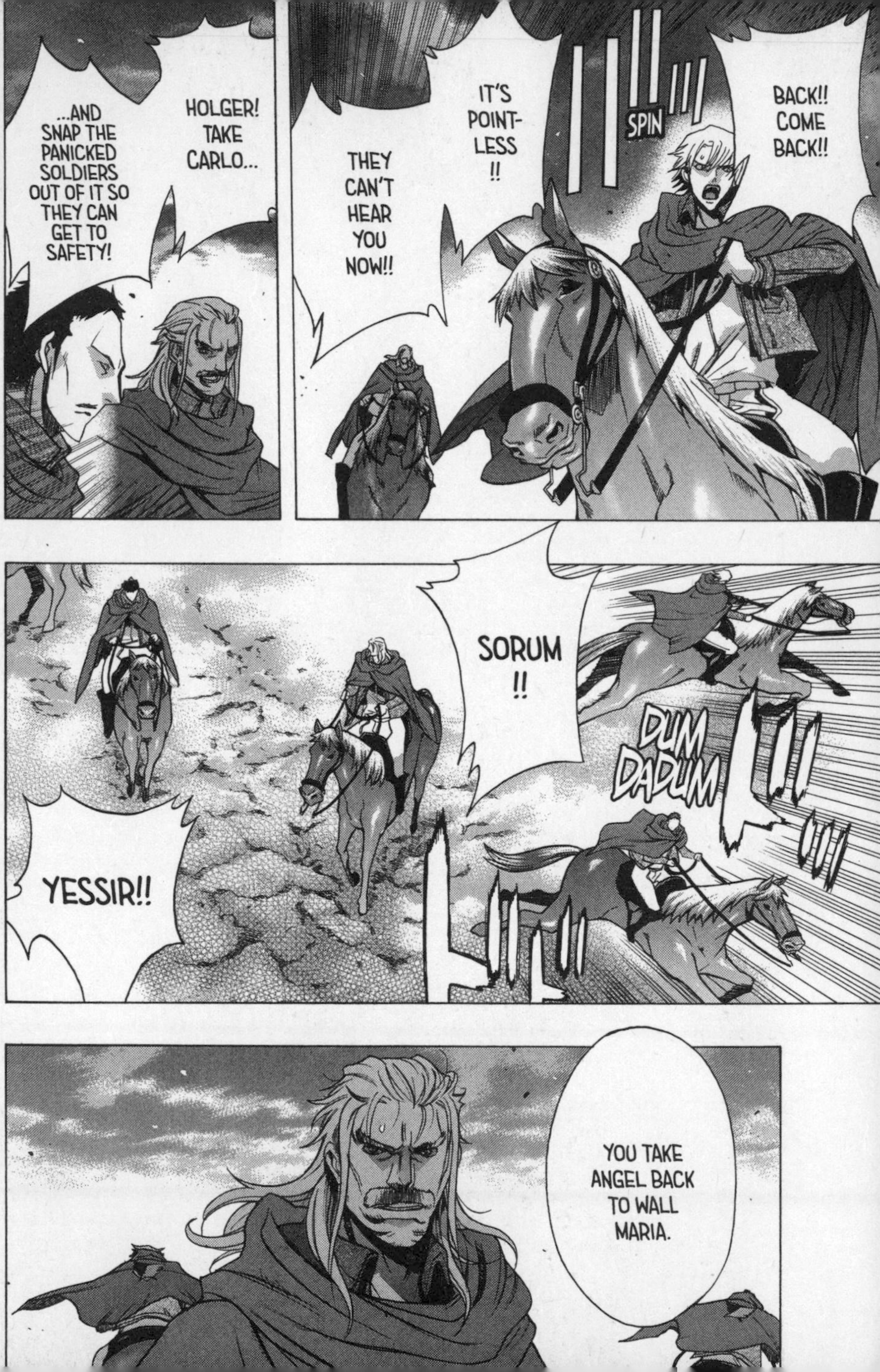
BACK!! COME BACK!!
SPIN
IT'S POINT-LESS !!
THEY CAN'T HEAR YOU NOW!!
HOLGER! TAKE CARLO...
...AND SNAP THE PANICKED SOLDIERS OUT OF IT SO THEY CAN GET TO SAFETY!
SORUM !!
DUM DADUM
YESSIR!!
YOU TAKE ANGEL BACK TO WALL MARIA.

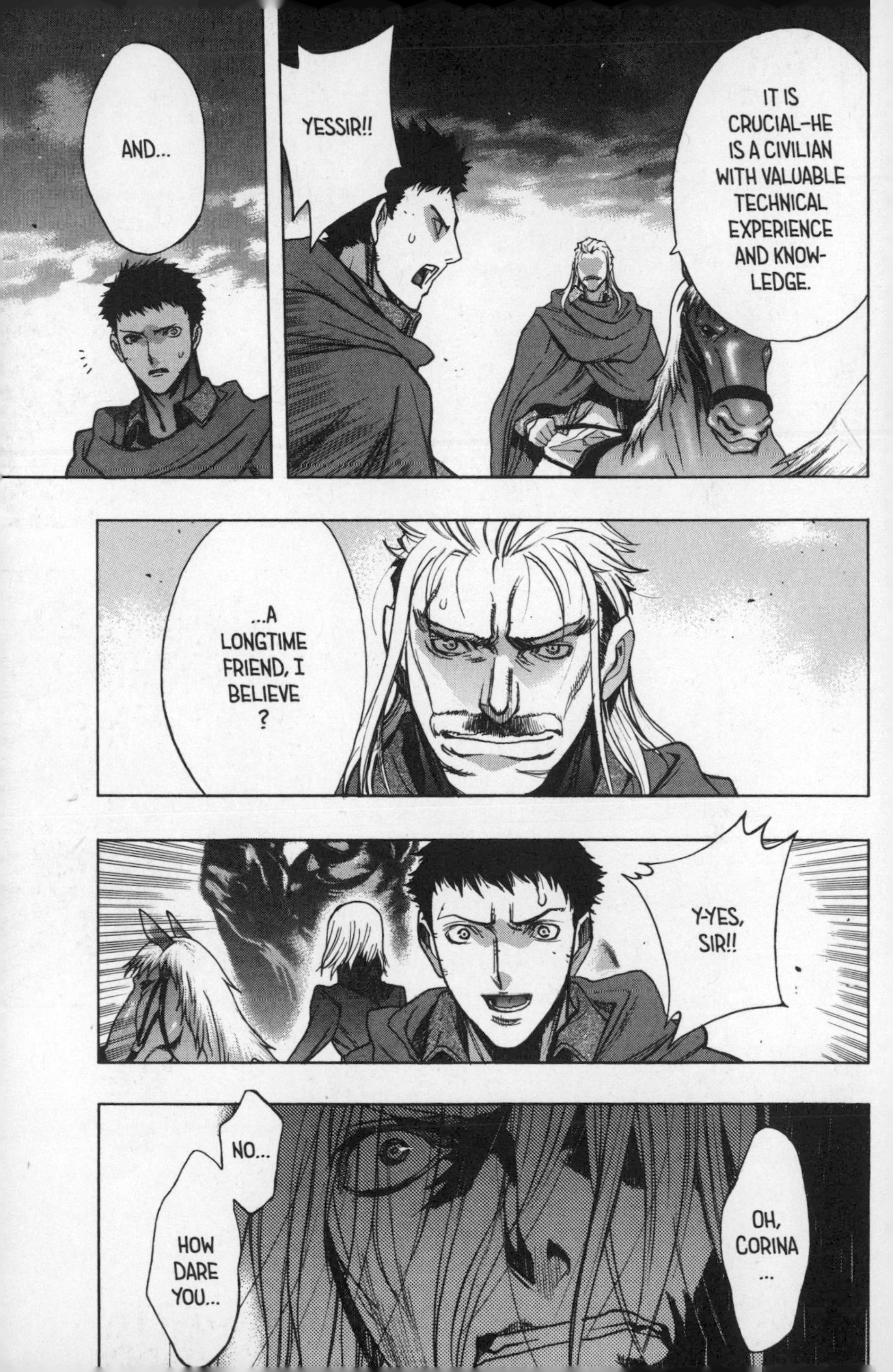
IT IS CRUCIAL—HE IS A CIVILIAN WITH VALUABLE TECHNICAL EXPERIENCE AND KNOW-LEDGE.
YESSIR!!
AND...
...A LONGTIME FRIEND, I BELIEVE ?
Y-YES, SIR!!
OH, CORINA ...
NO...
HOW DARE YOU...

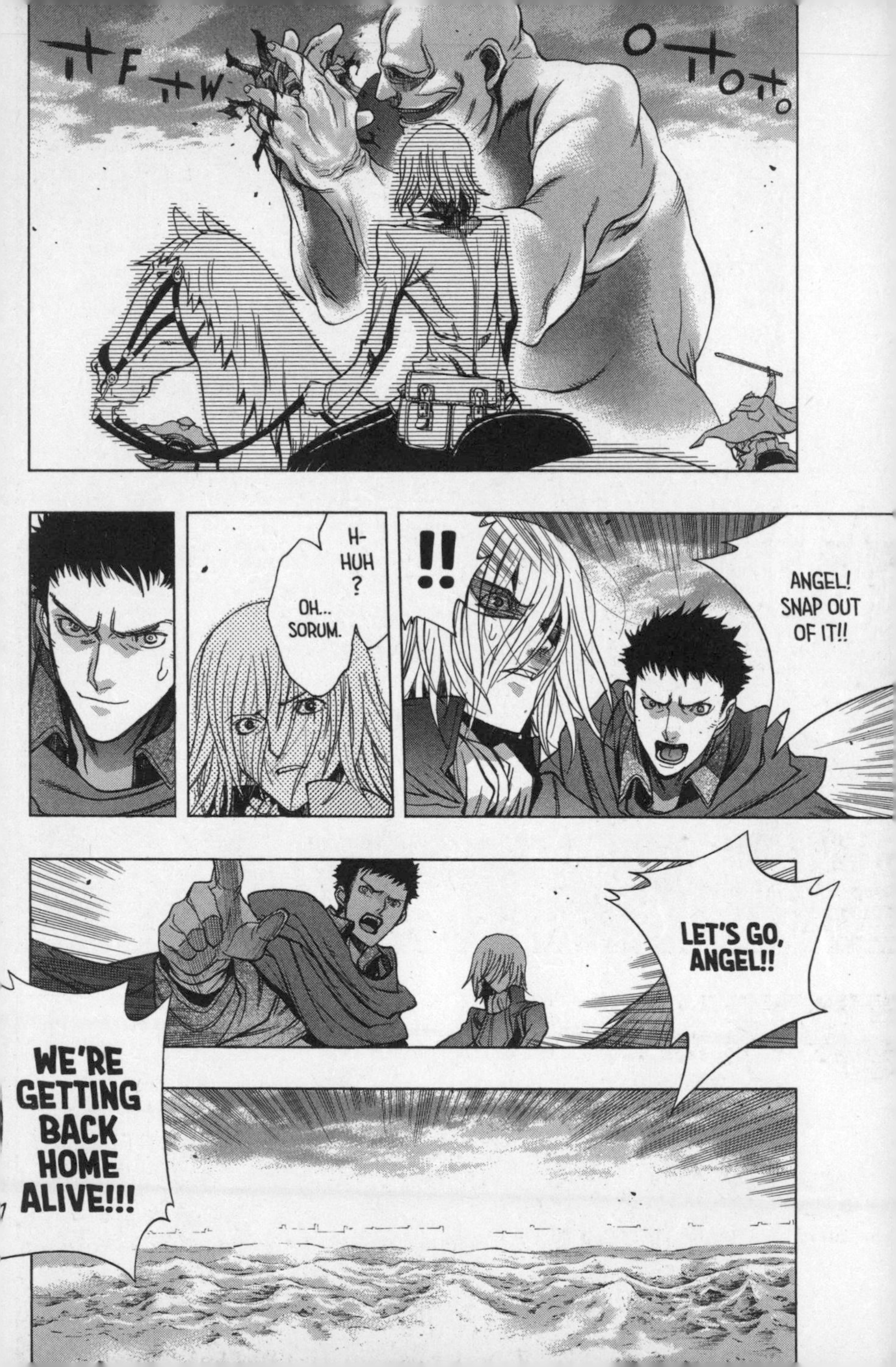
ANGEL! SNAP OUT OF IT!!
!!
H-HUH?
OH.. SORUM.
LET'S GO, ANGEL!!
WE'RE GETTING BACK HOME ALIVE!!!

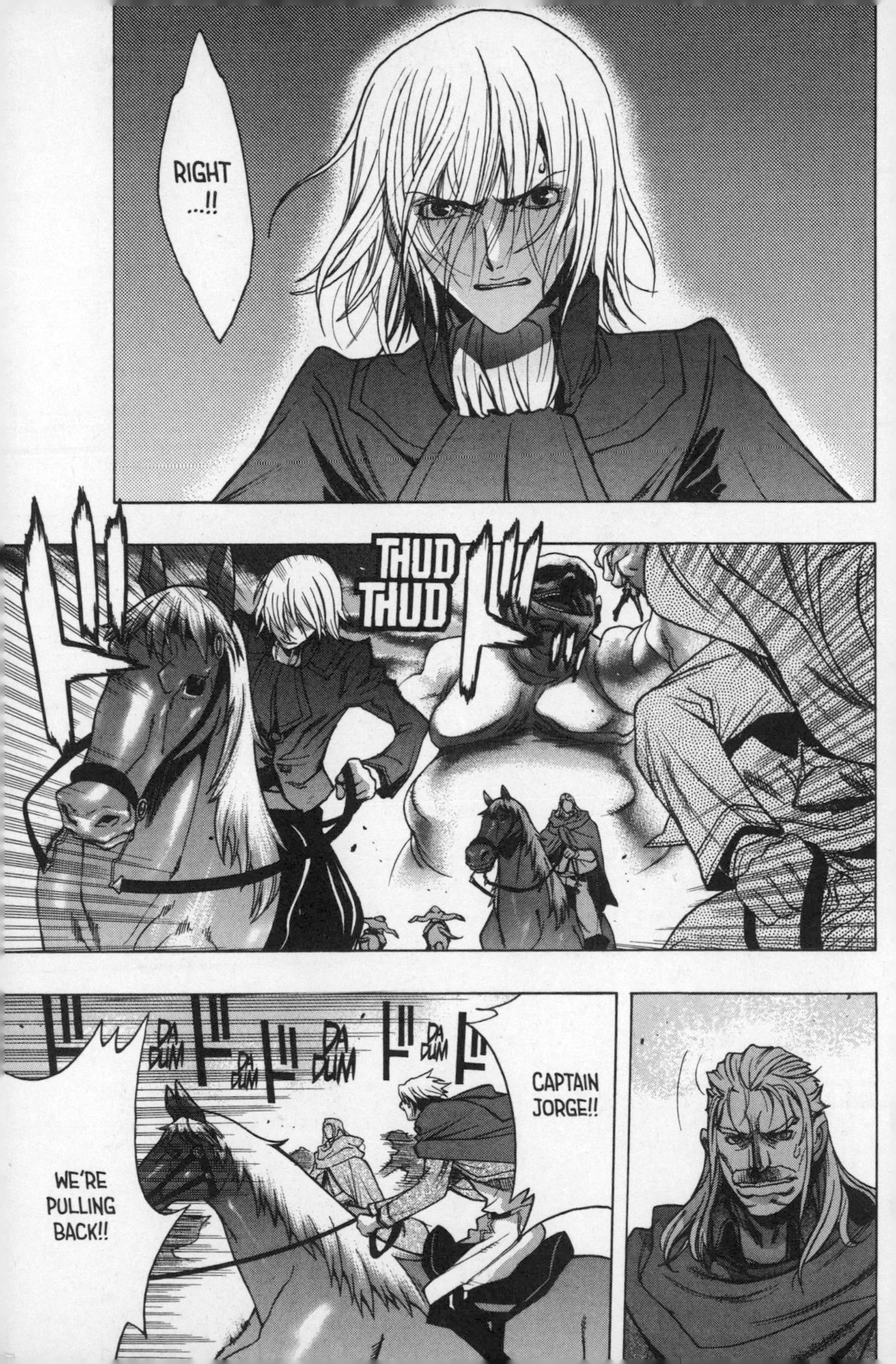
RIGHT ...!!
THUD THUD
CAPTAIN JORGE!!
DA DUM
DA DUM
DA DUM
DA DUM
WE'RE PULLING BACK!!

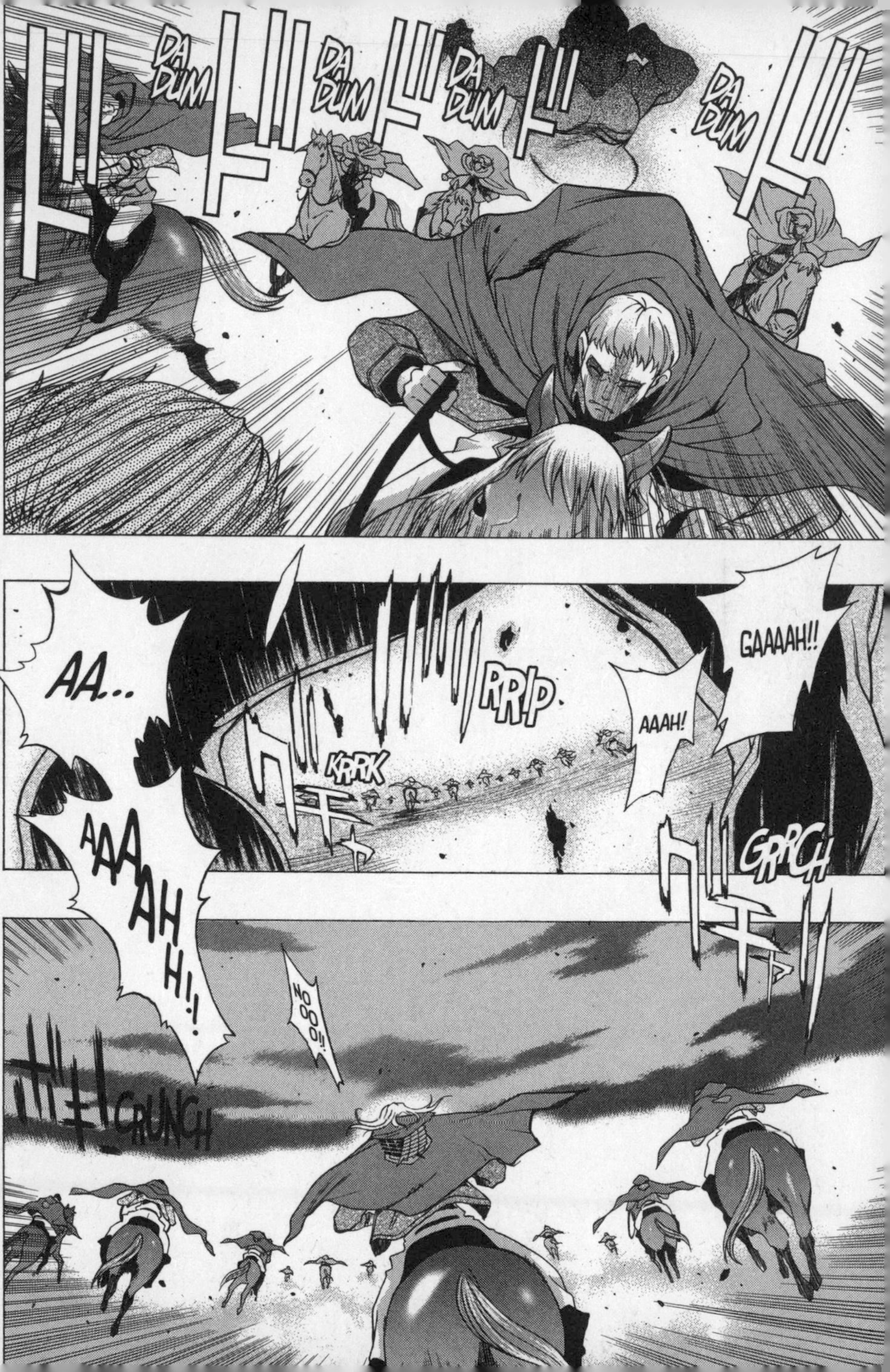
DA DUM
DA DUM
DA DUM
DA DUM
GAAAAH!!
RRIP
AAAH!
KRRK
AA...
GRRCH
AAAAAHH!!
NOOOO!!
CRUNCH

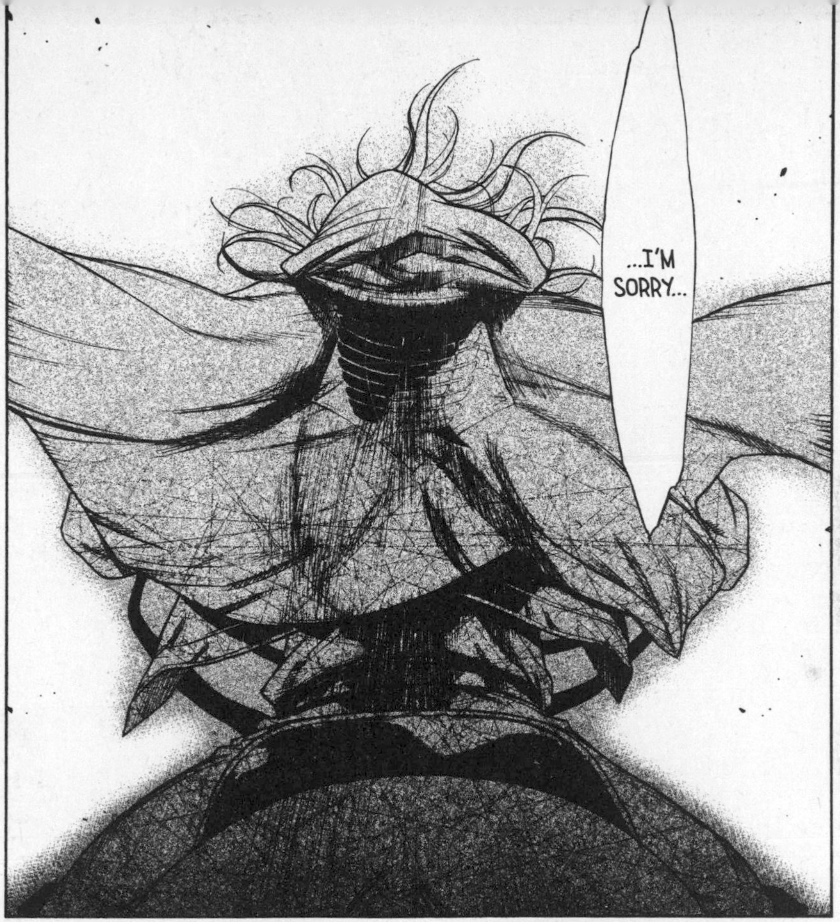
...I'M SORRY...
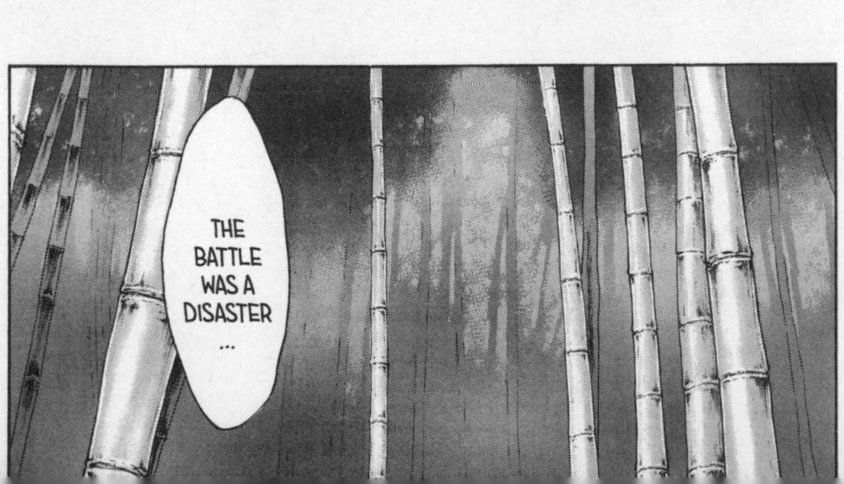
THE BATTLE WAS A DISASTER ...

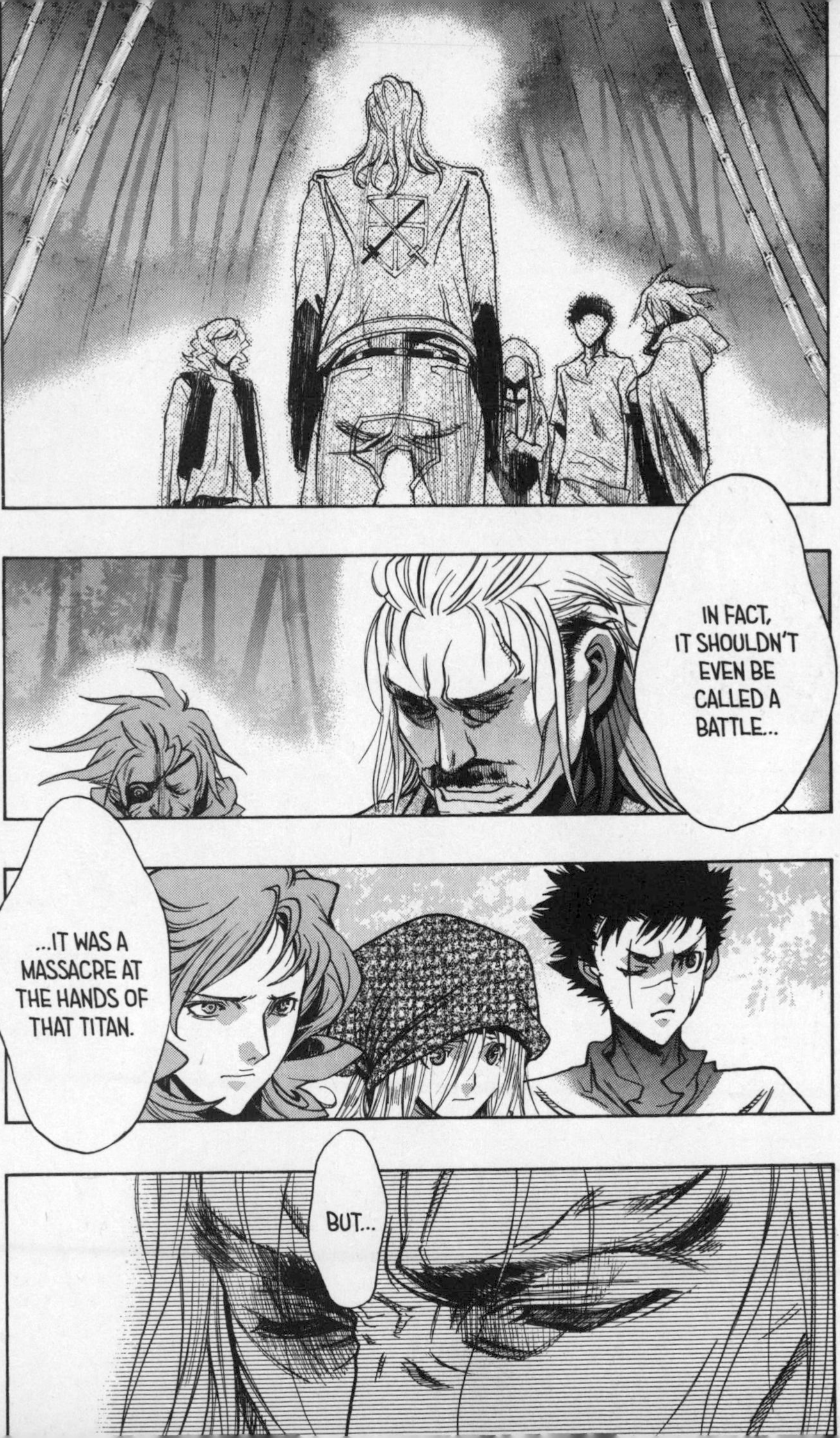
IN FACT, IT SHOULDN'T EVEN BE CALLED A BATTLE...
...IT WAS A MASSACRE AT THE HANDS OF THAT TITAN.
BUT...

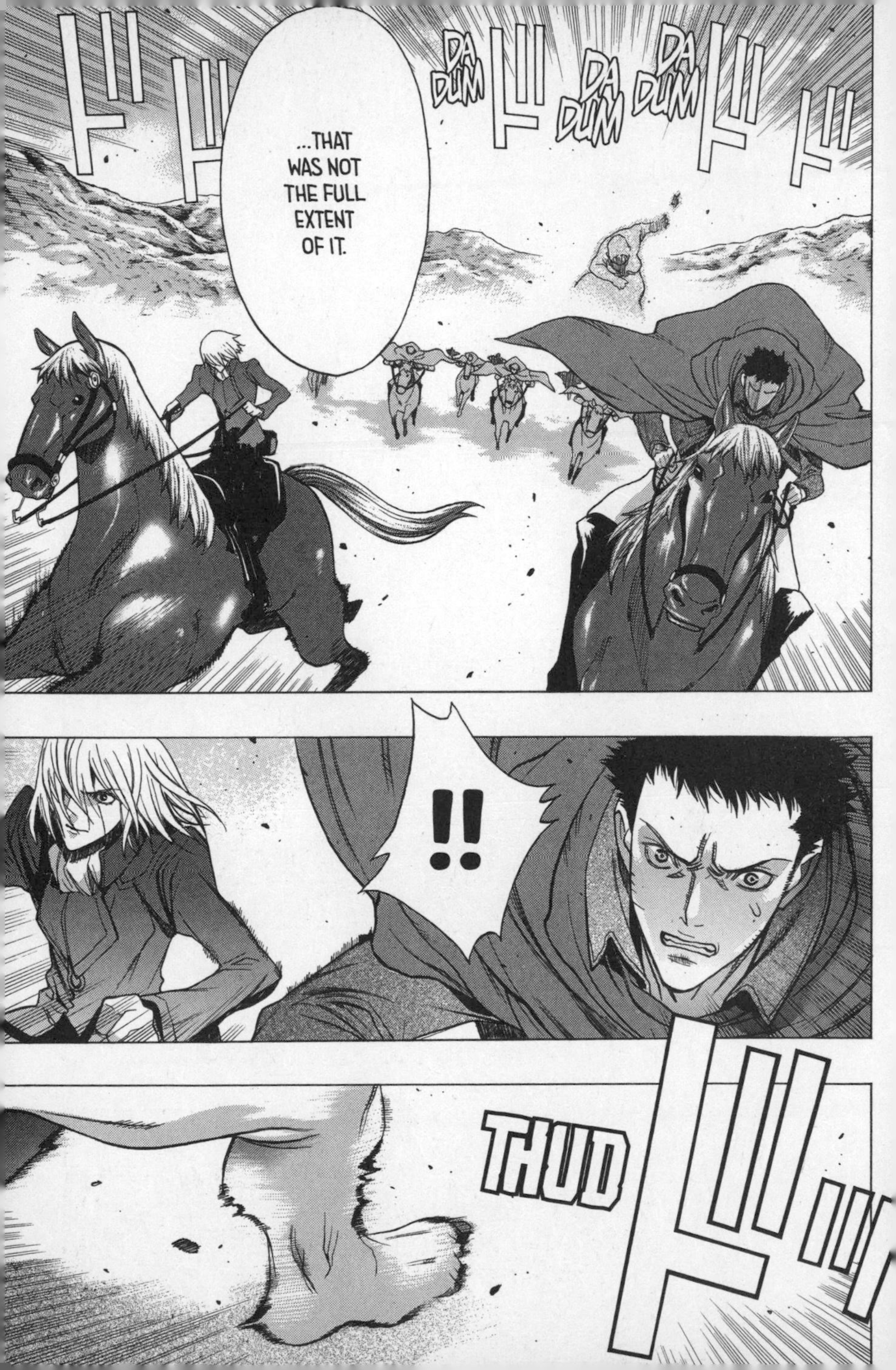
DA DUM
DA DUM
DA DUM
...THAT WAS NOT THE FULL EXTENT OF IT.
!!
THUD

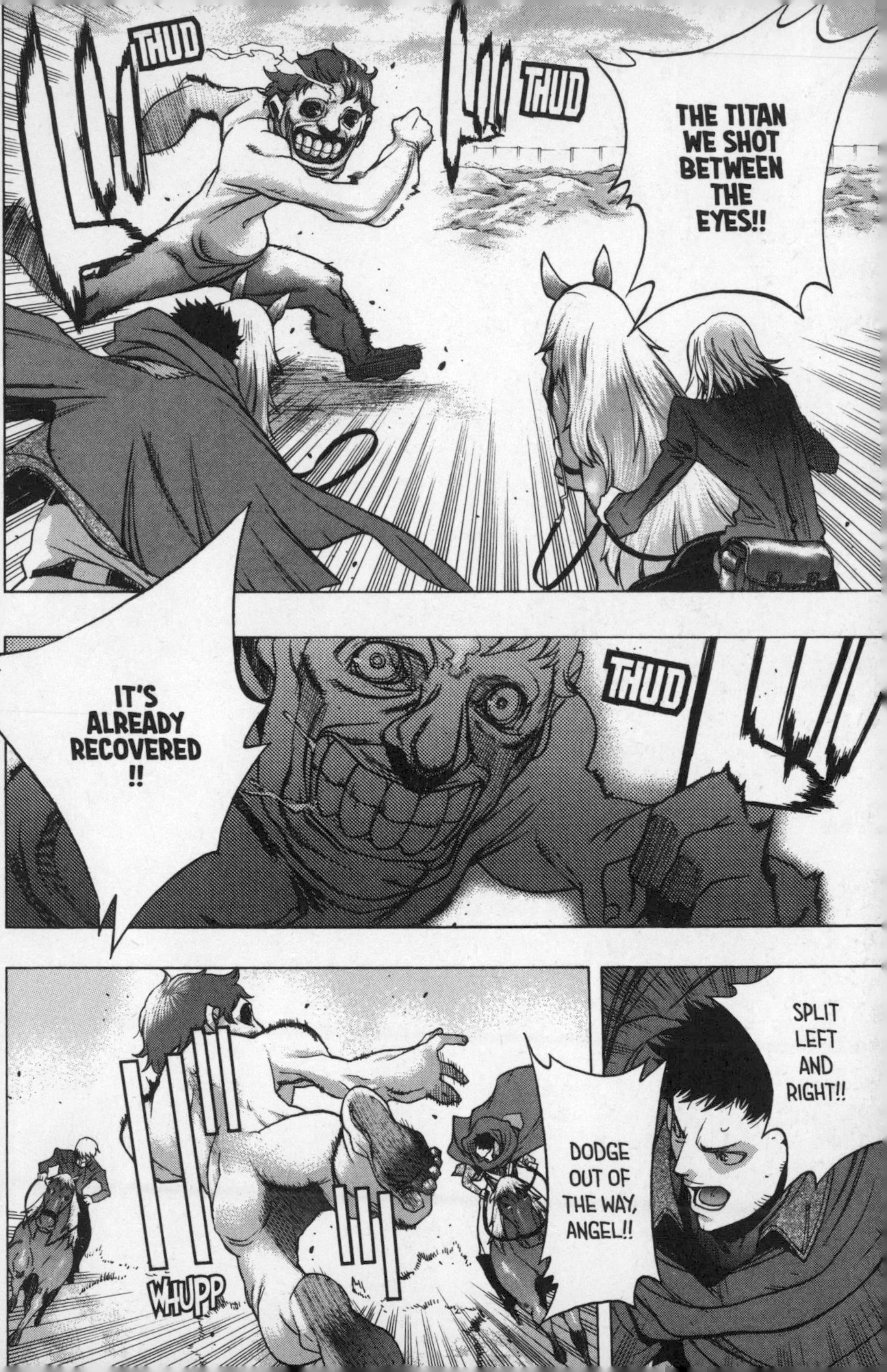
THE TITAN WE SHOT BETWEEN THE EYES!!
THUD
THUD
THUD
IT'S ALREADY RECOVERED !!
SPLIT LEFT AND RIGHT!!
DODGE OUT OF THE WAY, ANGEL!!
WHUPP

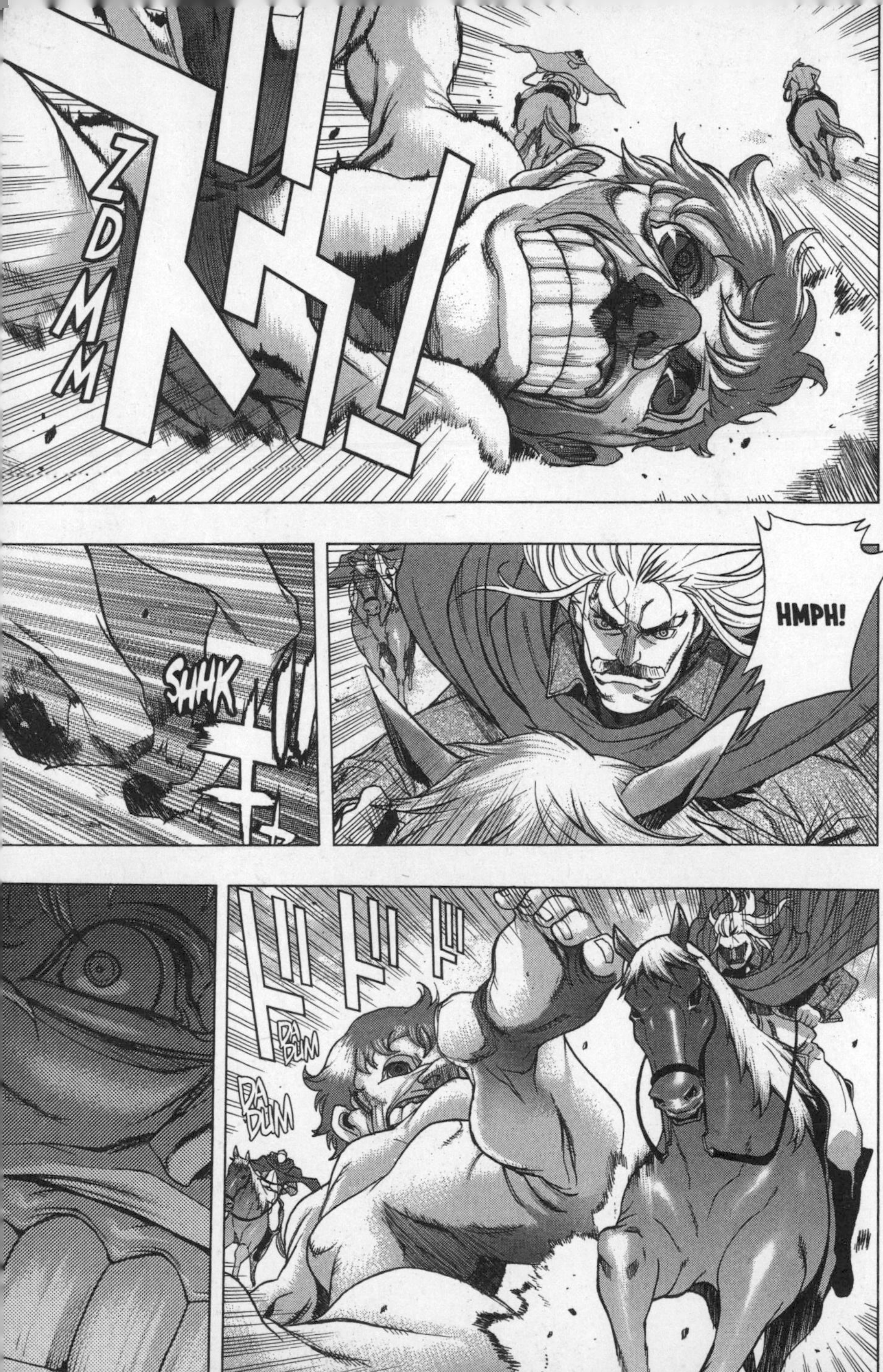
ZDMMM
HMPH!
SHHK
DA DUM
DA DUM

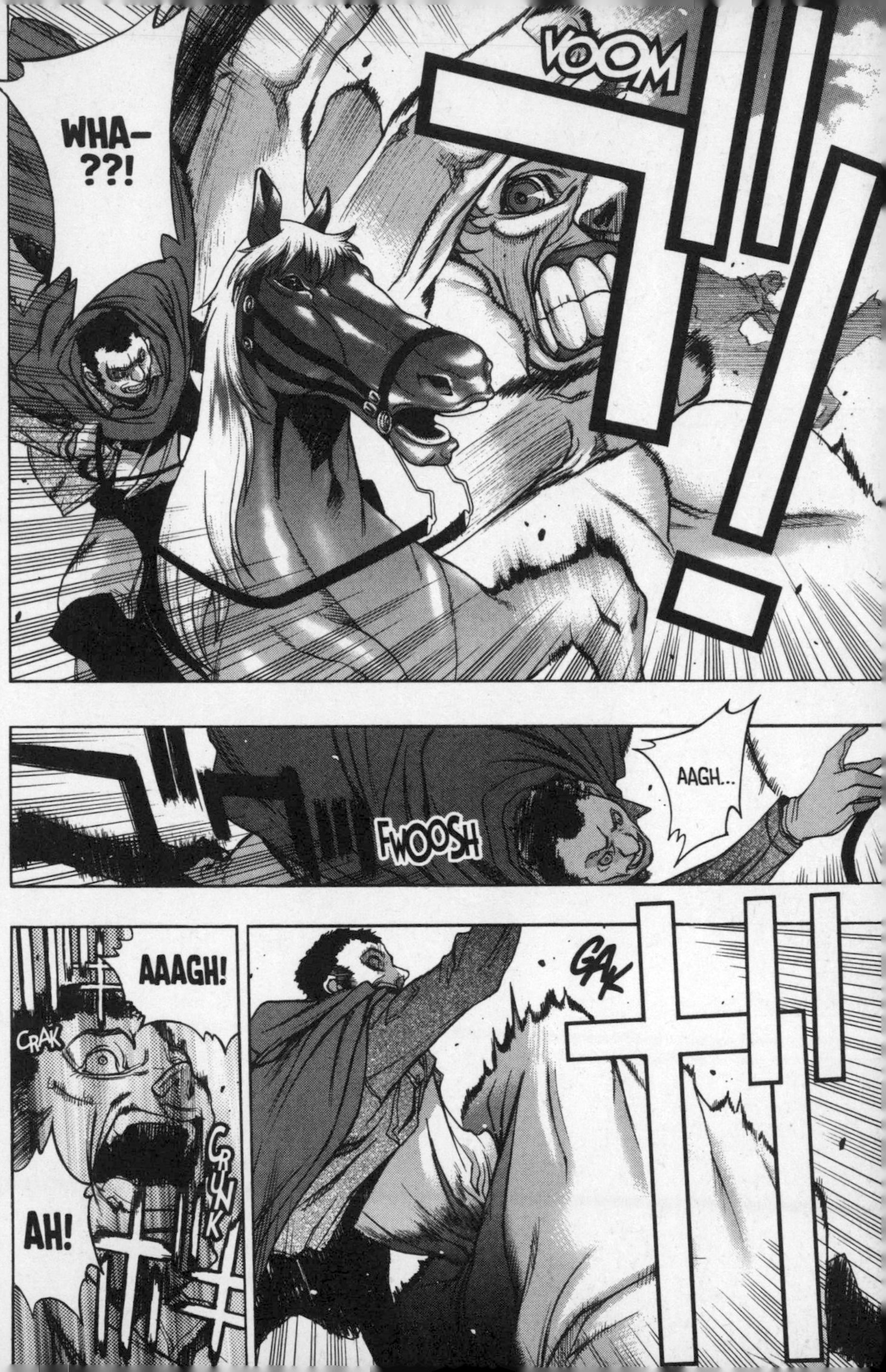
VOOM
WHA-
??!
AAGH...
FWOOSH
GAK
AAAGH!
CRAK
CRUNK
AH!

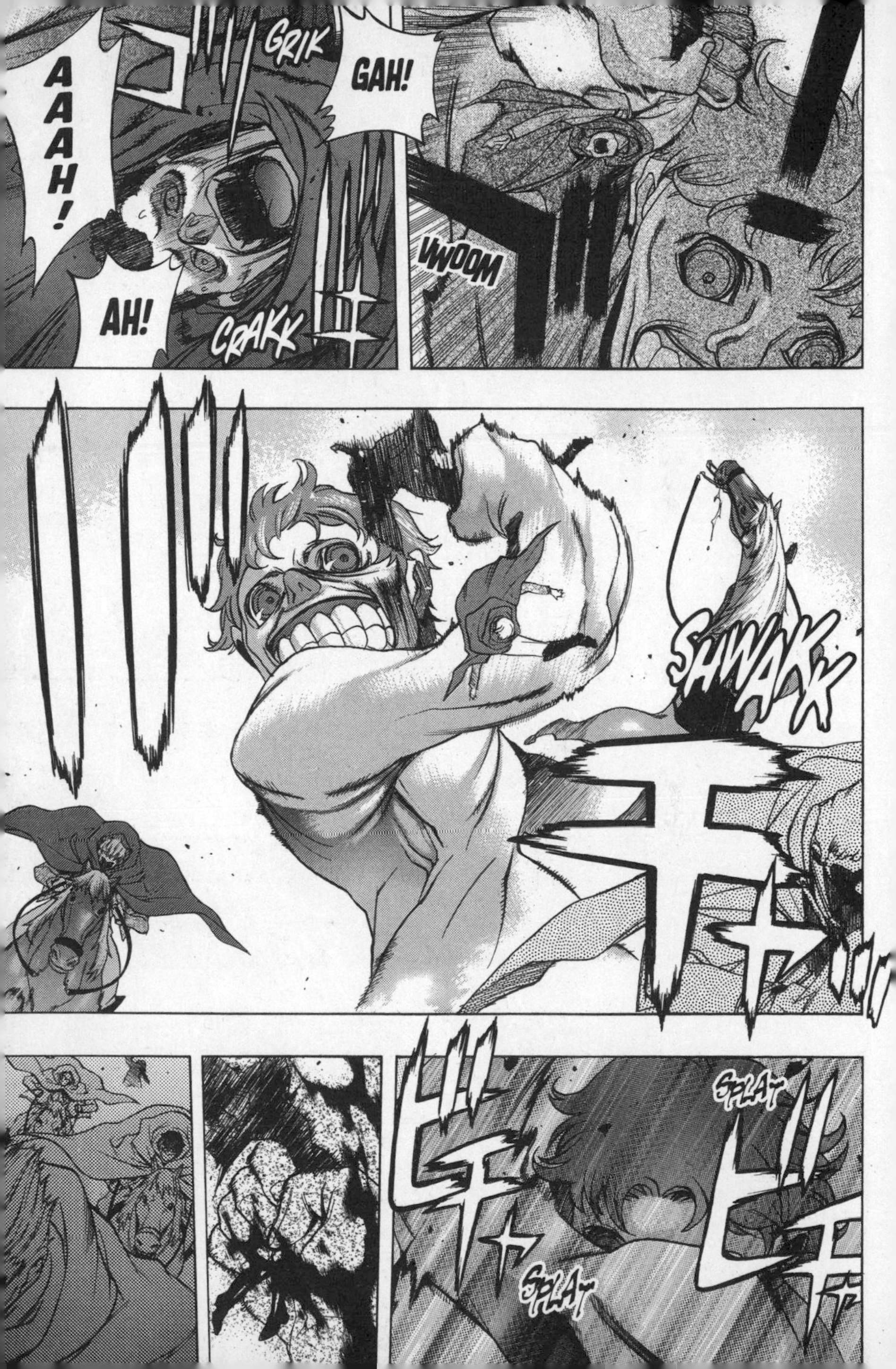
VWOOM
GRIK
GAH!
AAAAH!
AH!
CRAKK
SHWAKK
SPLAT
SPLAT

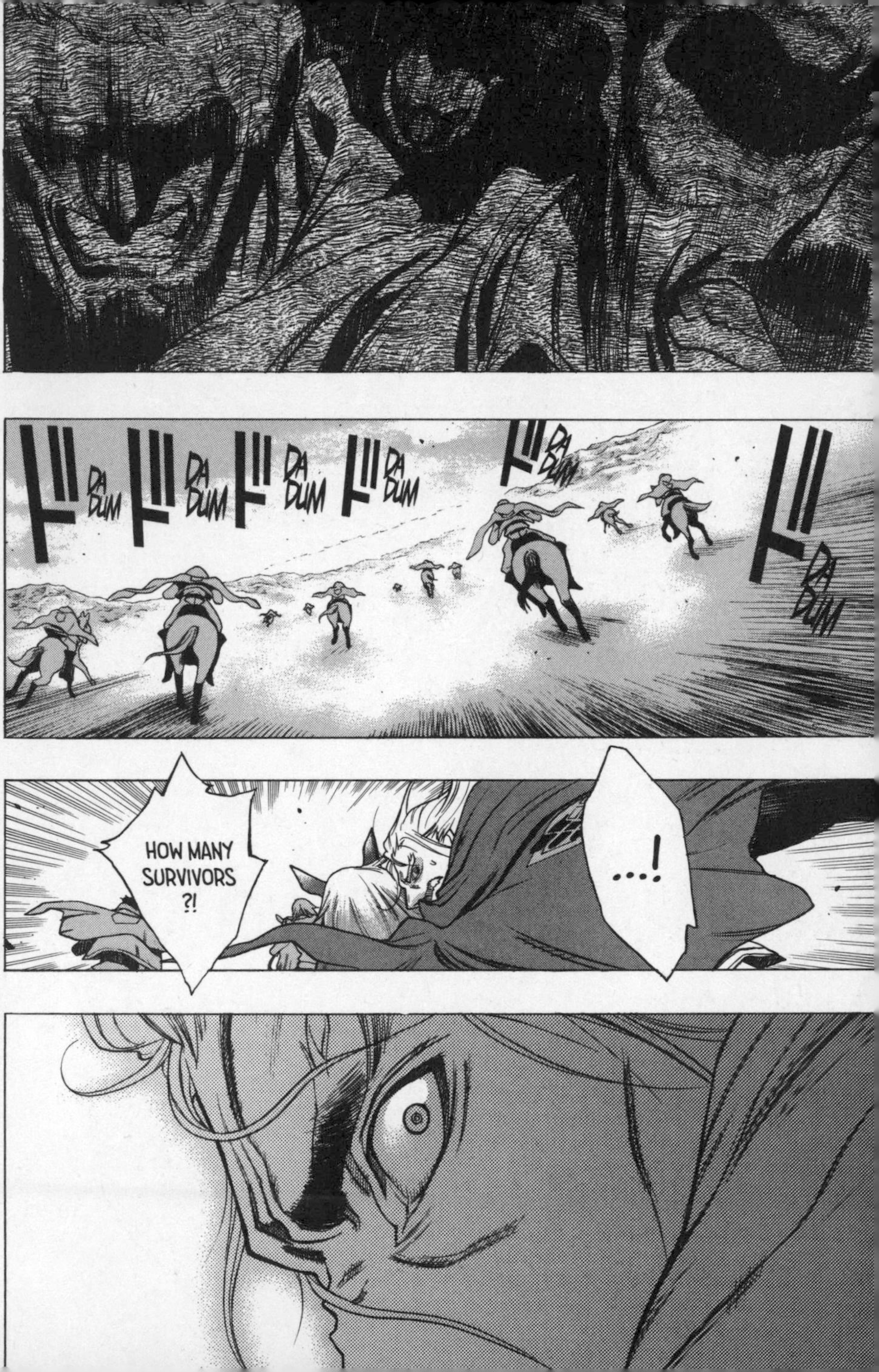
DA DUM
DA DUM
DA DUM
DA DUM
DA DUM
DA DUM
...!
HOW MANY SURVIVORS ?!

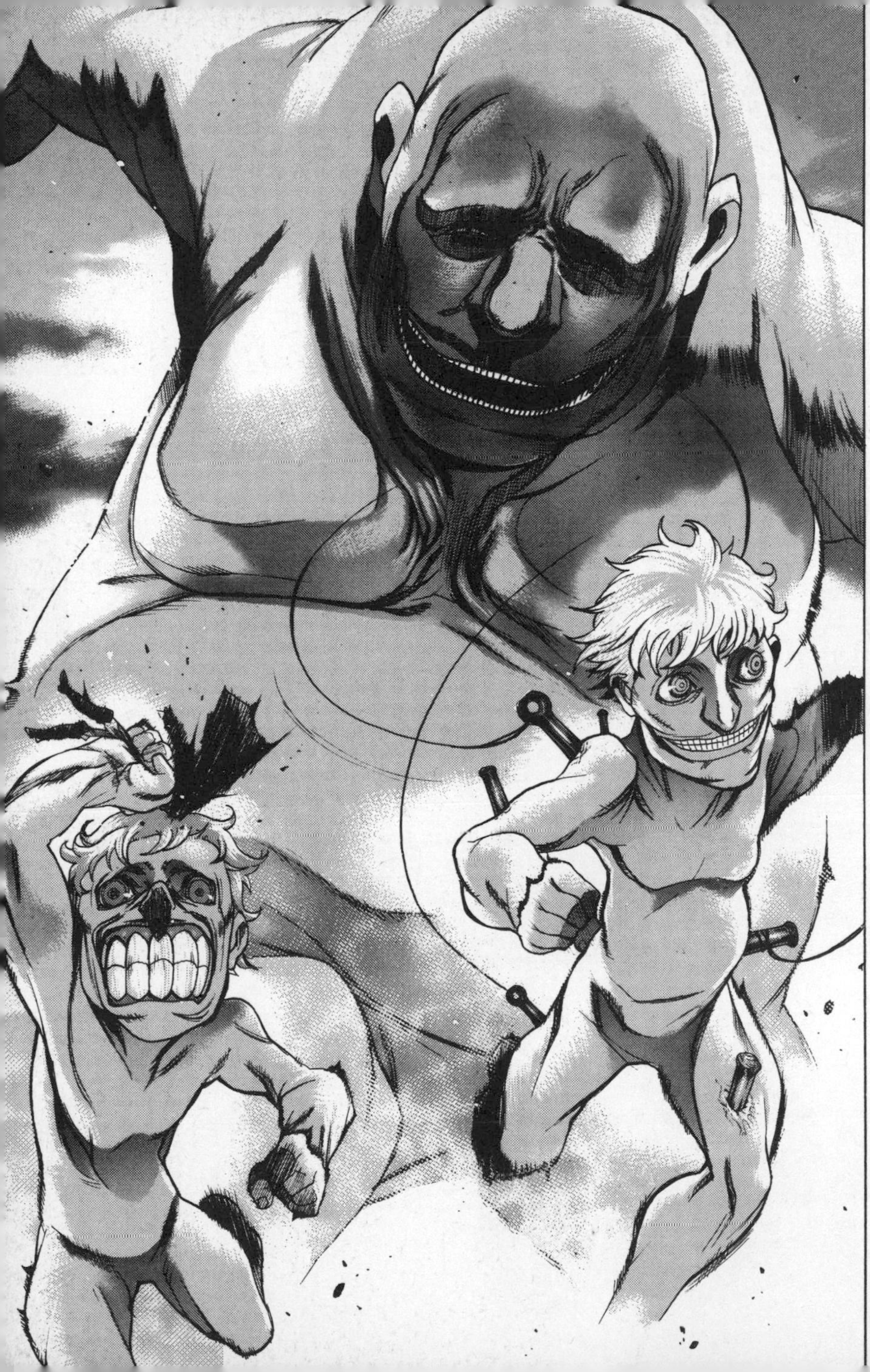

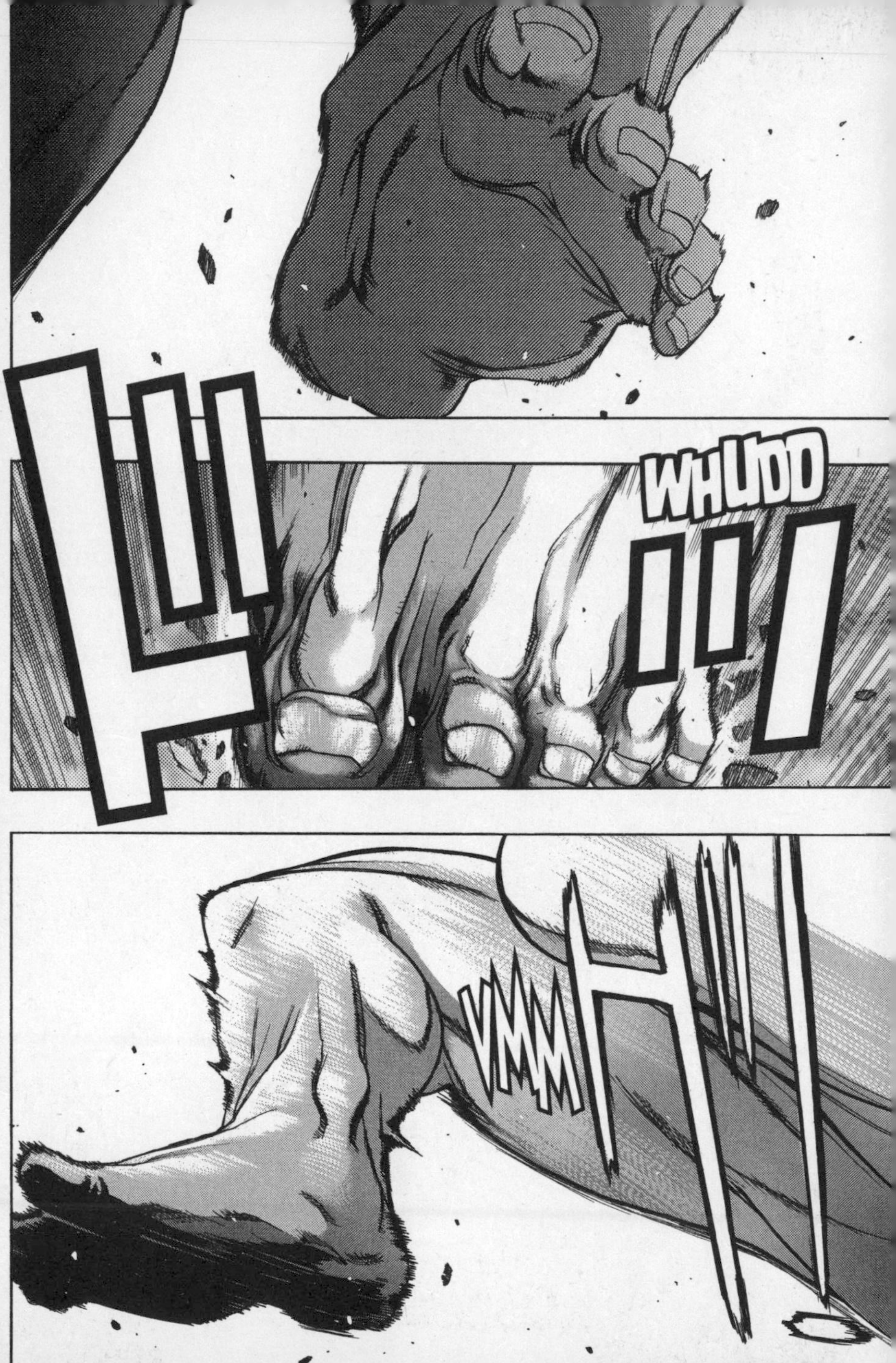
WHUDD
VMM

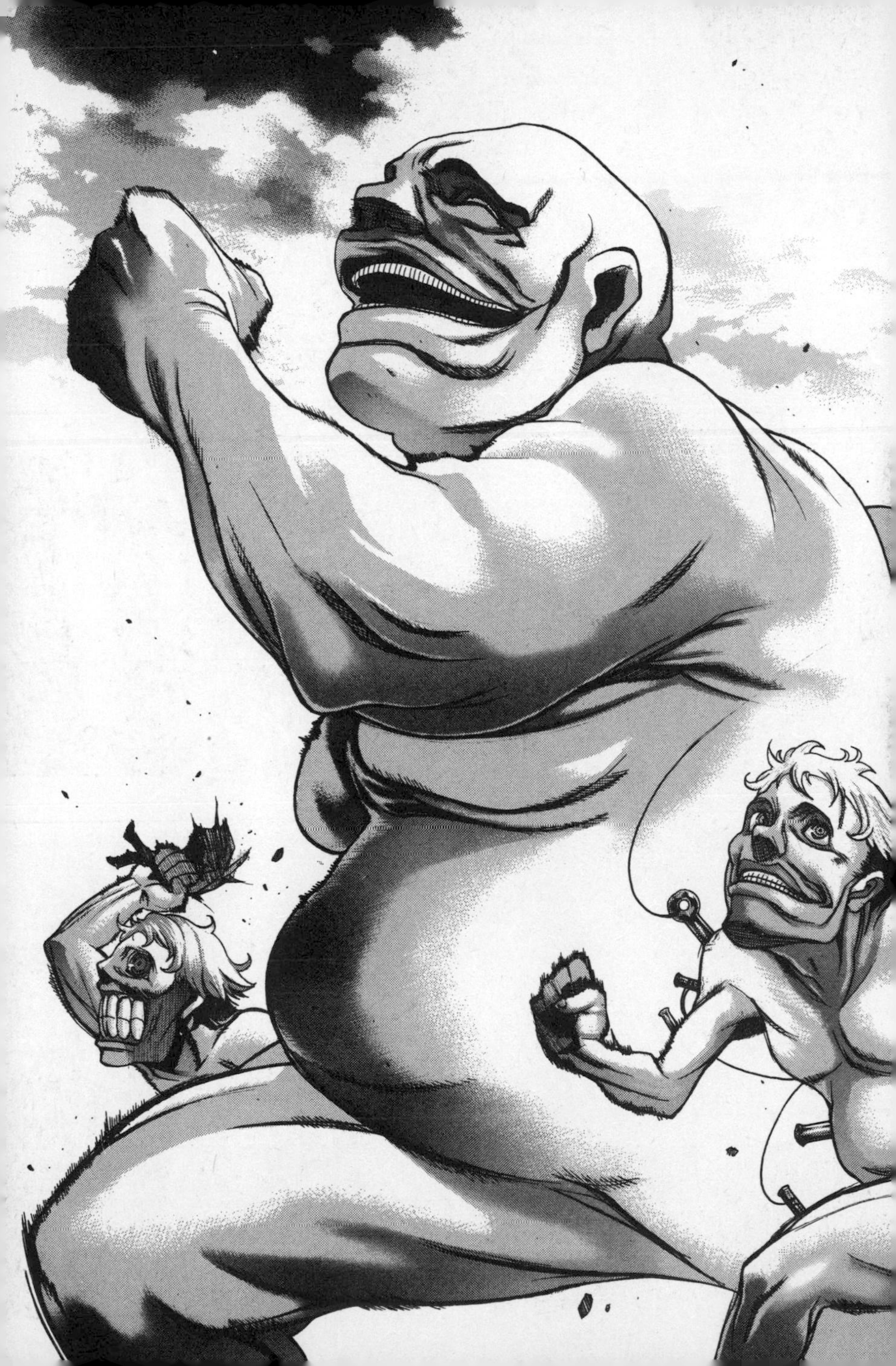

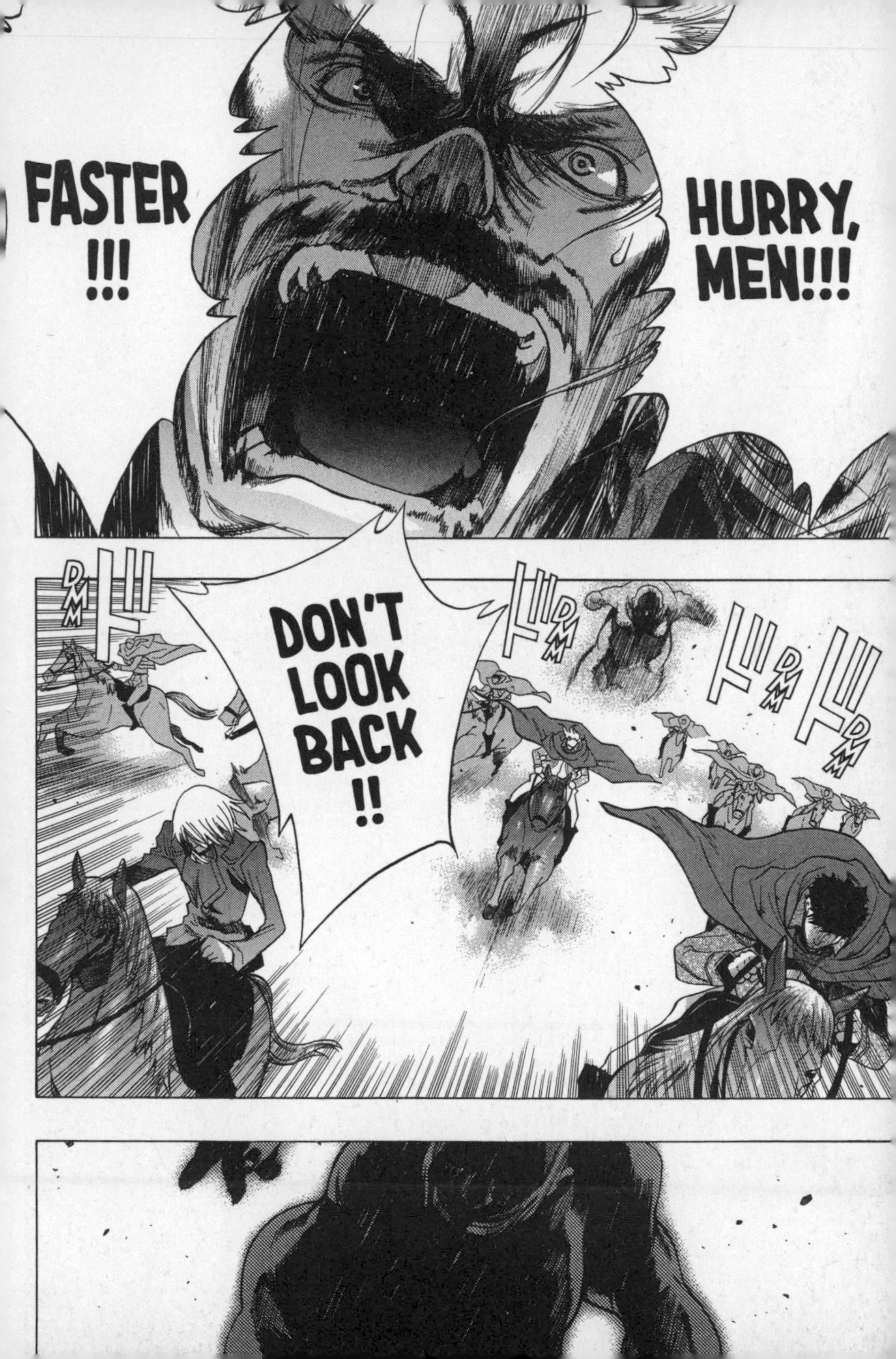
HURRY, MEN!!!
FASTER!!!
DMM
DMM
DMM
DON'T LOOK BACK!!
DMM

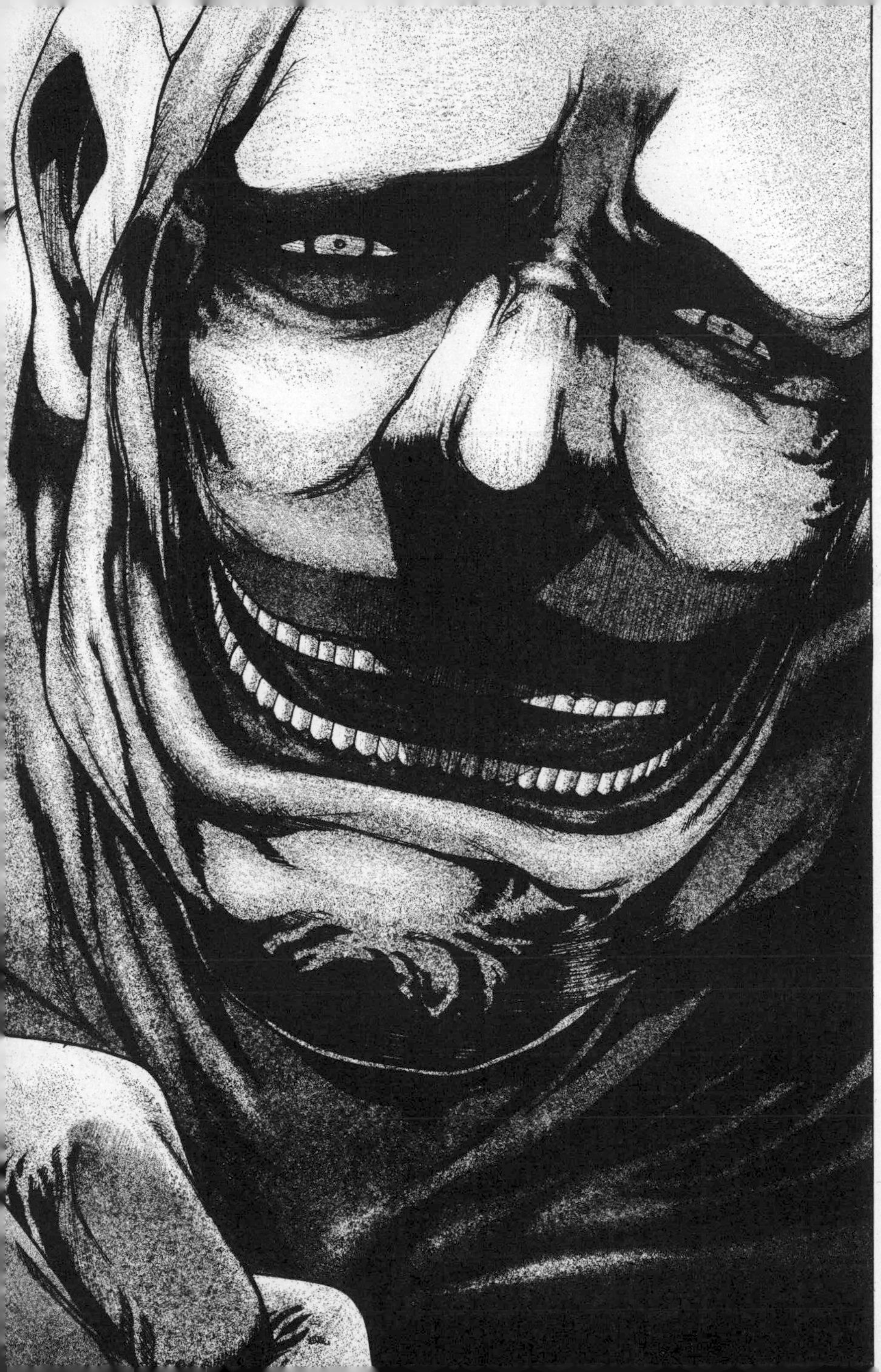

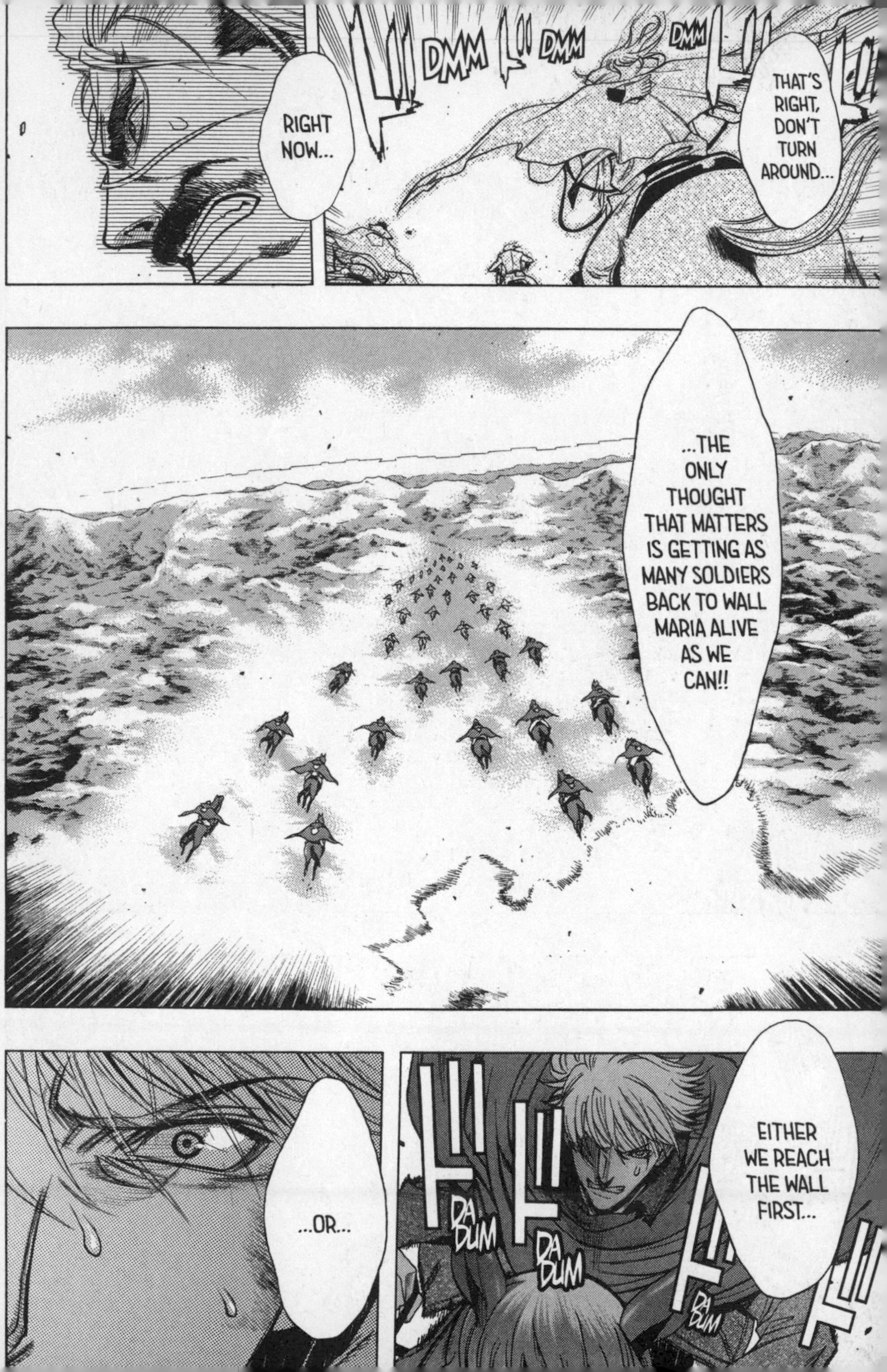
DMM
DMM
DMM
THAT'S RIGHT, DON'T TURN AROUND...
RIGHT NOW...
...THE ONLY THOUGHT THAT MATTERS IS GETTING AS MANY SOLDIERS BACK TO WALL MARIA ALIVE AS WE CAN!!
EITHER WE REACH THE WALL FIRST...
DA DUM
DA DUM
DA DUM
...OR...

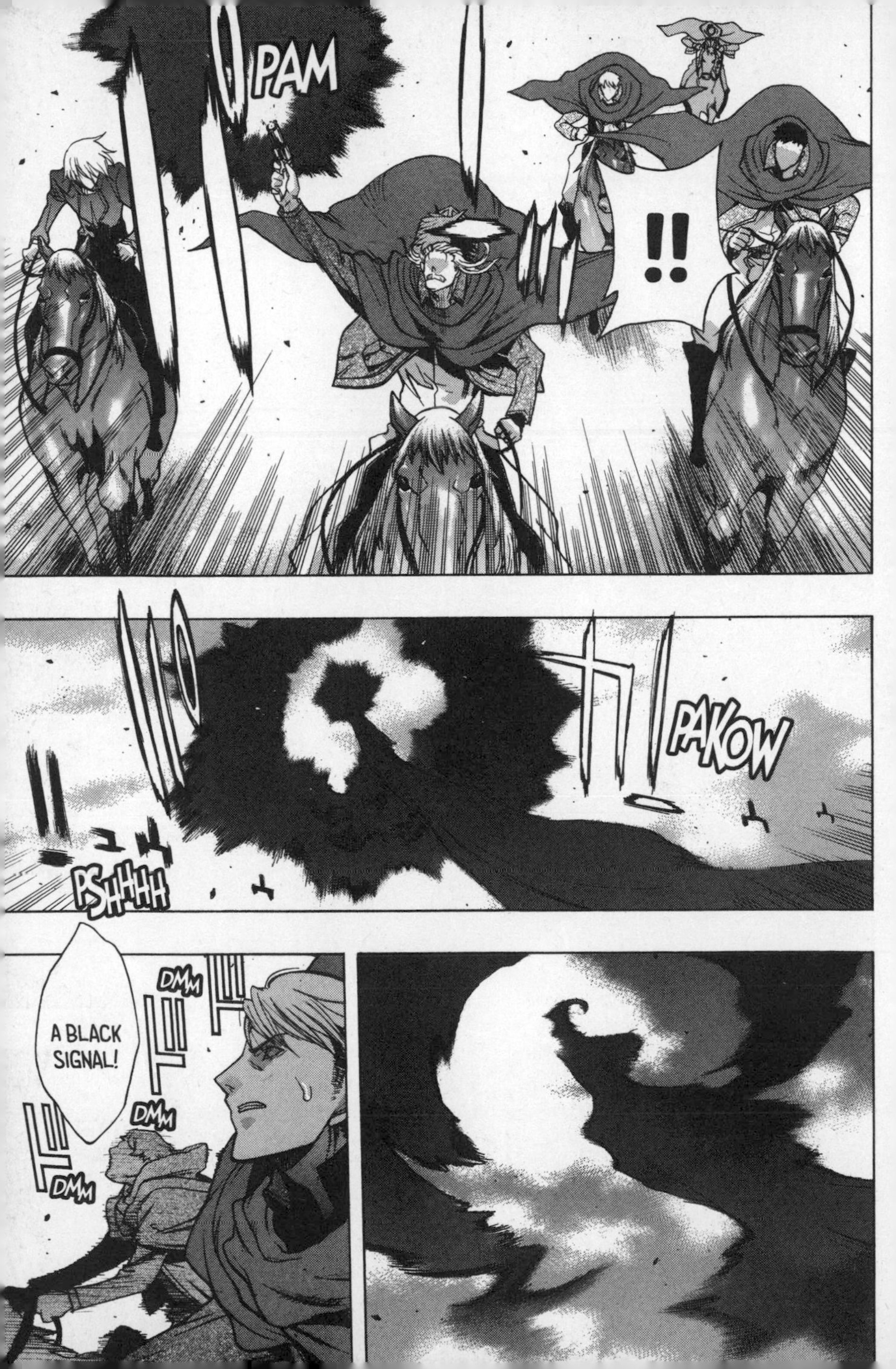
PAM
!!
PAKOW
PSHHHH
A BLACK SIGNAL!
DMM
DMM
DMM

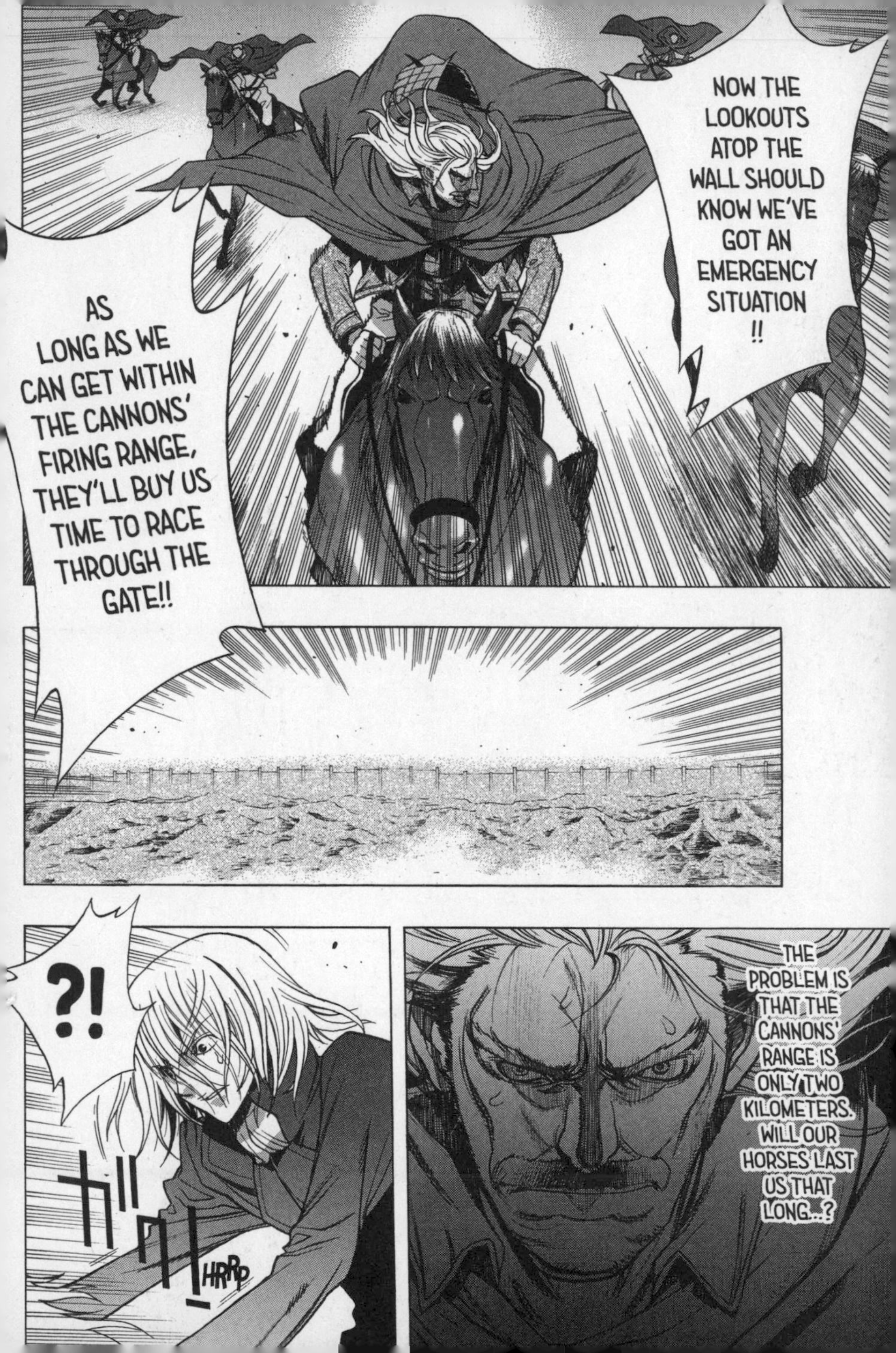
NOW THE LOOKOUTS ATOP THE WALL SHOULD KNOW WE'VE GOT AN EMERGENCY SITUATION !!
AS LONG AS WE CAN GET WITHIN THE CANNONS' FIRING RANGE, THEY'LL BUY US TIME TO RACE THROUGH THE GATE!!
THE PROBLEM IS THAT THE CANNONS' RANGE IS ONLY TWO KILOMETERS. WILL OUR HORSES LAST US THAT LONG...?
?!
HRRP

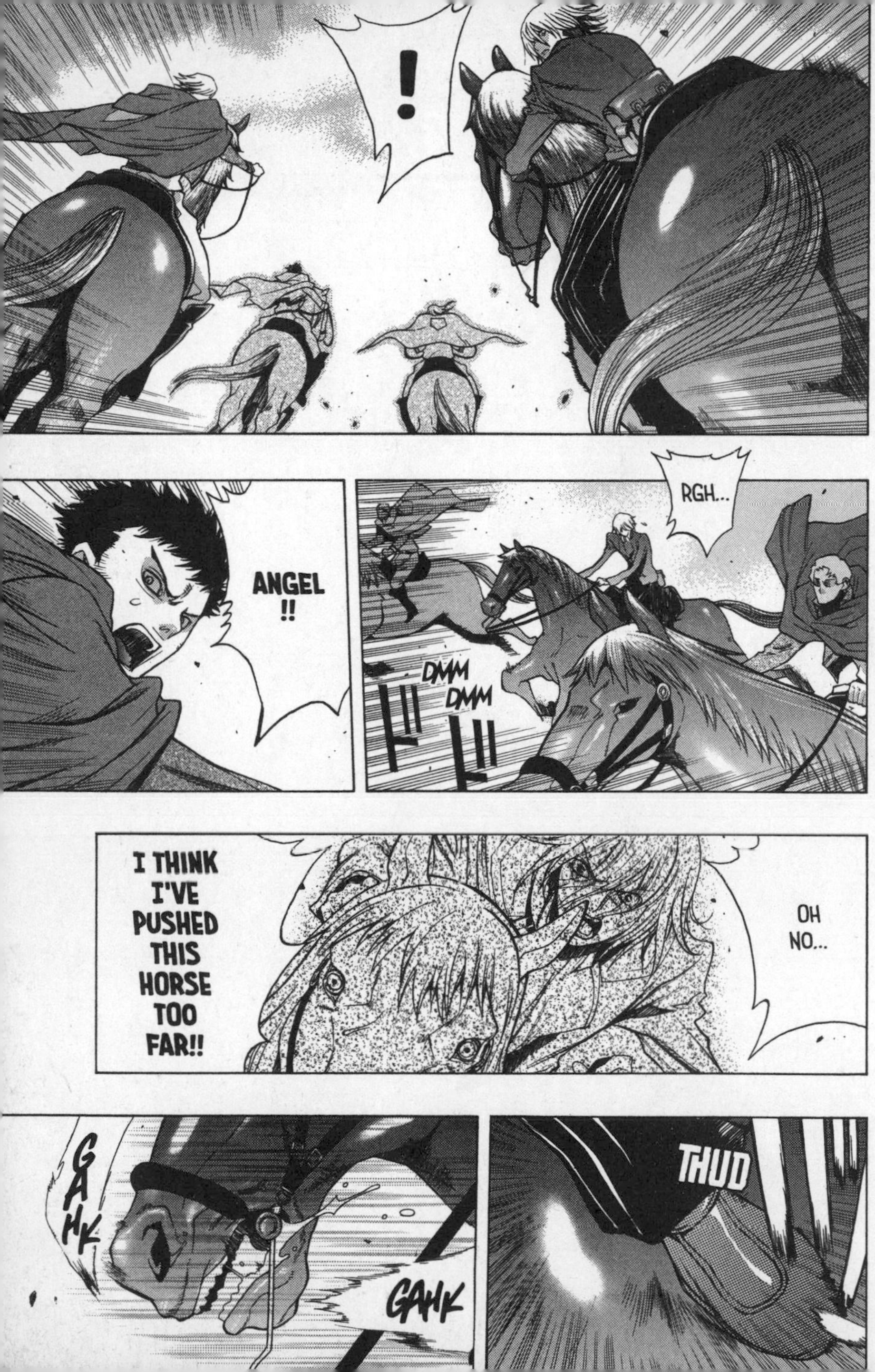
!
RGH...
DMM
DMM
ANGEL!!
OH NO...
I THINK I'VE PUSHED THIS HORSE TOO FAR!!
THUD
GAHK
GAHK

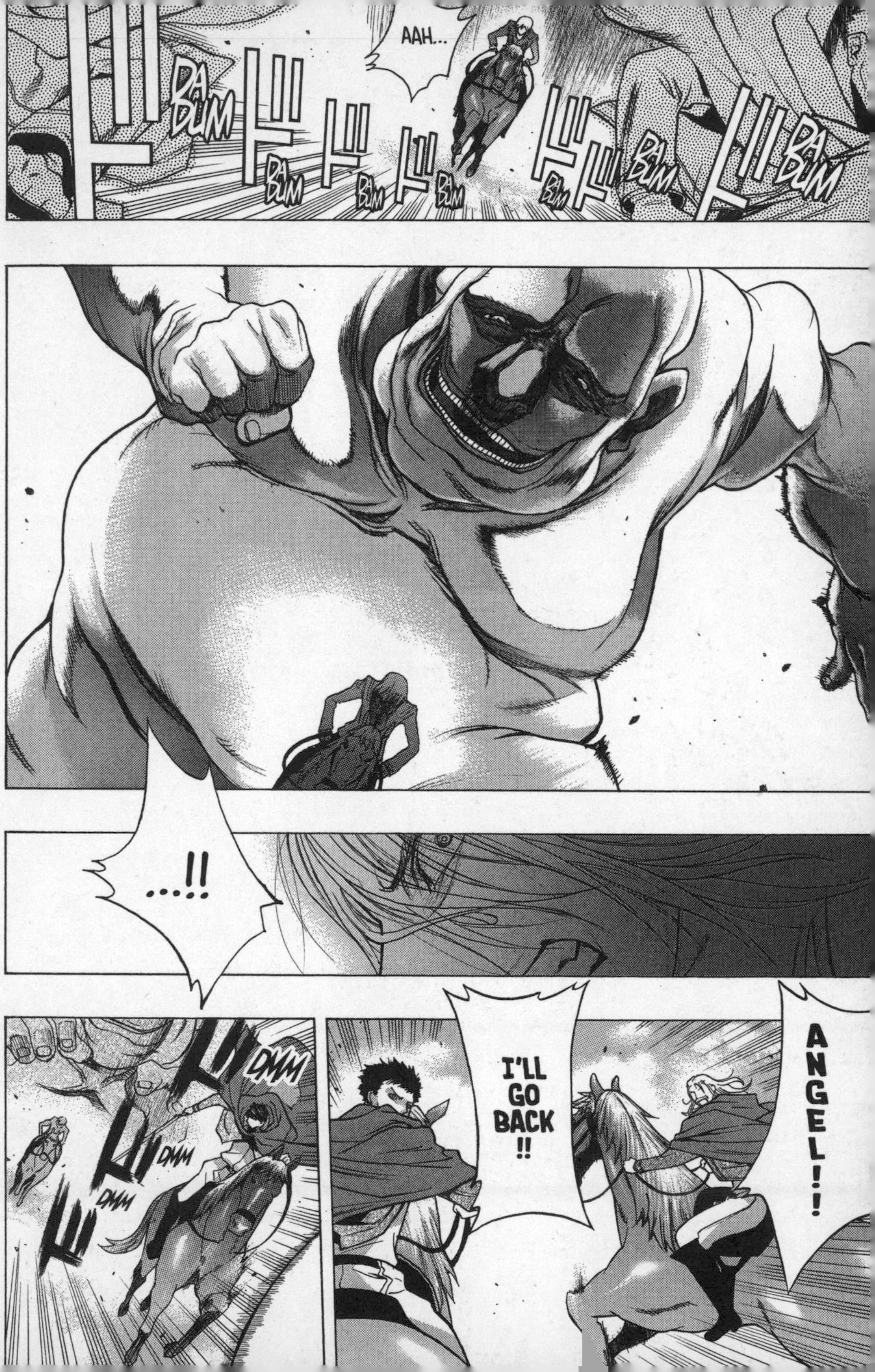
DA BUM
BA BUM
BUM
AAH...
BUM
BUM
BA BUM
DA BUM
...!!
ANGEL!!
I'LL GO BACK!!
DMM
DMM
DMM

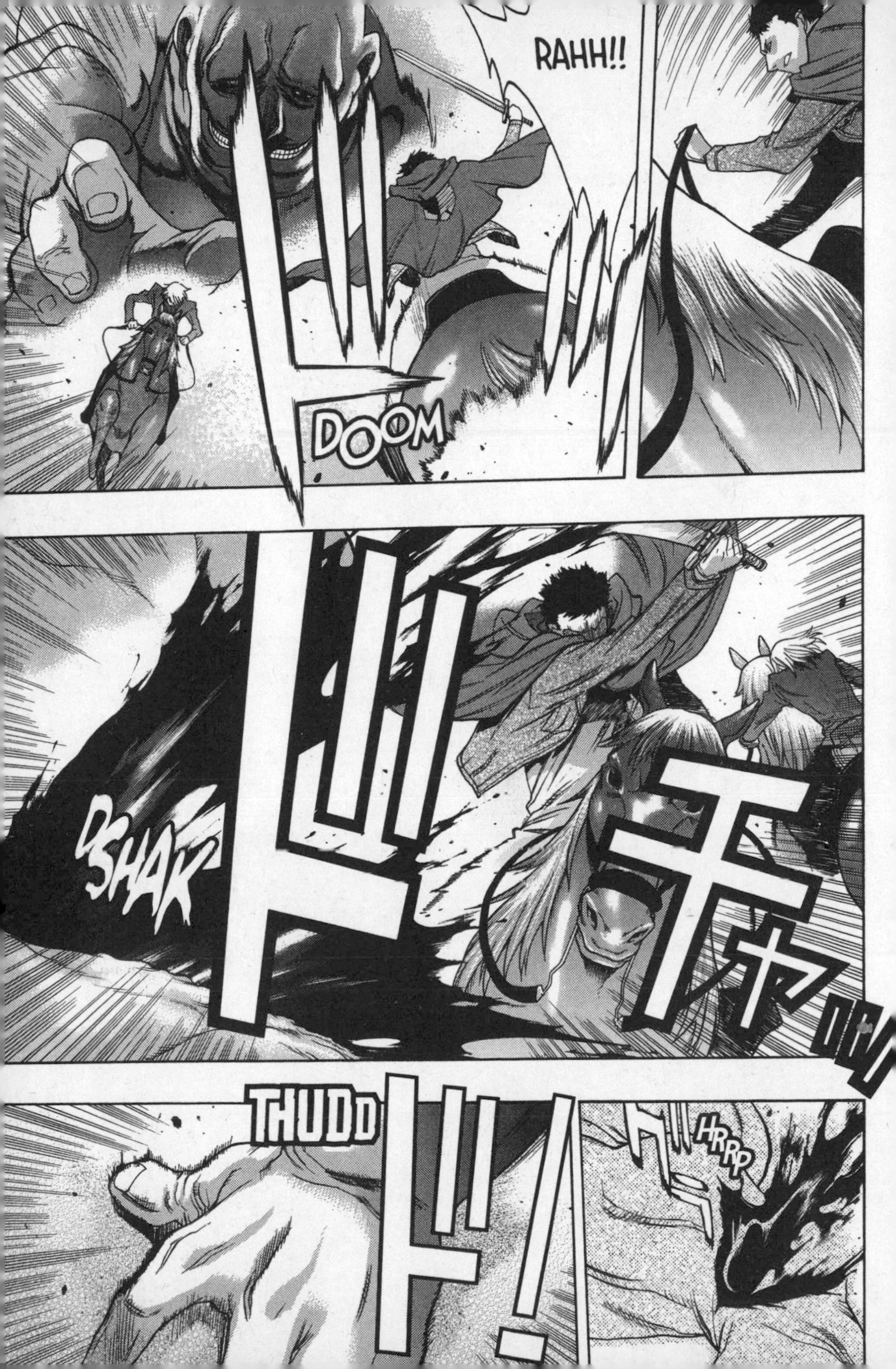
RAHH!!
DOOM
DSHAK
HRRP
THUDD

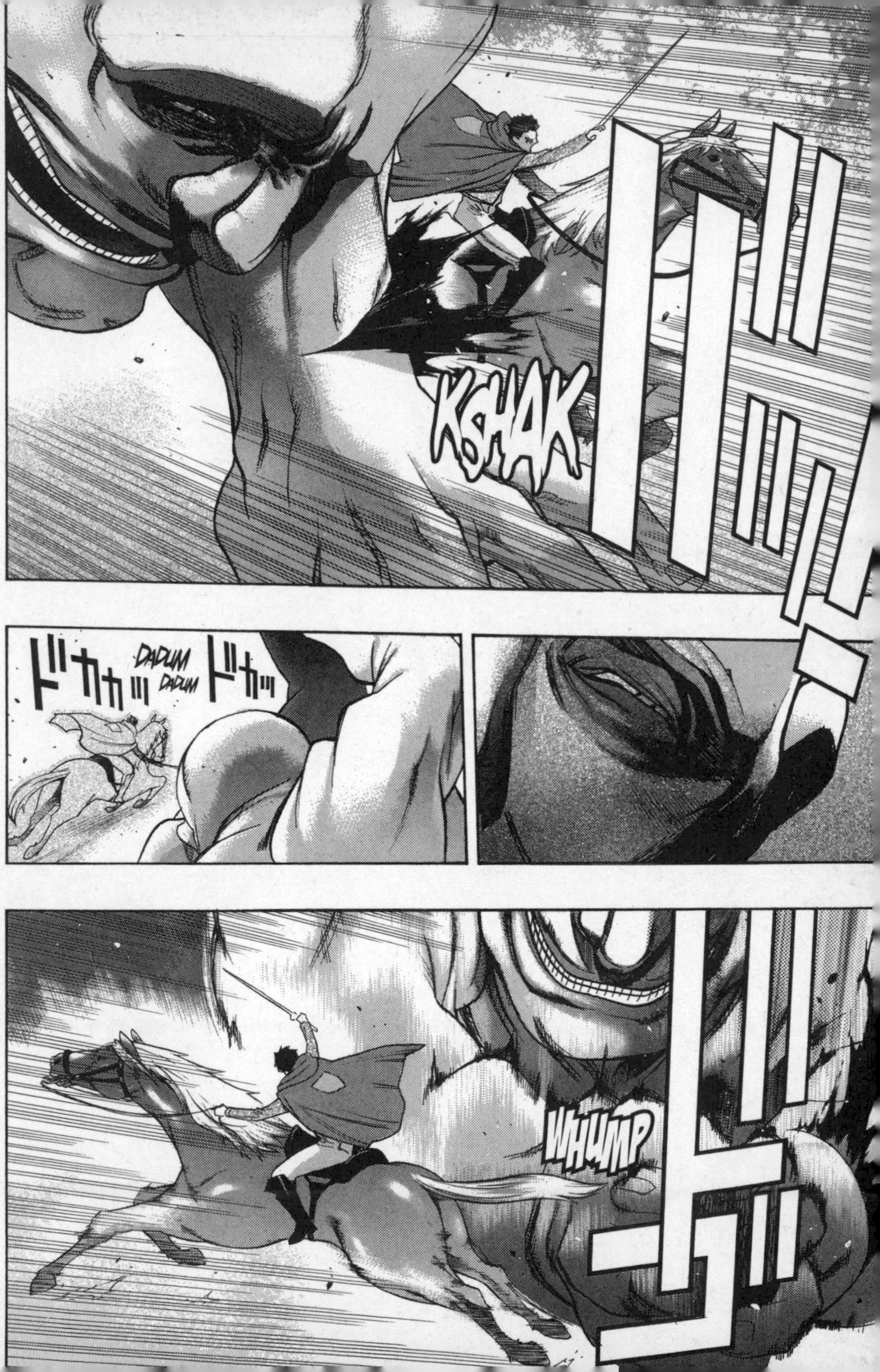
KSHAK
ドカカッ
DADUM DADUM
ドカッ
WHUMP

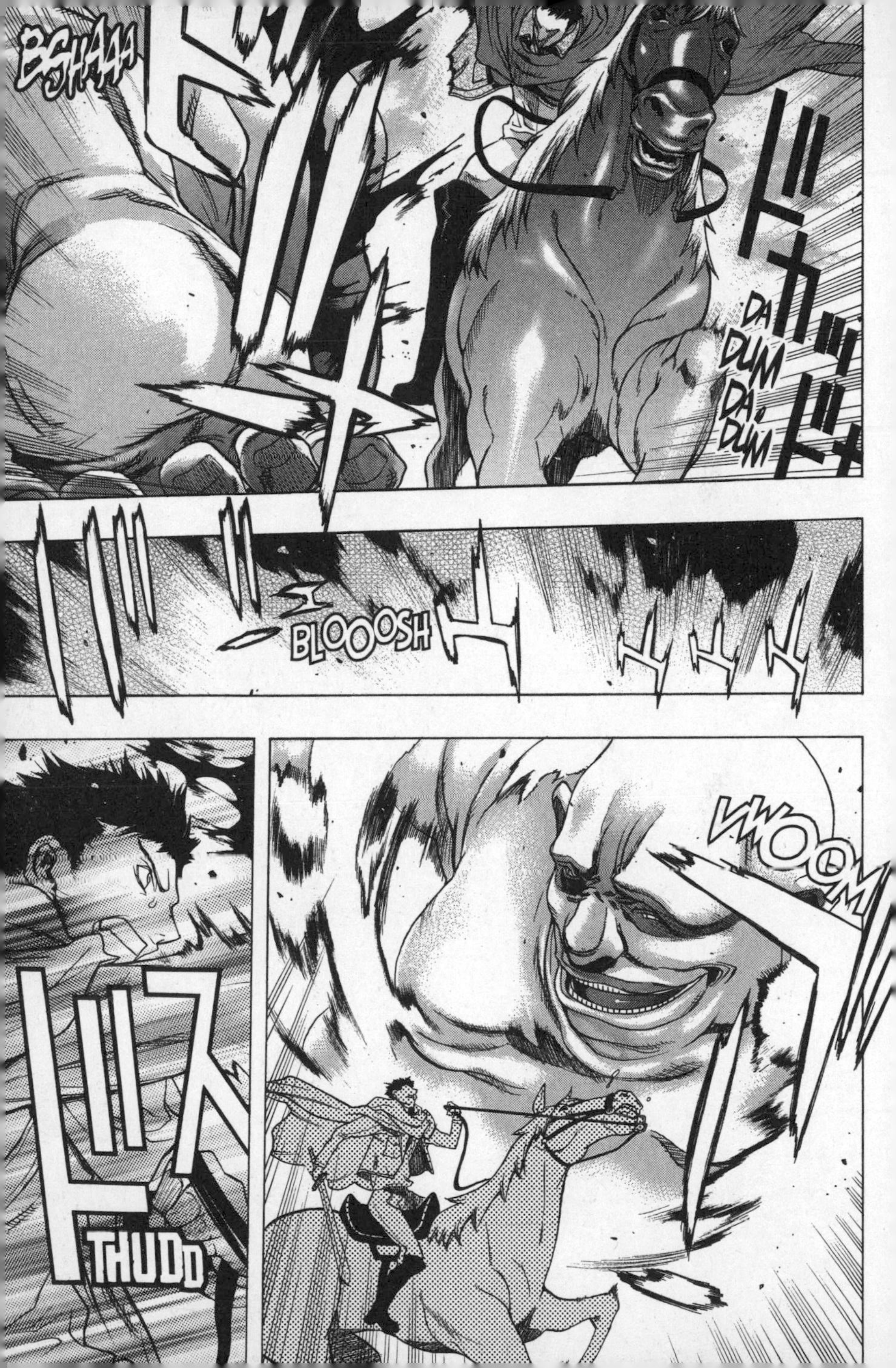
DA DUM DA DUM
BSHAAA
BLOOOSH
VWOOM
THUDD

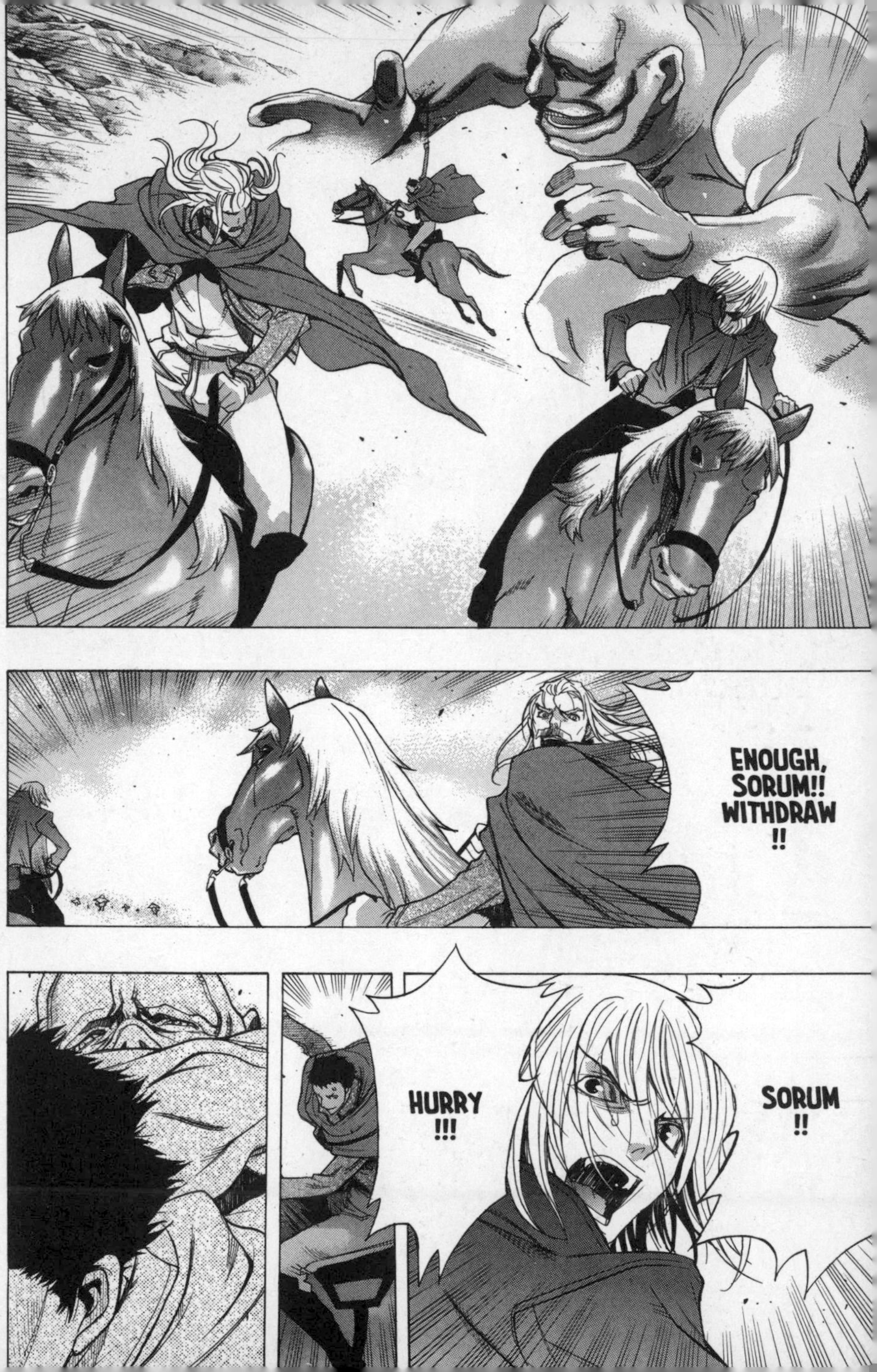
ENOUGH, SORUM!! WITHDRAW !!
SORUM !!
HURRY !!!

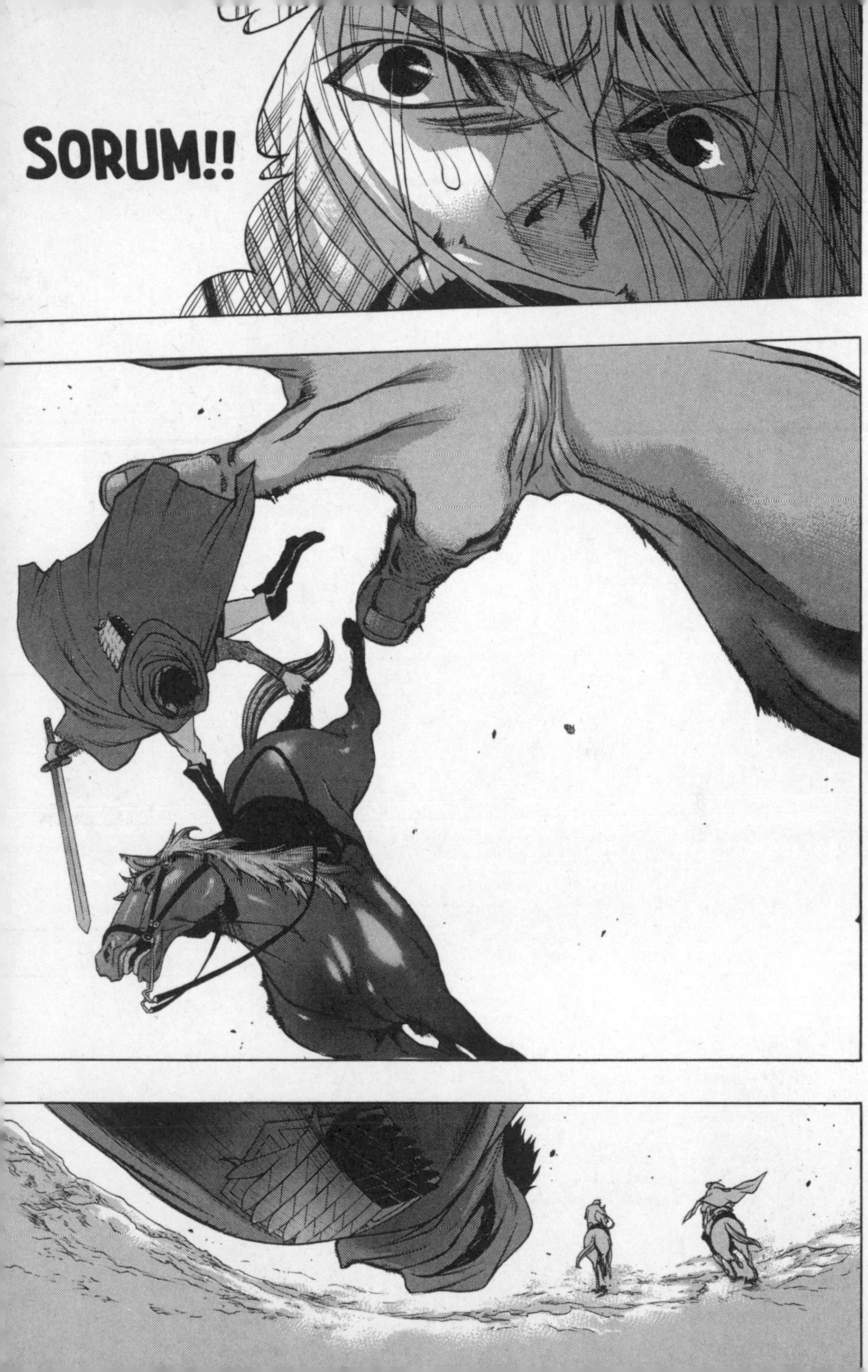
SORUM!!

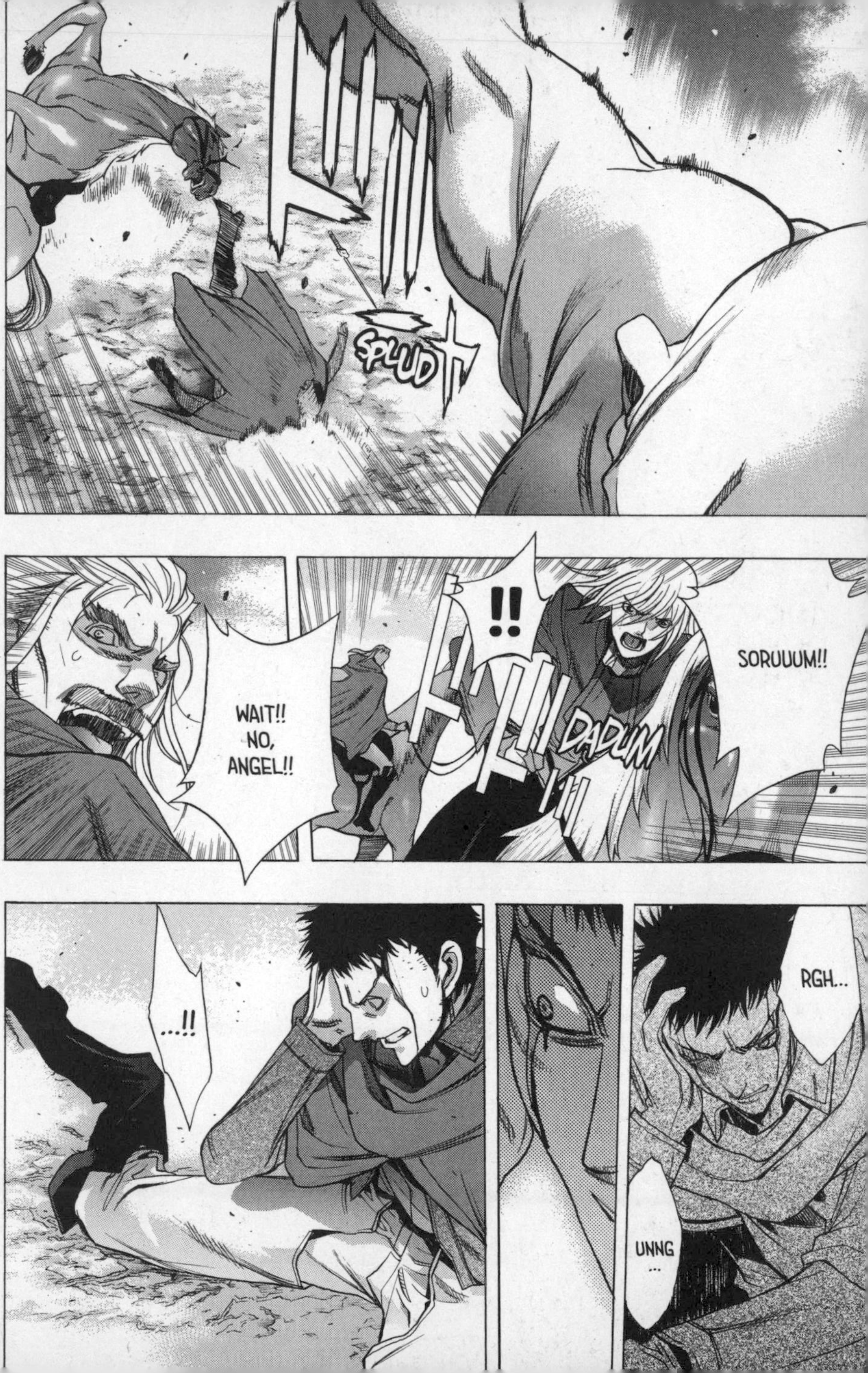
SPLUD
SORUUUM!!
!!
DADUM
WAIT!! NO, ANGEL!!
RGH...
UNNG ...
...!!

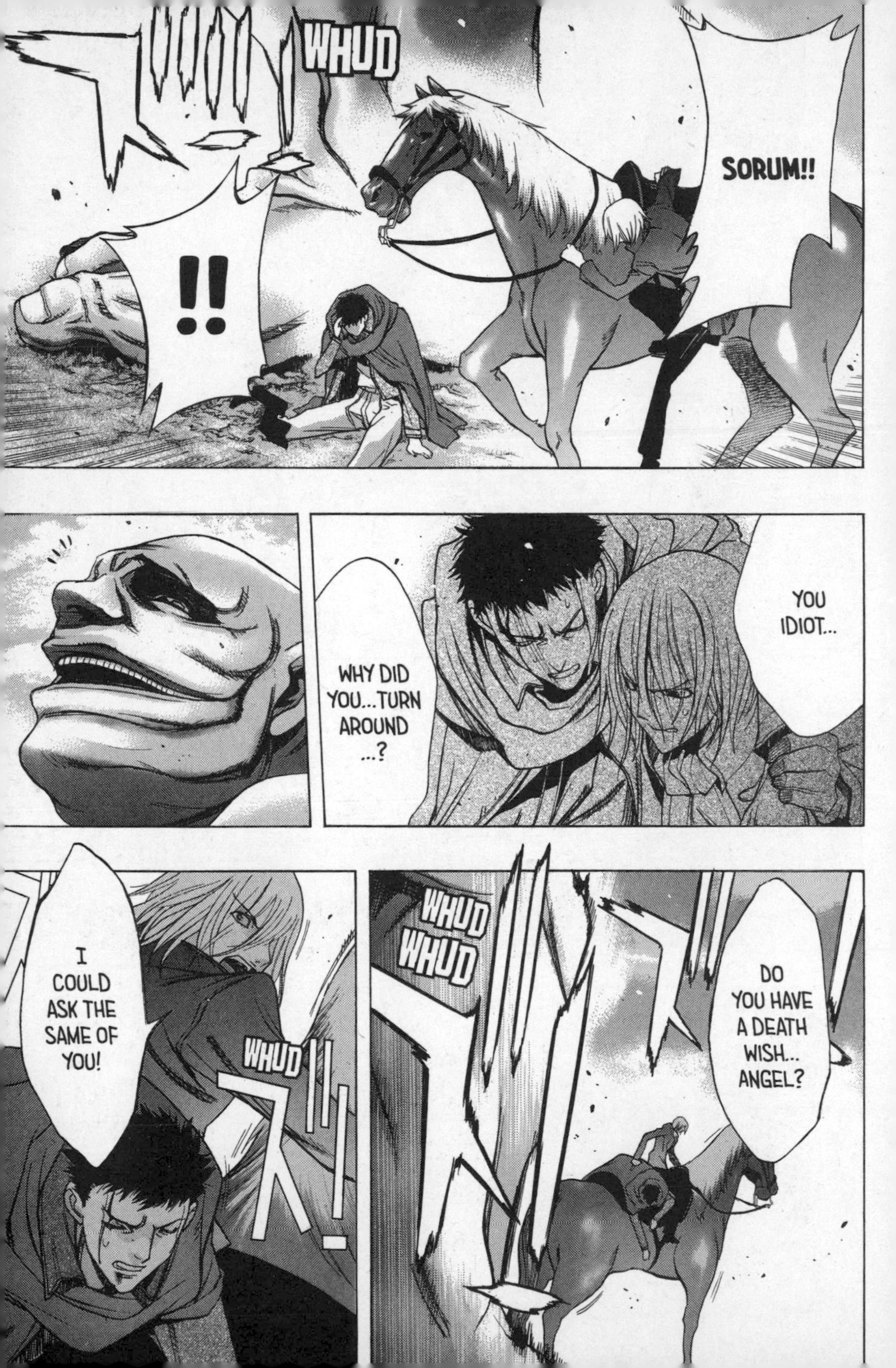
SORUM!!
WHUD
!!
YOU IDIOT...
WHY DID YOU...TURN AROUND ...?
DO YOU HAVE A DEATH WISH... ANGEL?
WHUD WHUD
I COULD ASK THE SAME OF YOU!
WHUD

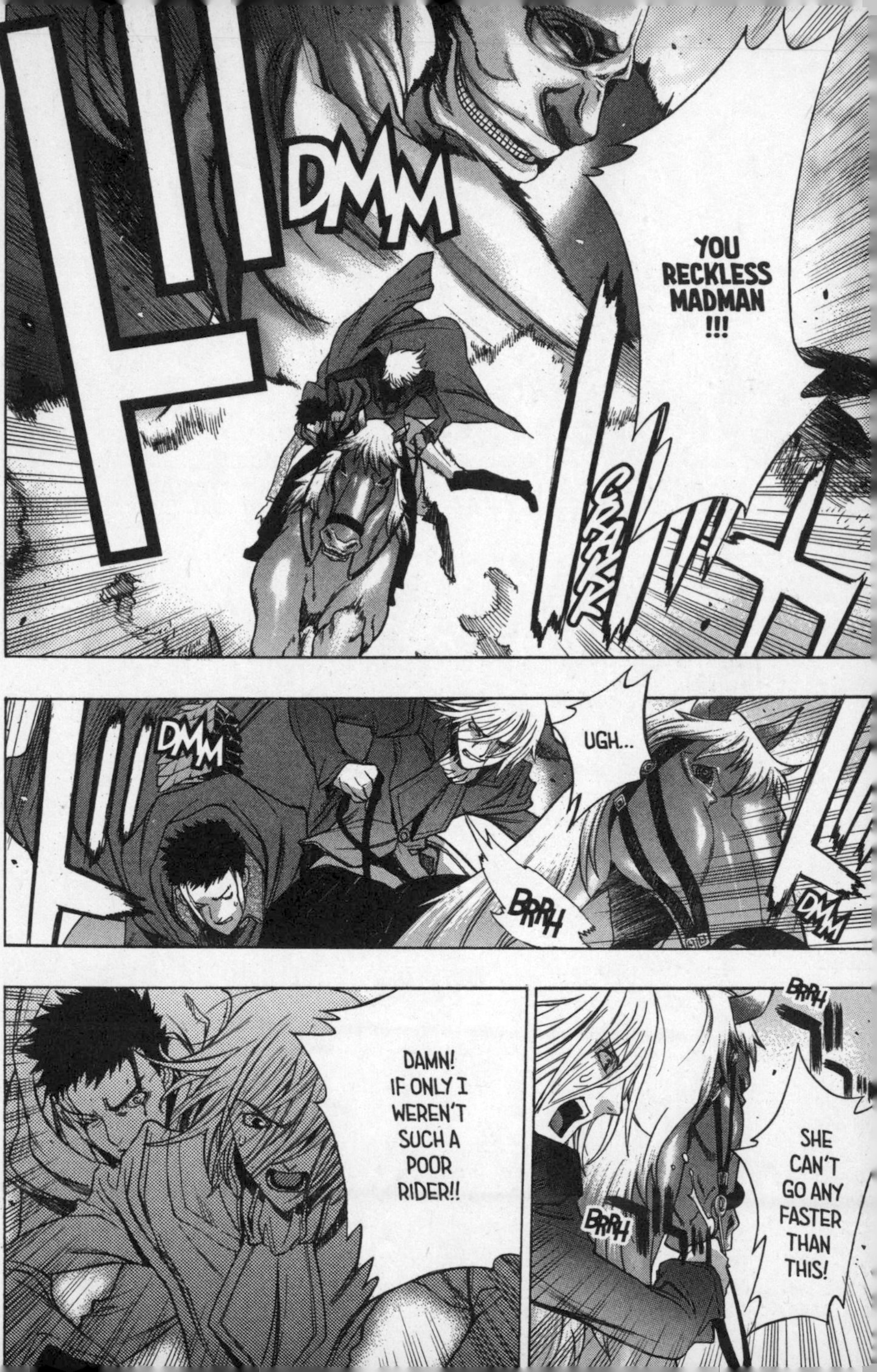
YOU RECKLESS MADMAN!!!
DMM
CRAKK
DMM
UGH...
BRRH
DMM
BRRH
SHE CAN'T GO ANY FASTER THAN THIS!
BRRH
DAMN! IF ONLY I WEREN'T SUCH A POOR RIDER!!

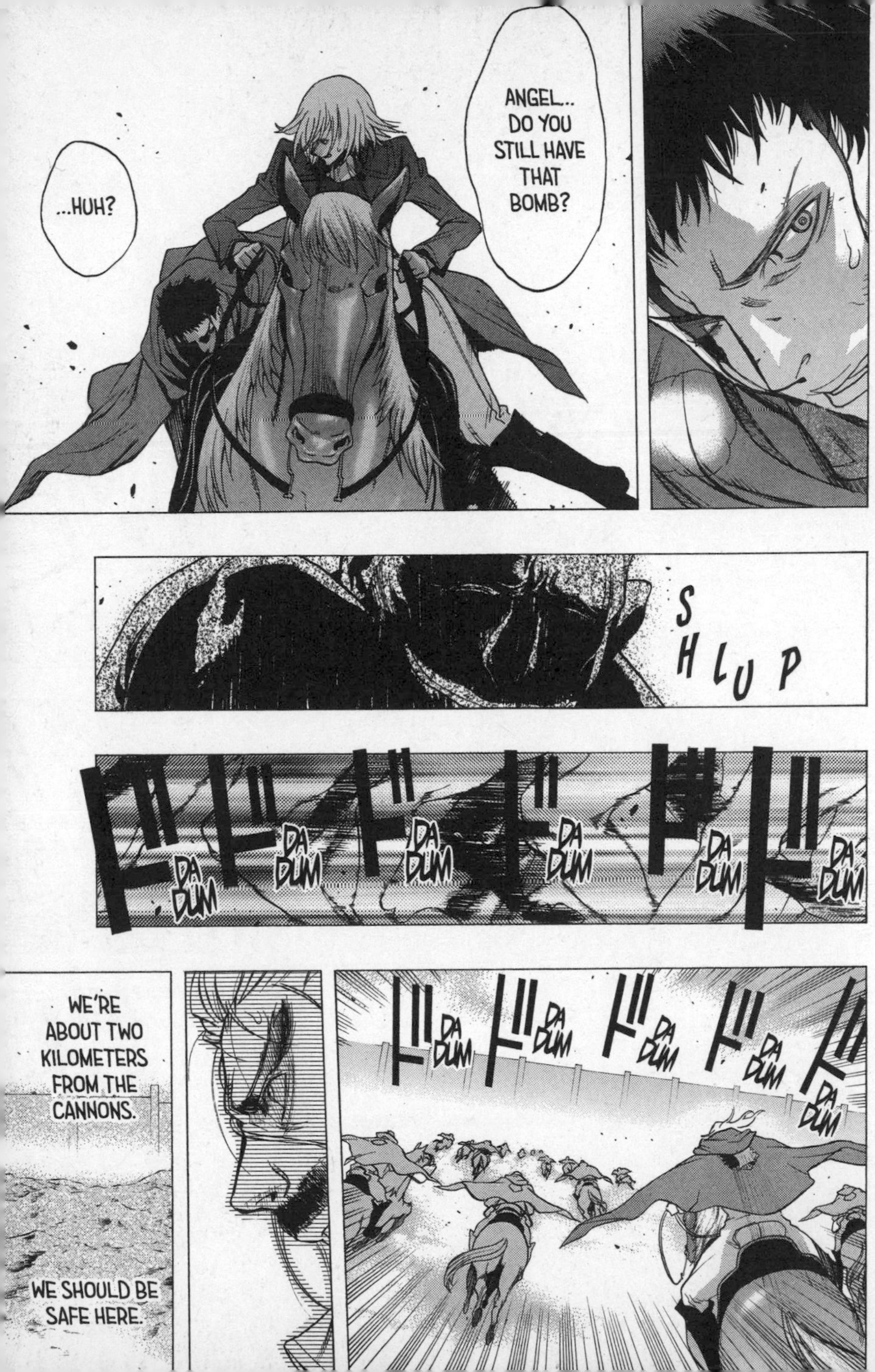
ANGEL... DO YOU STILL HAVE THAT BOMB?
...HUH?
SHLUP
DA DUM
DA DUM
DA DUM
DA DUM
DA DUM
DA DUM
DA DUM
DA DUM
DA DUM
DA DUM
WE'RE ABOUT TWO KILOMETERS FROM THE CANNONS.
WE SHOULD BE SAFE HERE.

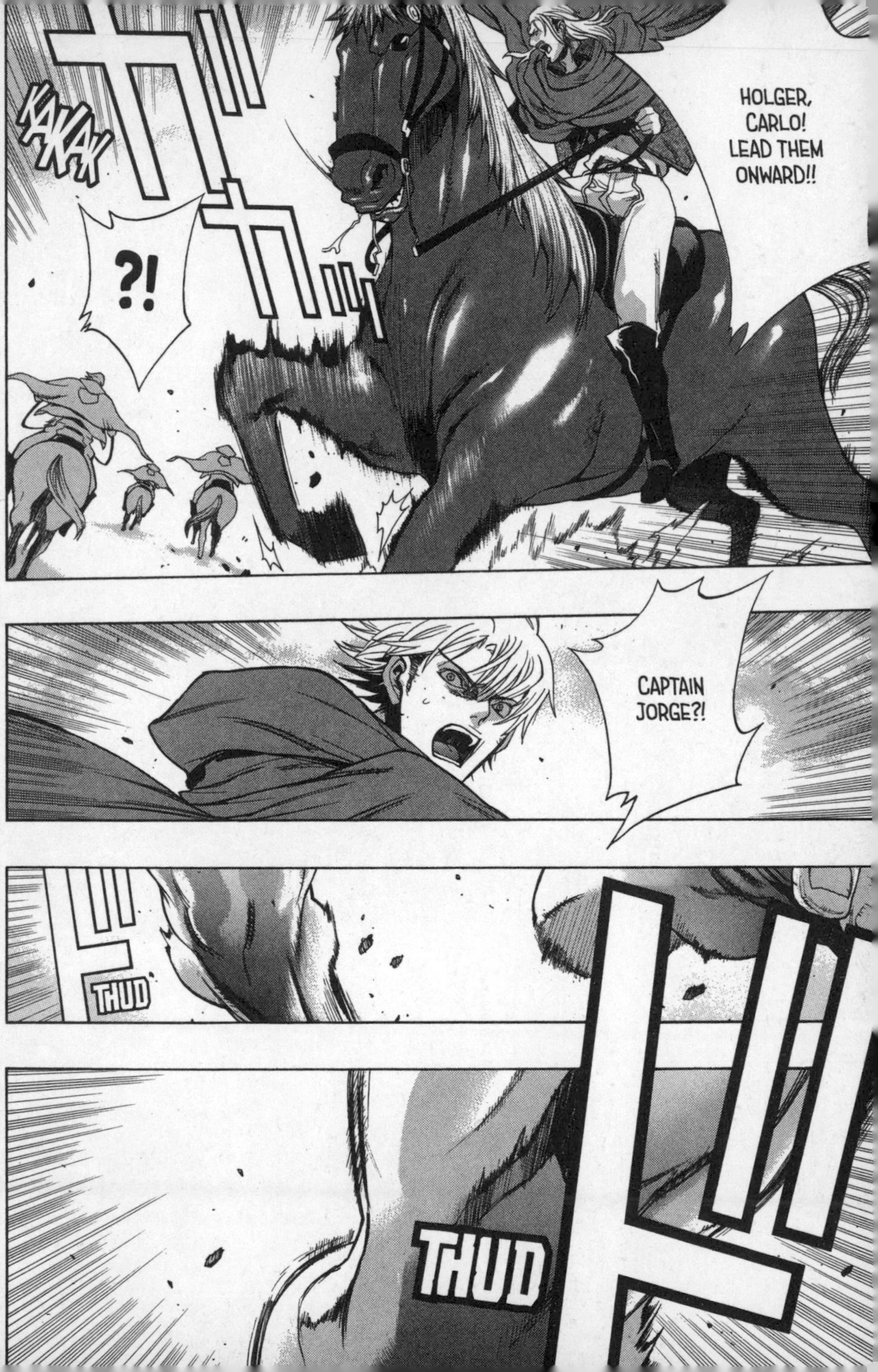
HOLGER, CARLO! LEAD THEM ONWARD!!
?!
KAKAK
CAPTAIN JORGE?!
THUD
THUD

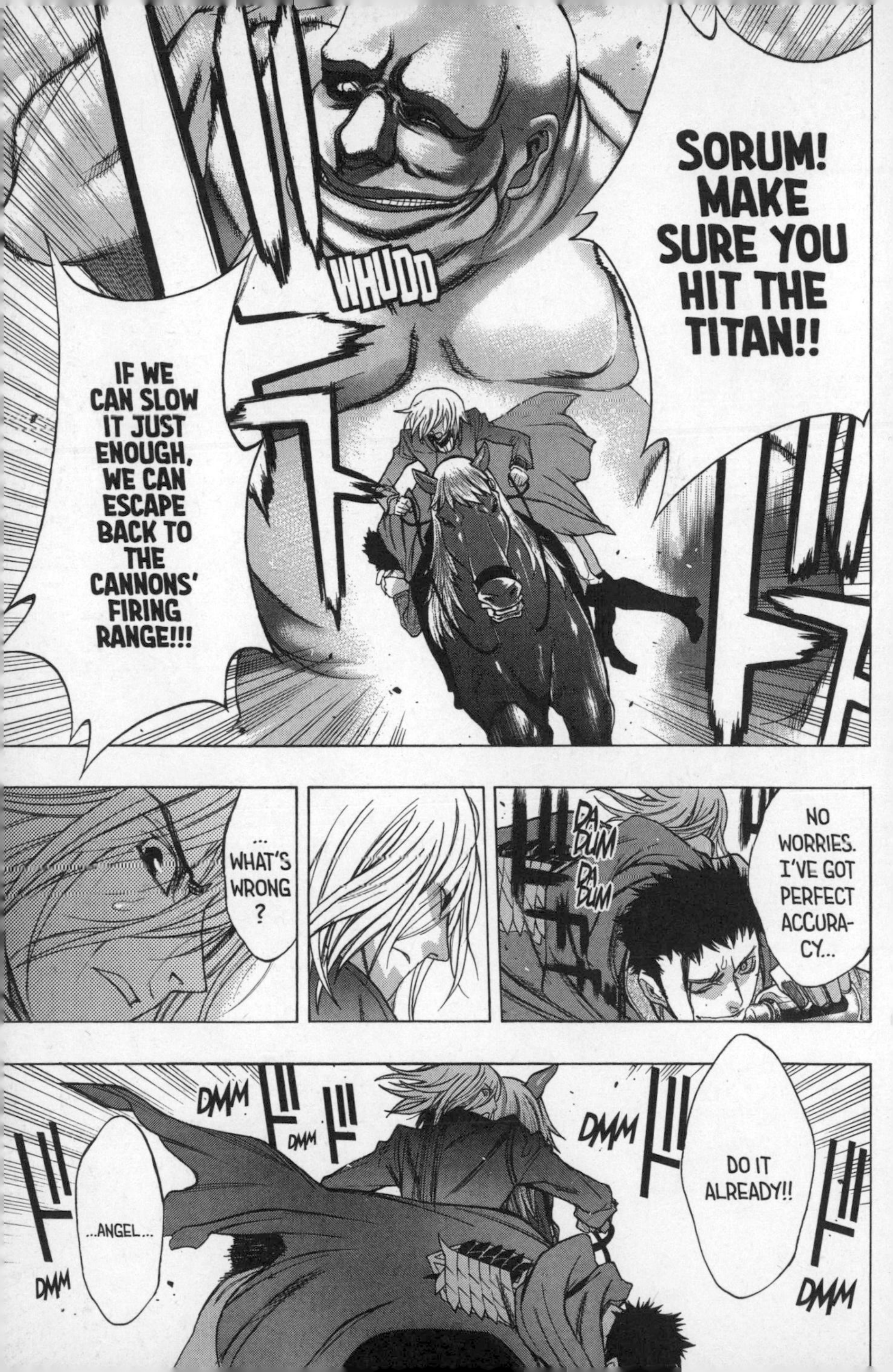
SORUM! MAKE SURE YOU HIT THE TITAN!!
WHUDD
IF WE CAN SLOW IT JUST ENOUGH, WE CAN ESCAPE BACK TO THE CANNONS' FIRING RANGE!!!
NO WORRIES. I'VE GOT PERFECT ACCURA-CY...
DA-DUM DA-DUM
...WHAT'S WRONG?
DO IT ALREADY!!
DMM DMM DMM DMM DMM
...ANGEL...

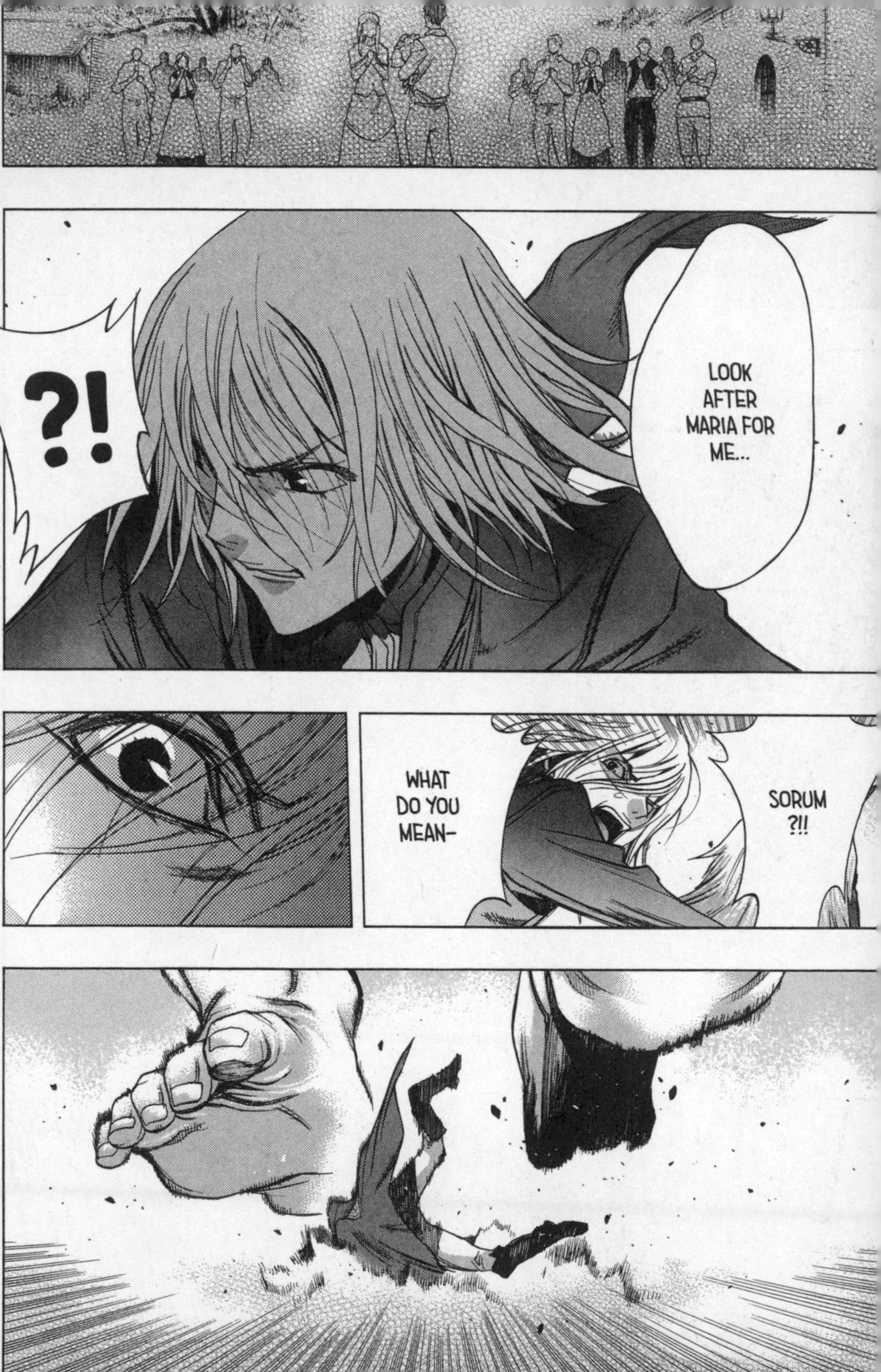
LOOK AFTER MARIA FOR ME...
?!
SORUM ?!!
WHAT DO YOU MEAN-

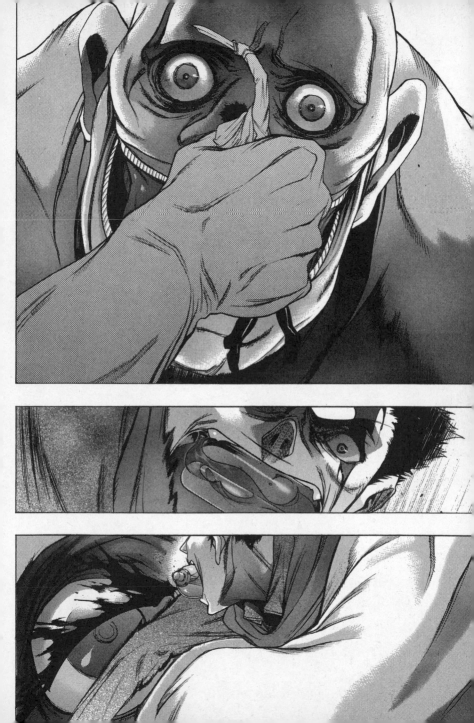

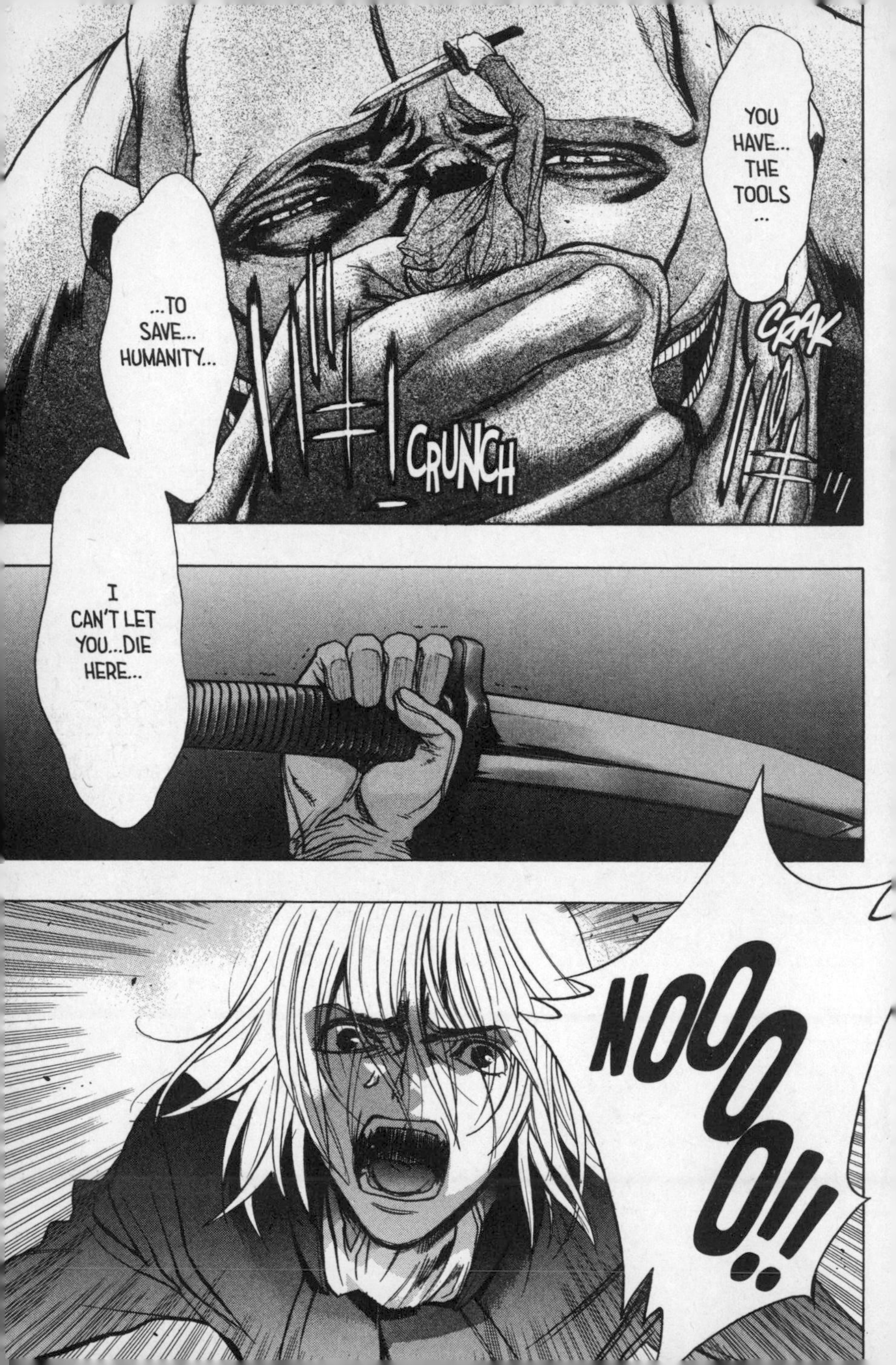
YOU HAVE... THE TOOLS ...
CRAK
...TO SAVE... HUMANITY...
CRUNCH
I CAN'T LET YOU...DIE HERE...
NOOOO!!

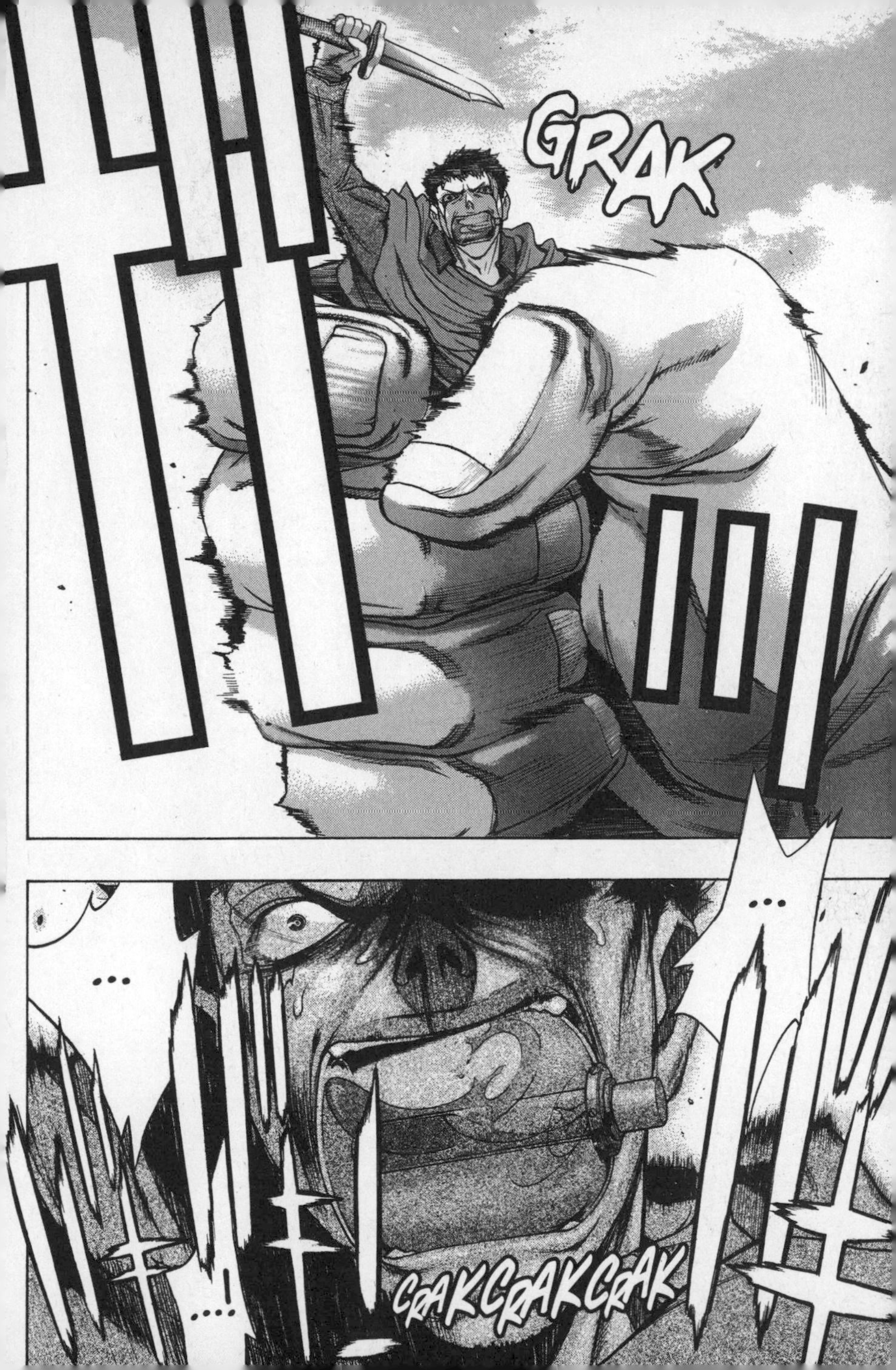
GRAK
...
...
CRAK CRAK CRAK
...!

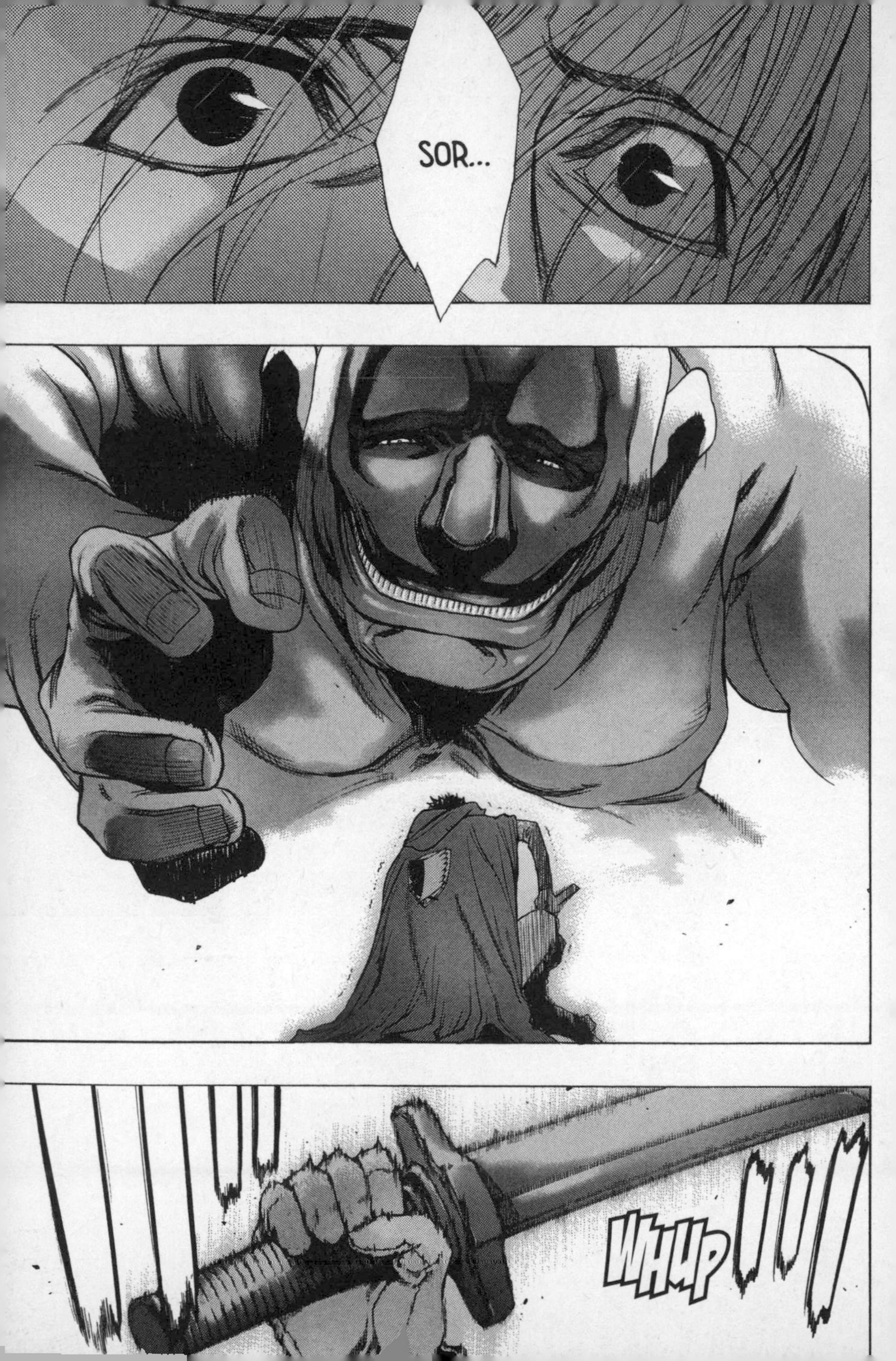
SOR...
WHUP

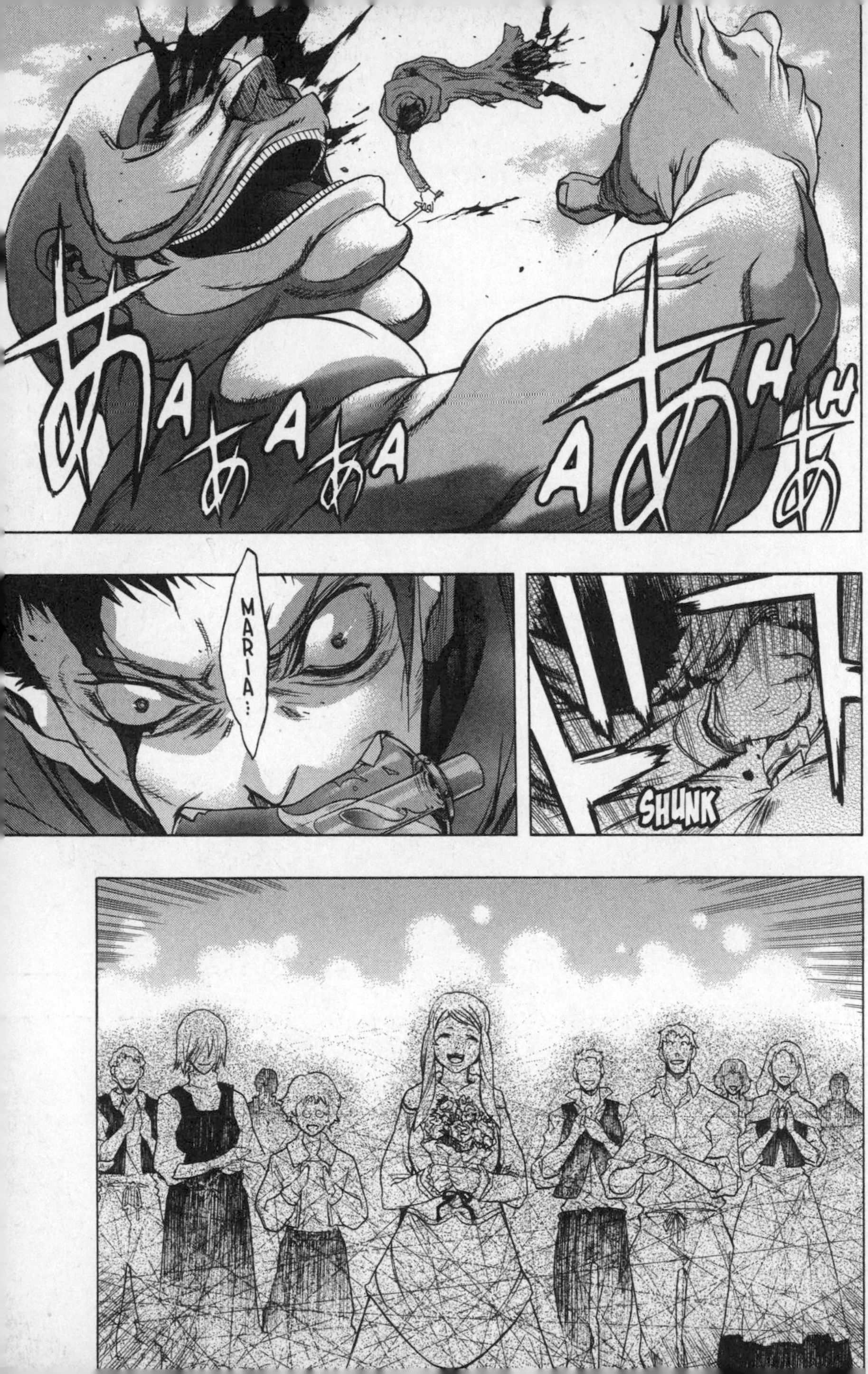

あAあAあA
AあHあH
SHUNK
MARIA...

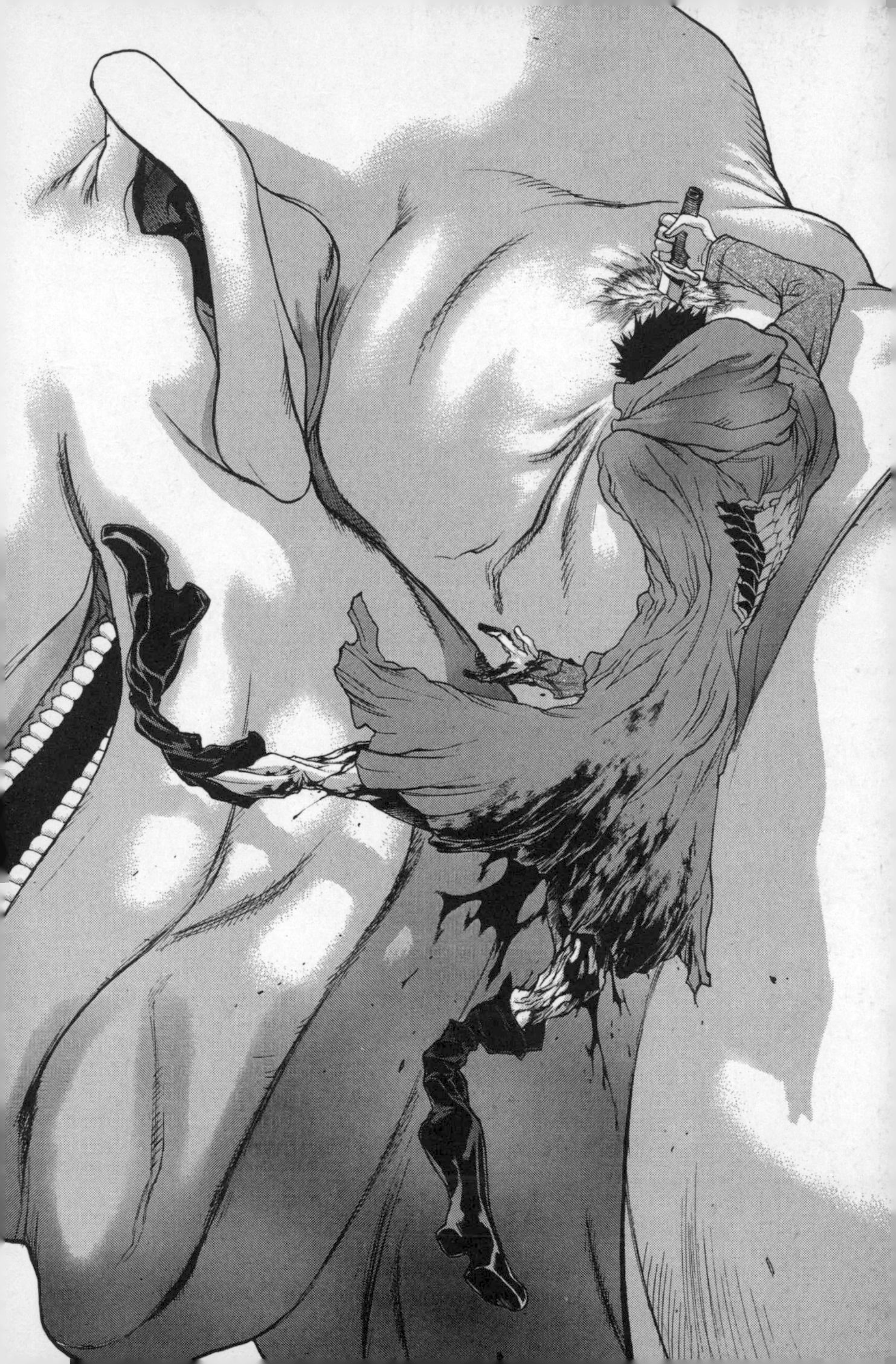

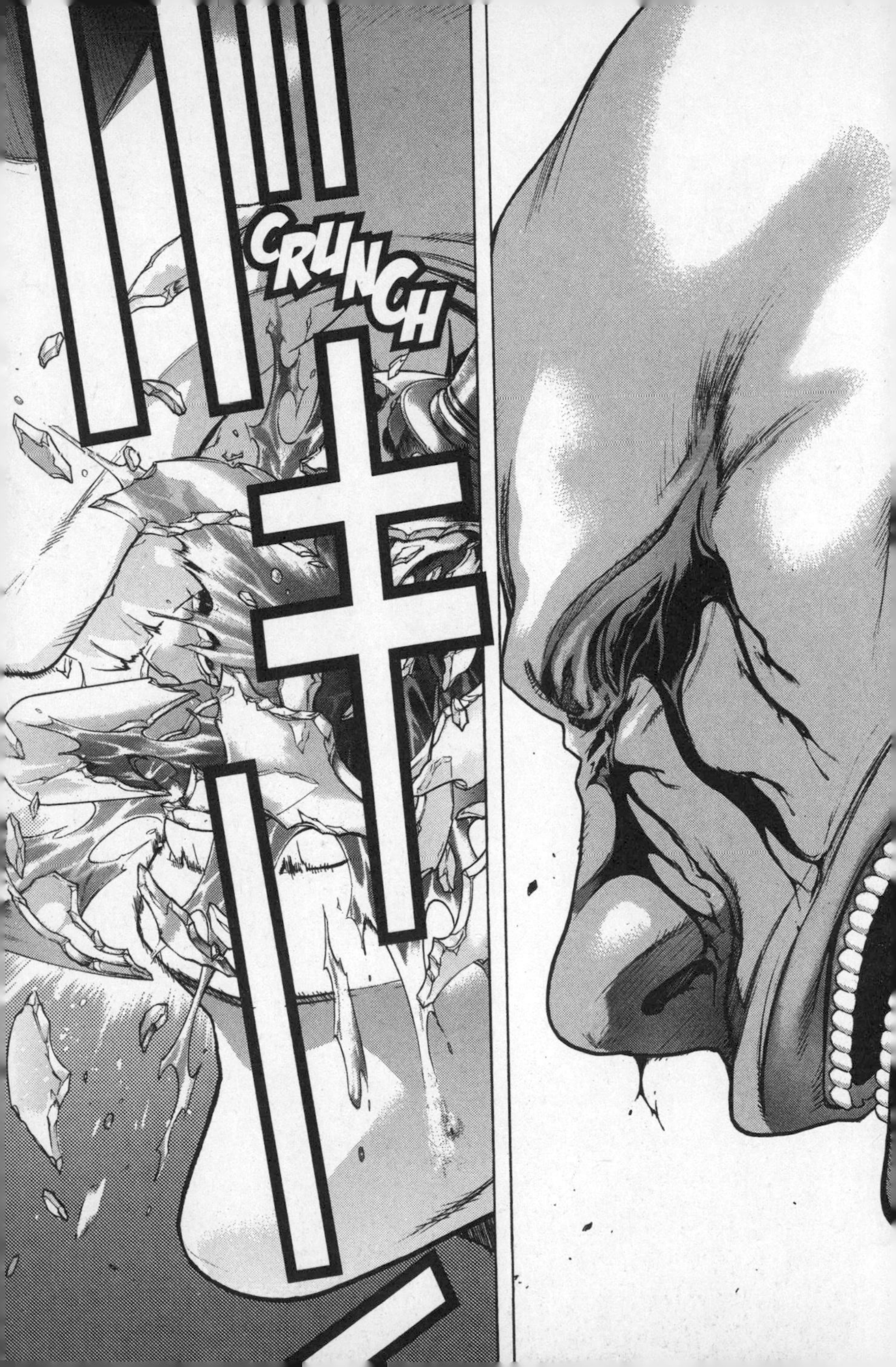
CRUNCH

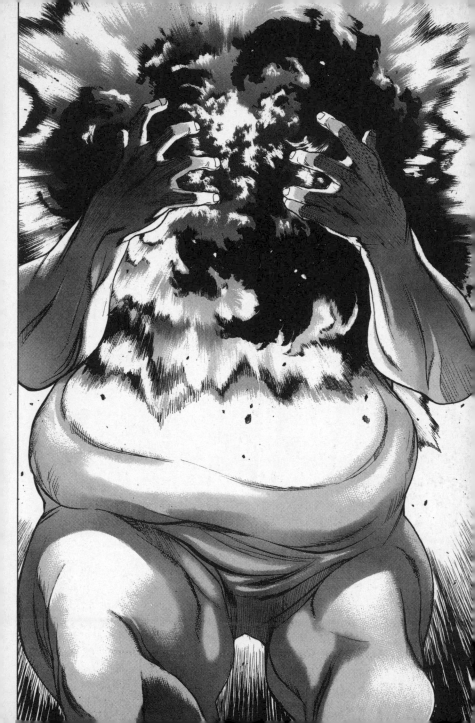

Chapter 18: Bacchanalia of Greed · End

ATTACK on TITAN

BEFORE THE FALL

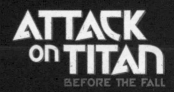

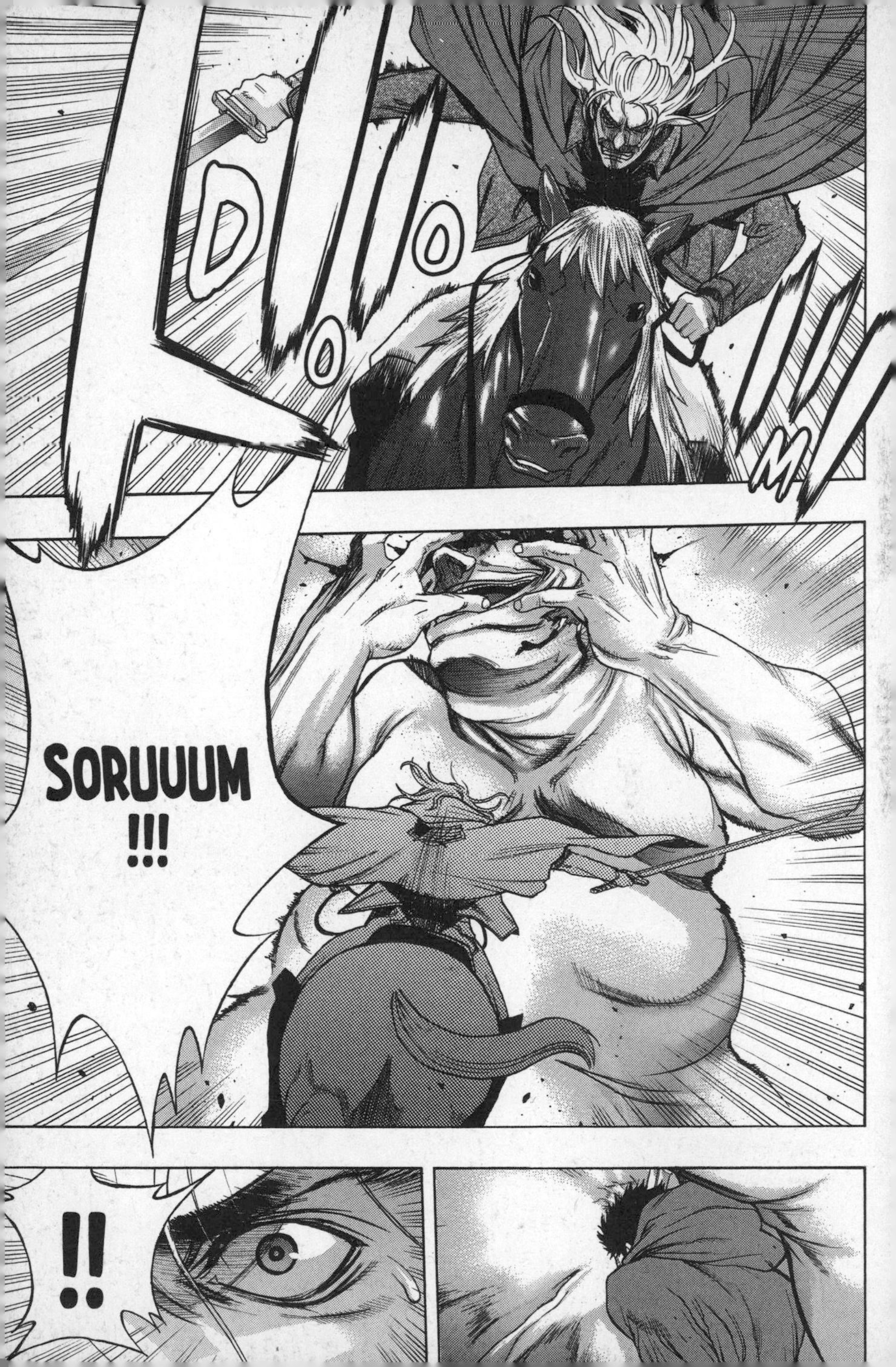
SORUUUM !!!
!!

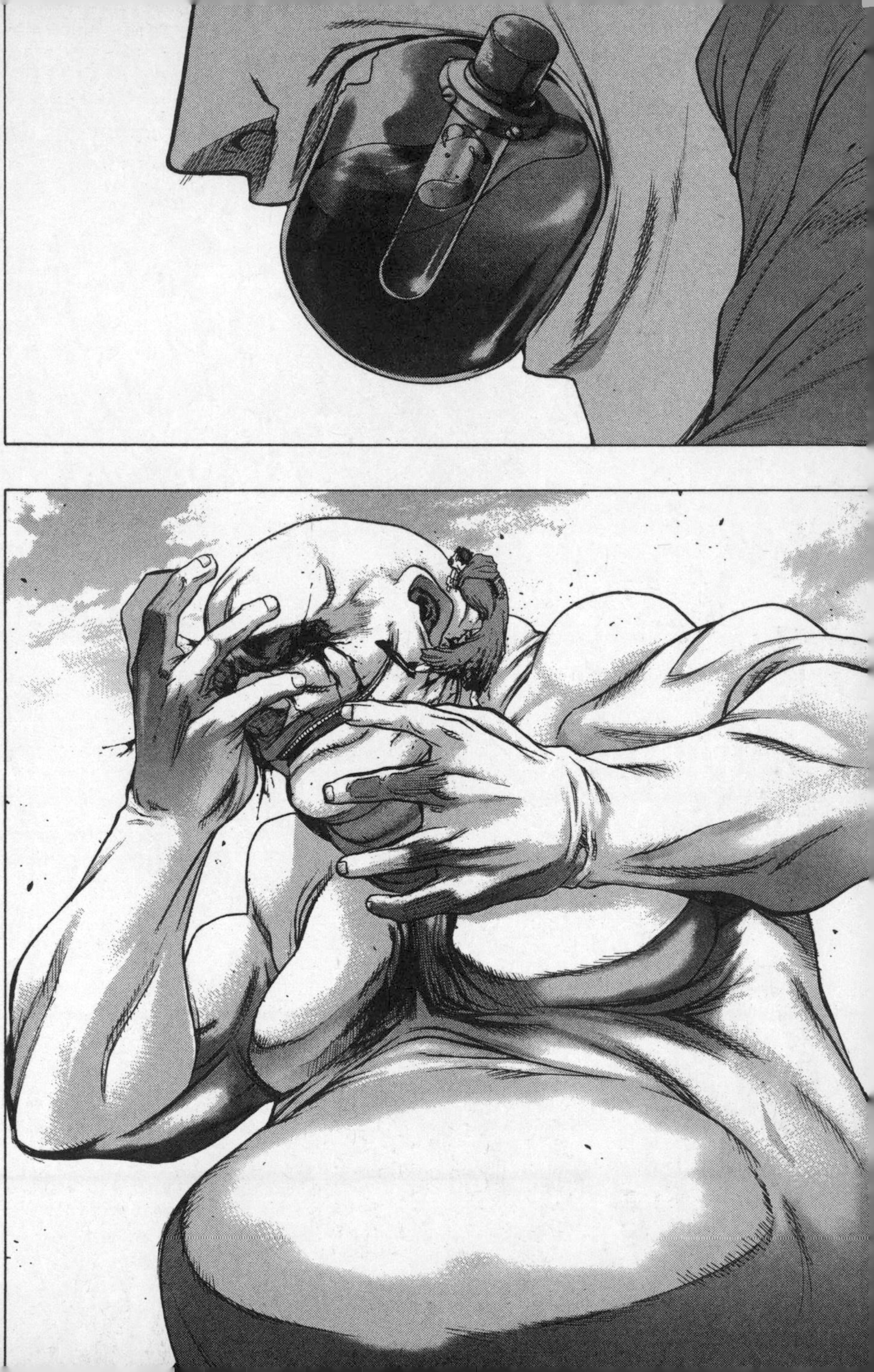

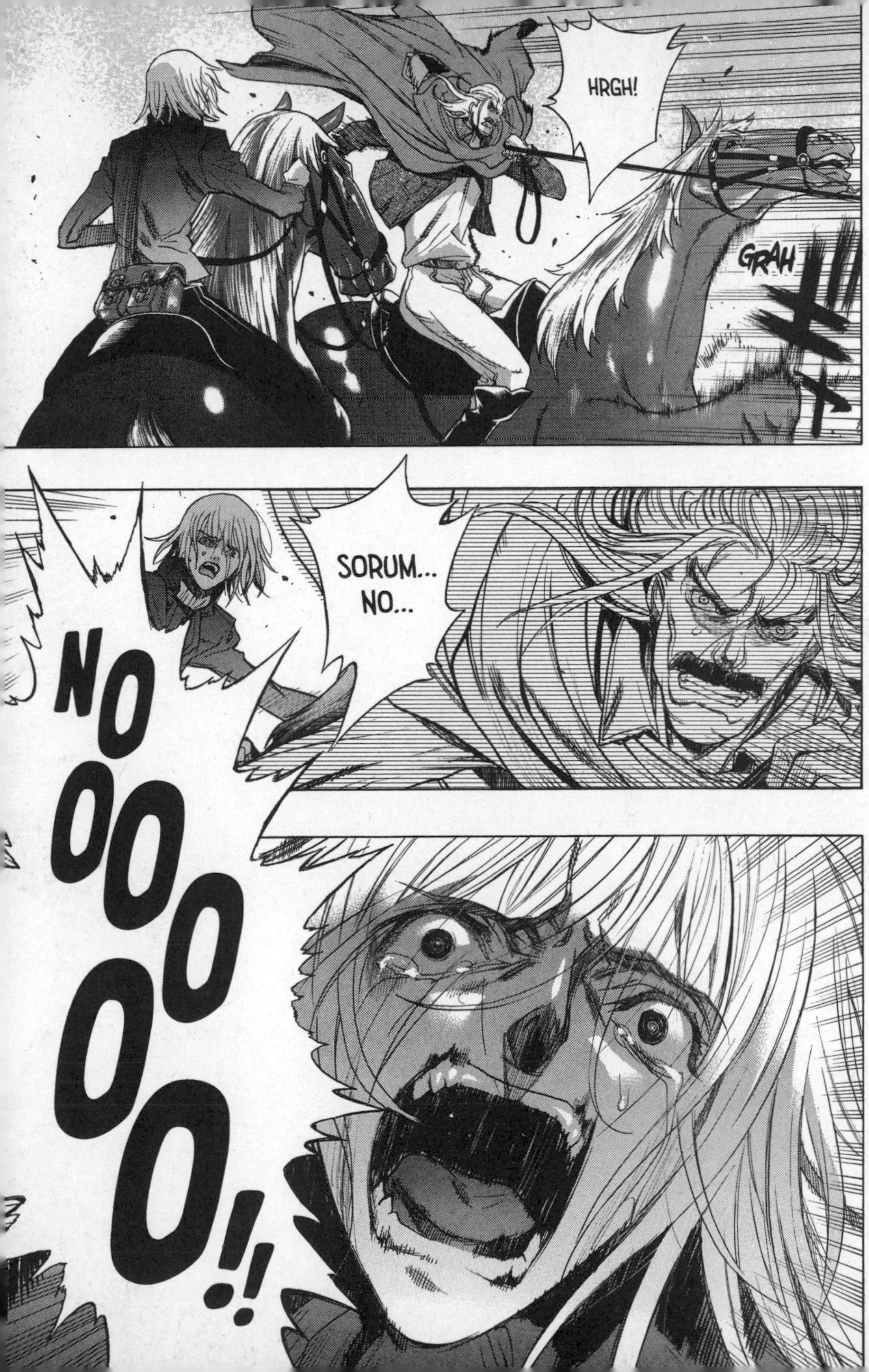
HRGH!
GRAH
SORUM... NO...
NOOOOOO!!

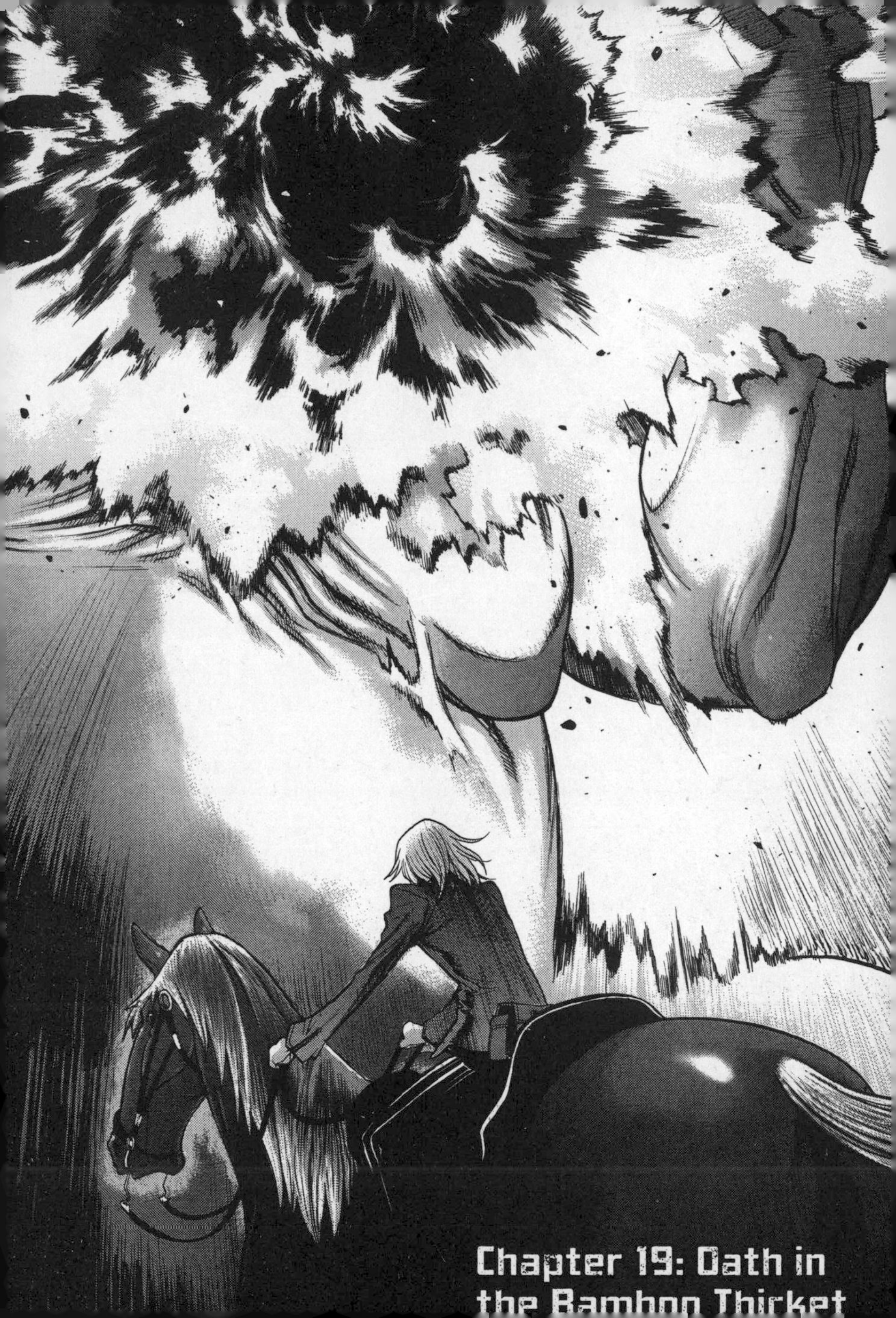

Chapter 19: Oath in the Bamboo Thicket

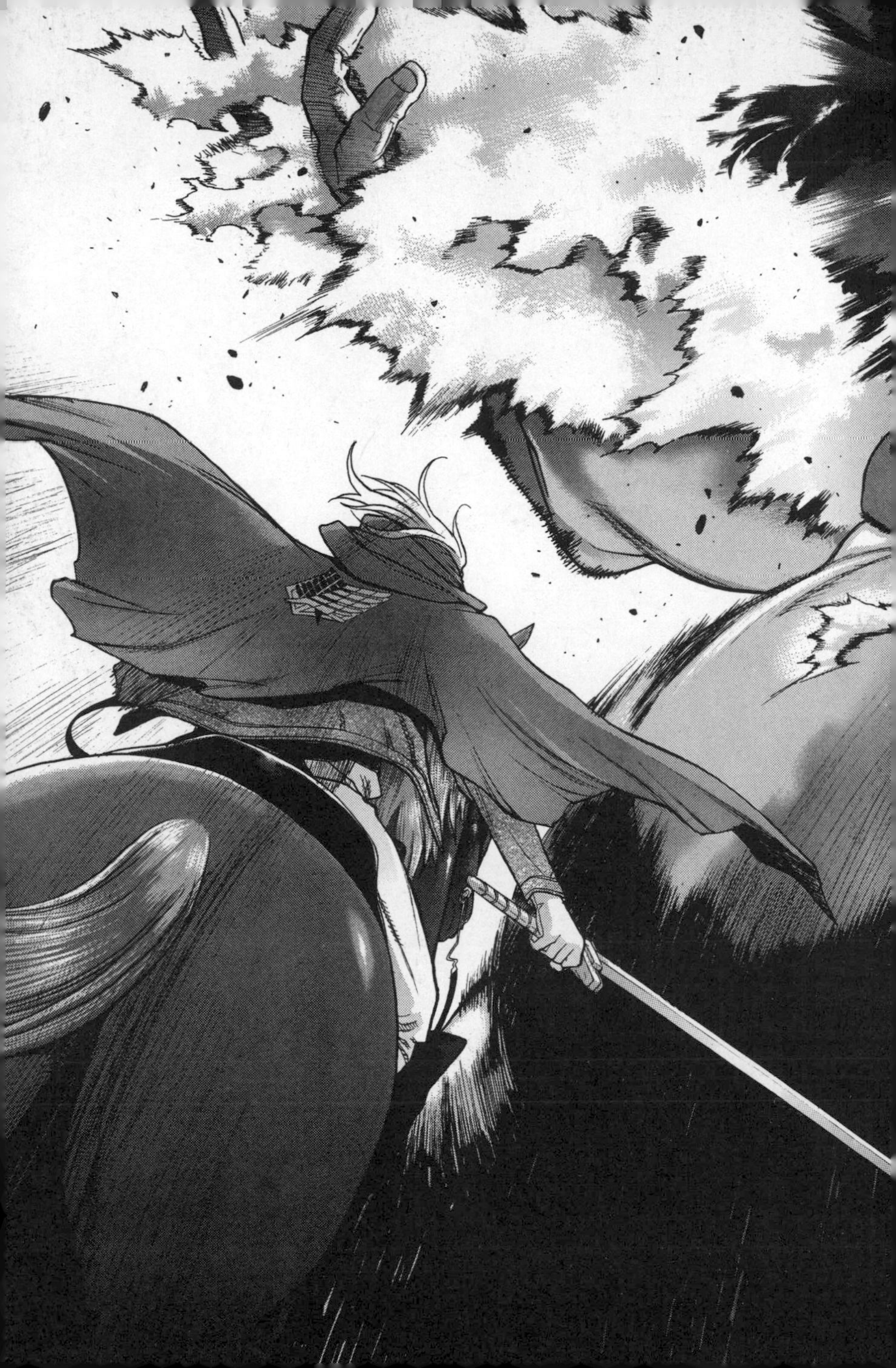

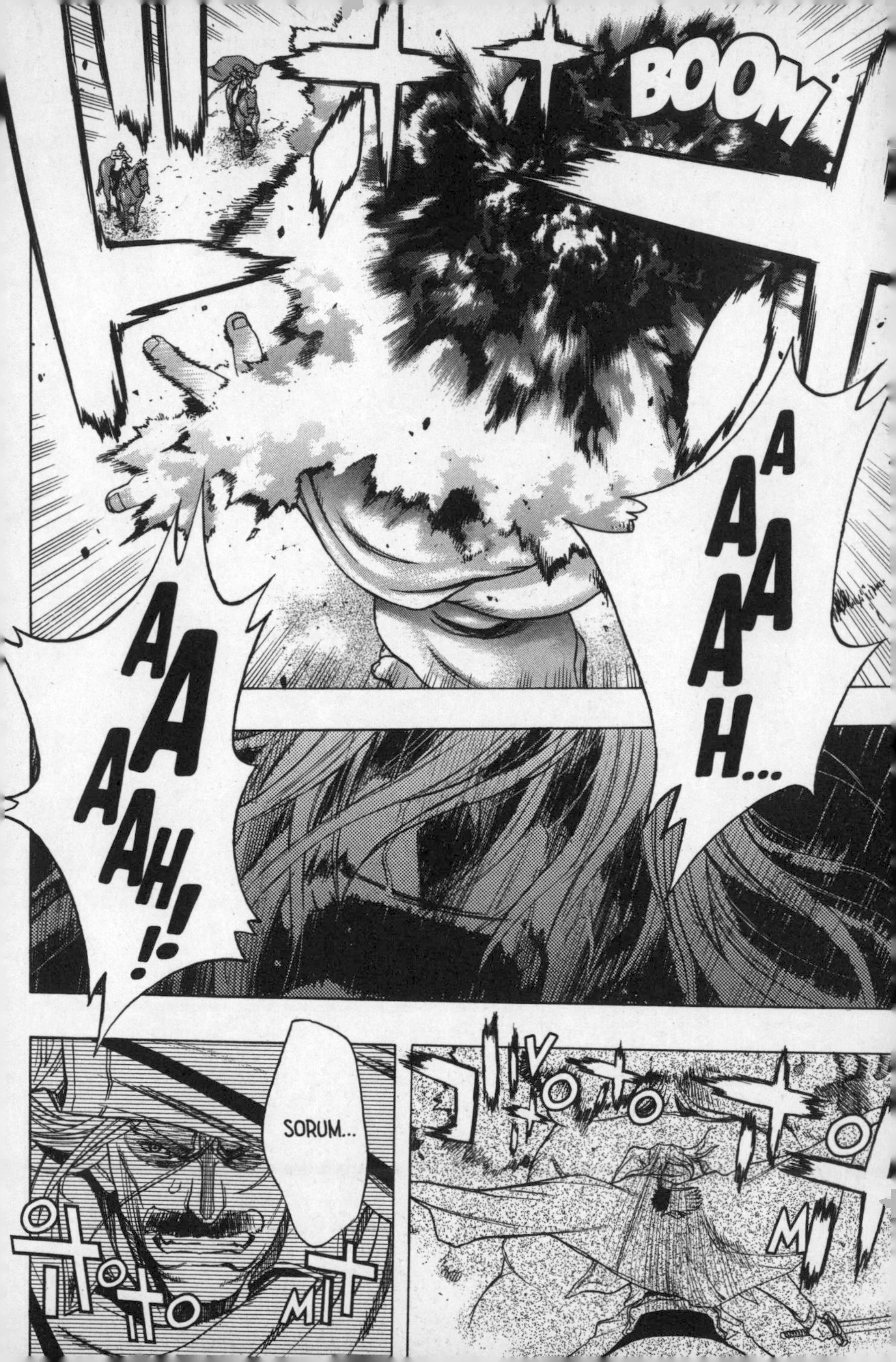
BOOM
AAAAAH...
AAAAAH!!
SORUM...

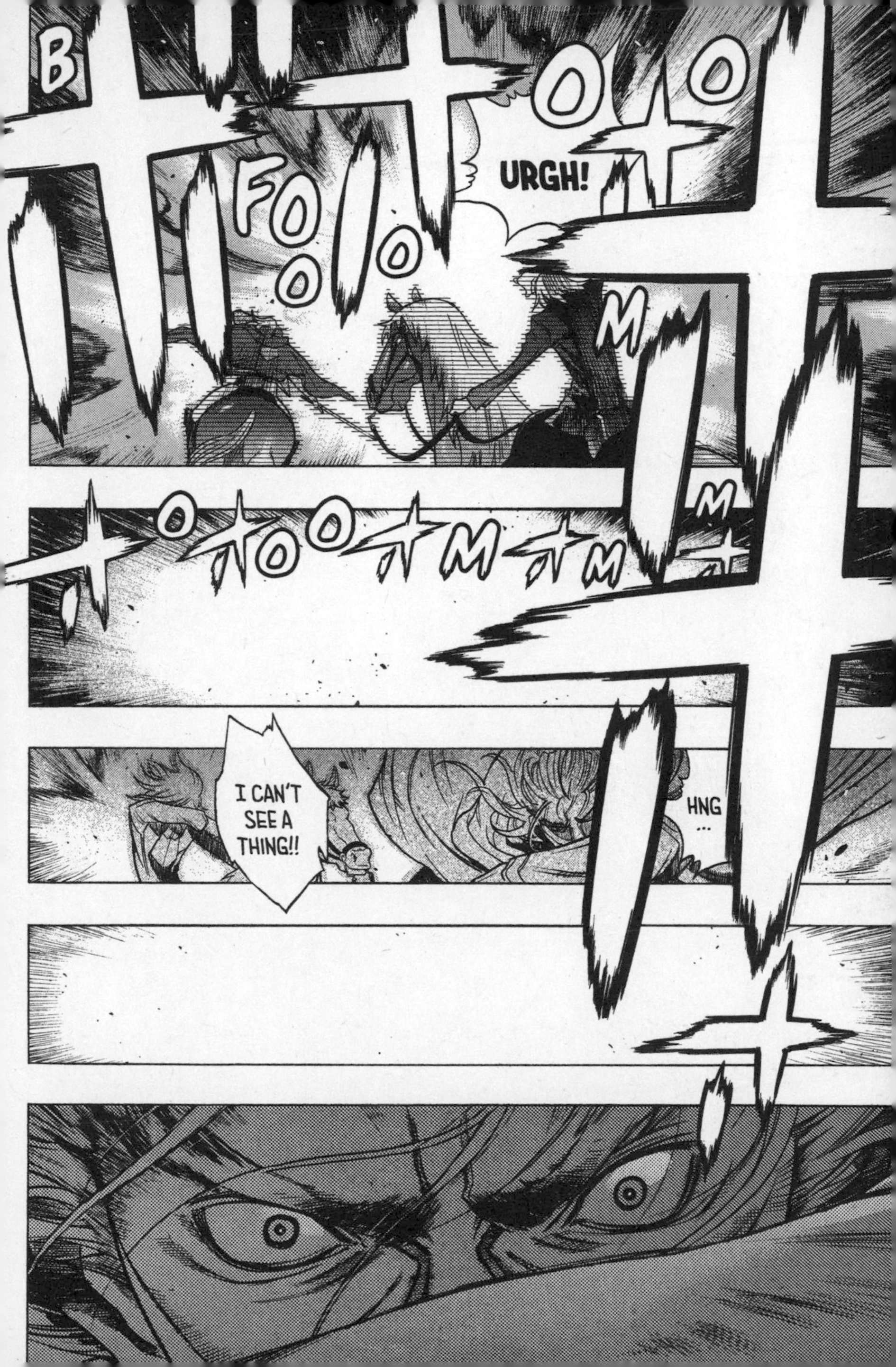
B
OO
URGH!
FOOOM
OOOMMMM
HNG ...
I CAN'T SEE A THING!!

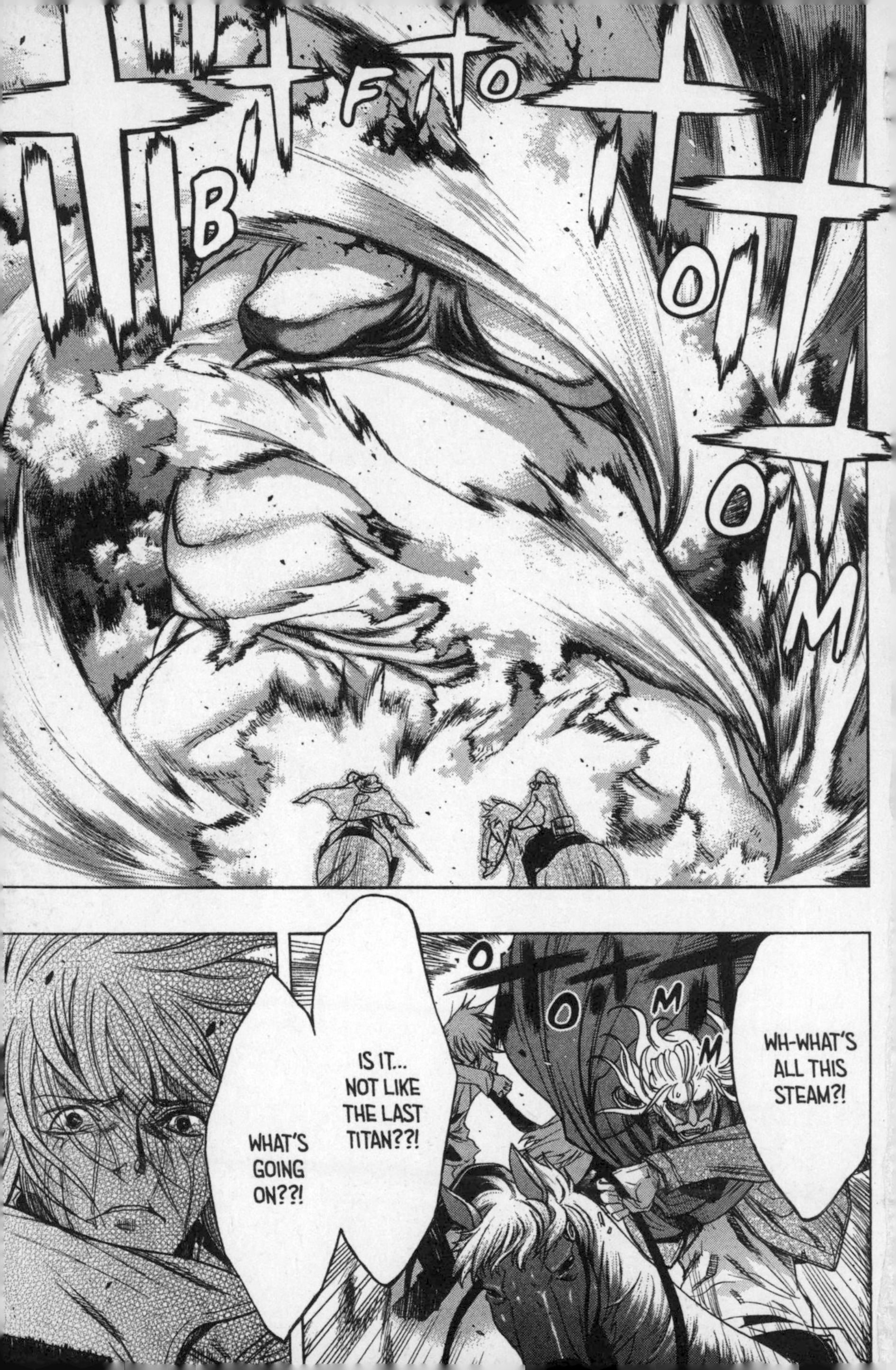
BFIOOOM
WH-WHAT'S ALL THIS STEAM?!
OOMMM
IS IT... NOT LIKE THE LAST TITAN??!
WHAT'S GOING ON??!

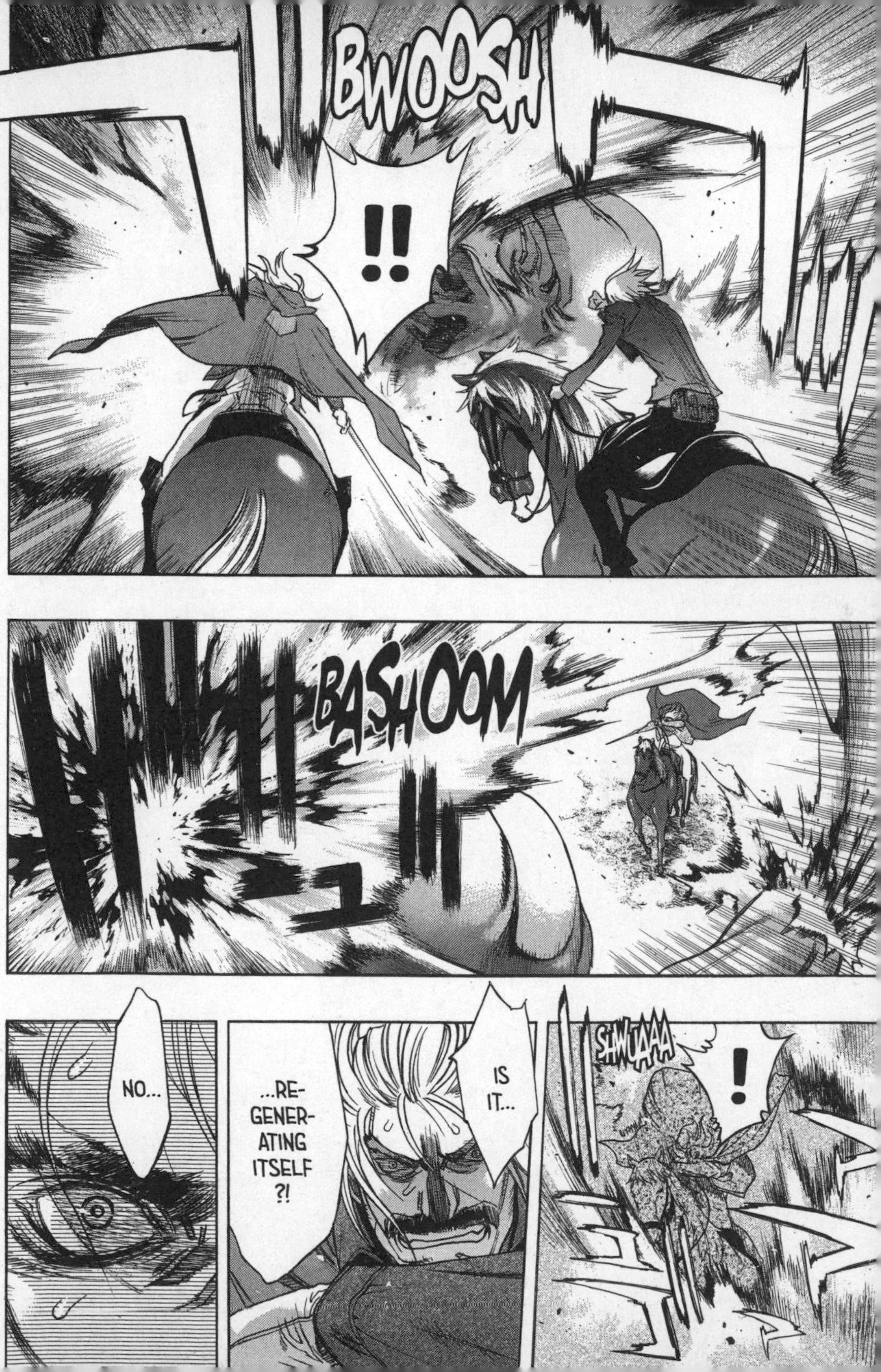
BWOOSH
!!
BASHOOM
SHWUAAA
!
IS IT...
...RE-GENERATING ITSELF?!
NO...

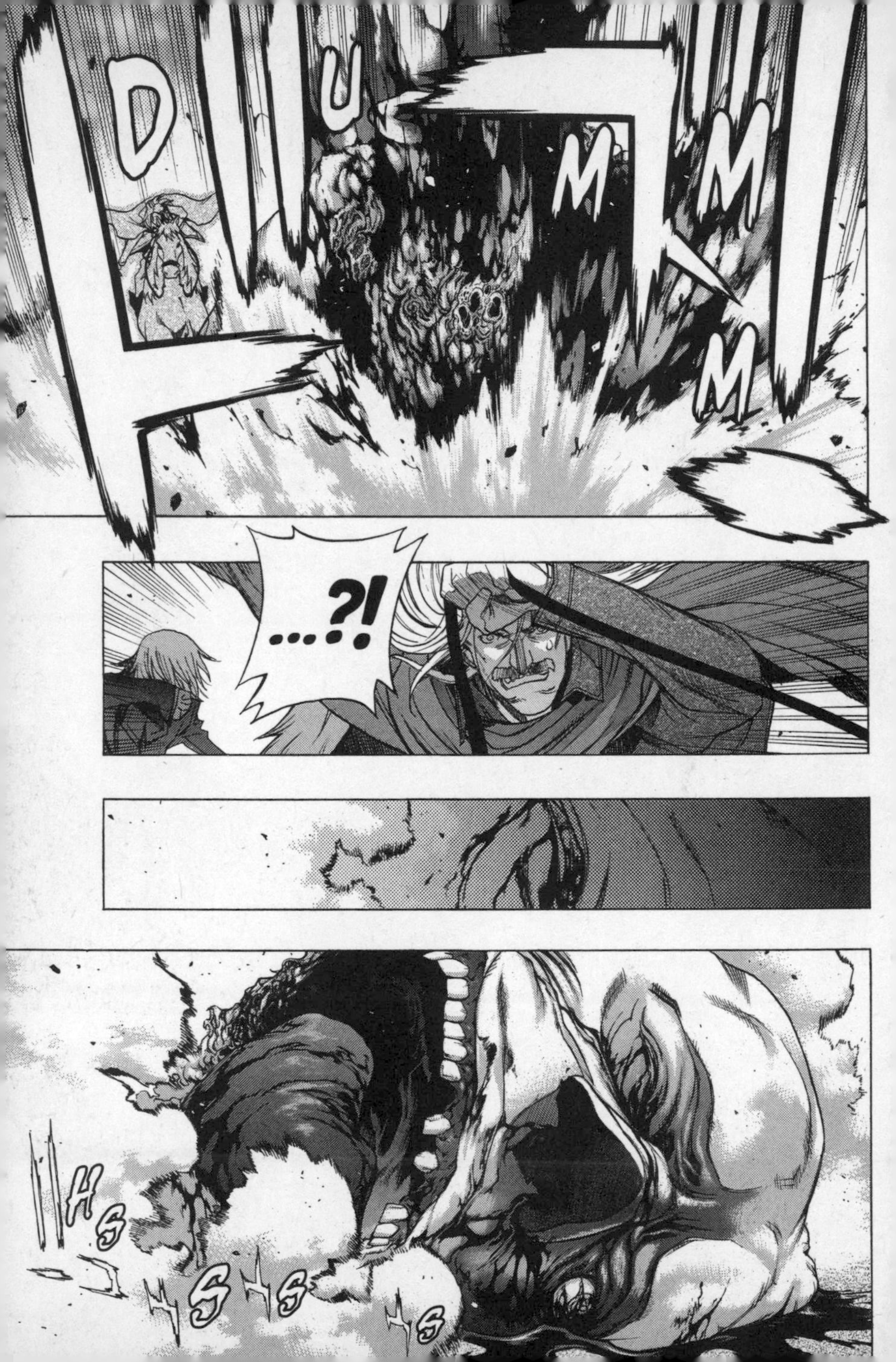
DUMMM
...?!
HSSSSSS

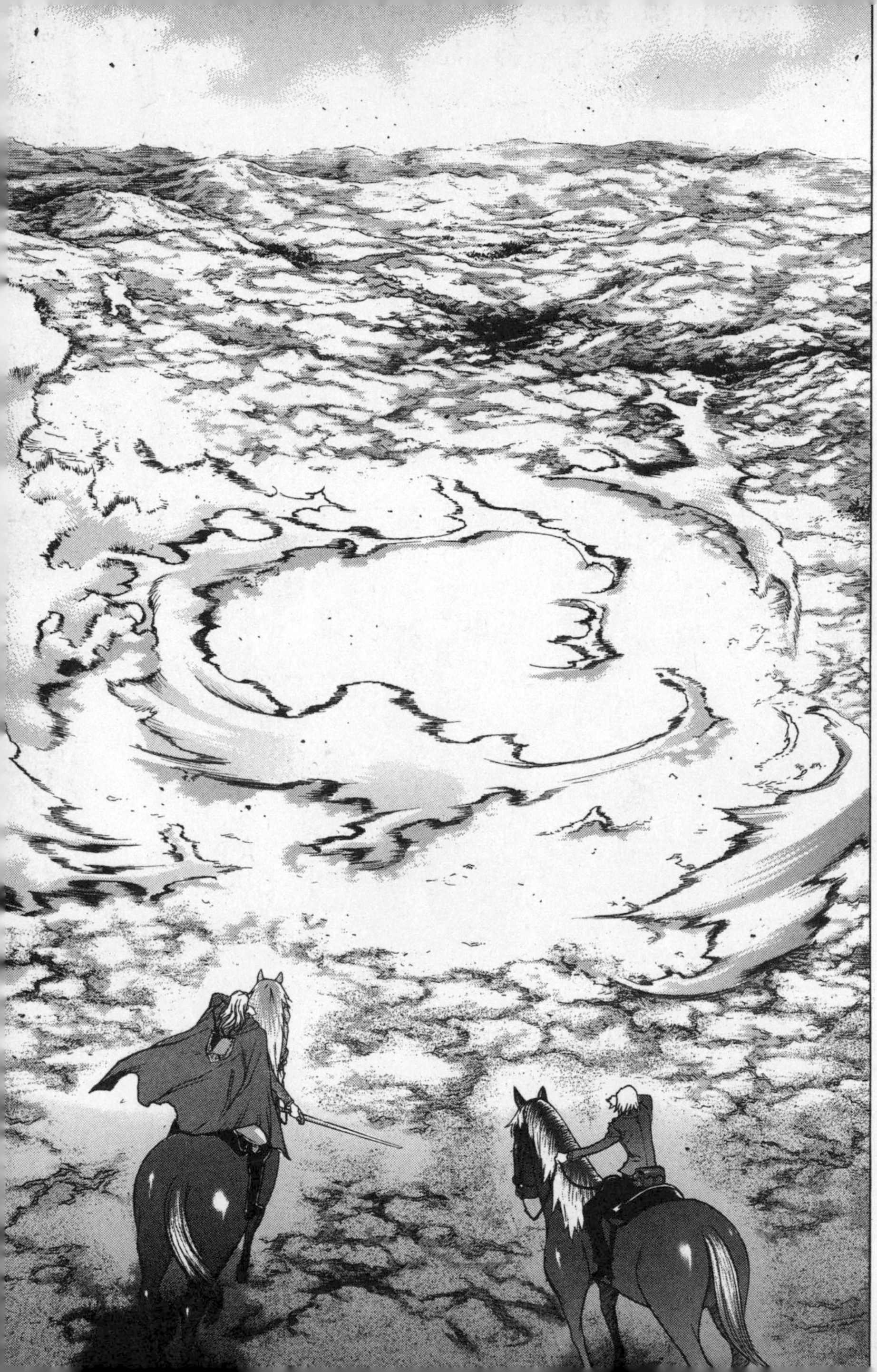

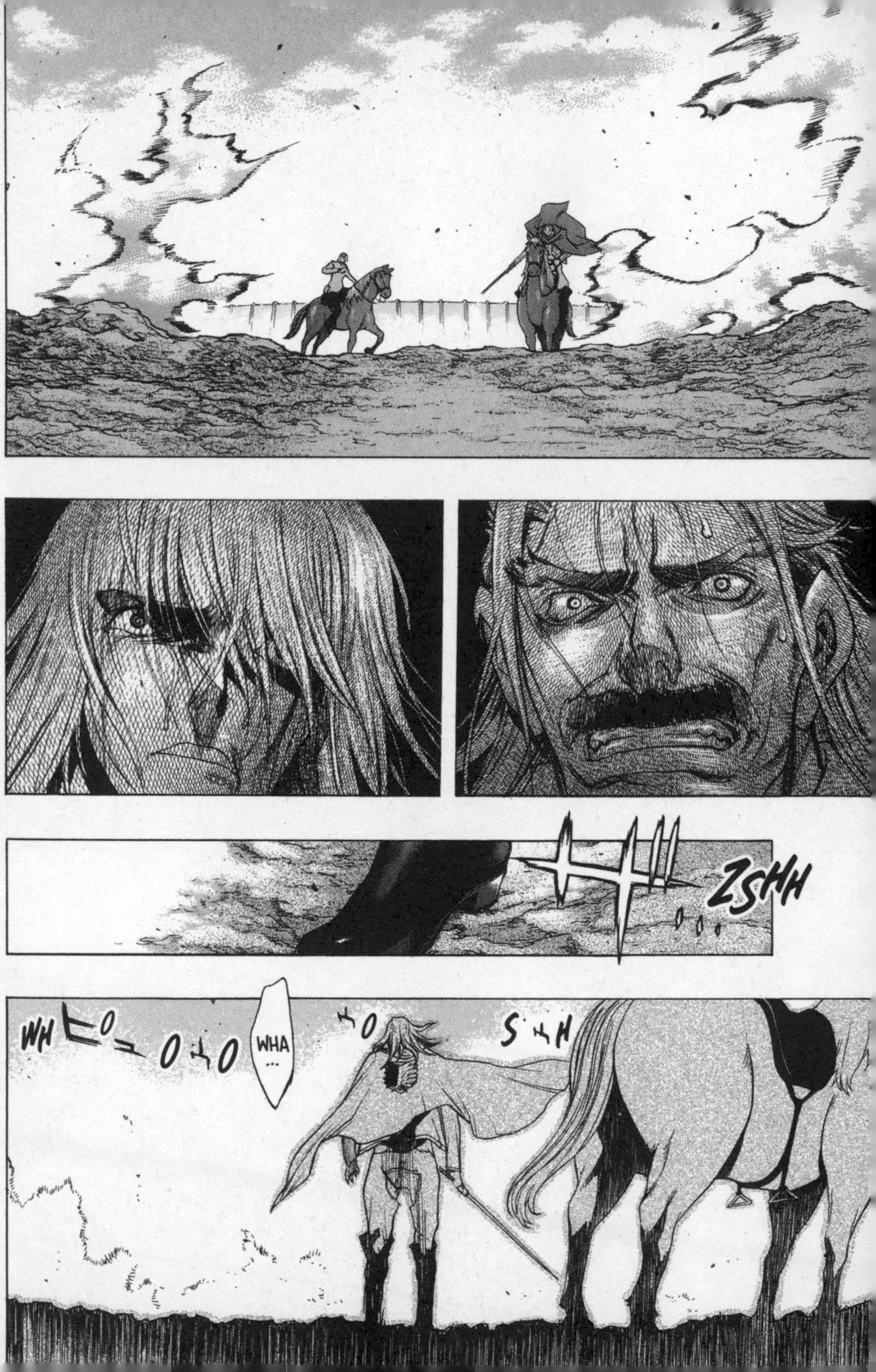
ZSHH
SHH
WHA...
WH

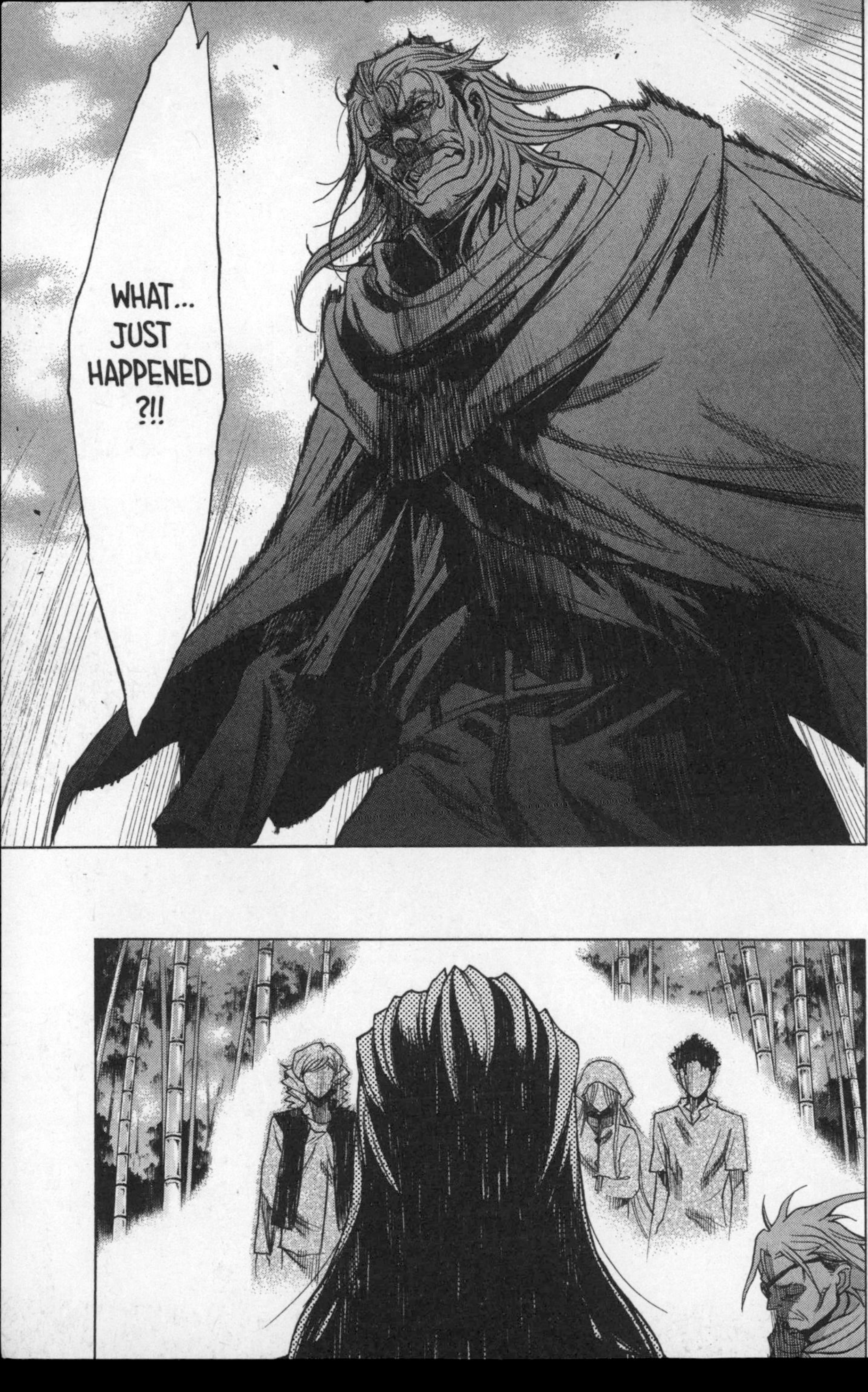
WHAT... JUST HAPPENED ?!!

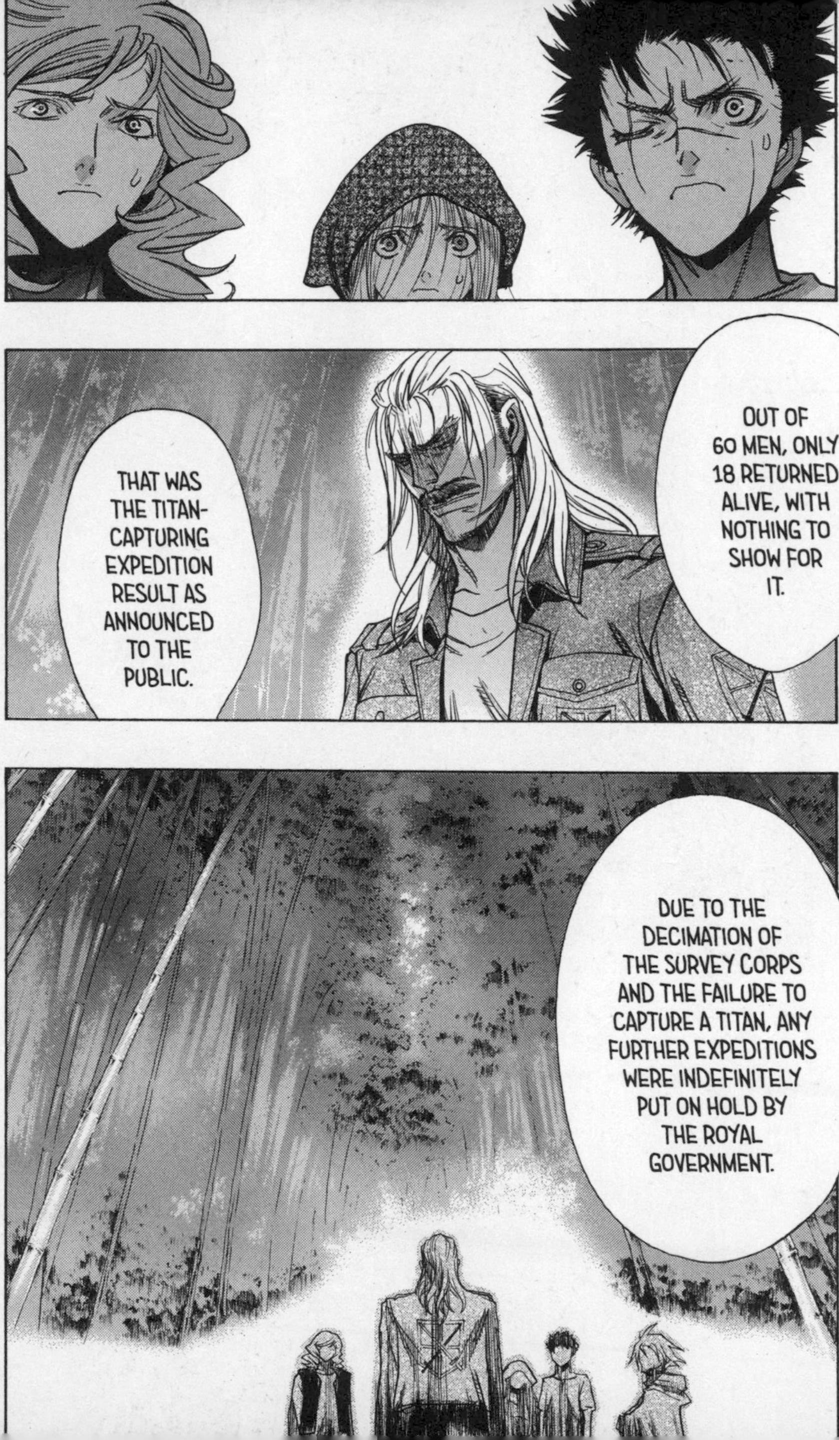
OUT OF 60 MEN, ONLY 18 RETURNED ALIVE, WITH NOTHING TO SHOW FOR IT.
THAT WAS THE TITAN-CAPTURING EXPEDITION RESULT AS ANNOUNCED TO THE PUBLIC.
DUE TO THE DECIMATION OF THE SURVEY CORPS AND THE FAILURE TO CAPTURE A TITAN, ANY FURTHER EXPEDITIONS WERE INDEFINITELY PUT ON HOLD BY THE ROYAL GOVERNMENT.

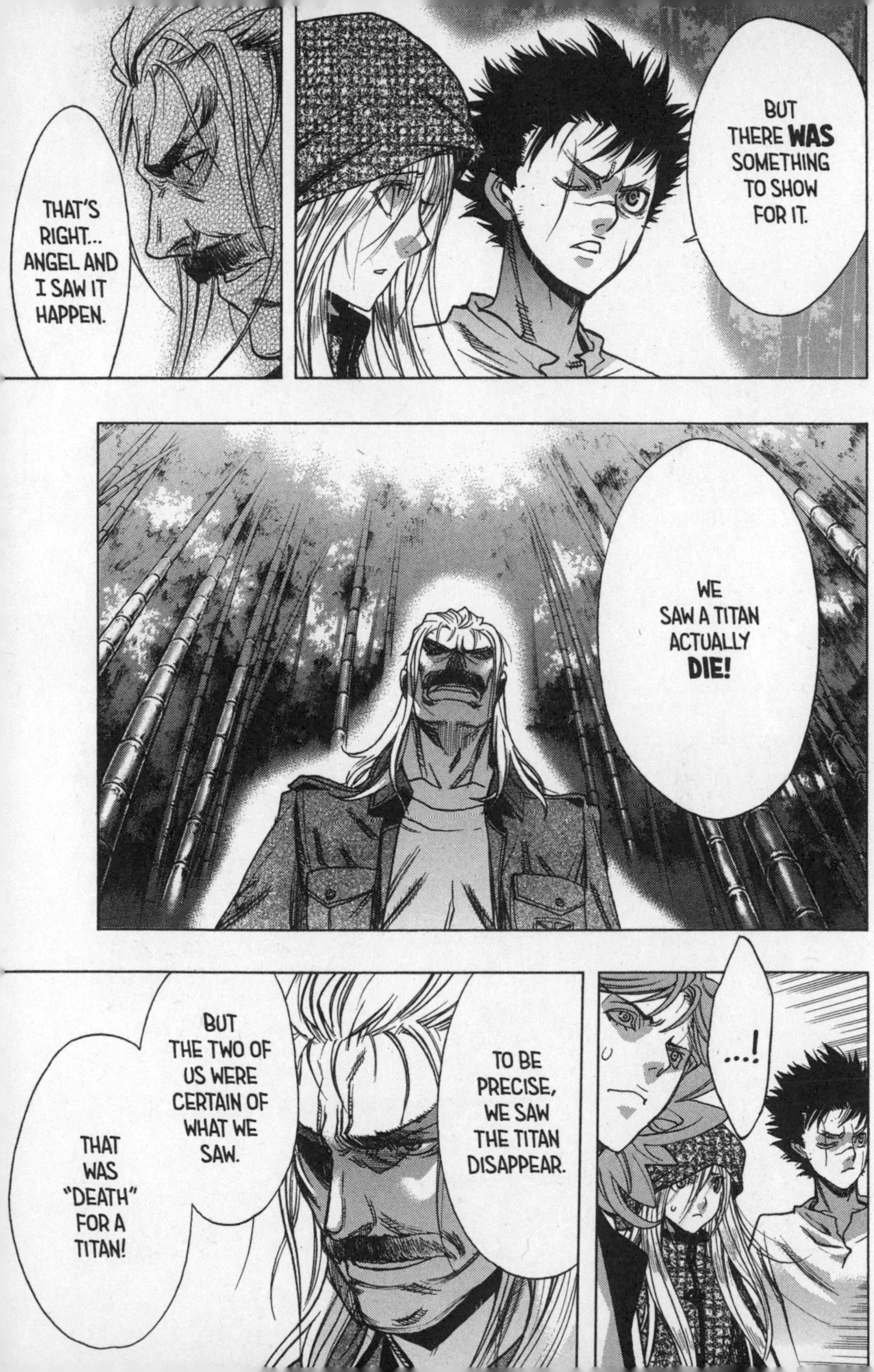
BUT THERE **WAS** SOMETHING TO SHOW FOR IT.
THAT'S RIGHT... ANGEL AND I SAW IT HAPPEN.
WE SAW A TITAN ACTUALLY **DIE!**
...!
TO BE PRECISE, WE SAW THE TITAN DISAPPEAR.
BUT THE TWO OF US WERE CERTAIN OF WHAT WE SAW.
THAT WAS "DEATH" FOR A TITAN!

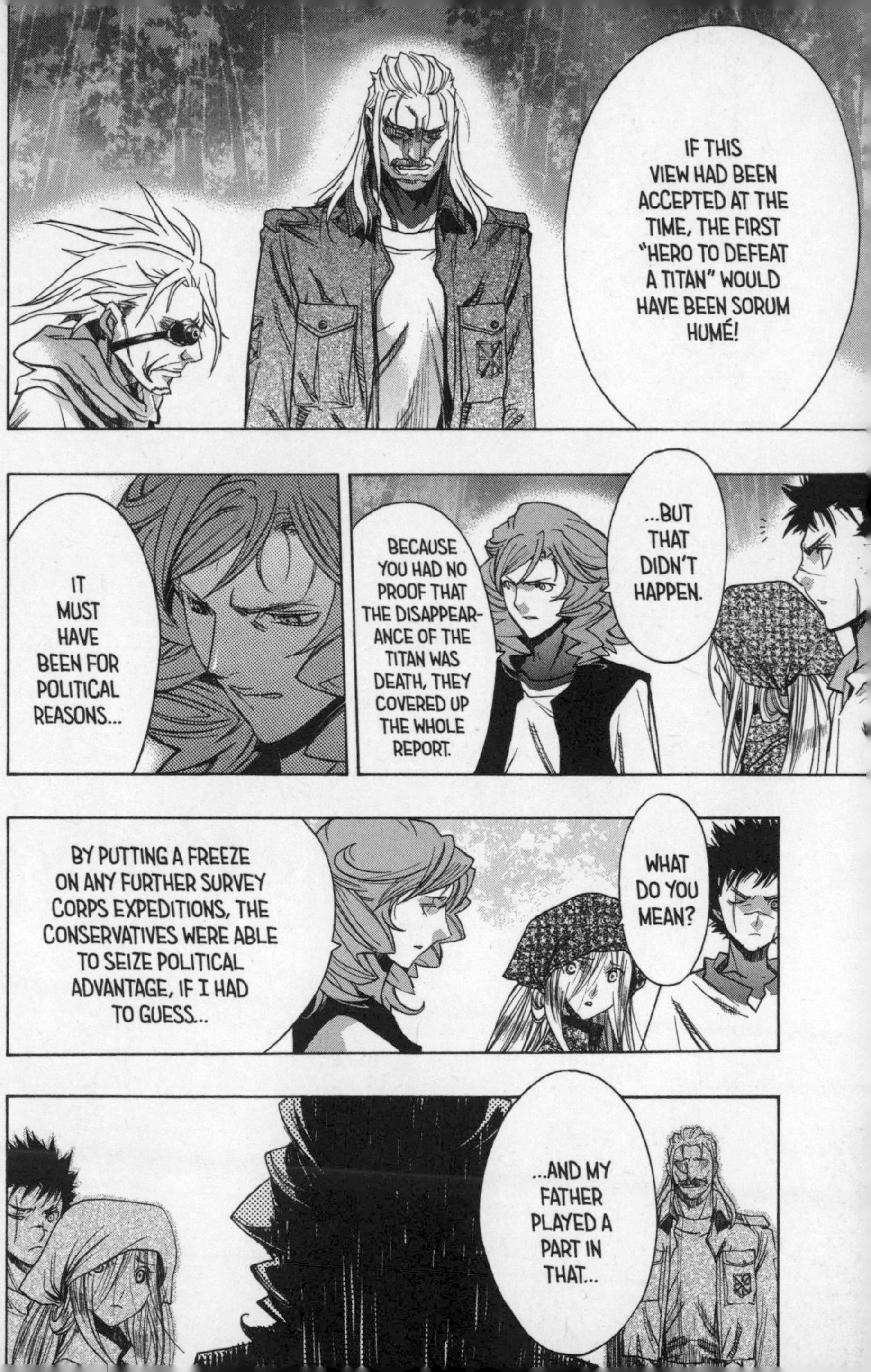
IF THIS VIEW HAD BEEN ACCEPTED AT THE TIME, THE FIRST "HERO TO DEFEAT A TITAN" WOULD HAVE BEEN SORUM HUMÉ!
...BUT THAT DIDN'T HAPPEN.
BECAUSE YOU HAD NO PROOF THAT THE DISAPPEAR-ANCE OF THE TITAN WAS DEATH, THEY COVERED UP THE WHOLE REPORT.
IT MUST HAVE BEEN FOR POLITICAL REASONS...
WHAT DO YOU MEAN?
BY PUTTING A FREEZE ON ANY FURTHER SURVEY CORPS EXPEDITIONS, THE CONSERVATIVES WERE ABLE TO SEIZE POLITICAL ADVANTAGE, IF I HAD TO GUESS...
...AND MY FATHER PLAYED A PART IN THAT...

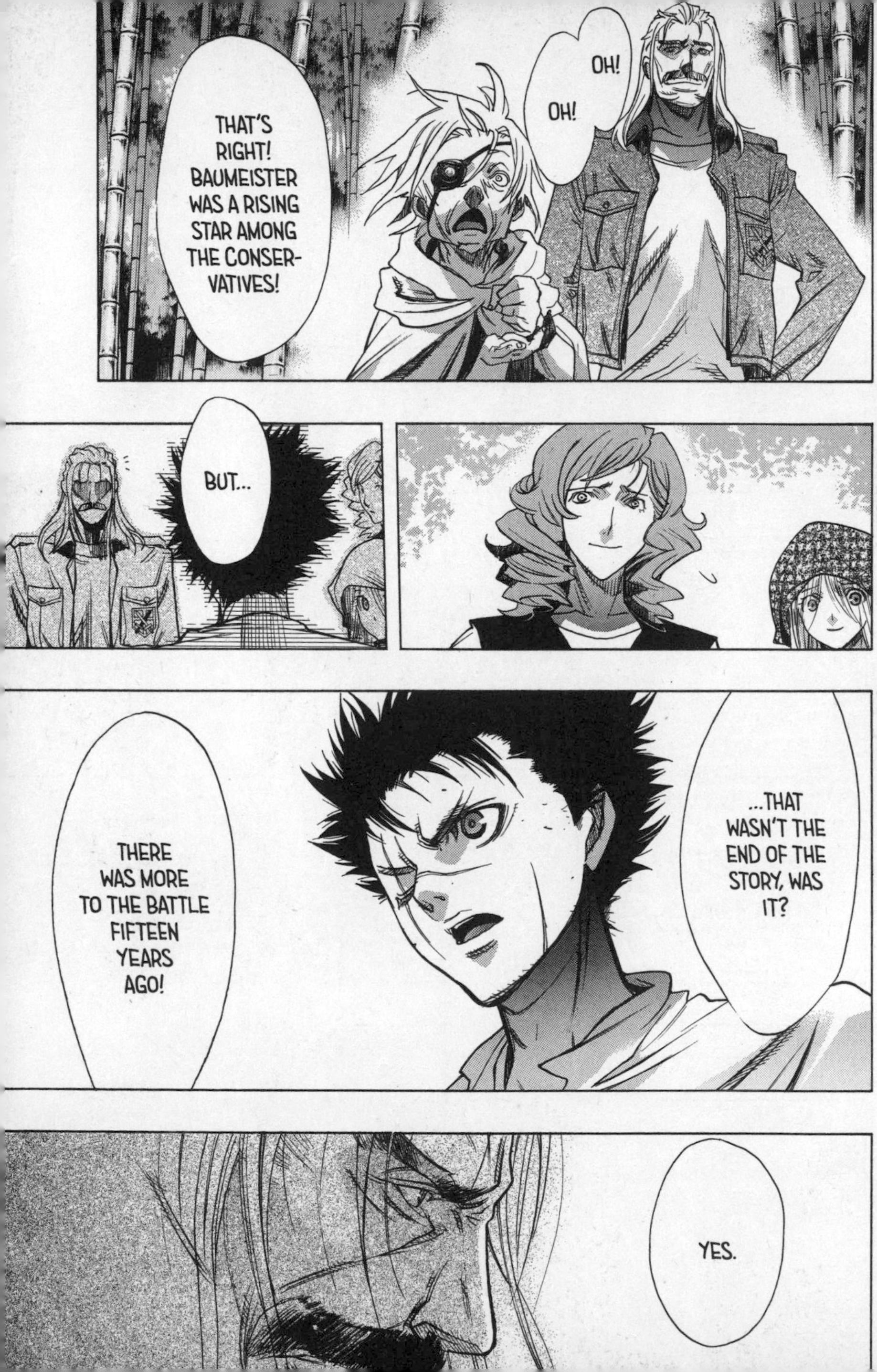
OH! OH!
THAT'S RIGHT! BAUMEISTER WAS A RISING STAR AMONG THE CONSER-VATIVES!
BUT...
...THAT WASN'T THE END OF THE STORY, WAS IT?
THERE WAS MORE TO THE BATTLE FIFTEEN YEARS AGO!
YES.

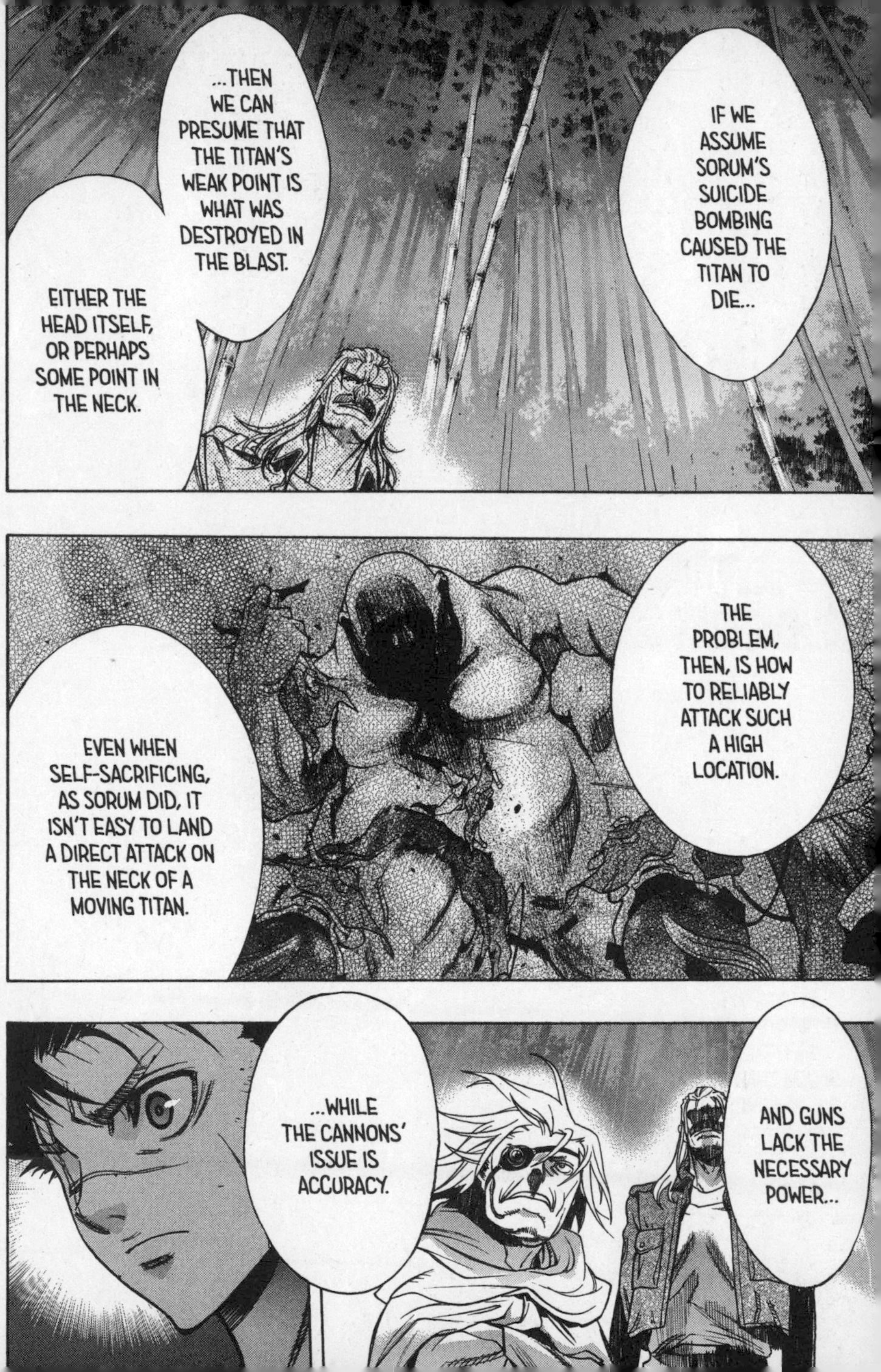
IF WE ASSUME SORUM'S SUICIDE BOMBING CAUSED THE TITAN TO DIE...
...THEN WE CAN PRESUME THAT THE TITAN'S WEAK POINT IS WHAT WAS DESTROYED IN THE BLAST.
EITHER THE HEAD ITSELF, OR PERHAPS SOME POINT IN THE NECK.
THE PROBLEM, THEN, IS HOW TO RELIABLY ATTACK SUCH A HIGH LOCATION.
EVEN WHEN SELF-SACRIFICING, AS SORUM DID, IT ISN'T EASY TO LAND A DIRECT ATTACK ON THE NECK OF A MOVING TITAN.
AND GUNS LACK THE NECESSARY POWER...
...WHILE THE CANNONS' ISSUE IS ACCURACY.

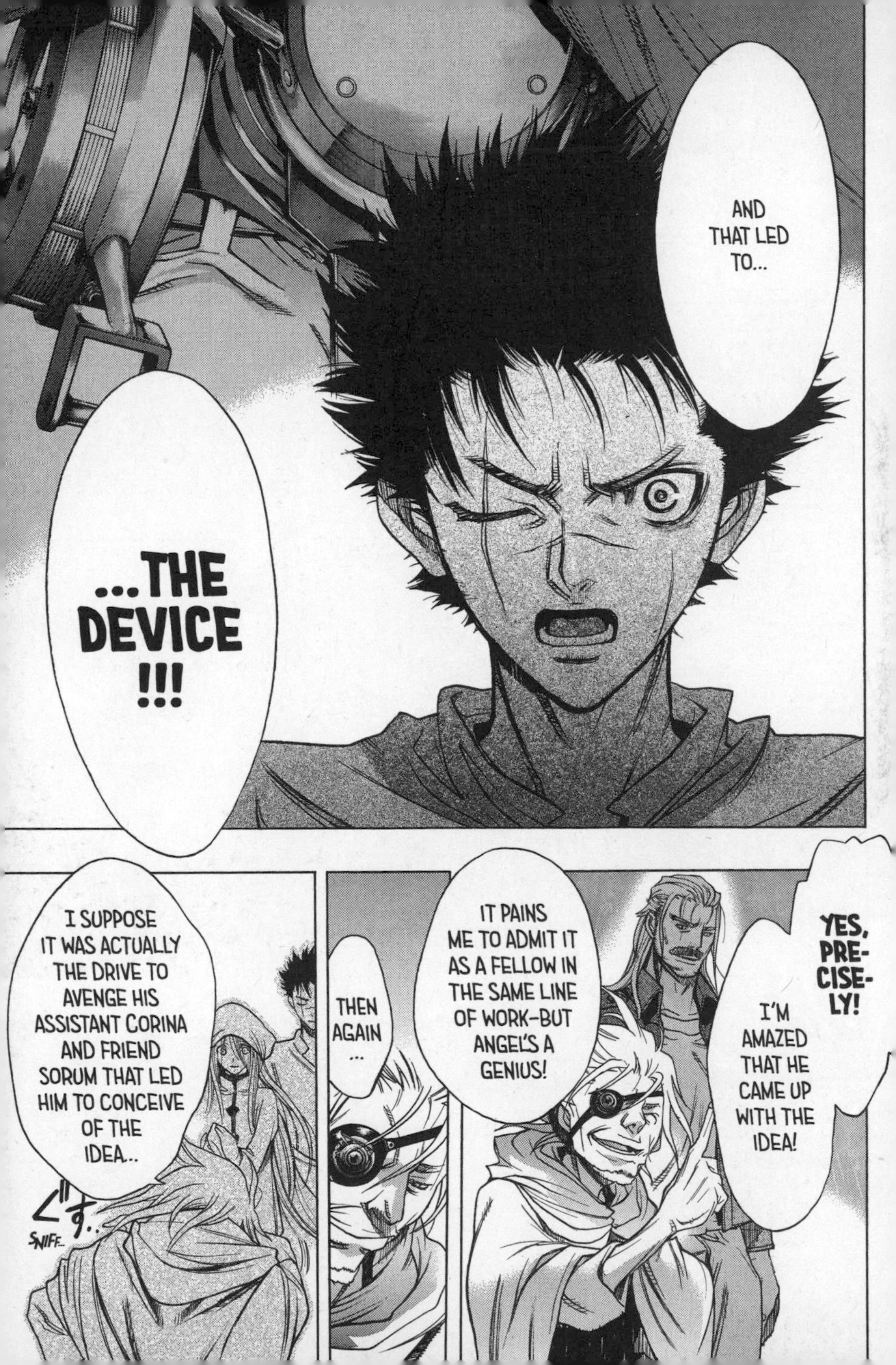

AND THAT LED TO...
...THE DEVICE!!!
YES, PRE-CISE-LY!
I'M AMAZED THAT HE CAME UP WITH THE IDEA!
IT PAINS ME TO ADMIT IT AS A FELLOW IN THE SAME LINE OF WORK—BUT ANGEL'S A GENIUS!
THEN AGAIN...
I SUPPOSE IT WAS ACTUALLY THE DRIVE TO AVENGE HIS ASSISTANT CORINA AND FRIEND SORUM THAT LED HIM TO CONCEIVE OF THE IDEA...
ぐす...
SNIFF...

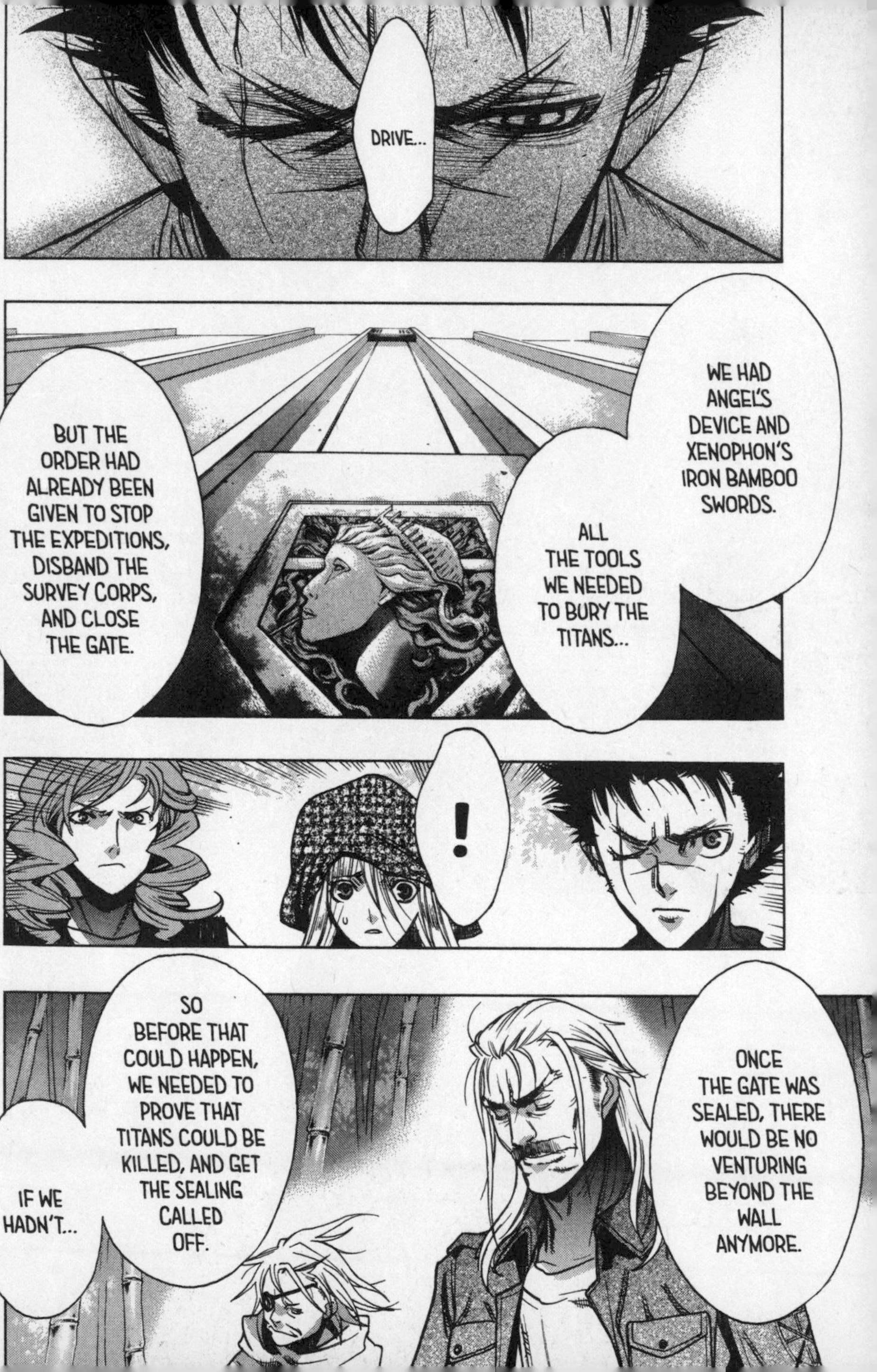
DRIVE...
WE HAD ANGEL'S DEVICE AND XENOPHON'S IRON BAMBOO SWORDS.
ALL THE TOOLS WE NEEDED TO BURY THE TITANS...
BUT THE ORDER HAD ALREADY BEEN GIVEN TO STOP THE EXPEDITIONS, DISBAND THE SURVEY CORPS, AND CLOSE THE GATE.
!
ONCE THE GATE WAS SEALED, THERE WOULD BE NO VENTURING BEYOND THE WALL ANYMORE.
SO BEFORE THAT COULD HAPPEN, WE NEEDED TO PROVE THAT TITANS COULD BE KILLED, AND GET THE SEALING CALLED OFF.
IF WE HADN'T...

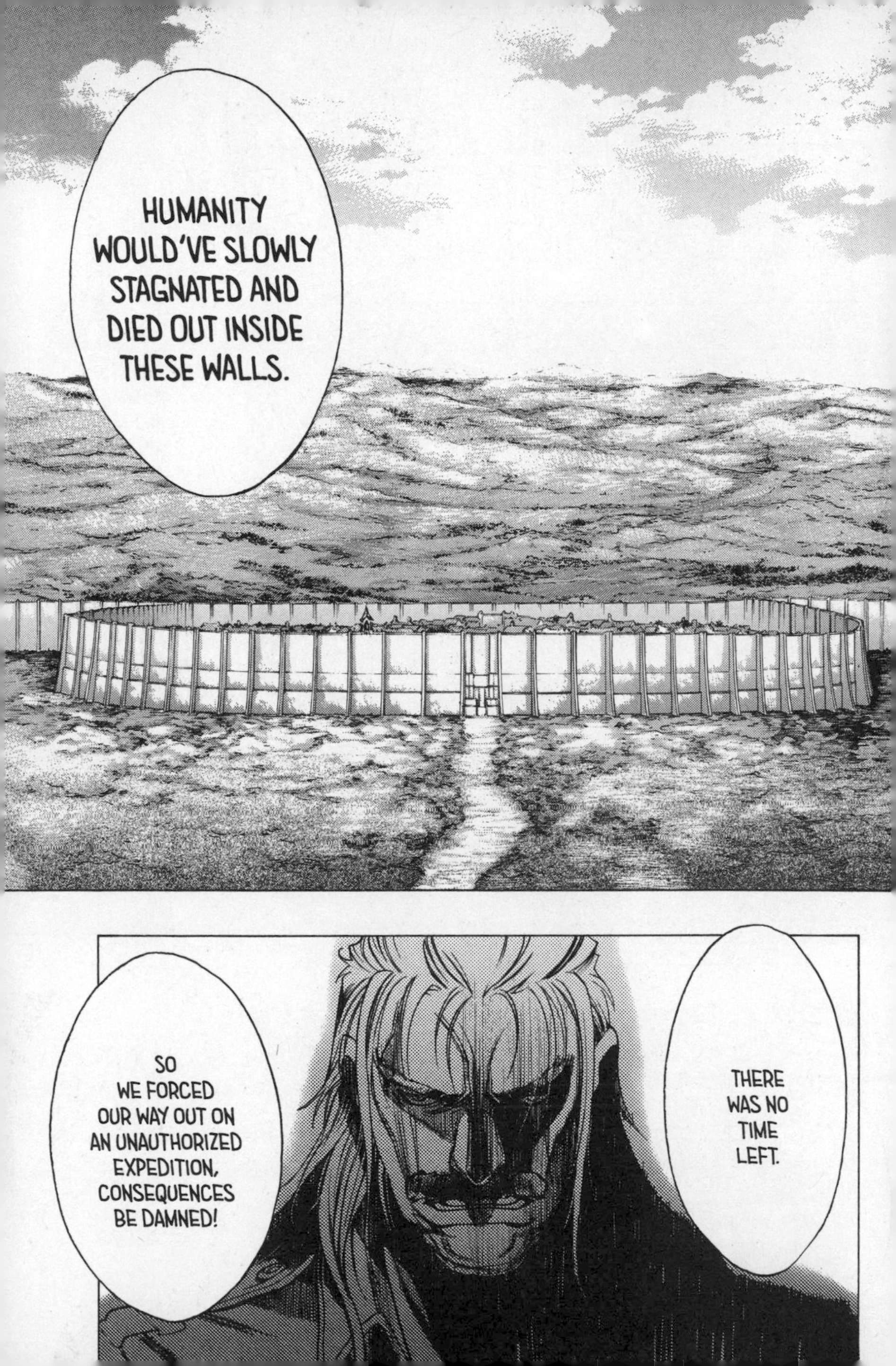
HUMANITY WOULD'VE SLOWLY STAGNATED AND DIED OUT INSIDE THESE WALLS.
THERE WAS NO TIME LEFT.
SO WE FORCED OUR WAY OUT ON AN UNAUTHORIZED EXPEDITION, CONSEQUENCES BE DAMNED!

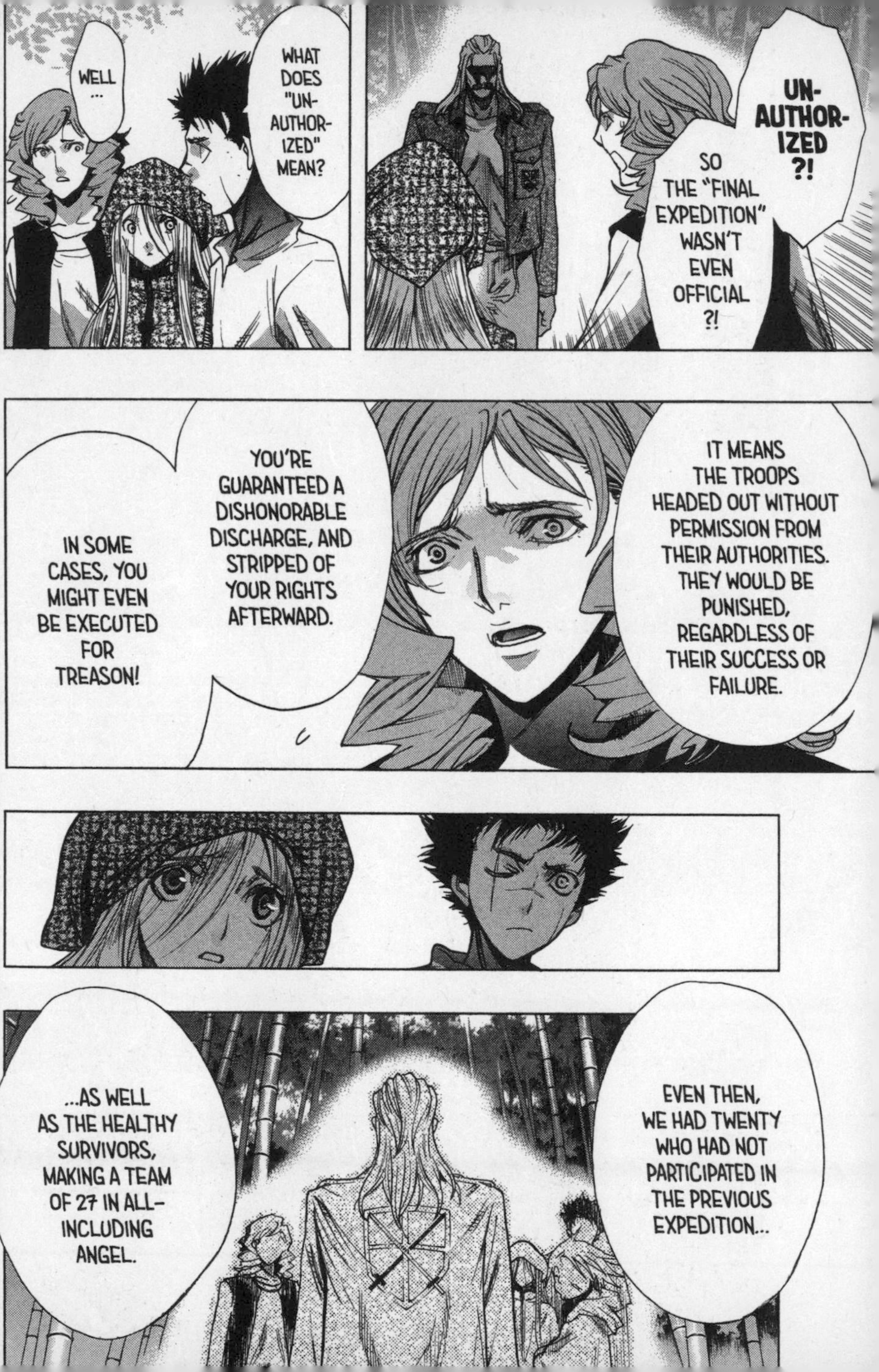
UN-AUTHORIZED?!
SO THE "FINAL EXPEDITION" WASN'T EVEN OFFICIAL?!
WHAT DOES "UN-AUTHORIZED" MEAN?
WELL...
IT MEANS THE TROOPS HEADED OUT WITHOUT PERMISSION FROM THEIR AUTHORITIES. THEY WOULD BE PUNISHED, REGARDLESS OF THEIR SUCCESS OR FAILURE.
YOU'RE GUARANTEED A DISHONORABLE DISCHARGE, AND STRIPPED OF YOUR RIGHTS AFTERWARD.
IN SOME CASES, YOU MIGHT EVEN BE EXECUTED FOR TREASON!
EVEN THEN, WE HAD TWENTY WHO HAD NOT PARTICIPATED IN THE PREVIOUS EXPEDITION...
...AS WELL AS THE HEALTHY SURVIVORS, MAKING A TEAM OF 27 IN ALL-INCLUDING ANGEL.

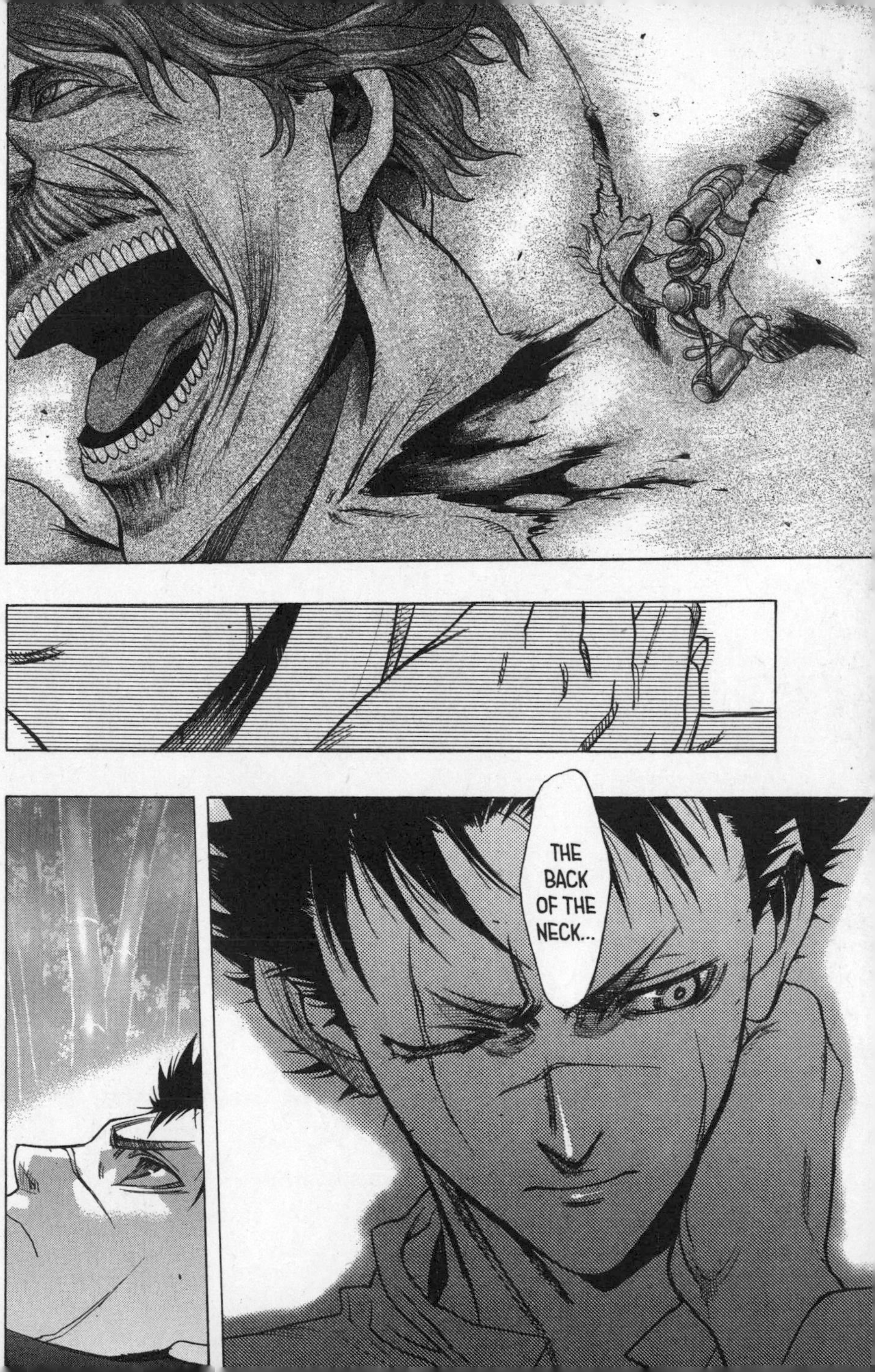
THE BACK OF THE NECK...

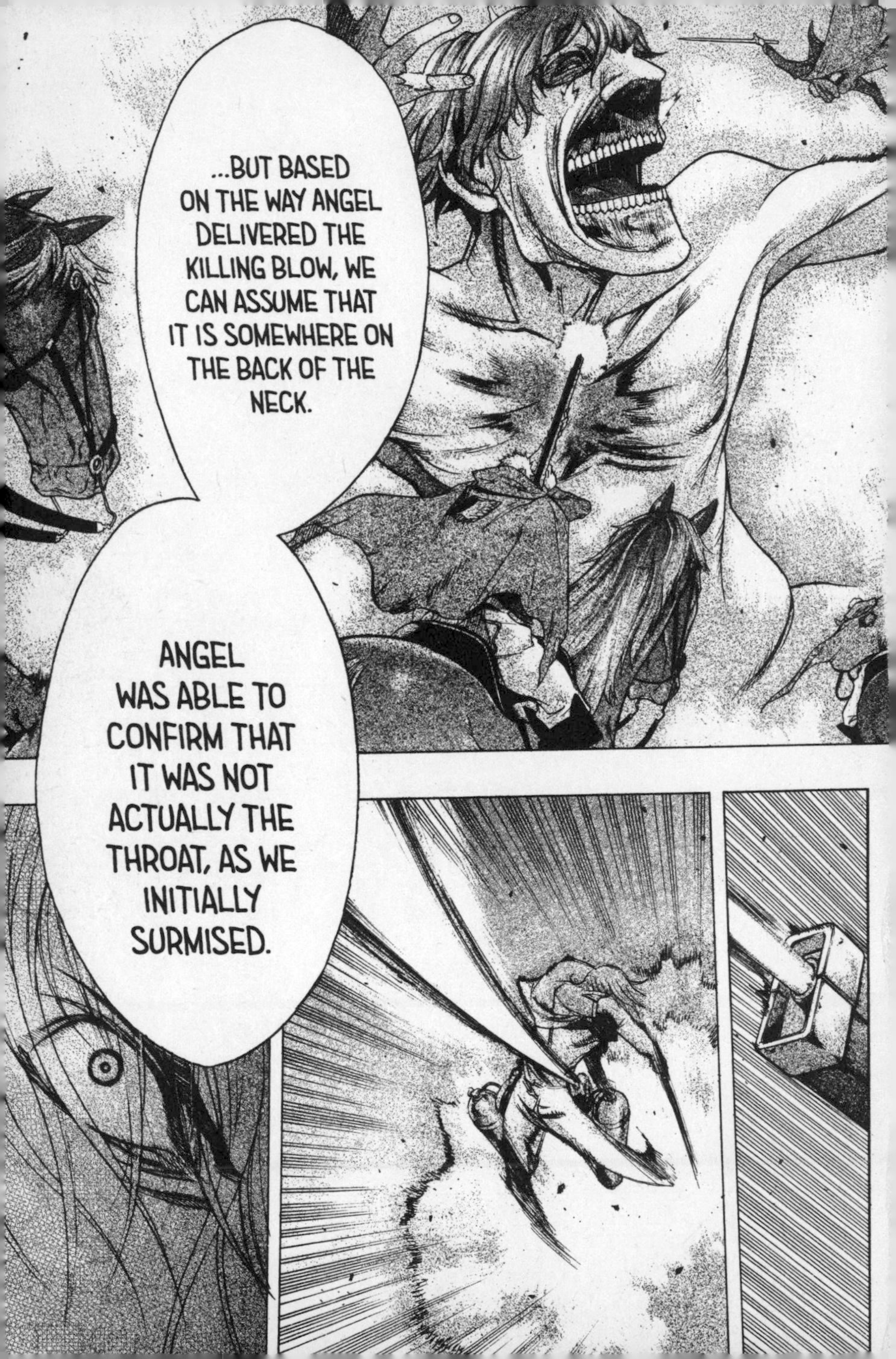
...BUT BASED ON THE WAY ANGEL DELIVERED THE KILLING BLOW, WE CAN ASSUME THAT IT IS SOMEWHERE ON THE BACK OF THE NECK.
ANGEL WAS ABLE TO CONFIRM THAT IT WAS NOT ACTUALLY THE THROAT, AS WE INITIALLY SURMISED.

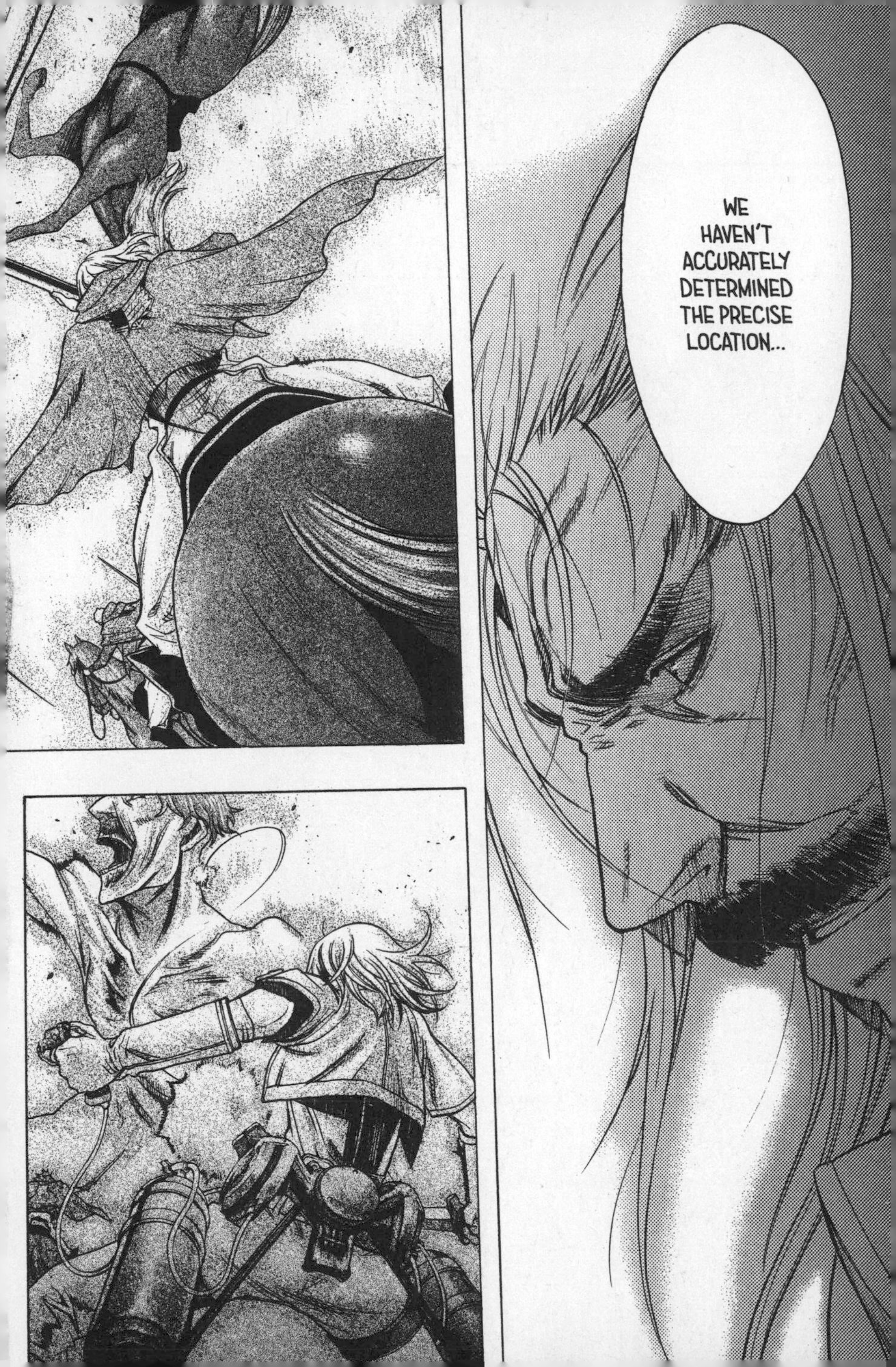
WE HAVEN'T ACCURATELY DETERMINED THE PRECISE LOCATION...

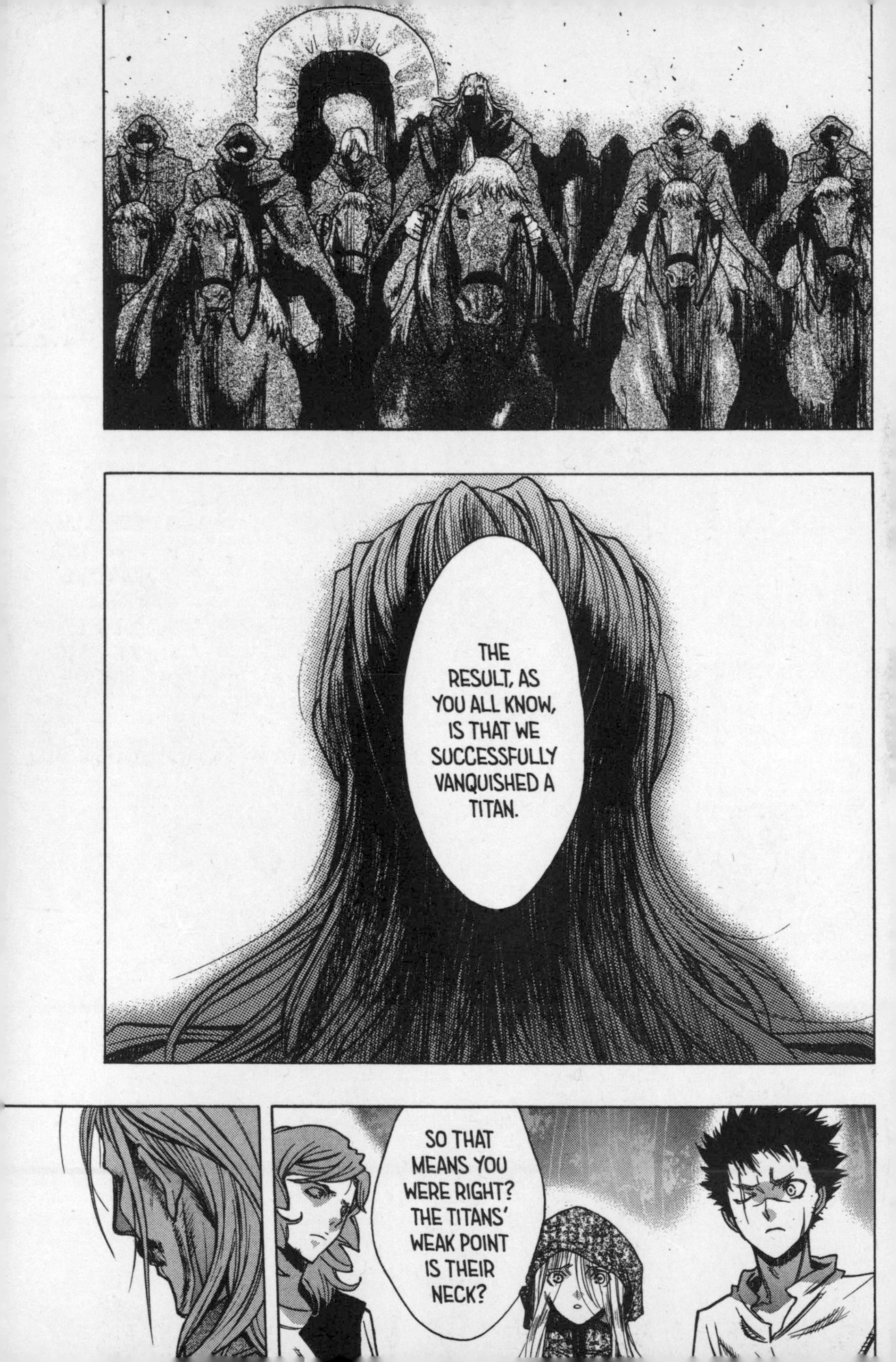
THE RESULT, AS YOU ALL KNOW, IS THAT WE SUCCESSFULLY VANQUISHED A TITAN.
SO THAT MEANS YOU WERE RIGHT? THE TITANS' WEAK POINT IS THEIR NECK?

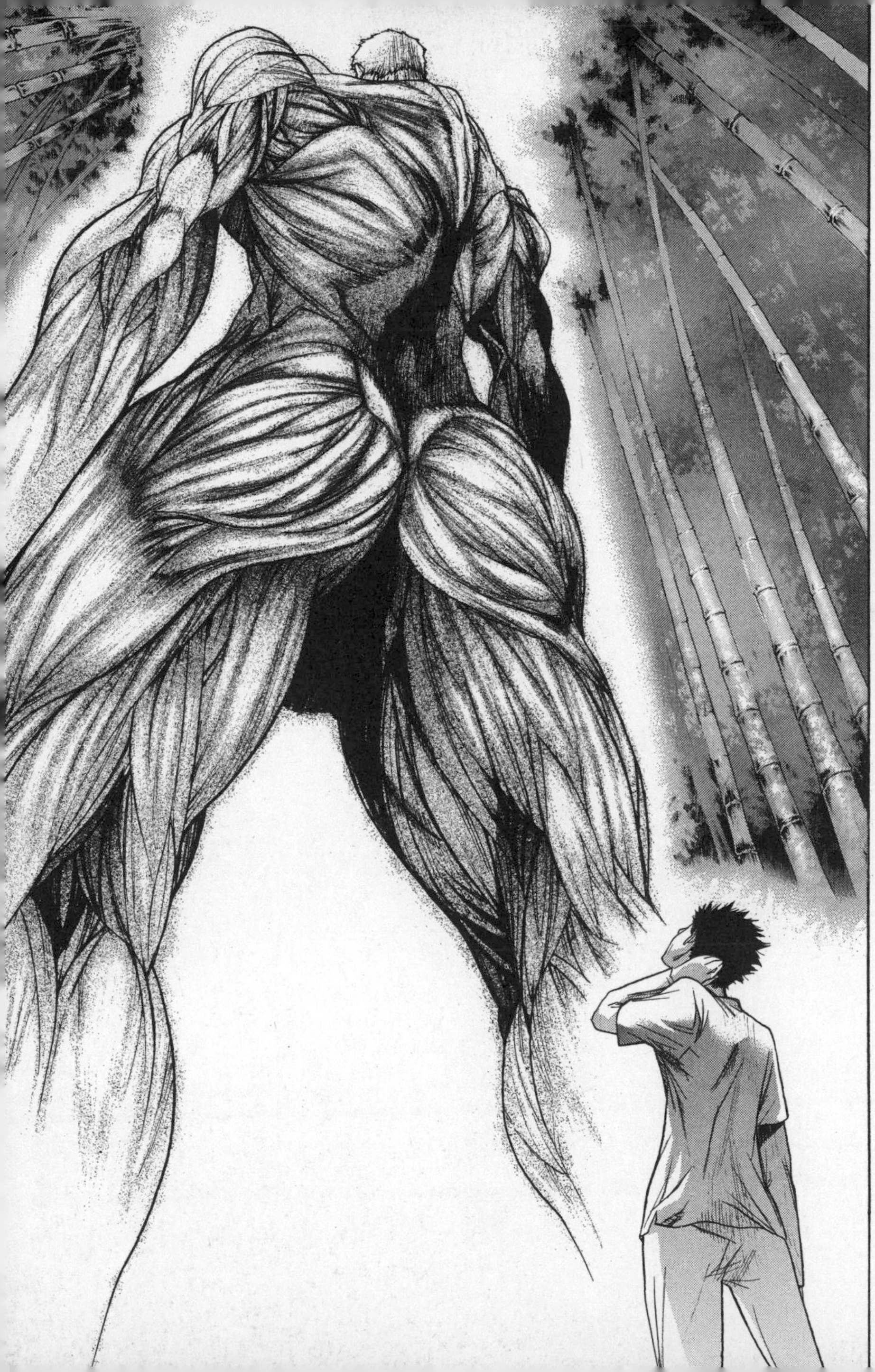

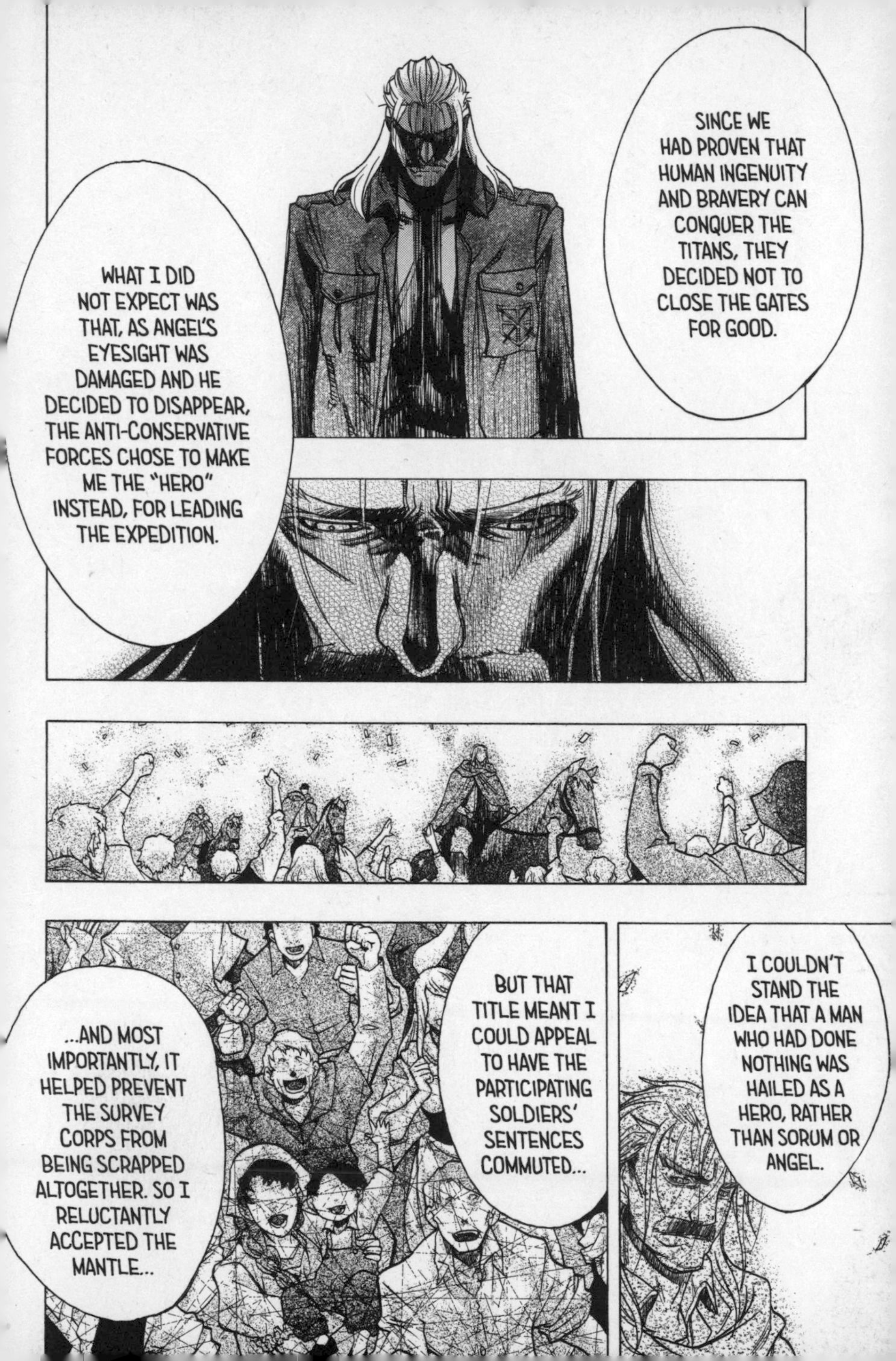
SINCE WE HAD PROVEN THAT HUMAN INGENUITY AND BRAVERY CAN CONQUER THE TITANS, THEY DECIDED NOT TO CLOSE THE GATES FOR GOOD.
WHAT I DID NOT EXPECT WAS THAT, AS ANGEL'S EYESIGHT WAS DAMAGED AND HE DECIDED TO DISAPPEAR, THE ANTI-CONSERVATIVE FORCES CHOSE TO MAKE ME THE "HERO" INSTEAD, FOR LEADING THE EXPEDITION.
I COULDN'T STAND THE IDEA THAT A MAN WHO HAD DONE NOTHING WAS HAILED AS A HERO, RATHER THAN SORUM OR ANGEL.
BUT THAT TITLE MEANT I COULD APPEAL TO HAVE THE PARTICIPATING SOLDIERS' SENTENCES COMMUTED...
...AND MOST IMPORTANTLY, IT HELPED PREVENT THE SURVEY CORPS FROM BEING SCRAPPED ALTOGETHER. SO I RELUCTANTLY ACCEPTED THE MANTLE...

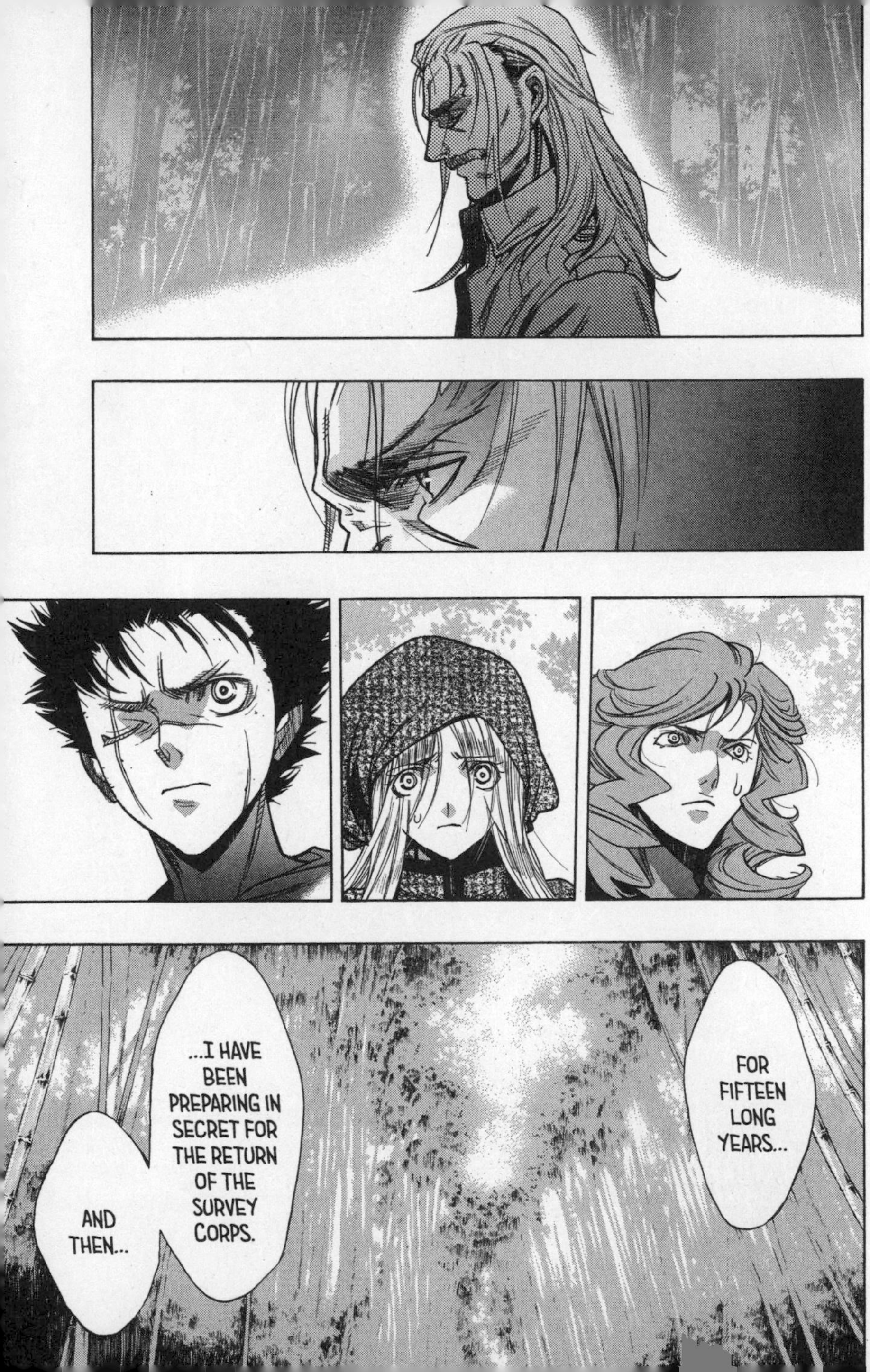
FOR FIFTEEN LONG YEARS...
...I HAVE BEEN PREPARING IN SECRET FOR THE RETURN OF THE SURVEY CORPS.
AND THEN...

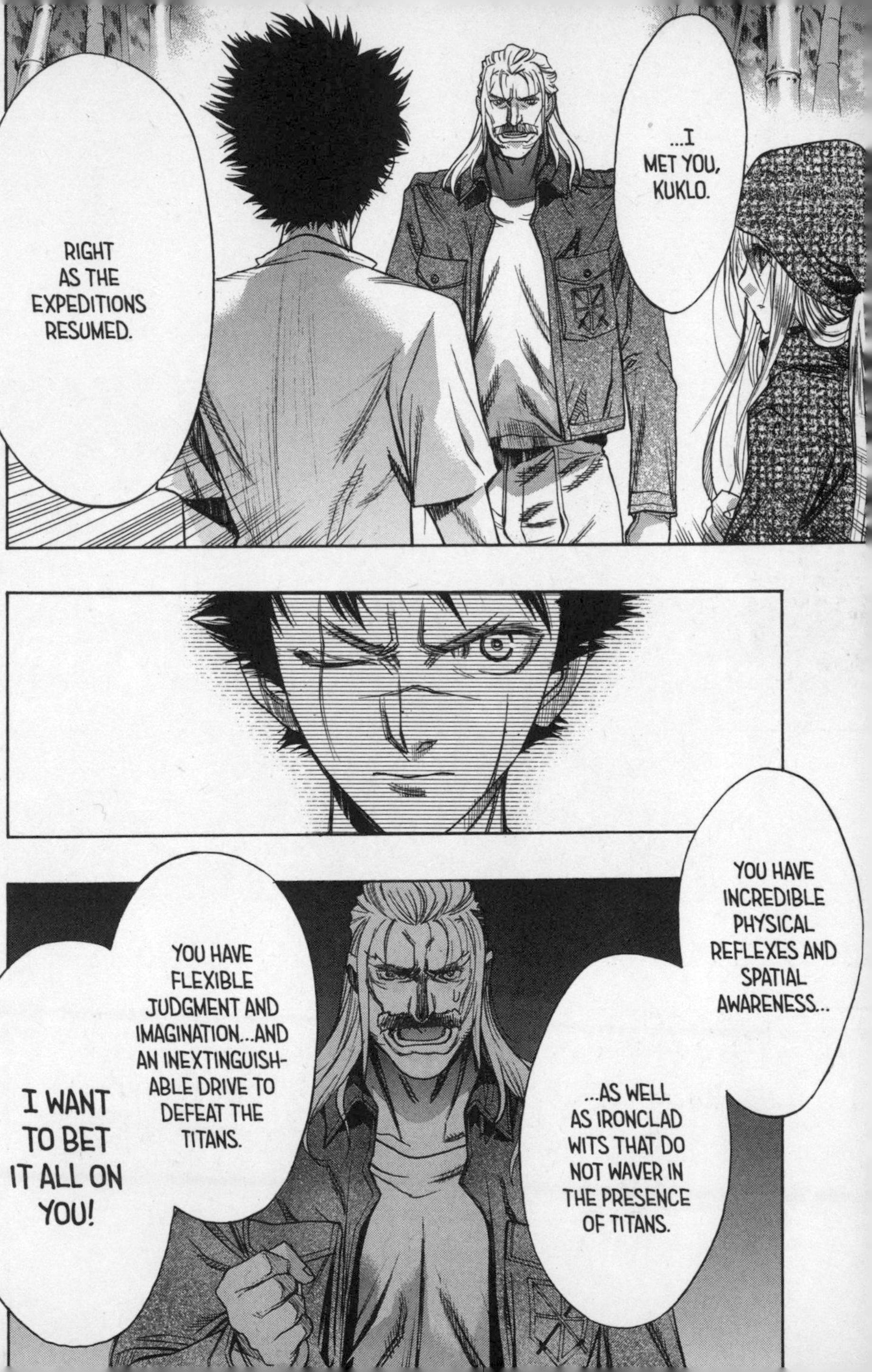
...I MET YOU, KUKLO.
RIGHT AS THE EXPEDITIONS RESUMED.
YOU HAVE INCREDIBLE PHYSICAL REFLEXES AND SPATIAL AWARENESS...
...AS WELL AS IRONCLAD WITS THAT DO NOT WAVER IN THE PRESENCE OF TITANS.
YOU HAVE FLEXIBLE JUDGMENT AND IMAGINATION...AND AN INEXTINGUISHABLE DRIVE TO DEFEAT THE TITANS.
I WANT TO BET IT ALL ON YOU!

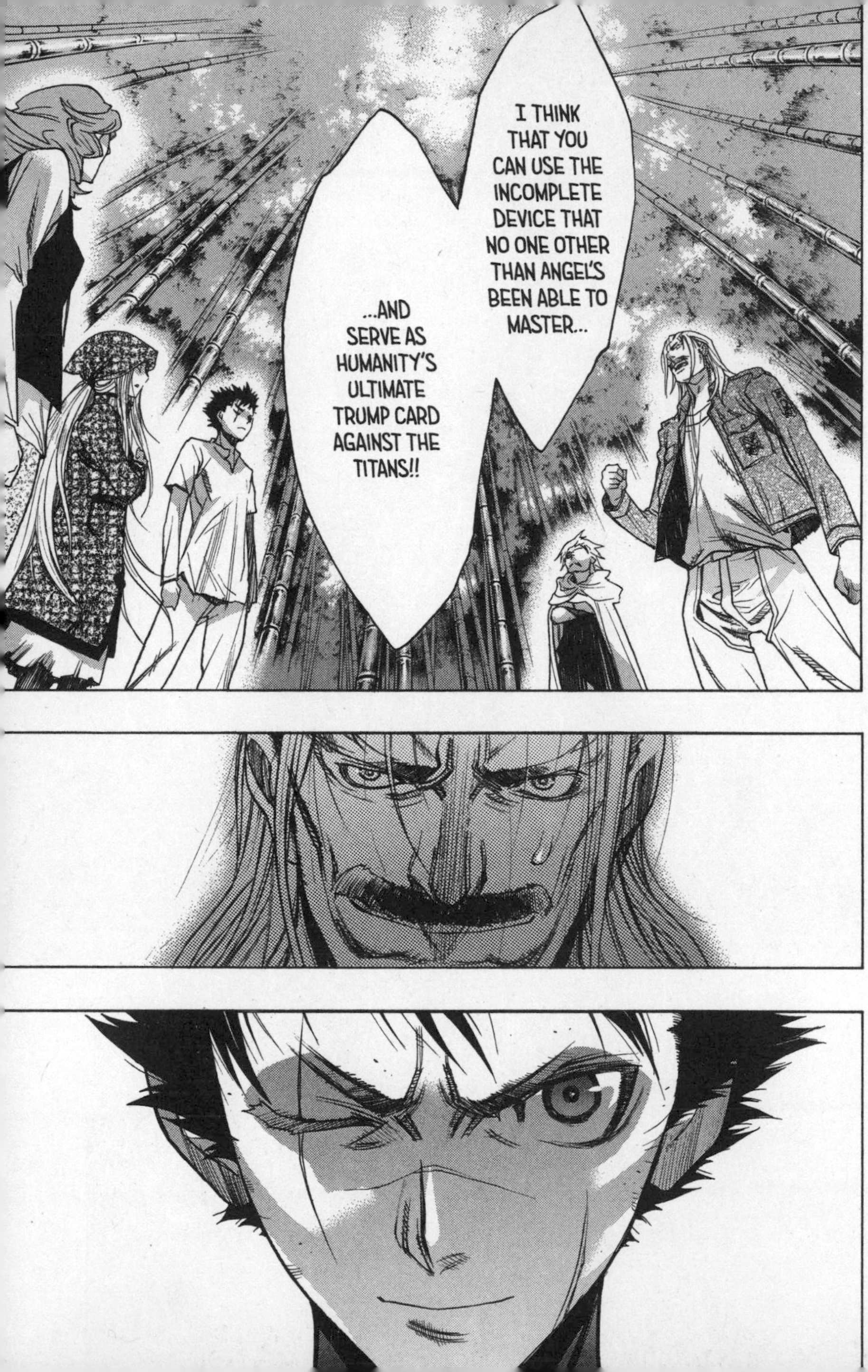
I THINK THAT YOU CAN USE THE INCOMPLETE DEVICE THAT NO ONE OTHER THAN ANGEL'S BEEN ABLE TO MASTER...
...AND SERVE AS HUMANITY'S ULTIMATE TRUMP CARD AGAINST THE TITANS!!

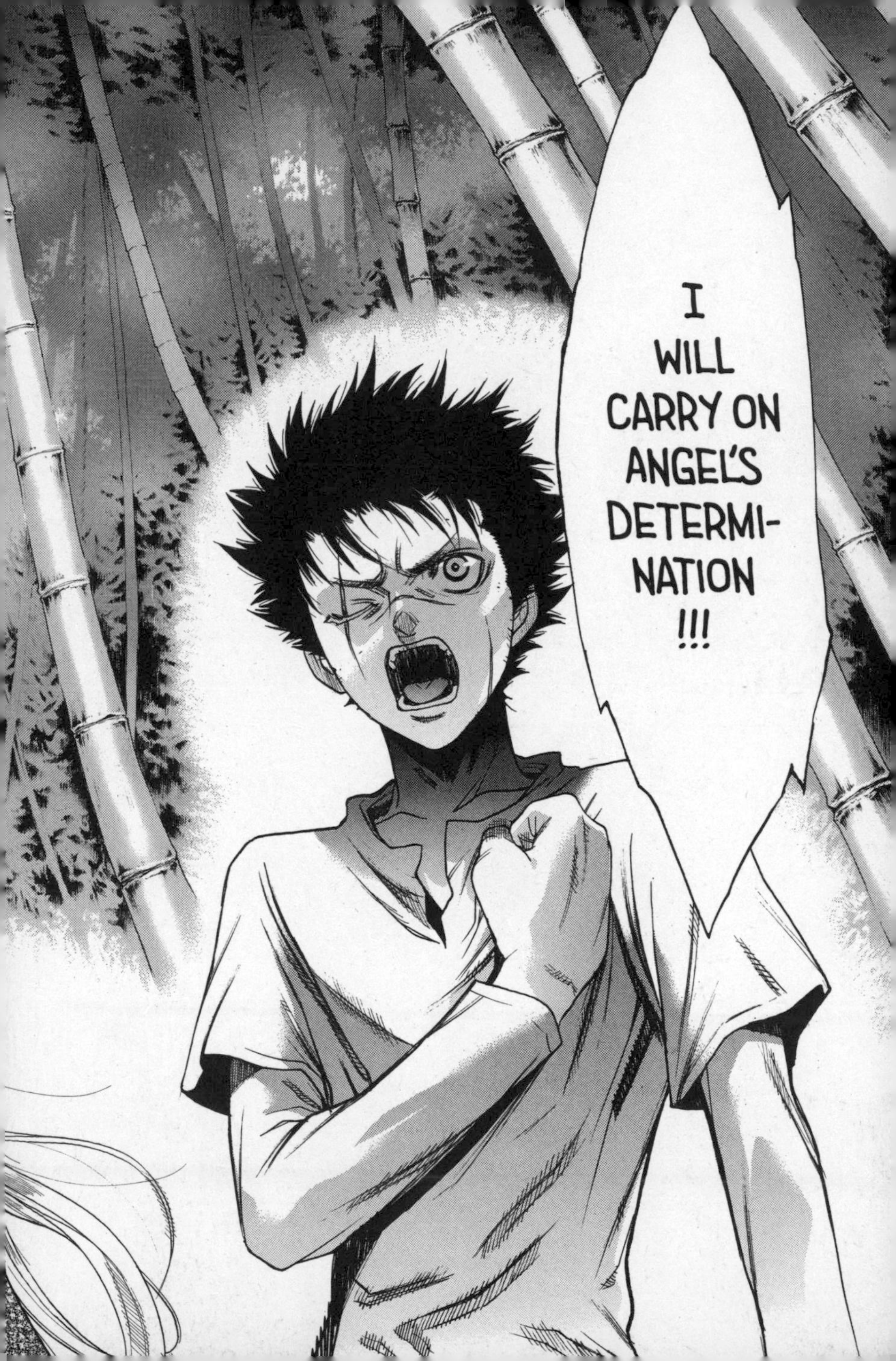
I WILL CARRY ON ANGEL'S DETERMINATION !!!

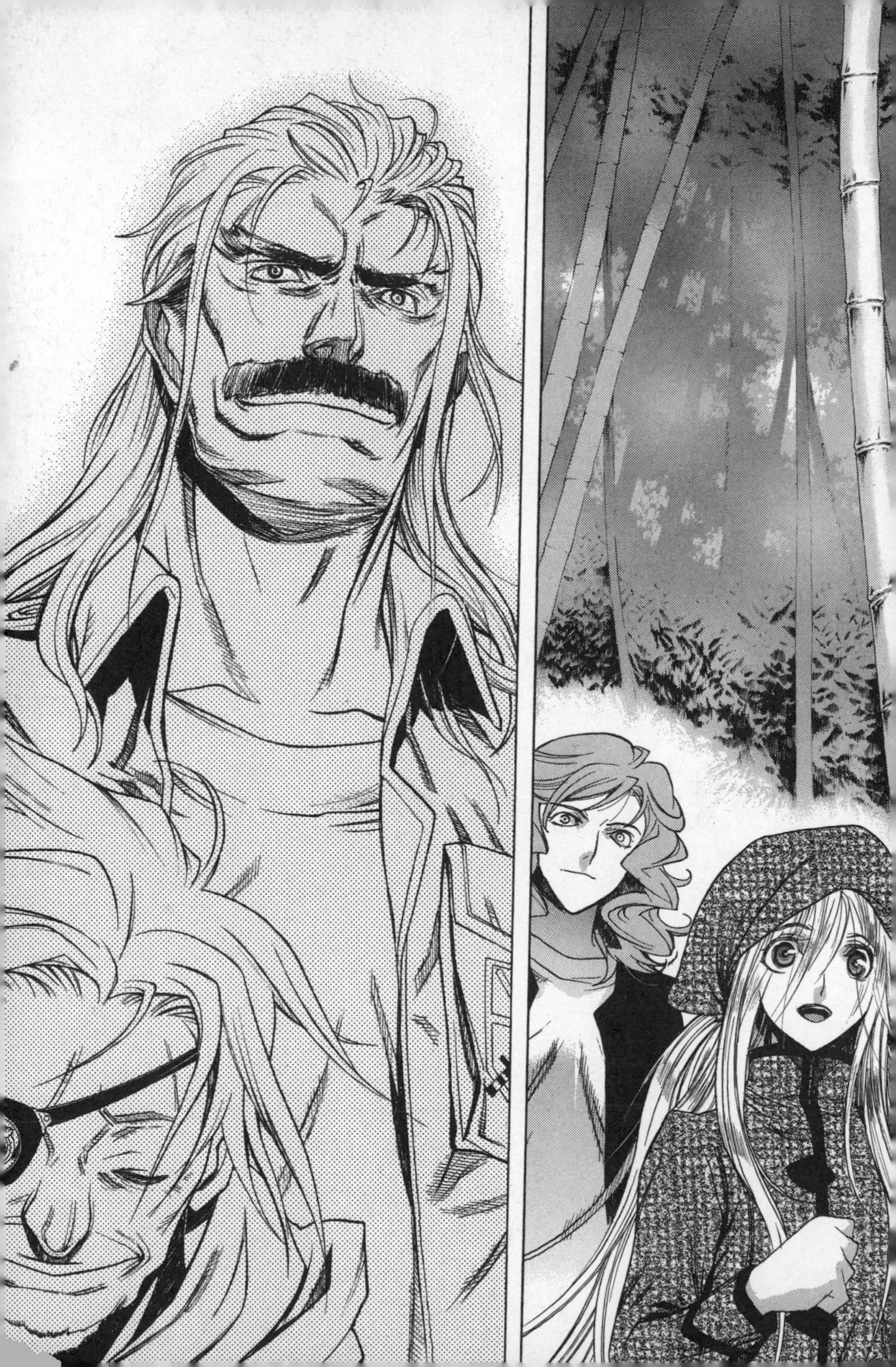

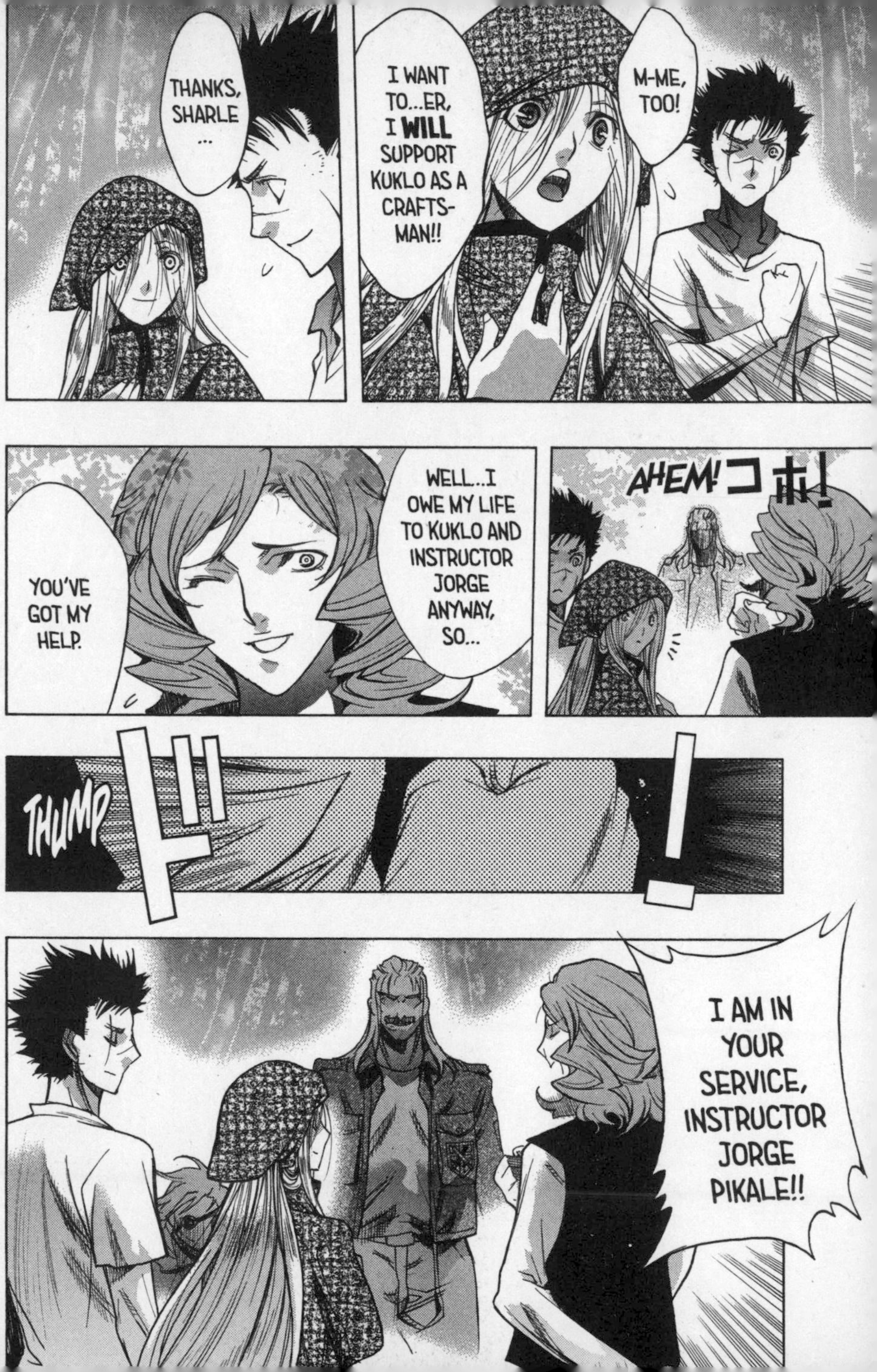
I WANT TO...ER, I **WILL** SUPPORT KUKLO AS A CRAFTS-MAN!!
M-ME, TOO!
THANKS, SHARLE ...
AHEM! コホ!
WELL...I OWE MY LIFE TO KUKLO AND INSTRUCTOR JORGE ANYWAY, SO...
YOU'VE GOT MY HELP.
THUMP ド
!
I AM IN YOUR SERVICE, INSTRUCTOR JORGE PIKALE!!

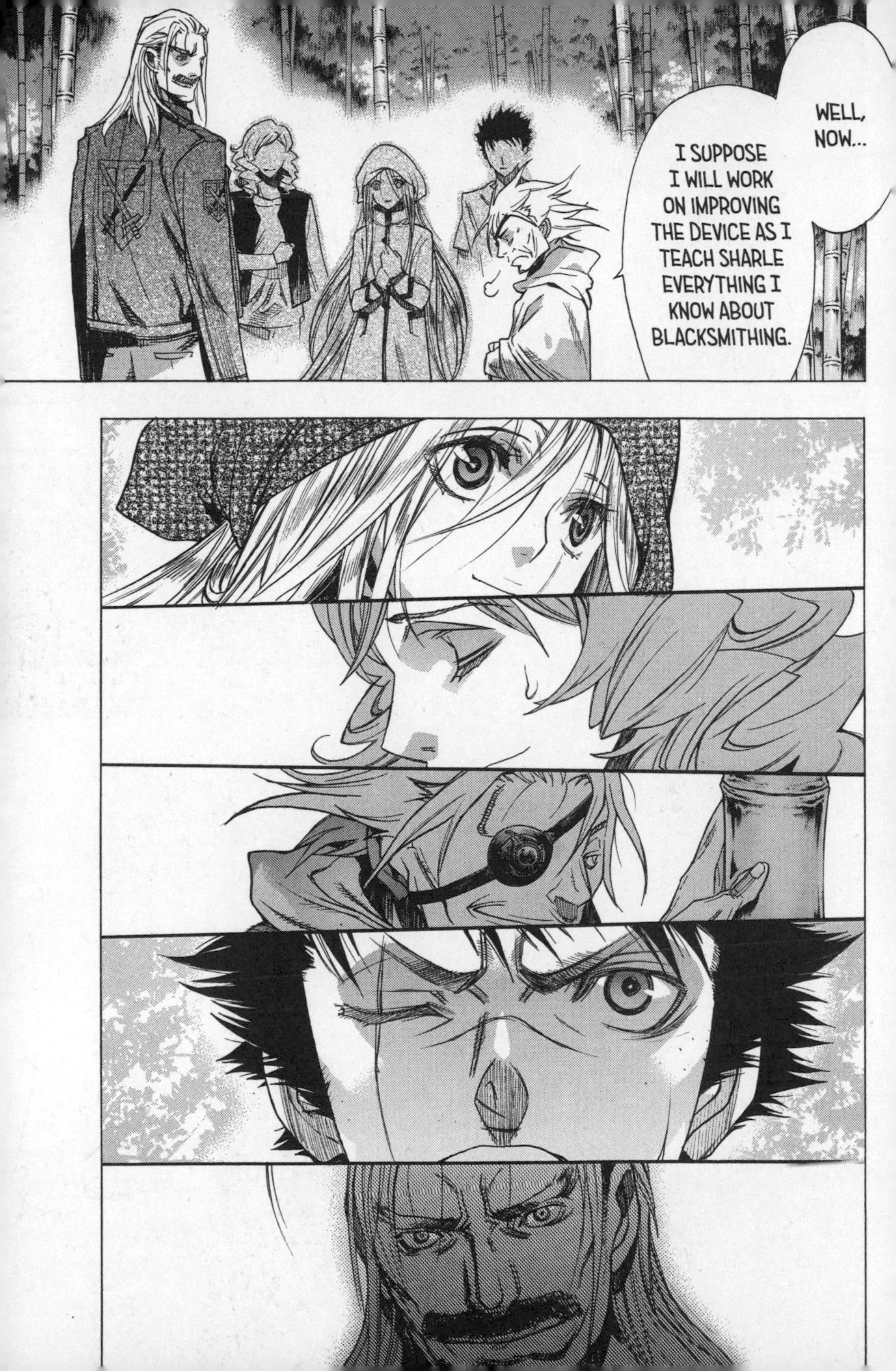
WELL, NOW...
I SUPPOSE I WILL WORK ON IMPROVING THE DEVICE AS I TEACH SHARLE EVERYTHING I KNOW ABOUT BLACKSMITHING.

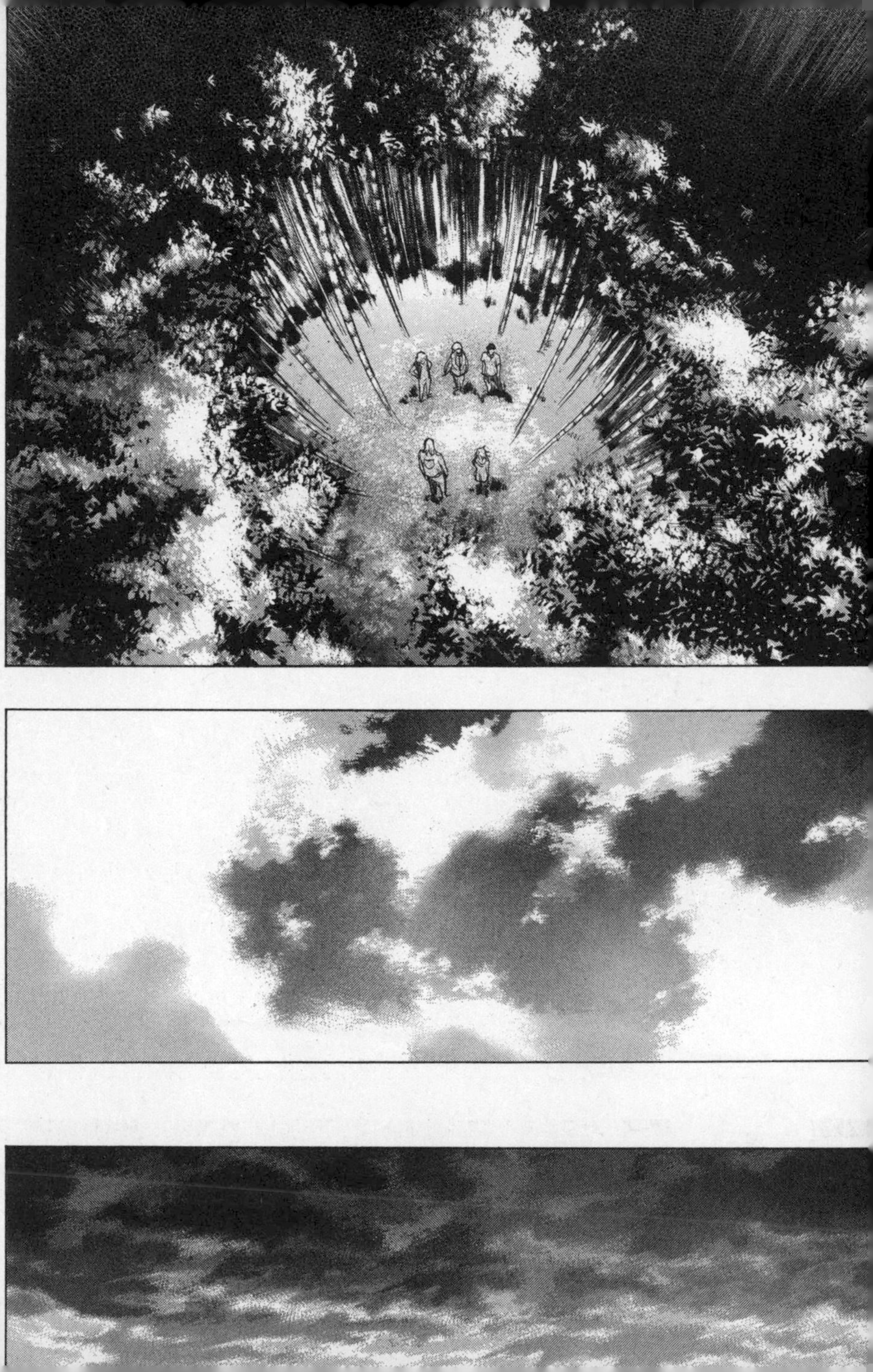

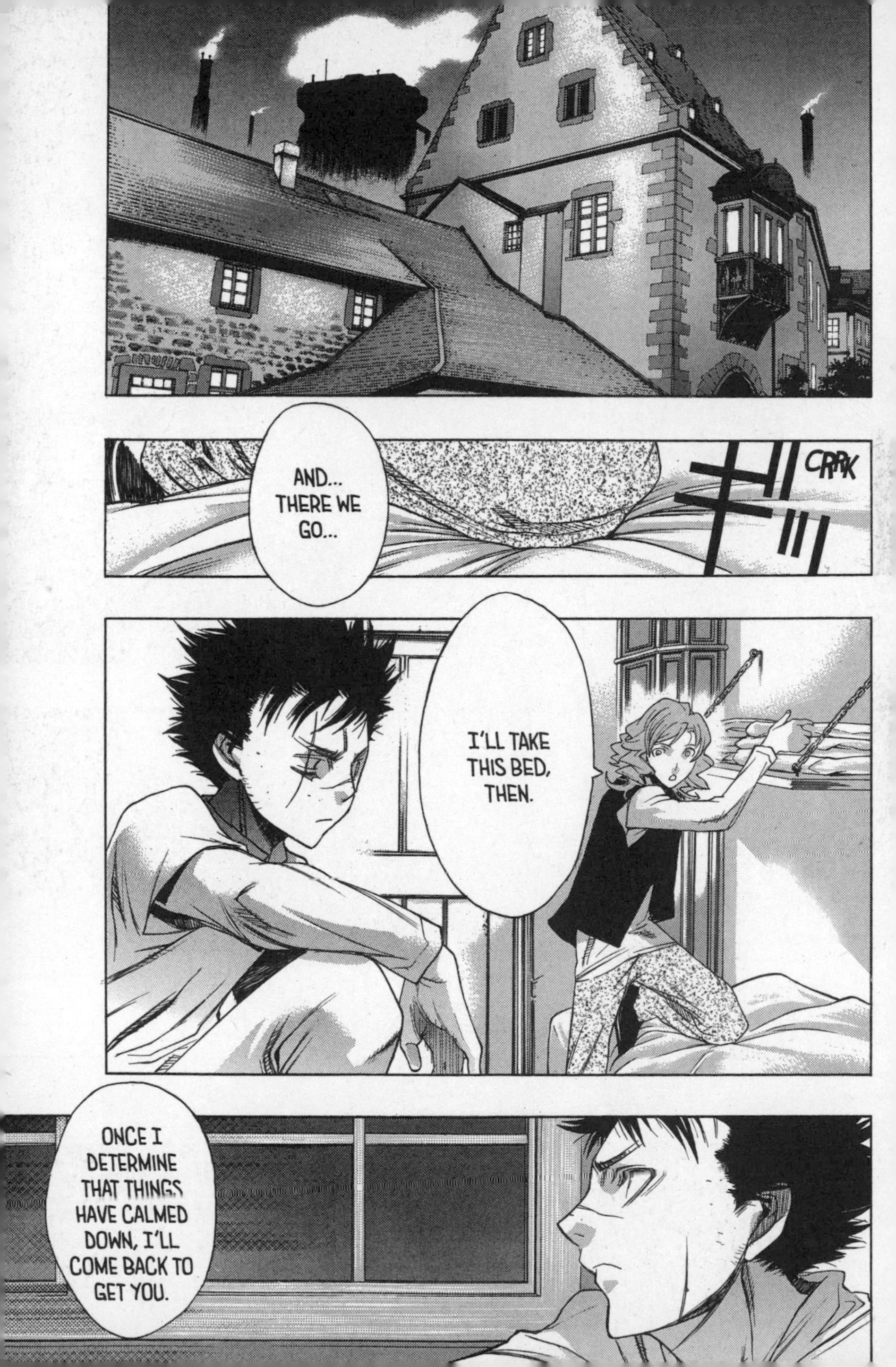
CRRK
AND... THERE WE GO...
I'LL TAKE THIS BED, THEN.
ONCE I DETERMINE THAT THINGS HAVE CALMED DOWN, I'LL COME BACK TO GET YOU.

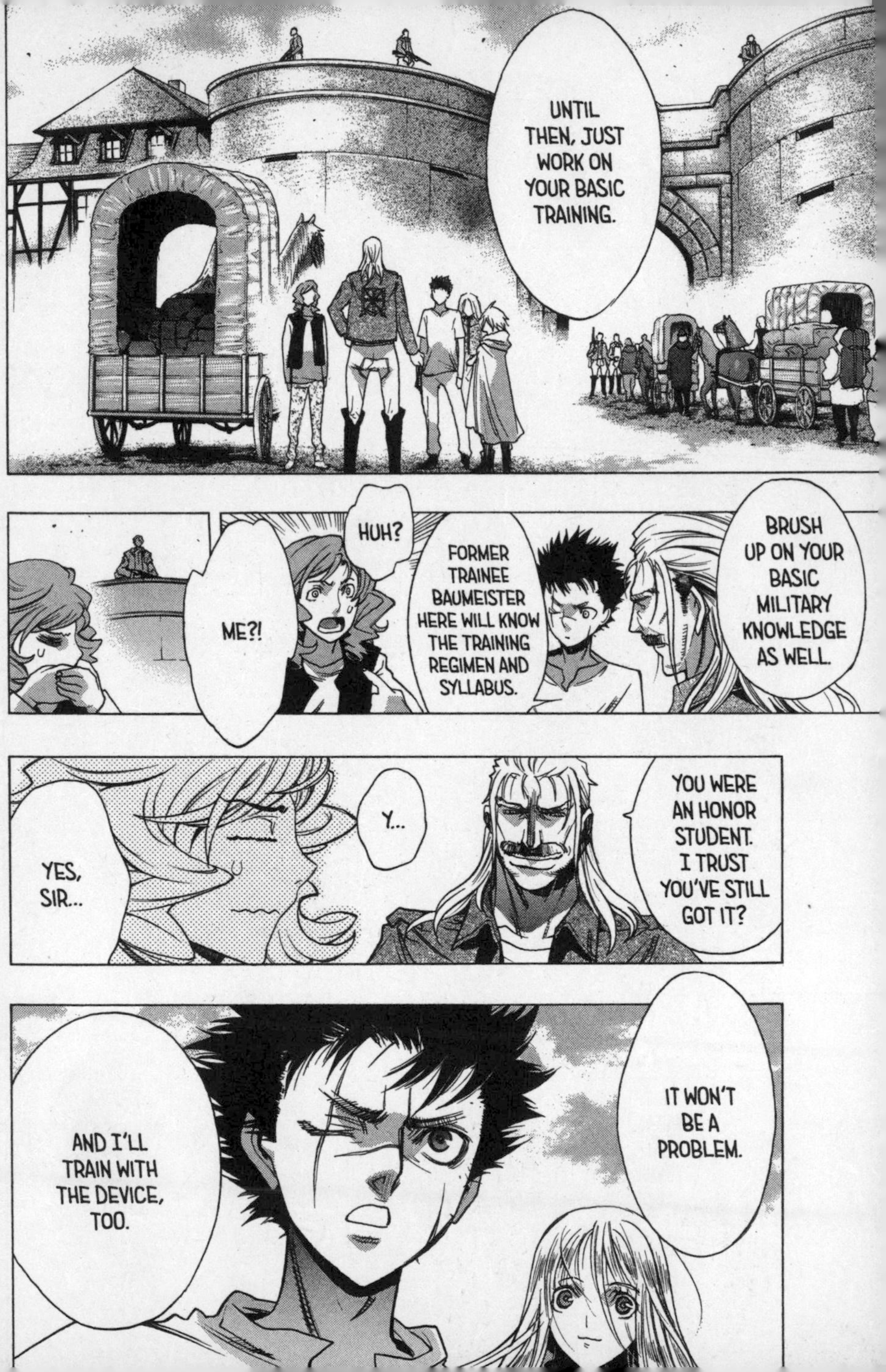
UNTIL THEN, JUST WORK ON YOUR BASIC TRAINING.
BRUSH UP ON YOUR BASIC MILITARY KNOWLEDGE AS WELL.
FORMER TRAINEE BAUMEISTER HERE WILL KNOW THE TRAINING REGIMEN AND SYLLABUS.
HUH?
ME?!
YOU WERE AN HONOR STUDENT. I TRUST YOU'VE STILL GOT IT?
Y...
YES, SIR...
IT WON'T BE A PROBLEM.
AND I'LL TRAIN WITH THE DEVICE, TOO.

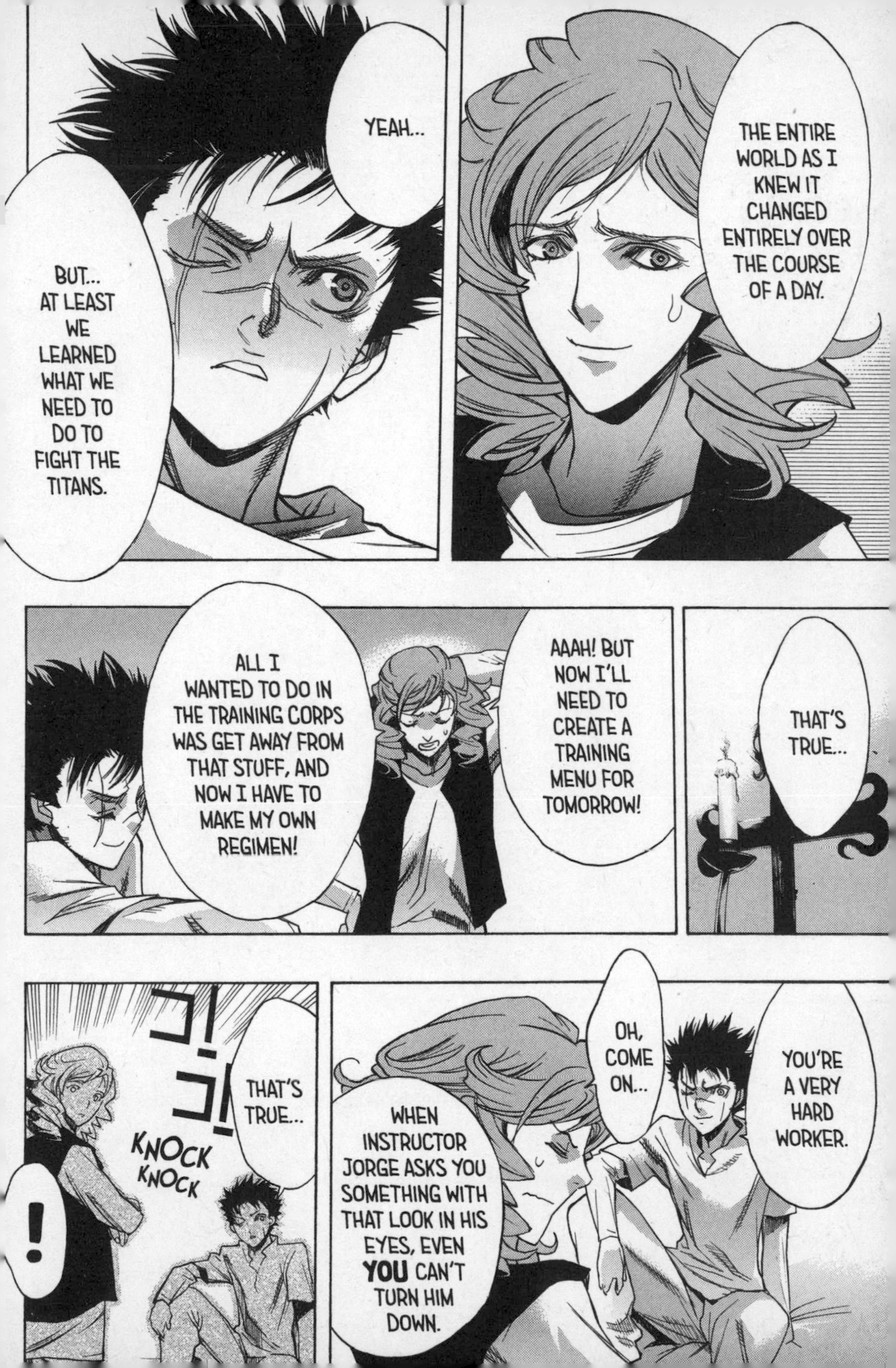

THE ENTIRE WORLD AS I KNEW IT CHANGED ENTIRELY OVER THE COURSE OF A DAY.
YEAH...
BUT... AT LEAST WE LEARNED WHAT WE NEED TO DO TO FIGHT THE TITANS.
THAT'S TRUE...
AAAH! BUT NOW I'LL NEED TO CREATE A TRAINING MENU FOR TOMORROW!
ALL I WANTED TO DO IN THE TRAINING CORPS WAS GET AWAY FROM THAT STUFF, AND NOW I HAVE TO MAKE MY OWN REGIMEN!
YOU'RE A VERY HARD WORKER.
OH, COME ON...
WHEN INSTRUCTOR JORGE ASKS YOU SOMETHING WITH THAT LOOK IN HIS EYES, EVEN **YOU** CAN'T TURN HIM DOWN.
THAT'S TRUE...
コ! コ!
KNOCK KNOCK
!

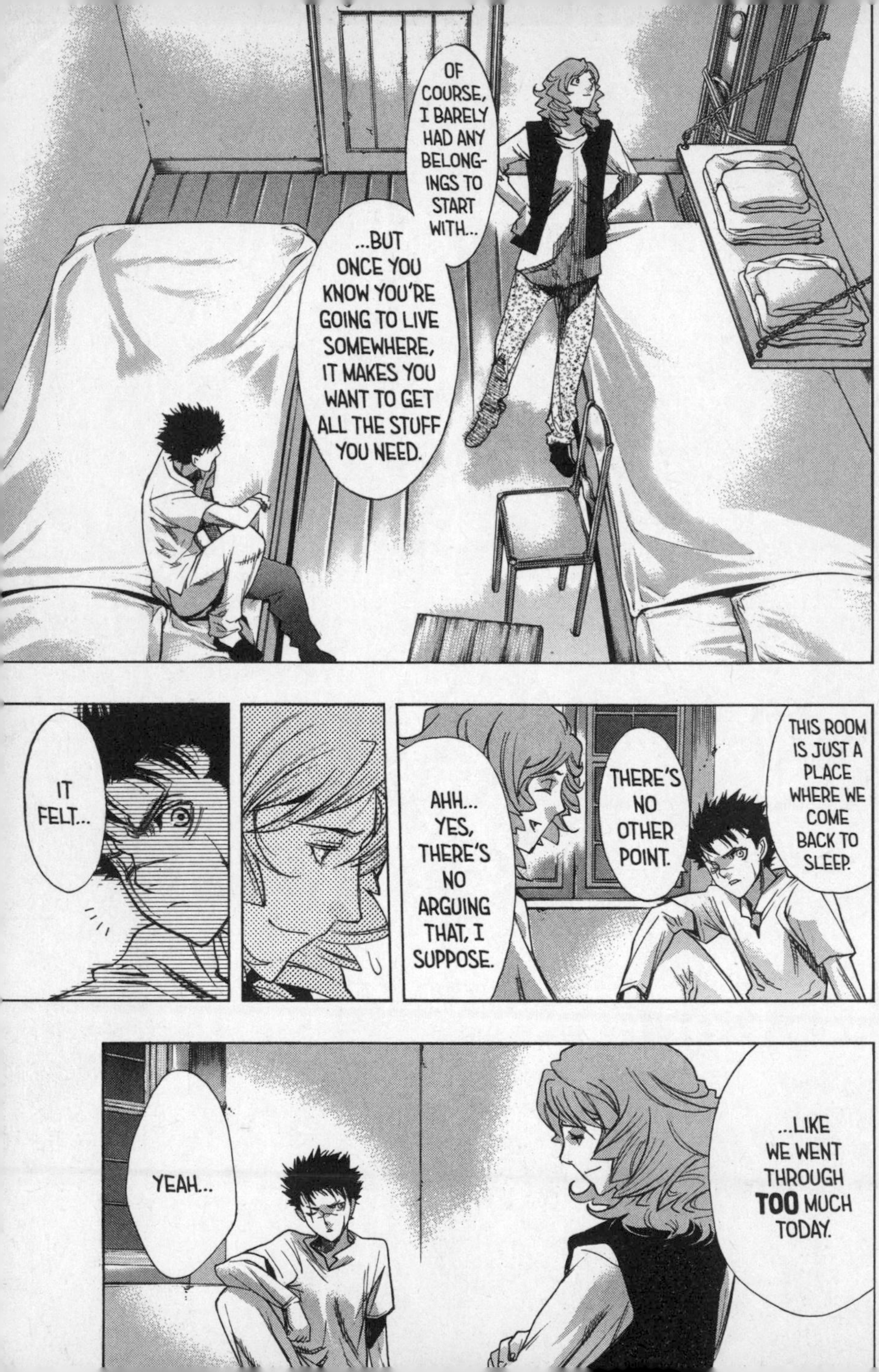
OF COURSE, I BARELY HAD ANY BELONGINGS TO START WITH...
...BUT ONCE YOU KNOW YOU'RE GOING TO LIVE SOMEWHERE, IT MAKES YOU WANT TO GET ALL THE STUFF YOU NEED.
THIS ROOM IS JUST A PLACE WHERE WE COME BACK TO SLEEP.
THERE'S NO OTHER POINT.
AHH... YES, THERE'S NO ARGUING THAT, I SUPPOSE.
IT FELT...
...LIKE WE WENT THROUGH **TOO** MUCH TODAY.
YEAH...

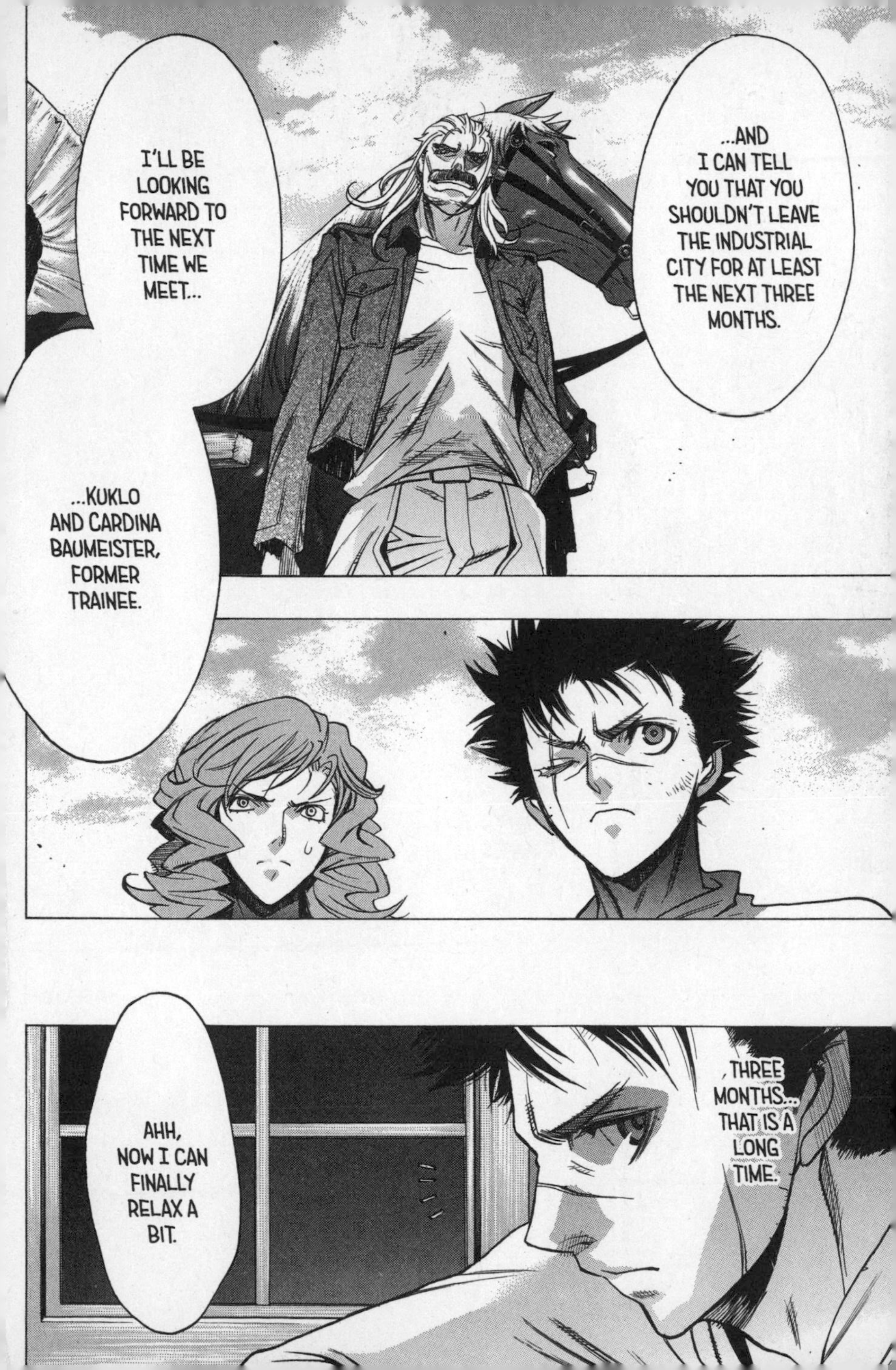
...AND I CAN TELL YOU THAT YOU SHOULDN'T LEAVE THE INDUSTRIAL CITY FOR AT LEAST THE NEXT THREE MONTHS.
I'LL BE LOOKING FORWARD TO THE NEXT TIME WE MEET...
...KUKLO AND CARDINA BAUMEISTER, FORMER TRAINEE.
THREE MONTHS... THAT IS A LONG TIME.
AHH, NOW I CAN FINALLY RELAX A BIT.

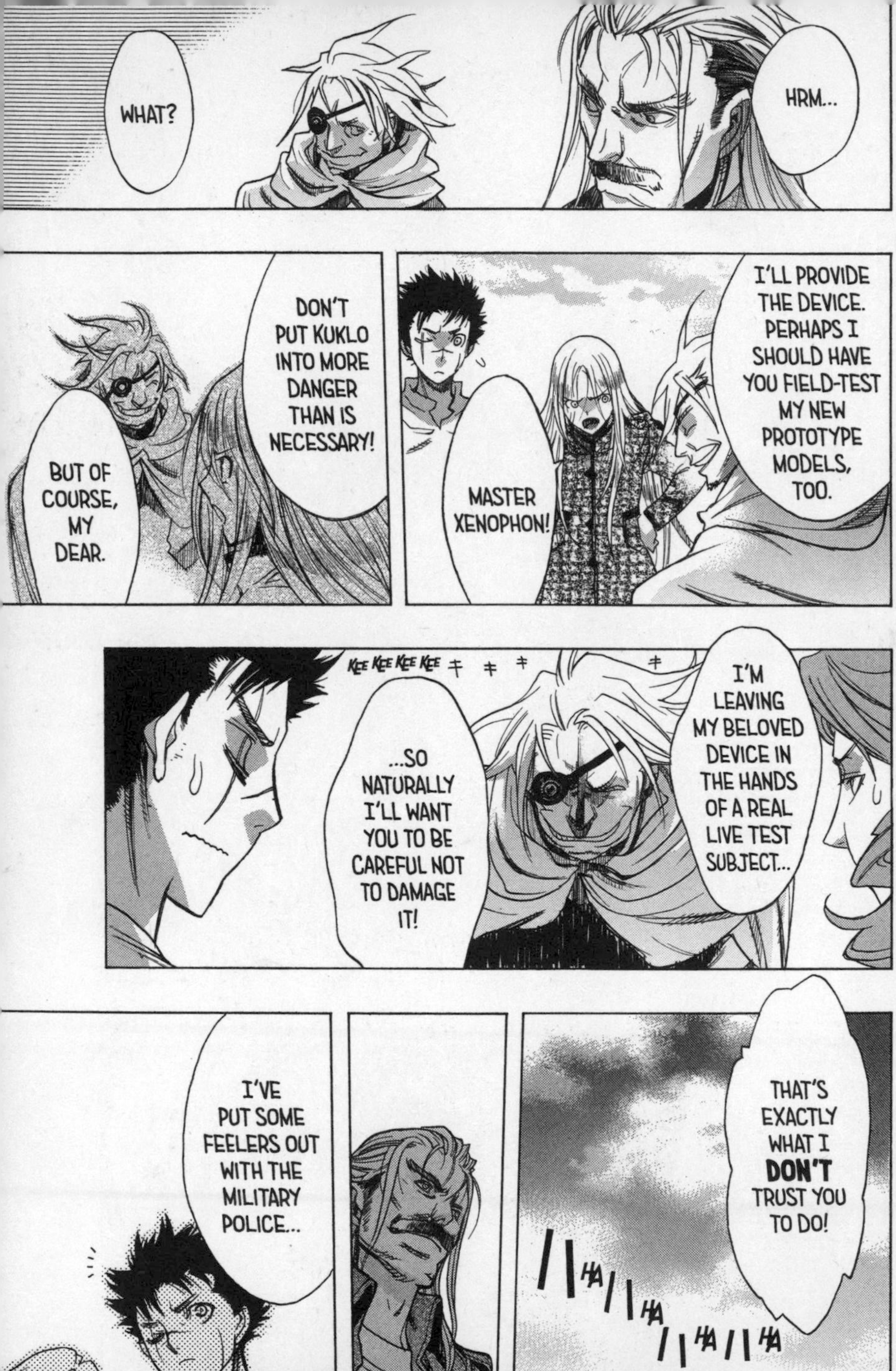
HRM...
WHAT?
I'LL PROVIDE THE DEVICE. PERHAPS I SHOULD HAVE YOU FIELD-TEST MY NEW PROTOTYPE MODELS, TOO.
MASTER XENOPHON!
DON'T PUT KUKLO INTO MORE DANGER THAN IS NECESSARY!
BUT OF COURSE, MY DEAR.
KEE KEE KEE KEE
キ キ キ キ
I'M LEAVING MY BELOVED DEVICE IN THE HANDS OF A REAL LIVE TEST SUBJECT...
...SO NATURALLY I'LL WANT YOU TO BE CAREFUL NOT TO DAMAGE IT!
THAT'S EXACTLY WHAT I **DON'T** TRUST YOU TO DO!
HA HA HA HA
I'VE PUT SOME FEELERS OUT WITH THE MILITARY POLICE...

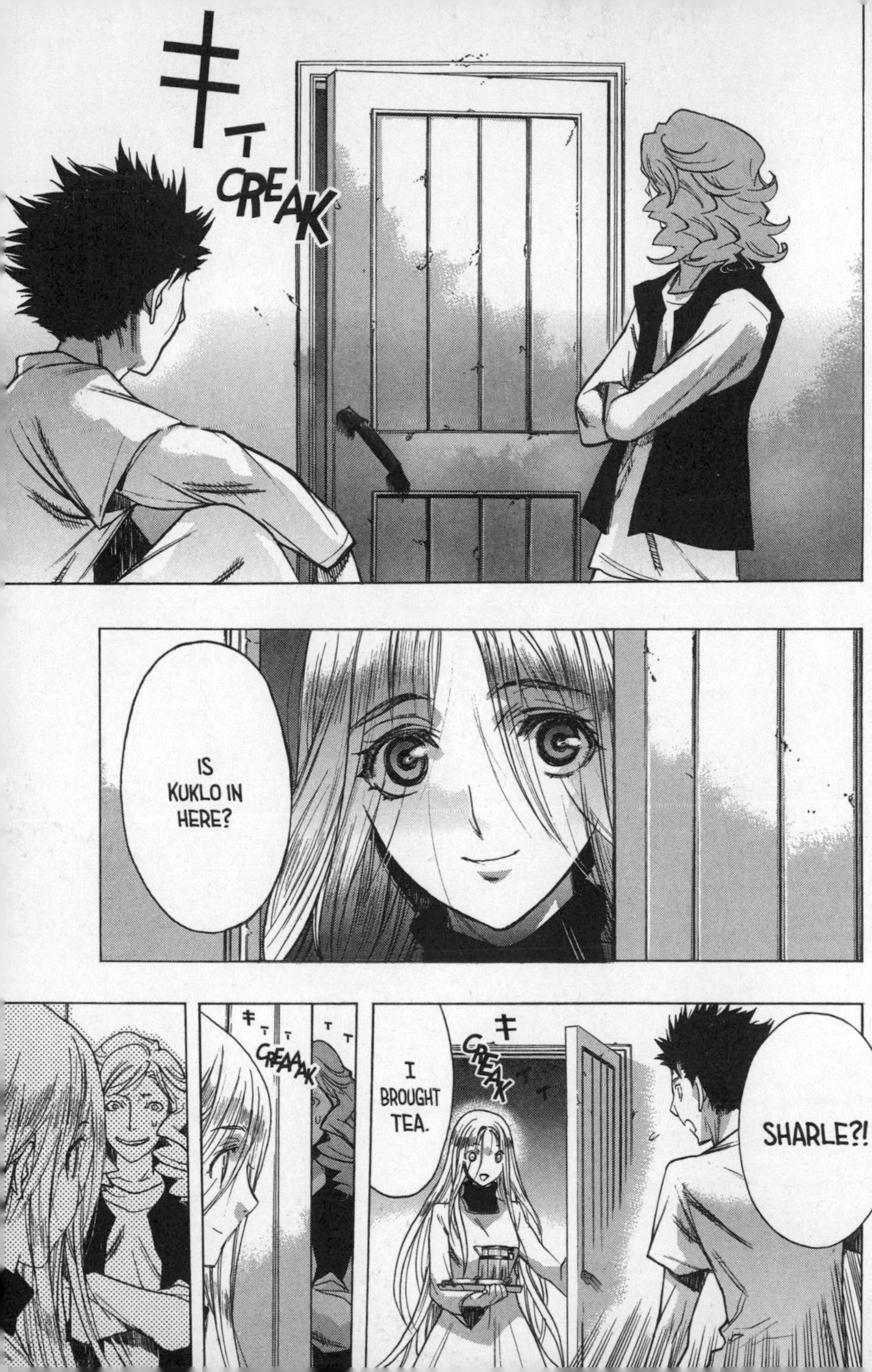

キ
CREAK
IS KUKLO IN HERE?
SHARLE?!
キ
CREAK
I BROUGHT TEA.
キ
CREAAAK

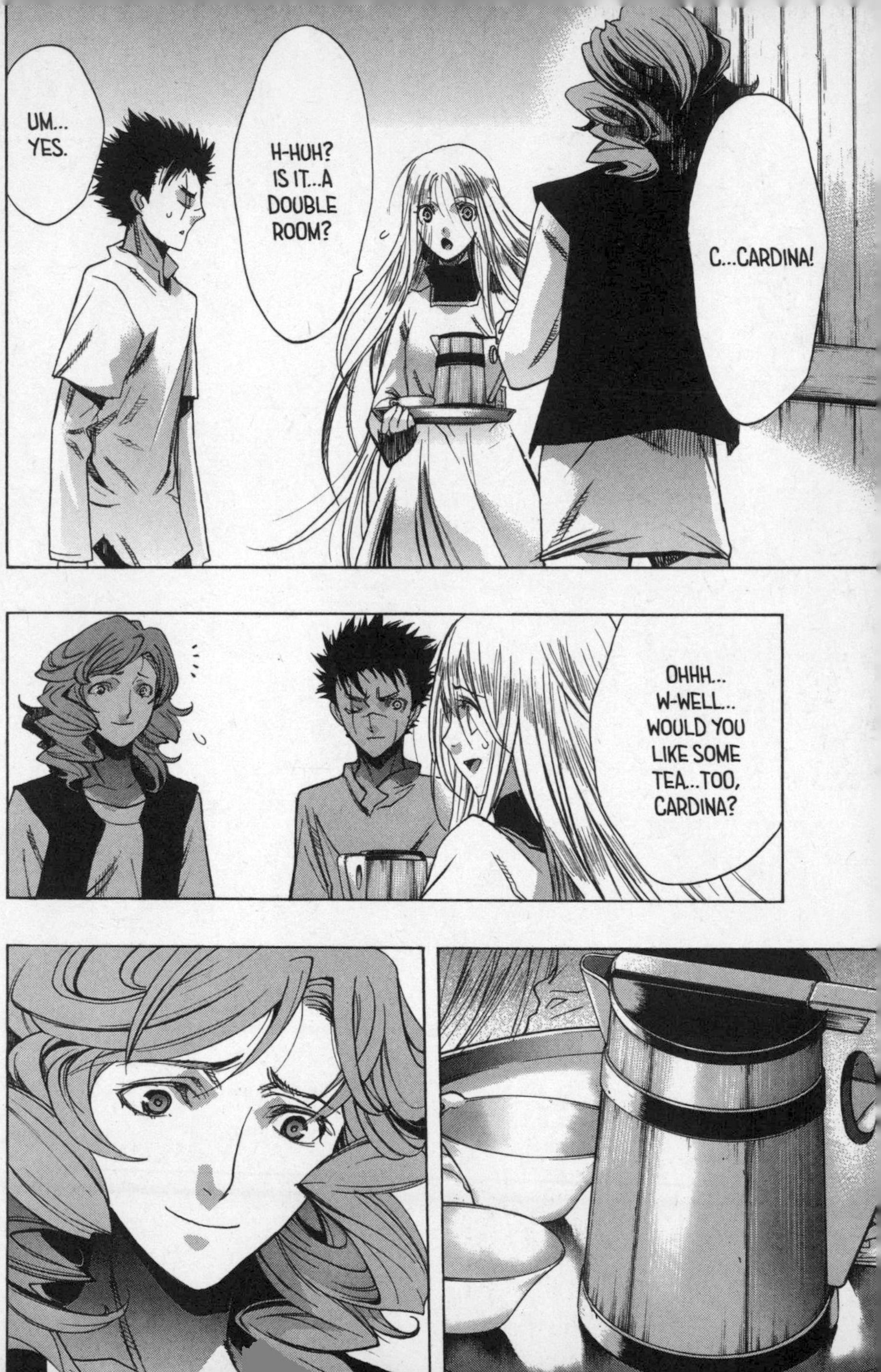
C...CARDINA!
H-HUH? IS IT...A DOUBLE ROOM?
UM... YES.
OHHH... W-WELL... WOULD YOU LIKE SOME TEA...TOO, CARDINA?

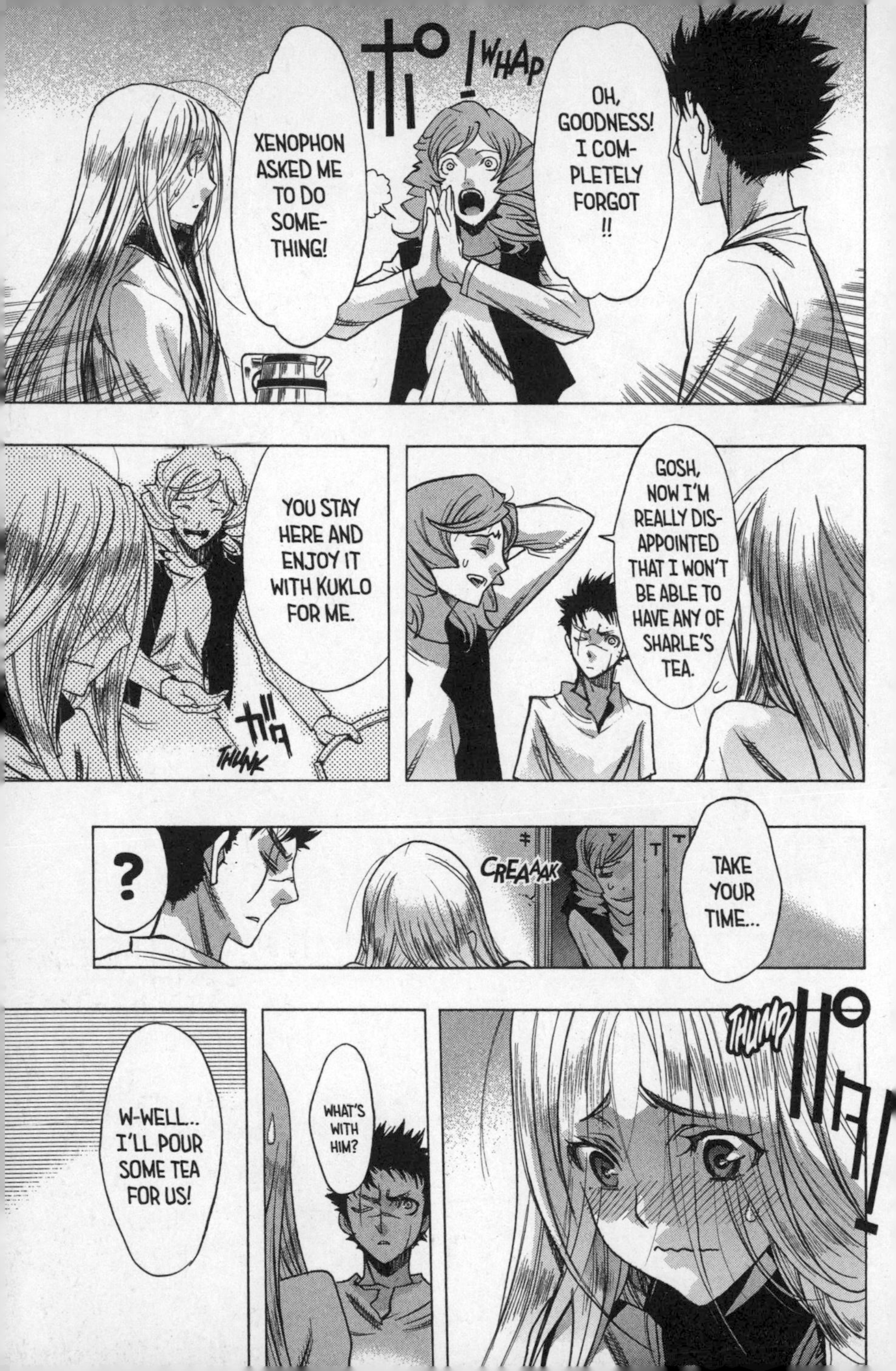
OH, GOODNESS! I COMPLETELY FORGOT !!
WHAP
XENOPHON ASKED ME TO DO SOMETHING!
GOSH, NOW I'M REALLY DISAPPOINTED THAT I WON'T BE ABLE TO HAVE ANY OF SHARLE'S TEA.
YOU STAY HERE AND ENJOY IT WITH KUKLO FOR ME.
THUNK
TAKE YOUR TIME...
CREAAAK
?
THUMP
WHAT'S WITH HIM?
W-WELL... I'LL POUR SOME TEA FOR US!

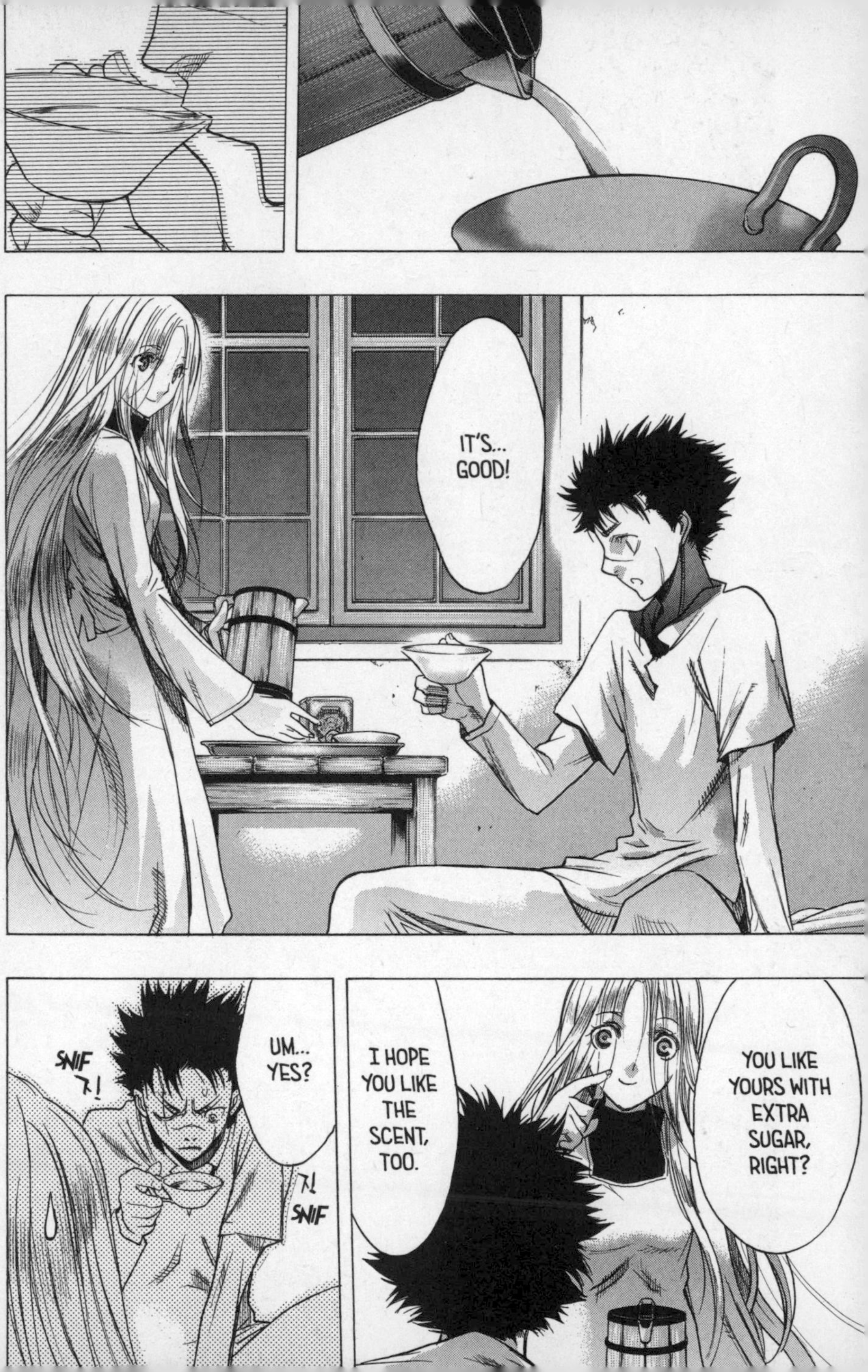

IT'S... GOOD!
YOU LIKE YOURS WITH EXTRA SUGAR, RIGHT?
I HOPE YOU LIKE THE SCENT, TOO.
UM... YES?
SNIF
SNIF

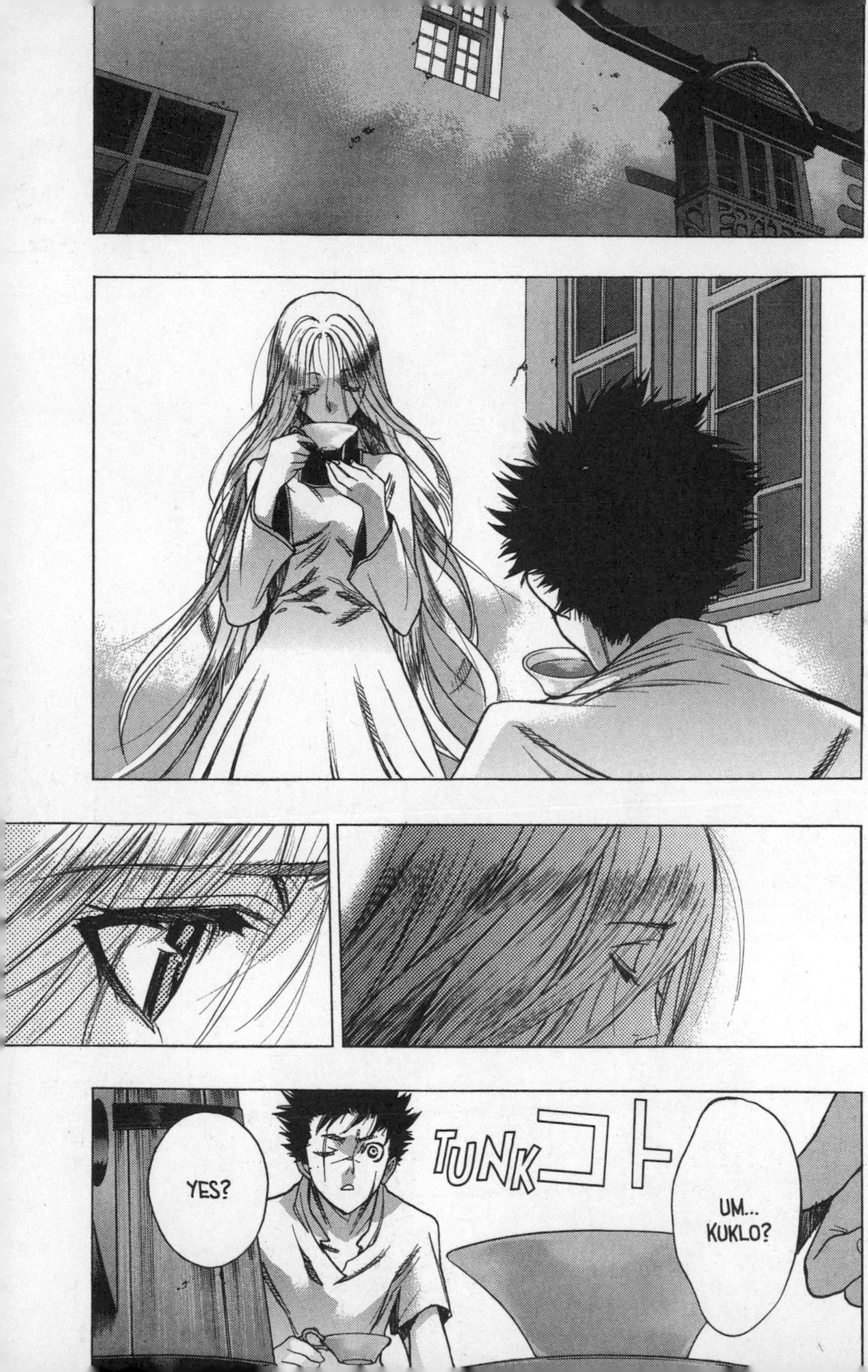
UM... KUKLO?
TUNK
コト
YES?

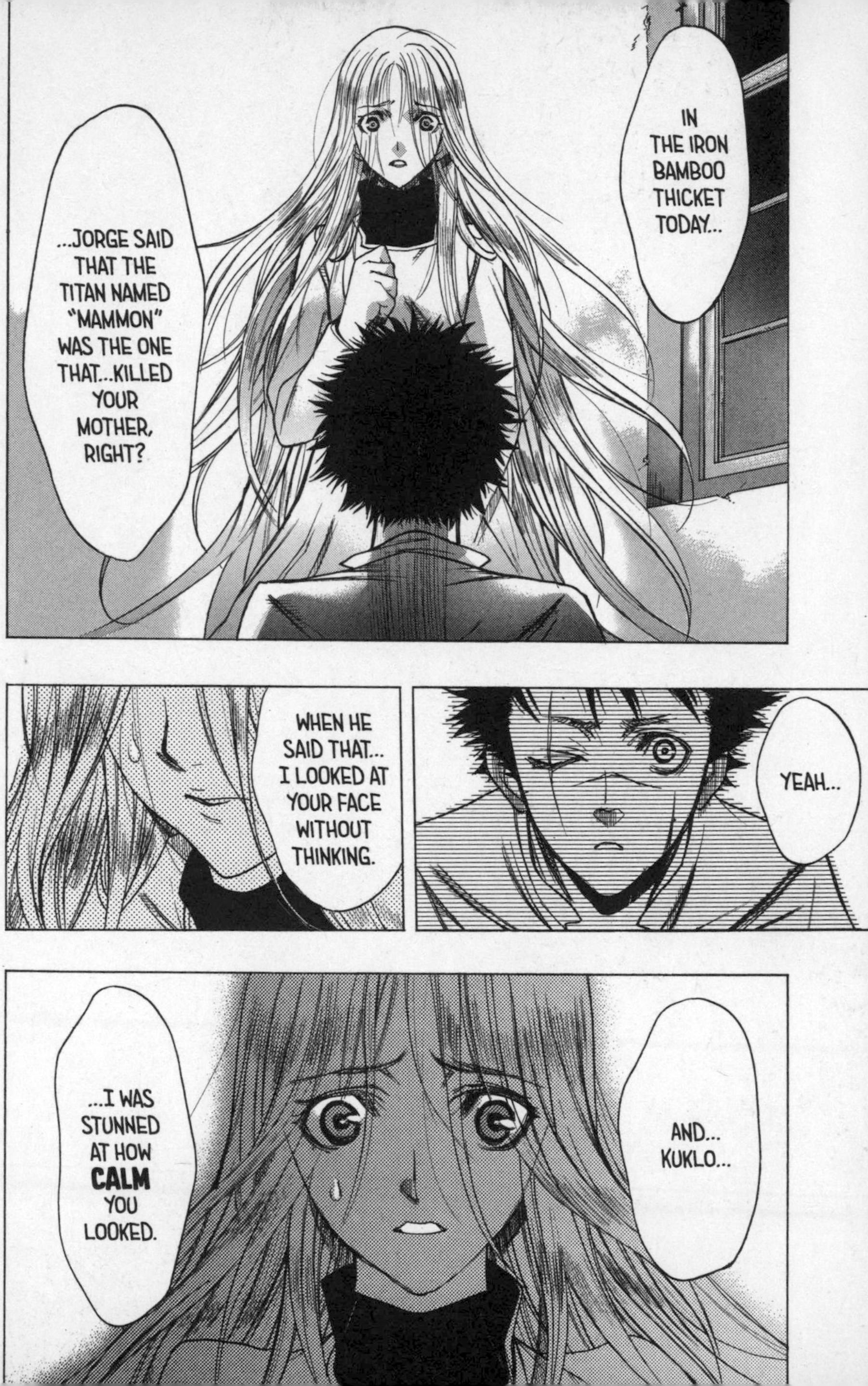
IN THE IRON BAMBOO THICKET TODAY...
...JORGE SAID THAT THE TITAN NAMED "MAMMON" WAS THE ONE THAT...KILLED YOUR MOTHER, RIGHT?
YEAH...
WHEN HE SAID THAT... I LOOKED AT YOUR FACE WITHOUT THINKING.
AND... KUKLO...
...I WAS STUNNED AT HOW **CALM** YOU LOOKED.

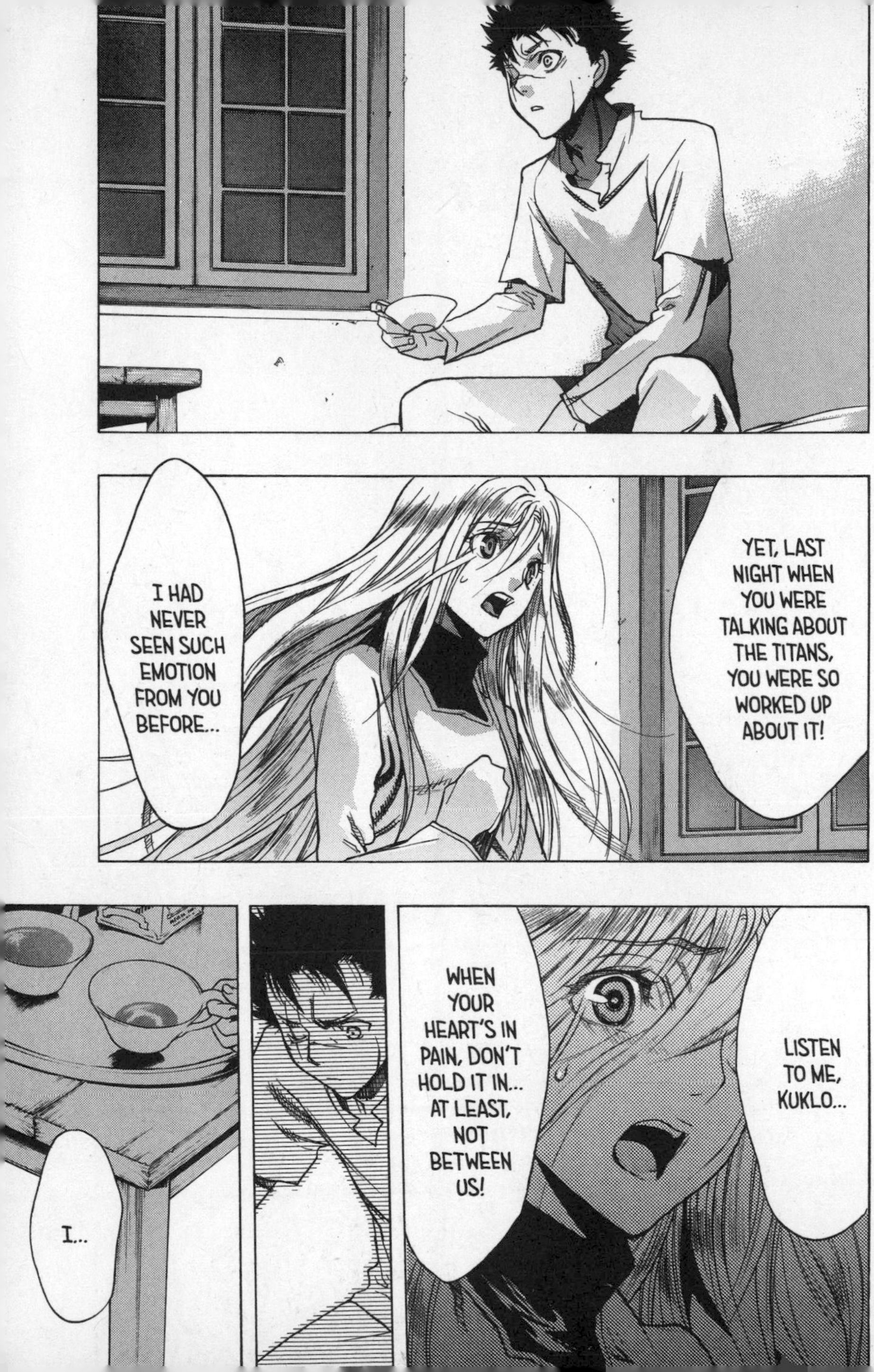
YET, LAST NIGHT WHEN YOU WERE TALKING ABOUT THE TITANS, YOU WERE SO WORKED UP ABOUT IT!
I HAD NEVER SEEN SUCH EMOTION FROM YOU BEFORE...
LISTEN TO ME, KUKLO...
WHEN YOUR HEART'S IN PAIN, DON'T HOLD IT IN... AT LEAST, NOT BETWEEN US!
I...

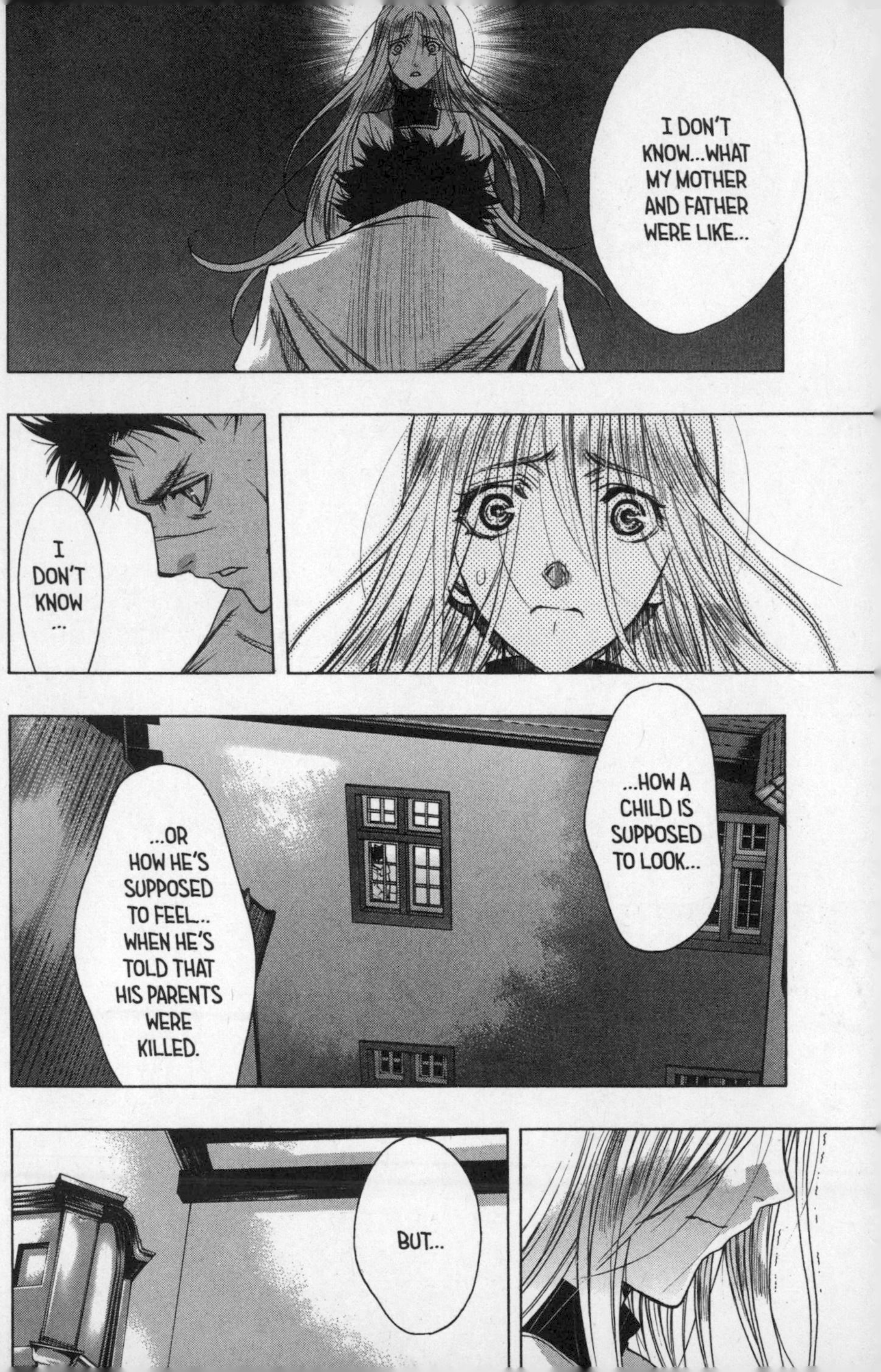
I DON'T KNOW...WHAT MY MOTHER AND FATHER WERE LIKE...
I DON'T KNOW ...
...HOW A CHILD IS SUPPOSED TO LOOK...
...OR HOW HE'S SUPPOSED TO FEEL... WHEN HE'S TOLD THAT HIS PARENTS WERE KILLED.
BUT...

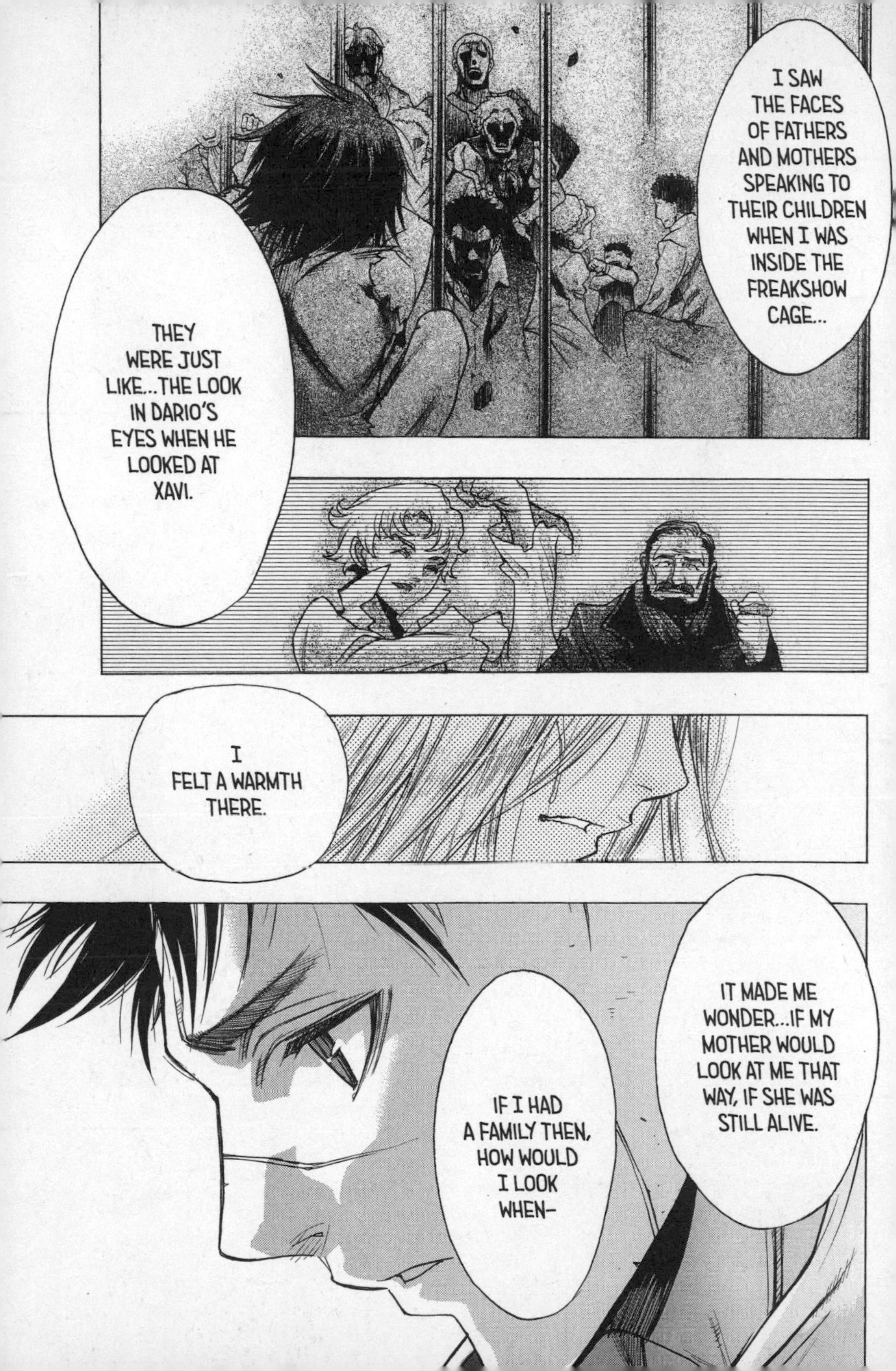
I SAW THE FACES OF FATHERS AND MOTHERS SPEAKING TO THEIR CHILDREN WHEN I WAS INSIDE THE FREAKSHOW CAGE...
THEY WERE JUST LIKE...THE LOOK IN DARIO'S EYES WHEN HE LOOKED AT XAVI.
I FELT A WARMTH THERE.
IT MADE ME WONDER...IF MY MOTHER WOULD LOOK AT ME THAT WAY, IF SHE WAS STILL ALIVE.
IF I HAD A FAMILY THEN, HOW WOULD I LOOK WHEN-

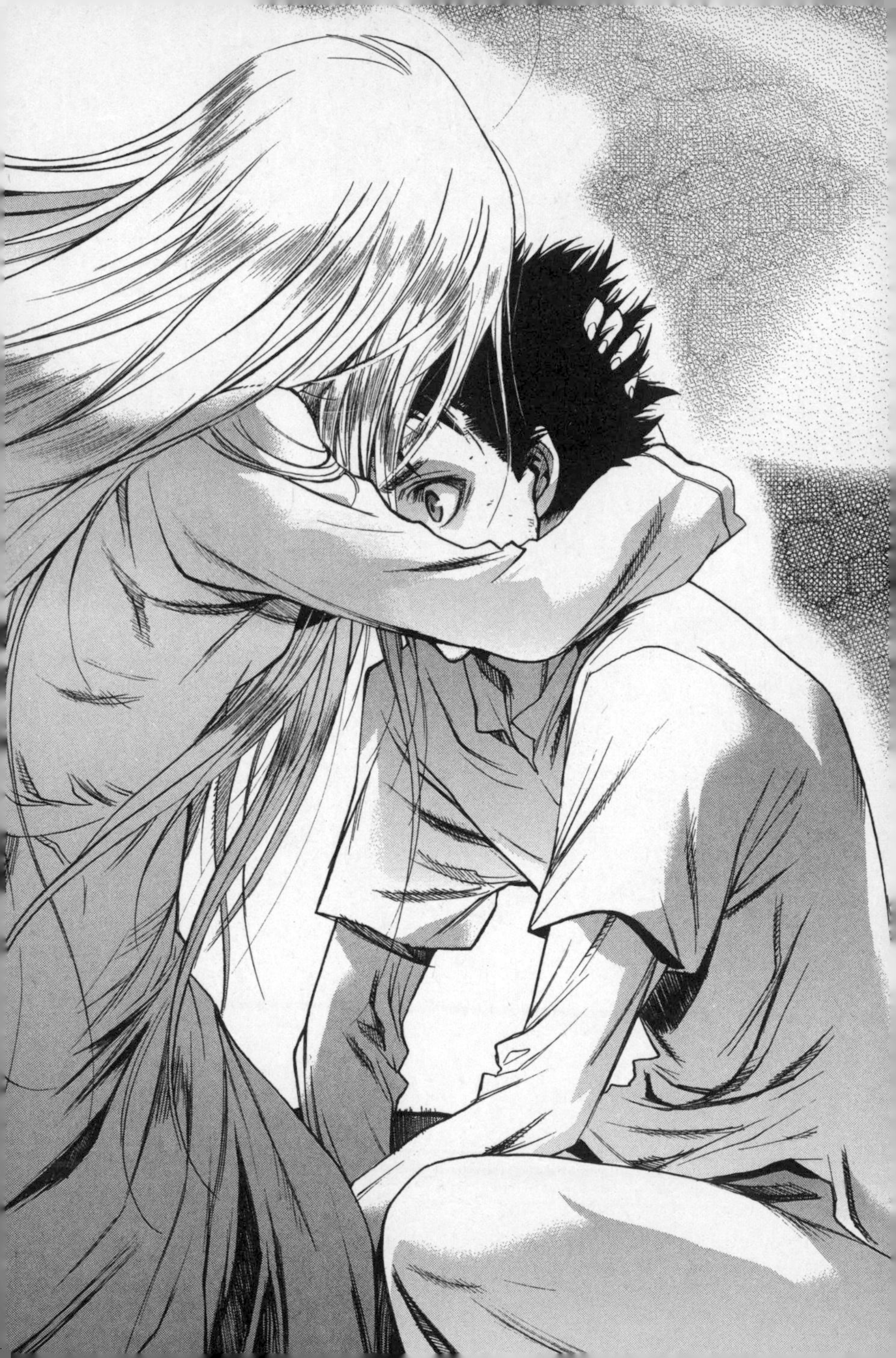

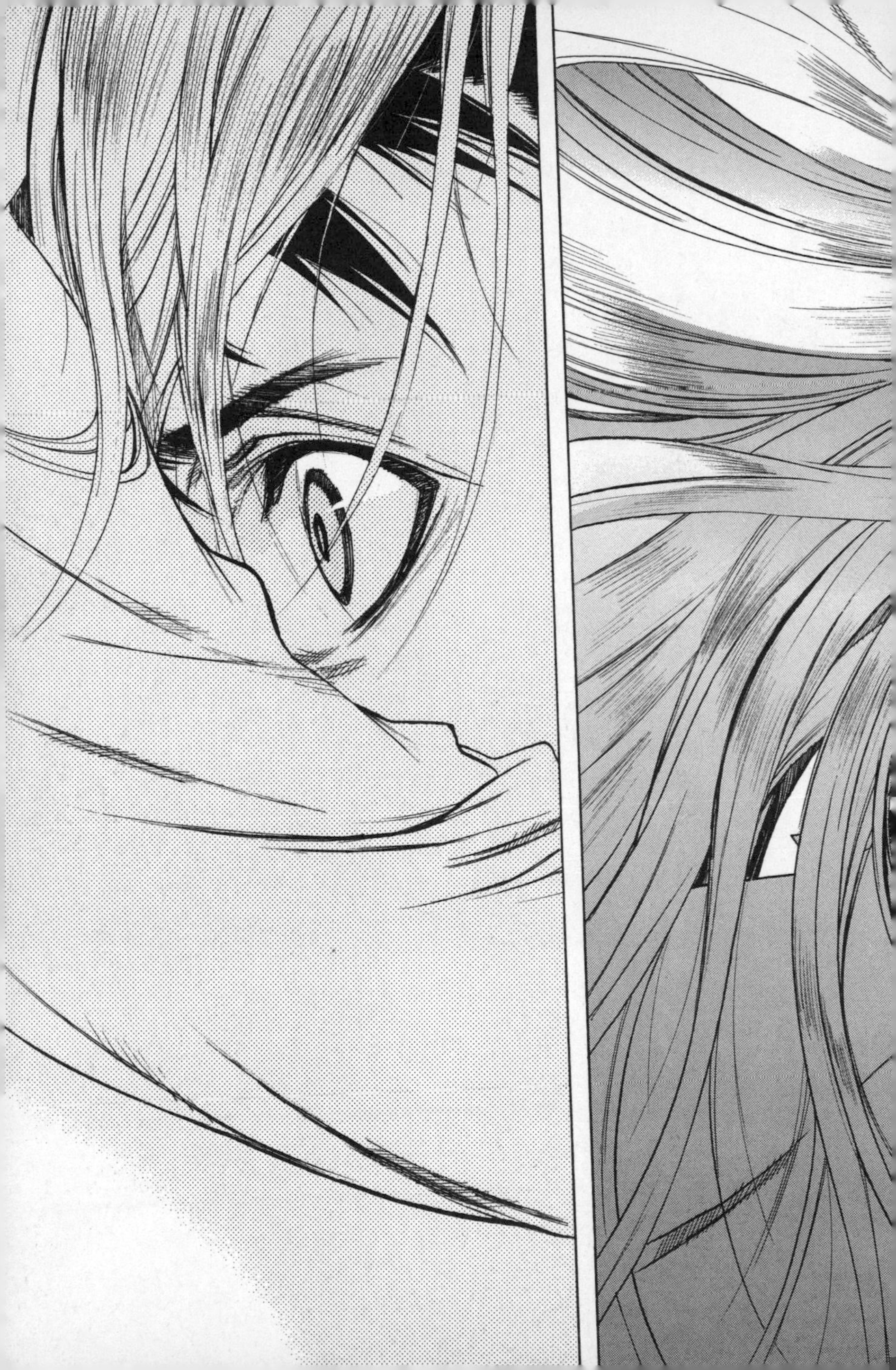

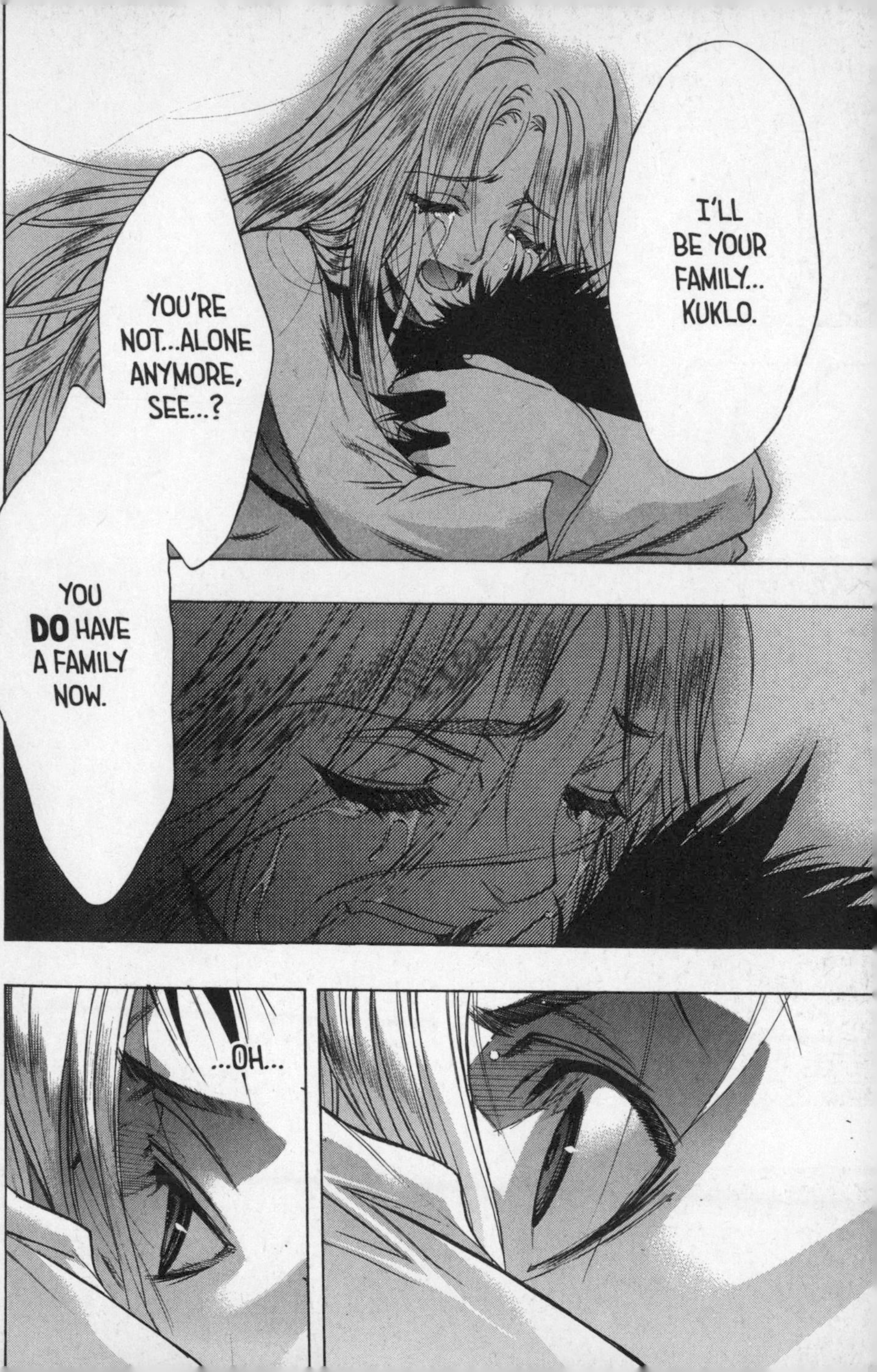
I'LL BE YOUR FAMILY... KUKLO.
YOU'RE NOT...ALONE ANYMORE, SEE...?
YOU **DO** HAVE A FAMILY NOW.
...OH...

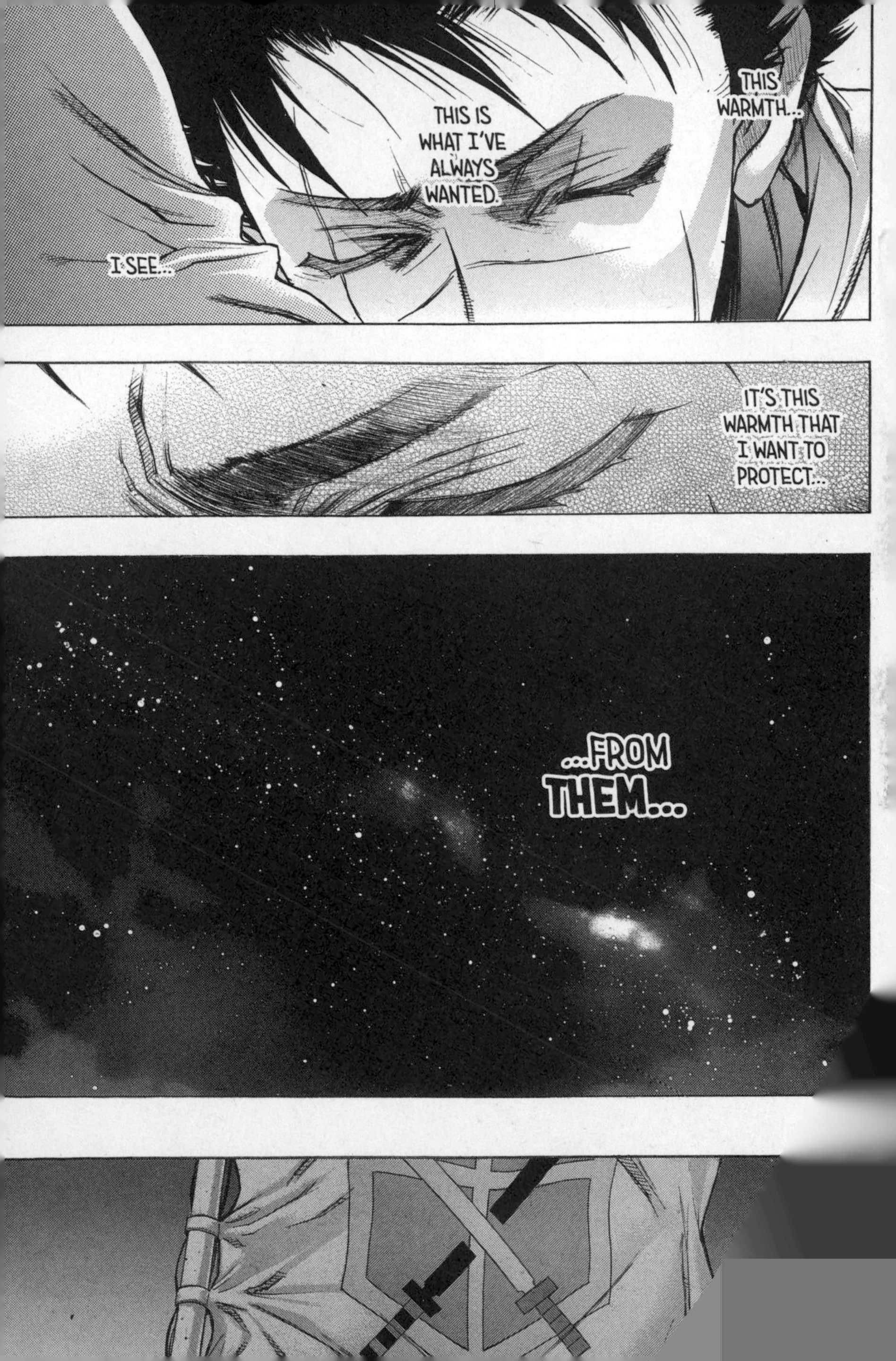
THIS WARMTH...
THIS IS WHAT I'VE ALWAYS WANTED.
I SEE...
IT'S THIS WARMTH THAT I WANT TO PROTECT...
...FROM THEM...

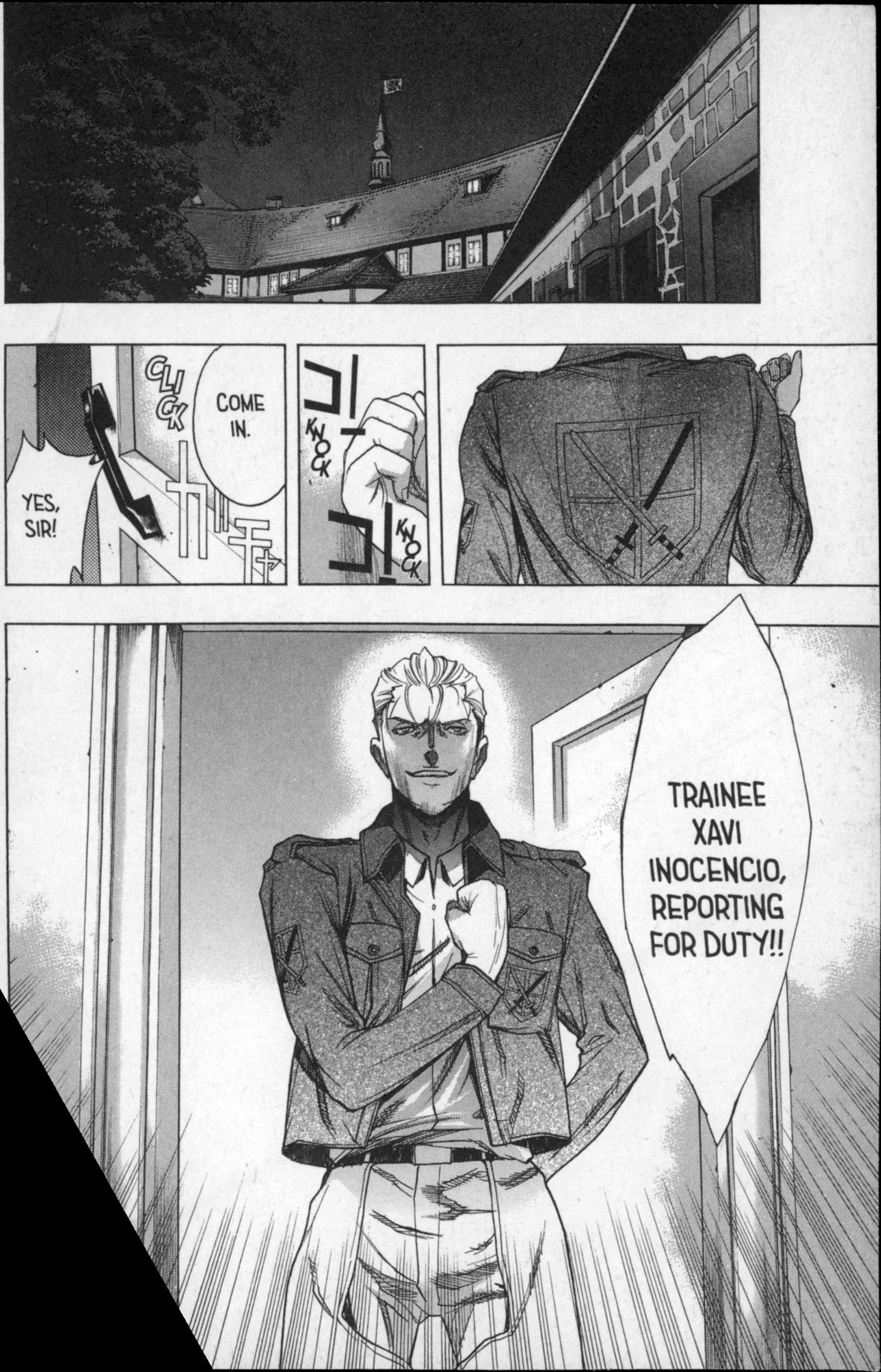

KNOCK
KNOCK
COME IN.
CLICK
YES, SIR!
TRAINEE XAVI INOCENCIO, REPORTING FOR DUTY!!

Chapter 19: Oath in the Bamboo Thicket · End

ATTACK on TITAN

BEFORE THE FALL

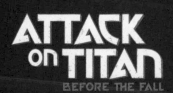

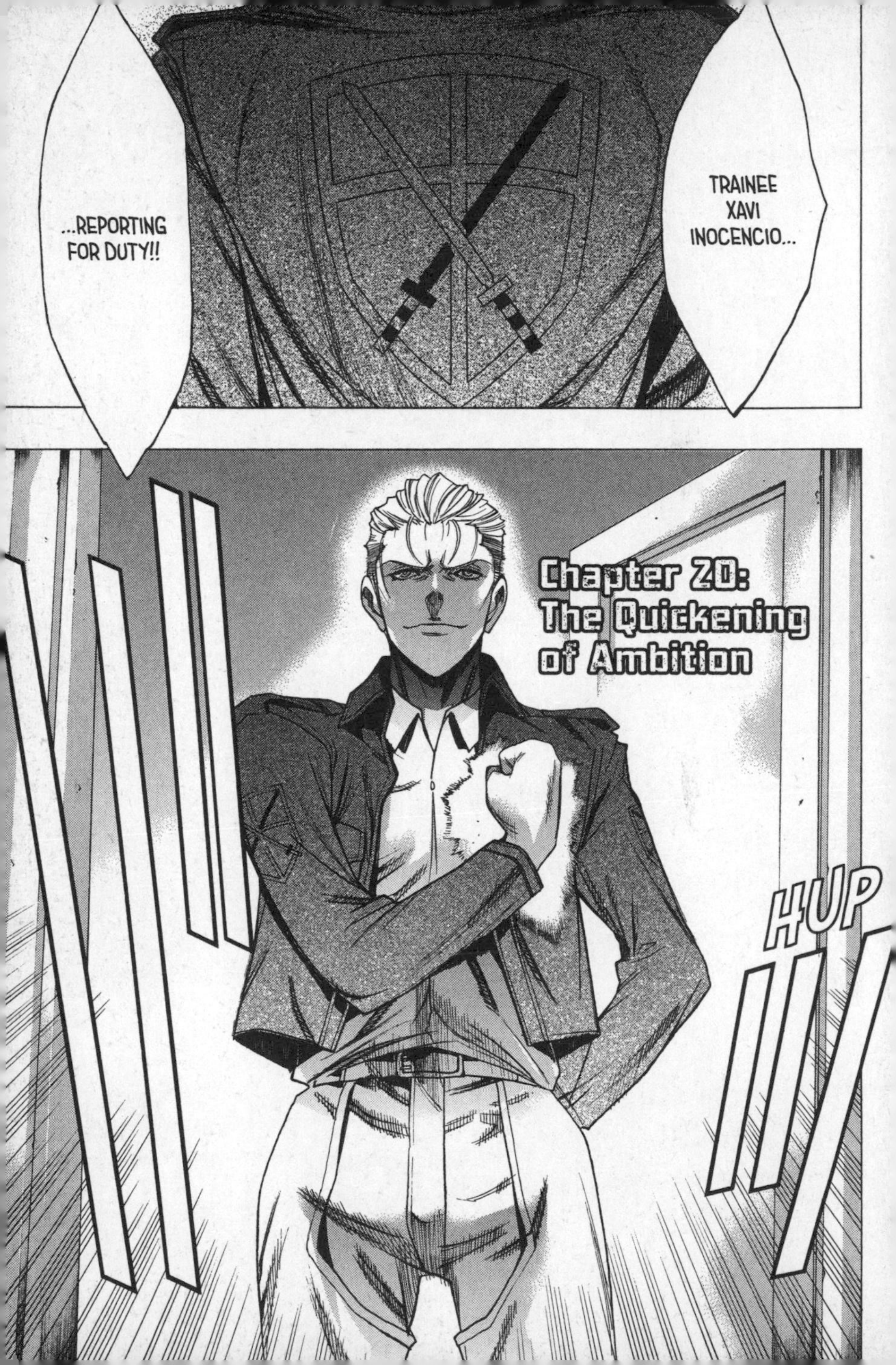
TRAINEE XAVI INOCENCIO...
...REPORTING FOR DUTY!!
Chapter 20: The Quickening of Ambition
HUP

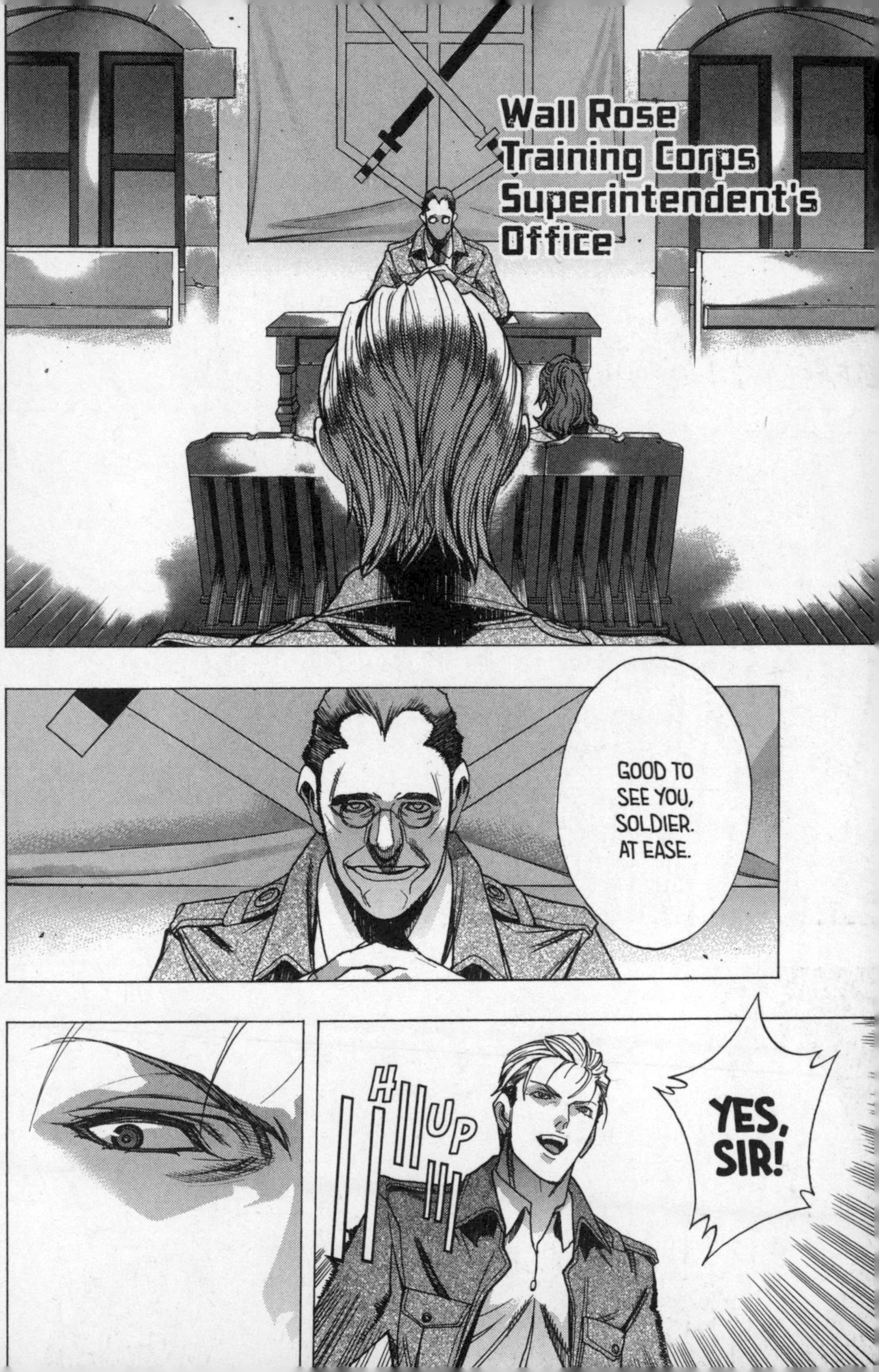
Wall Rose Training Corps Superintendent's Office
GOOD TO SEE YOU, SOLDIER. AT EASE.
YES, SIR!
HUP

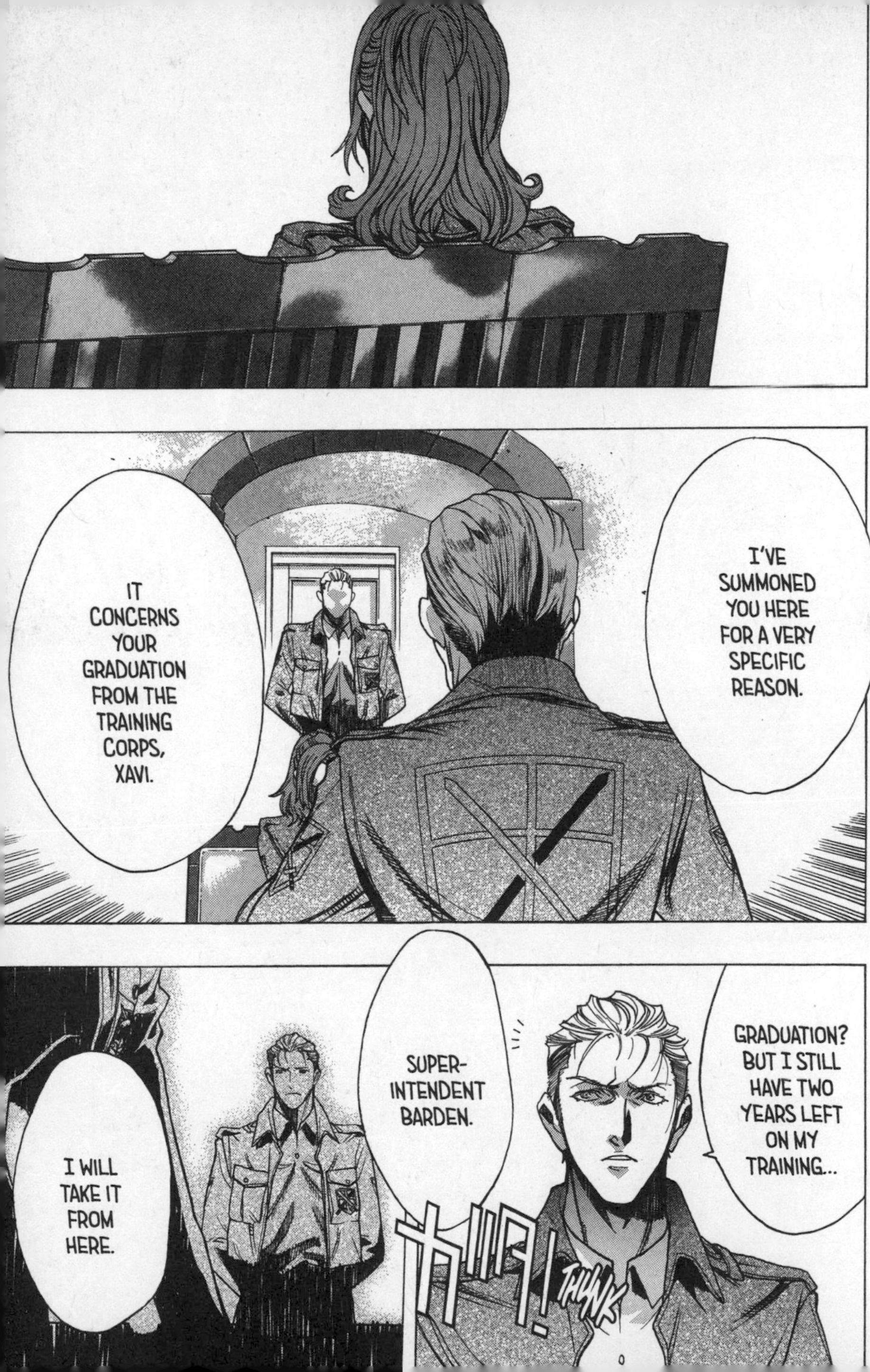
I'VE SUMMONED YOU HERE FOR A VERY SPECIFIC REASON.
IT CONCERNS YOUR GRADUATION FROM THE TRAINING CORPS, XAVI.
GRADUATION? BUT I STILL HAVE TWO YEARS LEFT ON MY TRAINING...
SUPER-INTENDENT BARDEN.
THUNK
I WILL TAKE IT FROM HERE.

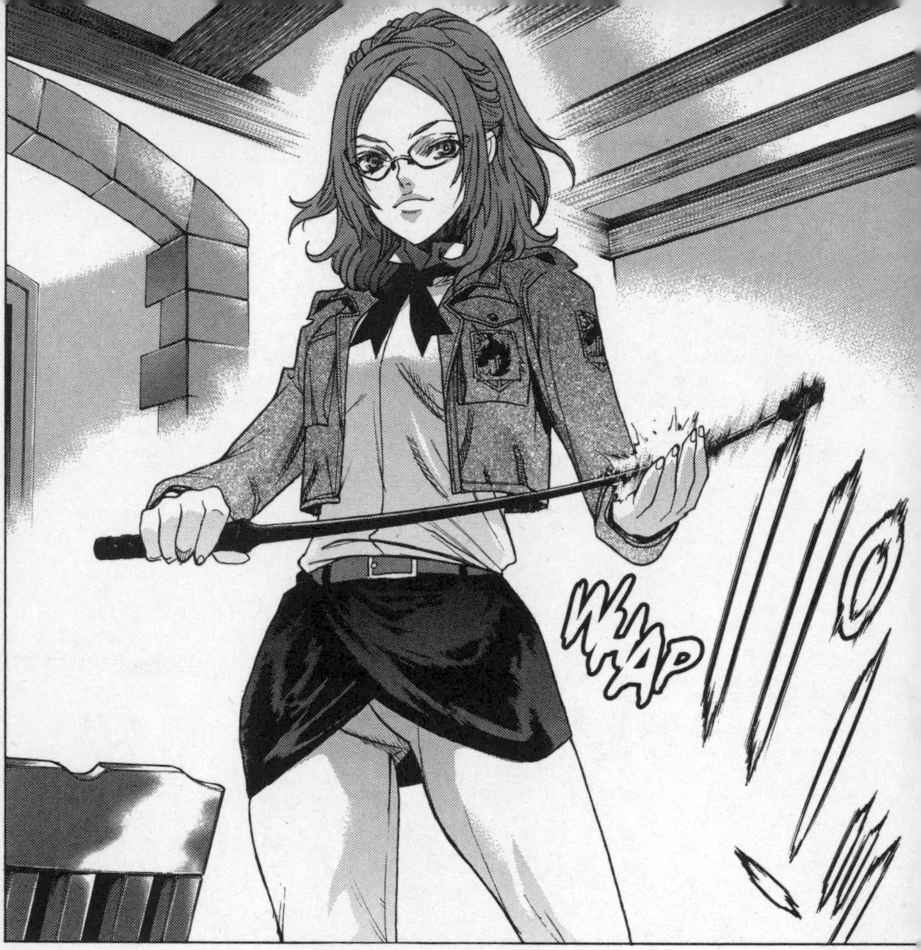
WHAP
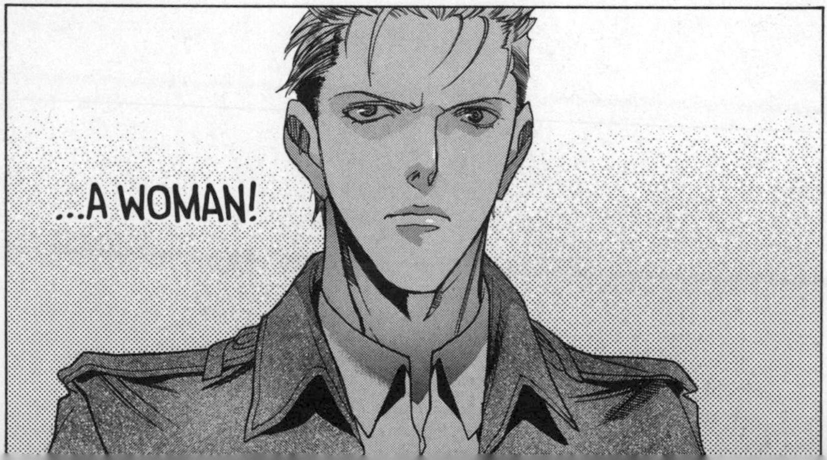
...A WOMAN!

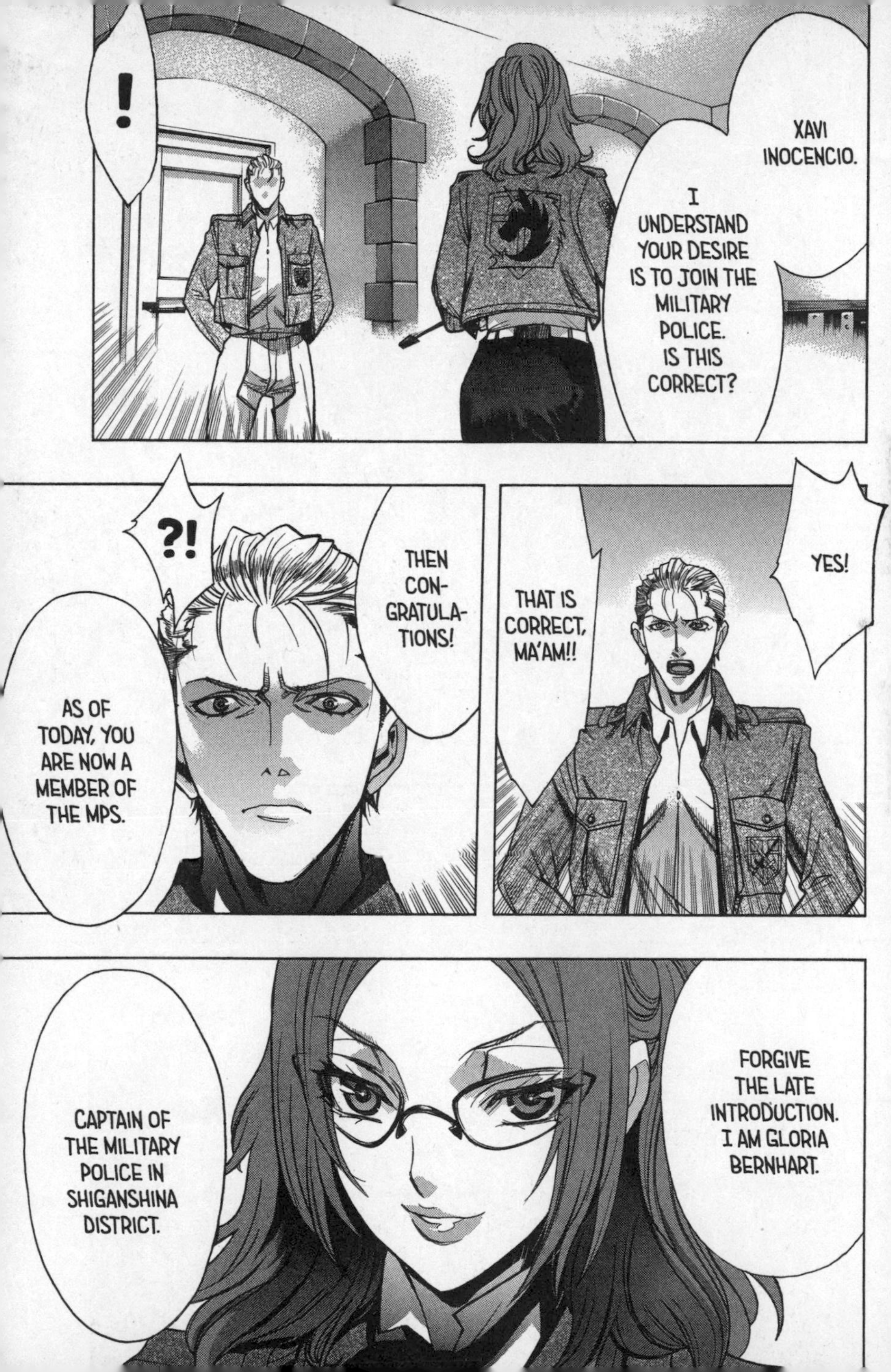
XAVI INOCENCIO.
I UNDERSTAND YOUR DESIRE IS TO JOIN THE MILITARY POLICE. IS THIS CORRECT?
!
YES!
THAT IS CORRECT, MA'AM!!
THEN CON-GRATULA-TIONS!
?!
AS OF TODAY, YOU ARE NOW A MEMBER OF THE MPS.
FORGIVE THE LATE INTRODUCTION. I AM GLORIA BERNHART.
CAPTAIN OF THE MILITARY POLICE IN SHIGANSHINA DISTRICT.

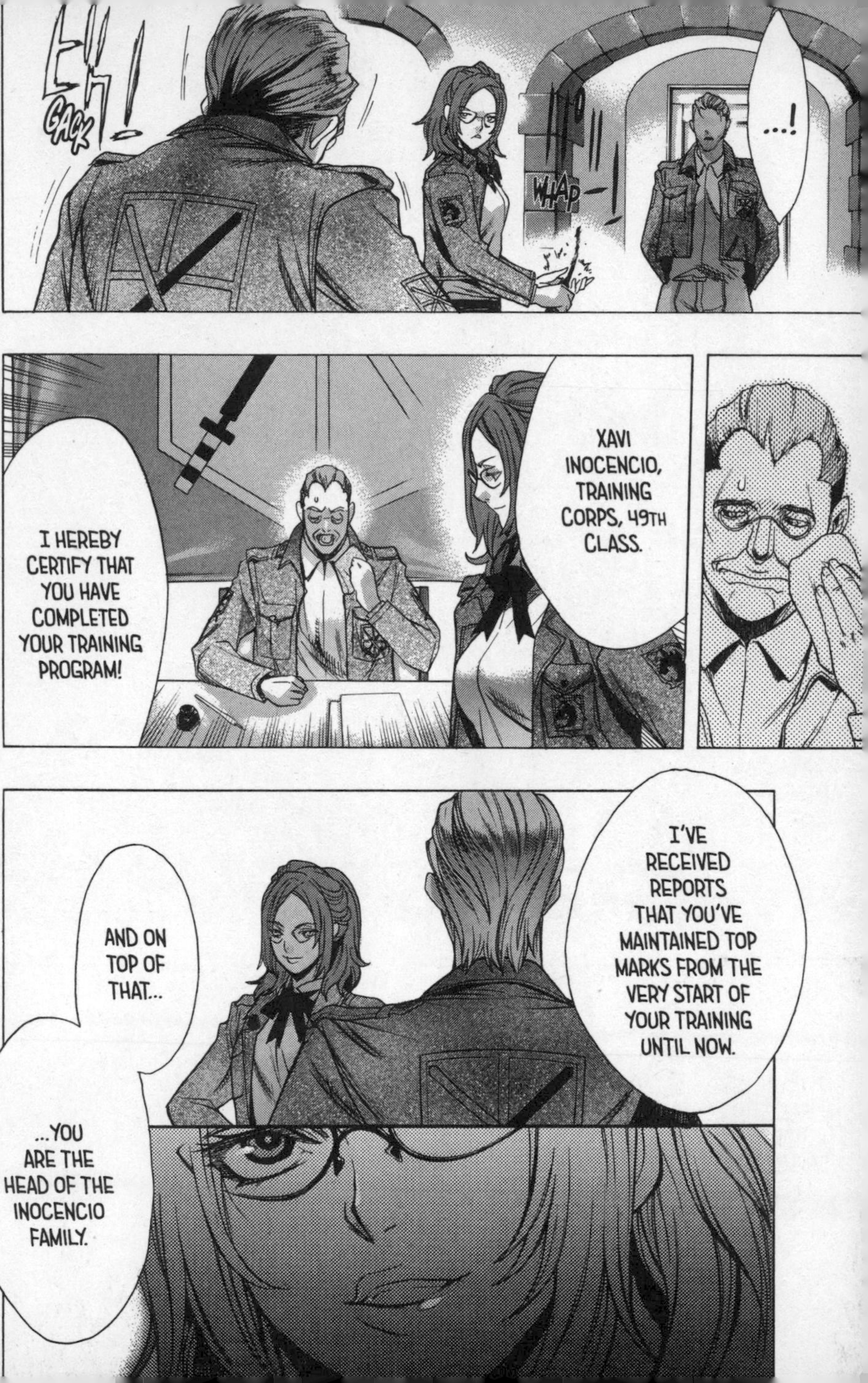
...!
WHAP
GACK
XAVI INOCENCIO, TRAINING CORPS, 49TH CLASS.
I HEREBY CERTIFY THAT YOU HAVE COMPLETED YOUR TRAINING PROGRAM!
I'VE RECEIVED REPORTS THAT YOU'VE MAINTAINED TOP MARKS FROM THE VERY START OF YOUR TRAINING UNTIL NOW.
AND ON TOP OF THAT...
...YOU ARE THE HEAD OF THE INOCENCIO FAMILY.

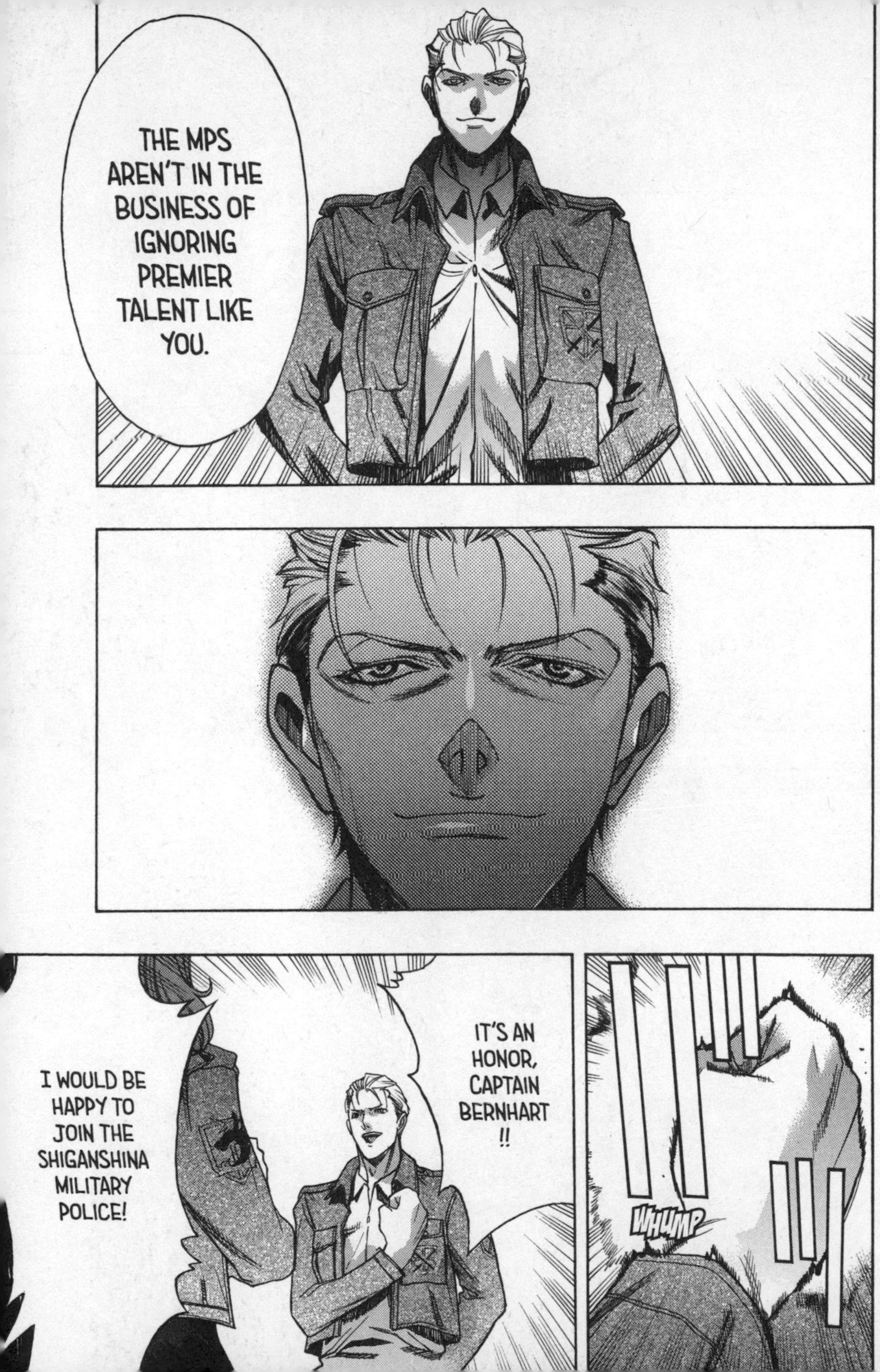
THE MPS AREN'T IN THE BUSINESS OF IGNORING PREMIER TALENT LIKE YOU.
WHUMP
IT'S AN HONOR, CAPTAIN BERNHART!!
I WOULD BE HAPPY TO JOIN THE SHIGANSHINA MILITARY POLICE!

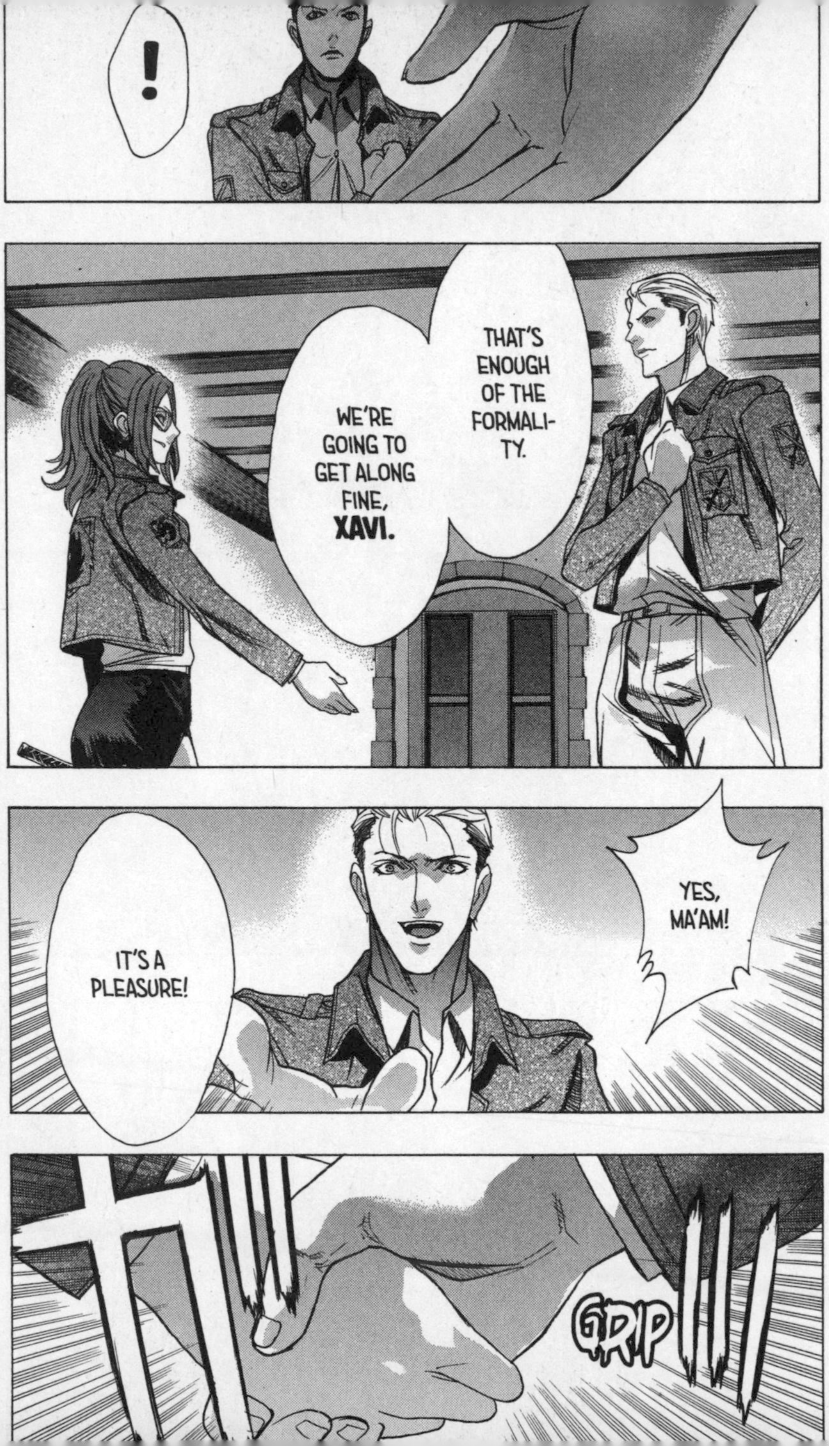
!
THAT'S ENOUGH OF THE FORMALI-TY.
WE'RE GOING TO GET ALONG FINE, XAVI.
YES, MA'AM!
IT'S A PLEASURE!
GRIP

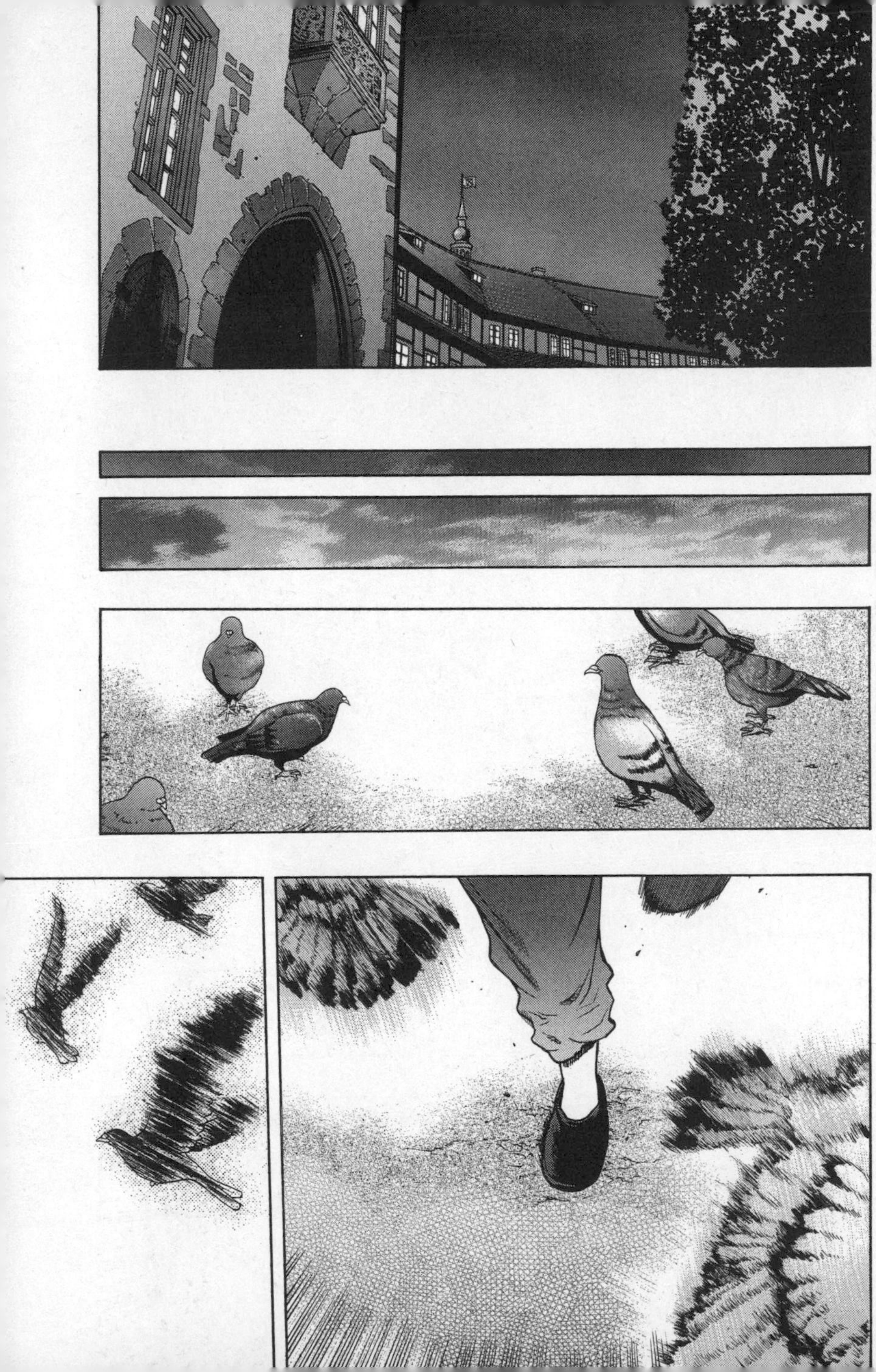

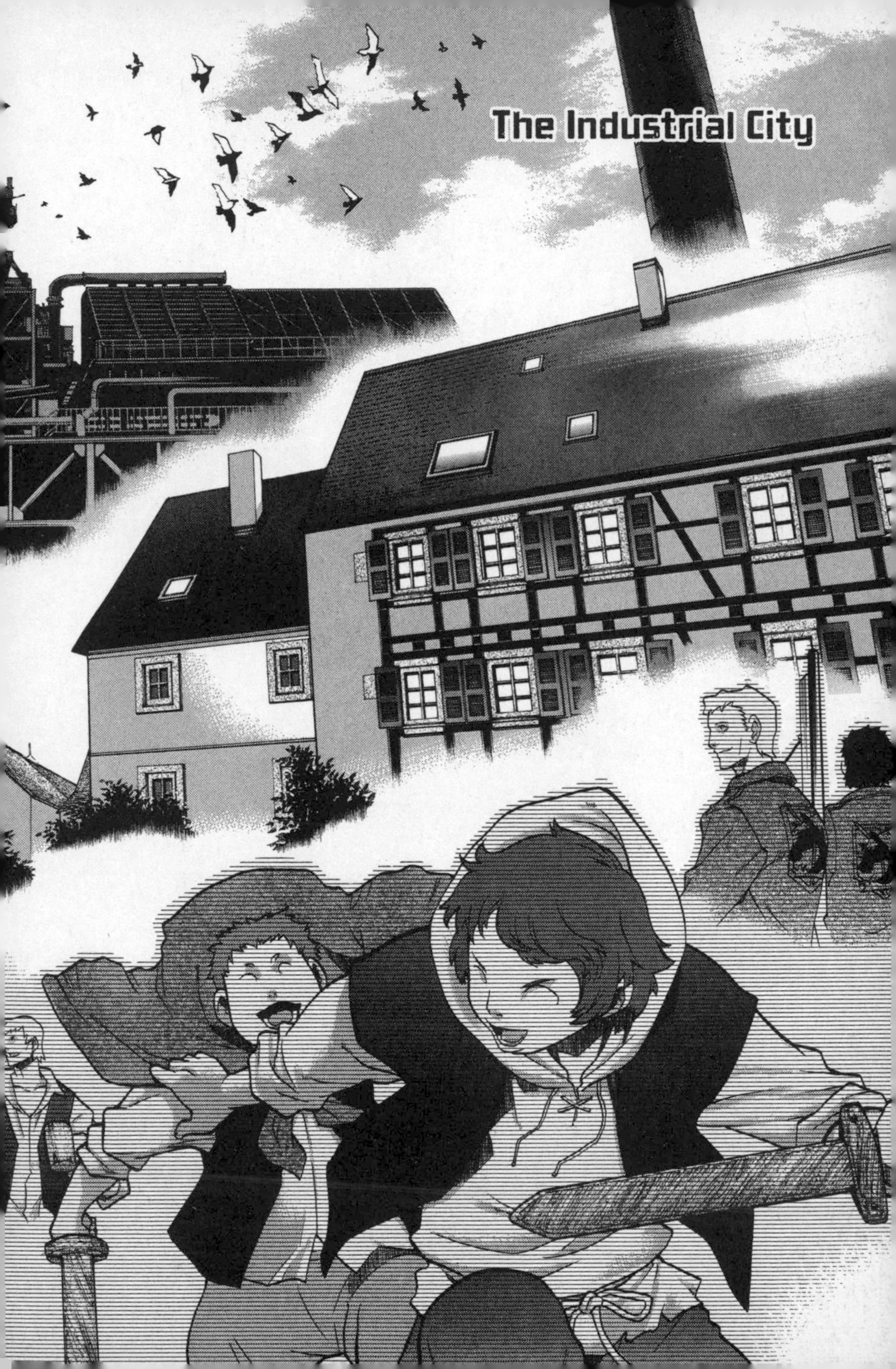
The Industrial City

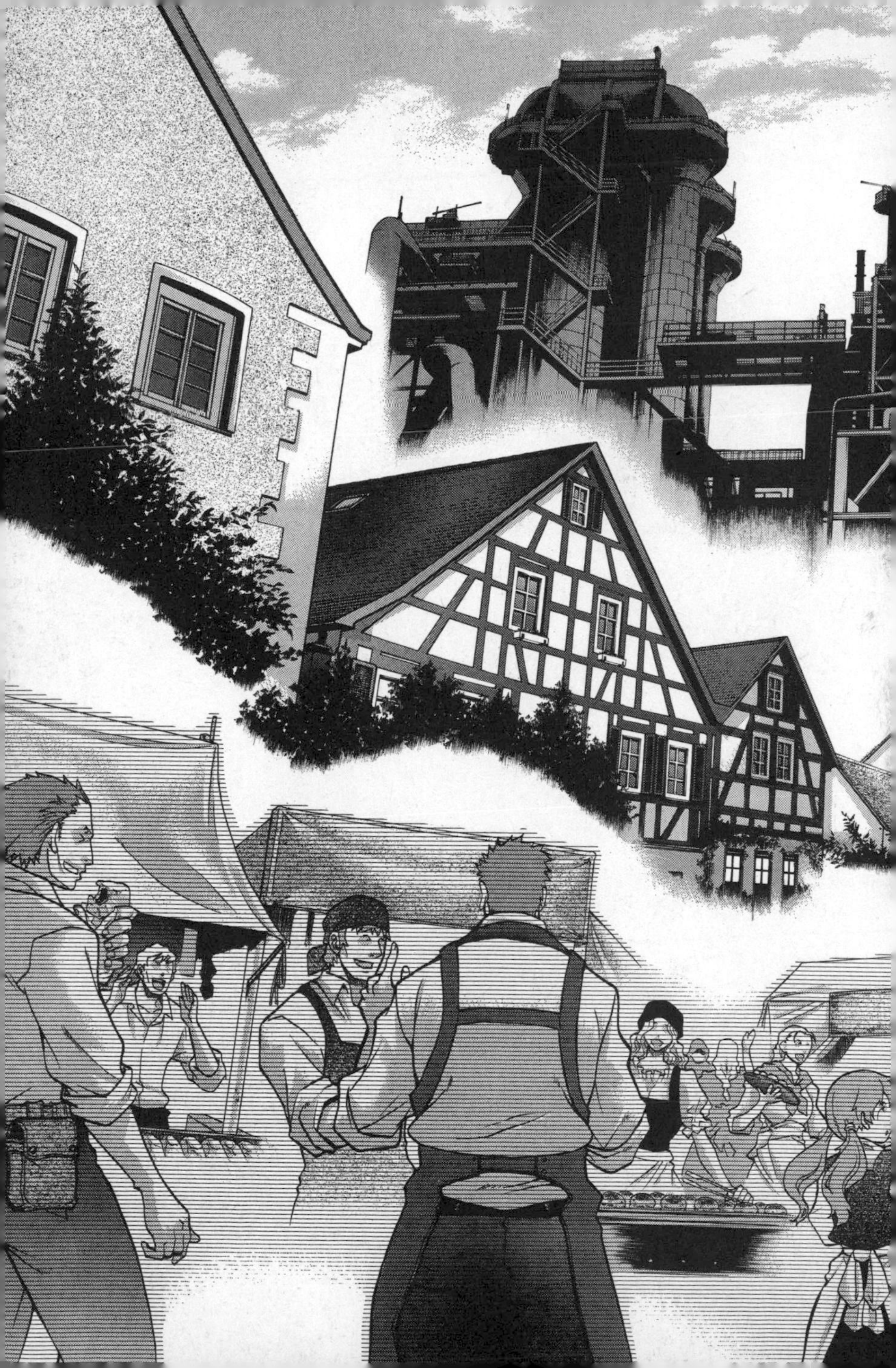

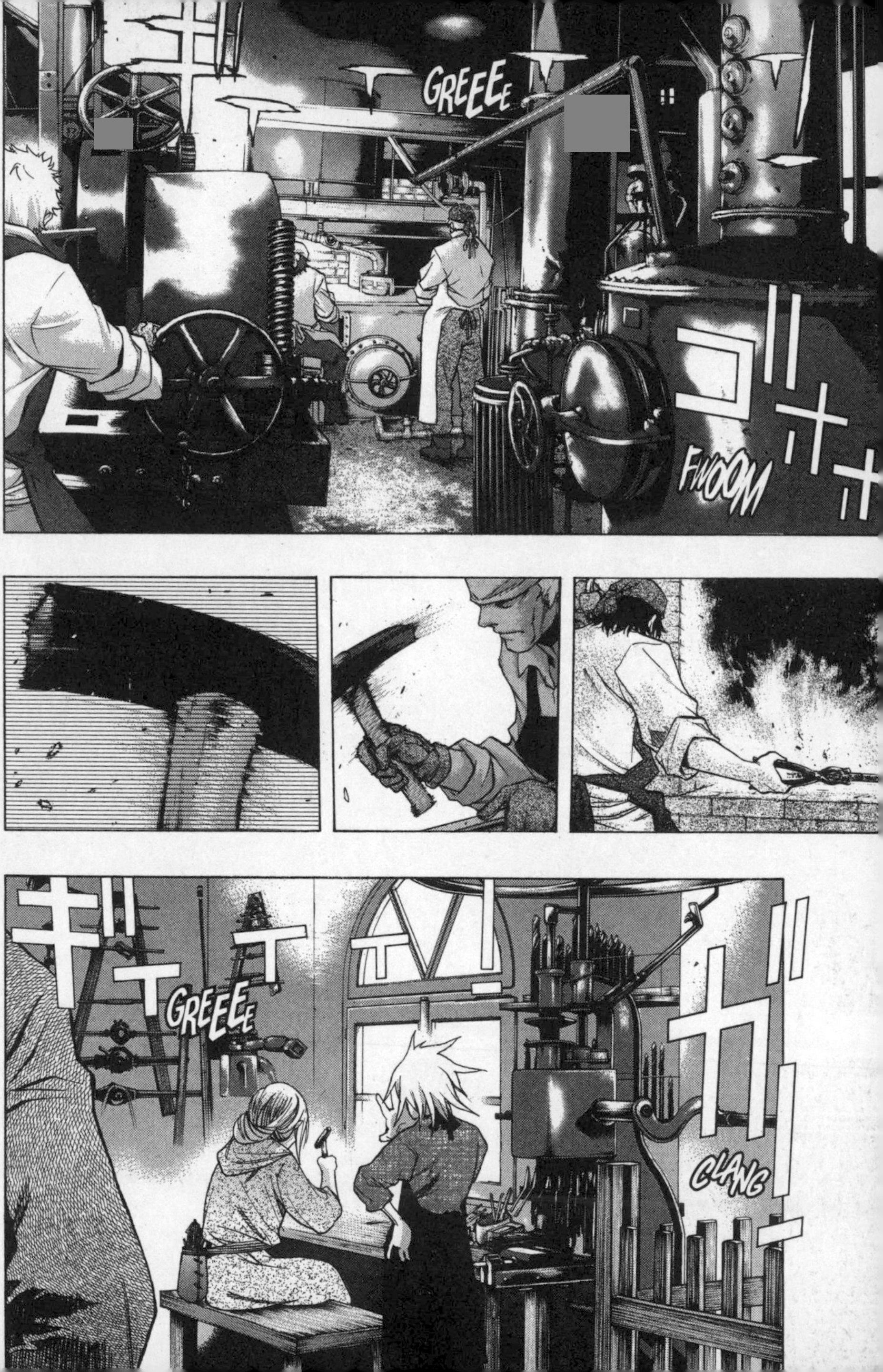
GREEEe
FWOOM
GREEEe
CLANG

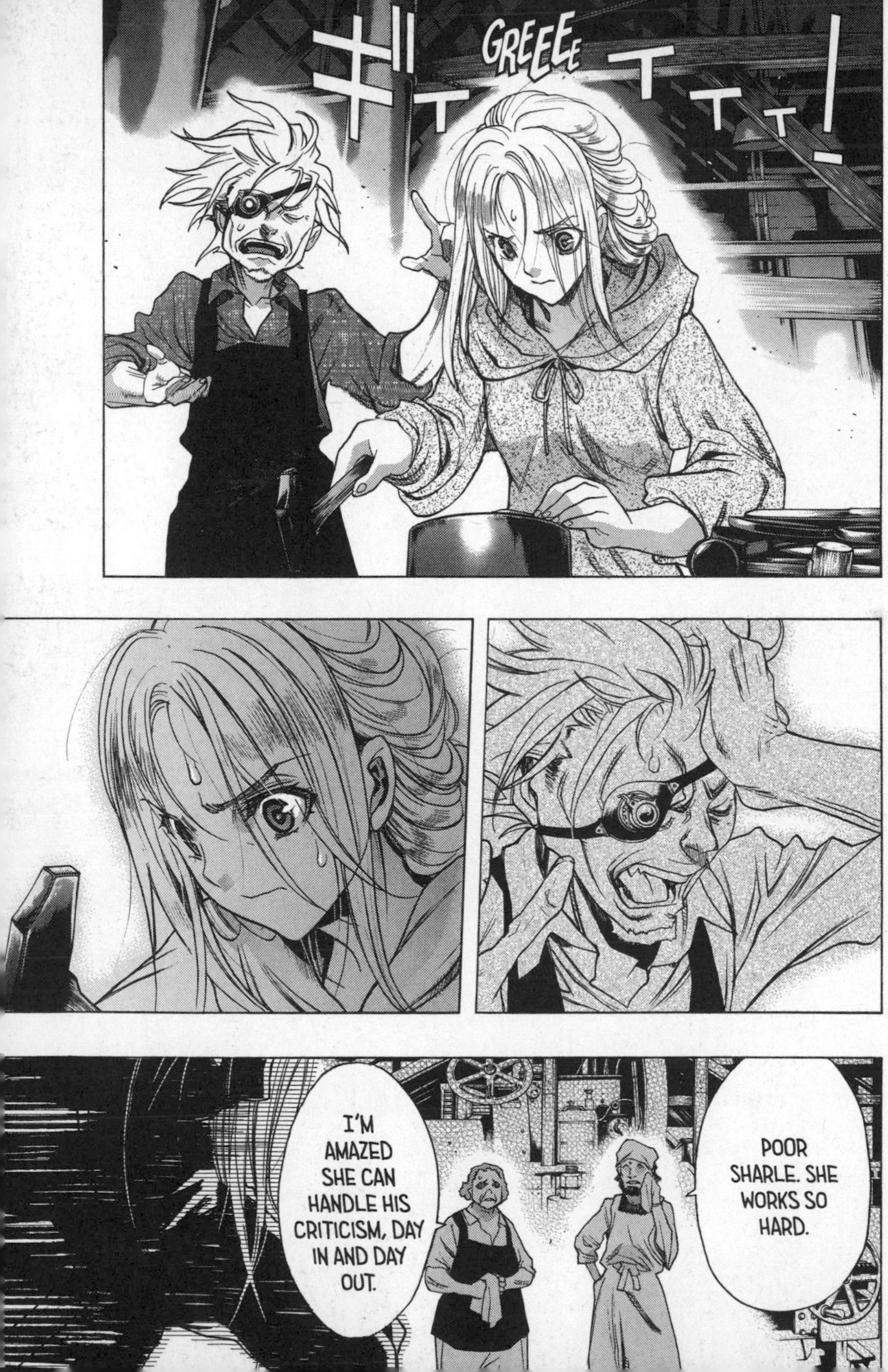
GREEEE
POOR SHARLE. SHE WORKS SO HARD.
I'M AMAZED SHE CAN HANDLE HIS CRITICISM, DAY IN AND DAY OUT.

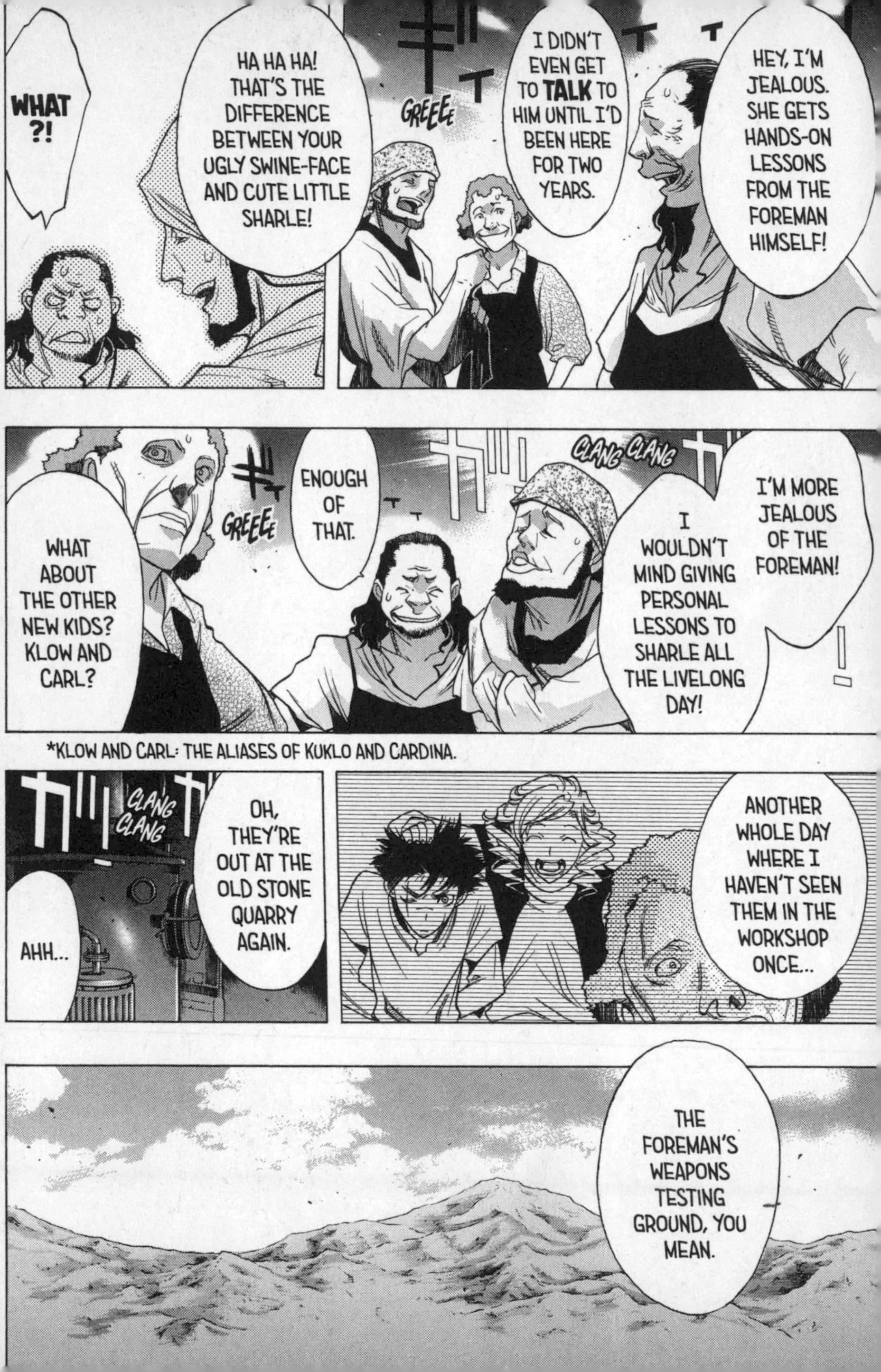
HEY, I'M JEALOUS. SHE GETS HANDS-ON LESSONS FROM THE FOREMAN HIMSELF!
I DIDN'T EVEN GET TO **TALK** TO HIM UNTIL I'D BEEN HERE FOR TWO YEARS.
GREEEE
HA HA HA! THAT'S THE DIFFERENCE BETWEEN YOUR UGLY SWINE-FACE AND CUTE LITTLE SHARLE!
WHAT ?!
CLANG CLANG
I'M MORE JEALOUS OF THE FOREMAN!
!
I WOULDN'T MIND GIVING PERSONAL LESSONS TO SHARLE ALL THE LIVELONG DAY!
ENOUGH OF THAT.
GREEEE
WHAT ABOUT THE OTHER NEW KIDS? KLOW AND CARL?
ANOTHER WHOLE DAY WHERE I HAVEN'T SEEN THEM IN THE WORKSHOP ONCE...
CLANG CLANG
OH, THEY'RE OUT AT THE OLD STONE QUARRY AGAIN.
AHH...
THE FOREMAN'S WEAPONS TESTING GROUND, YOU MEAN.

*KLOW AND CARL: THE ALIASES OF KUKLO AND CARDINA.

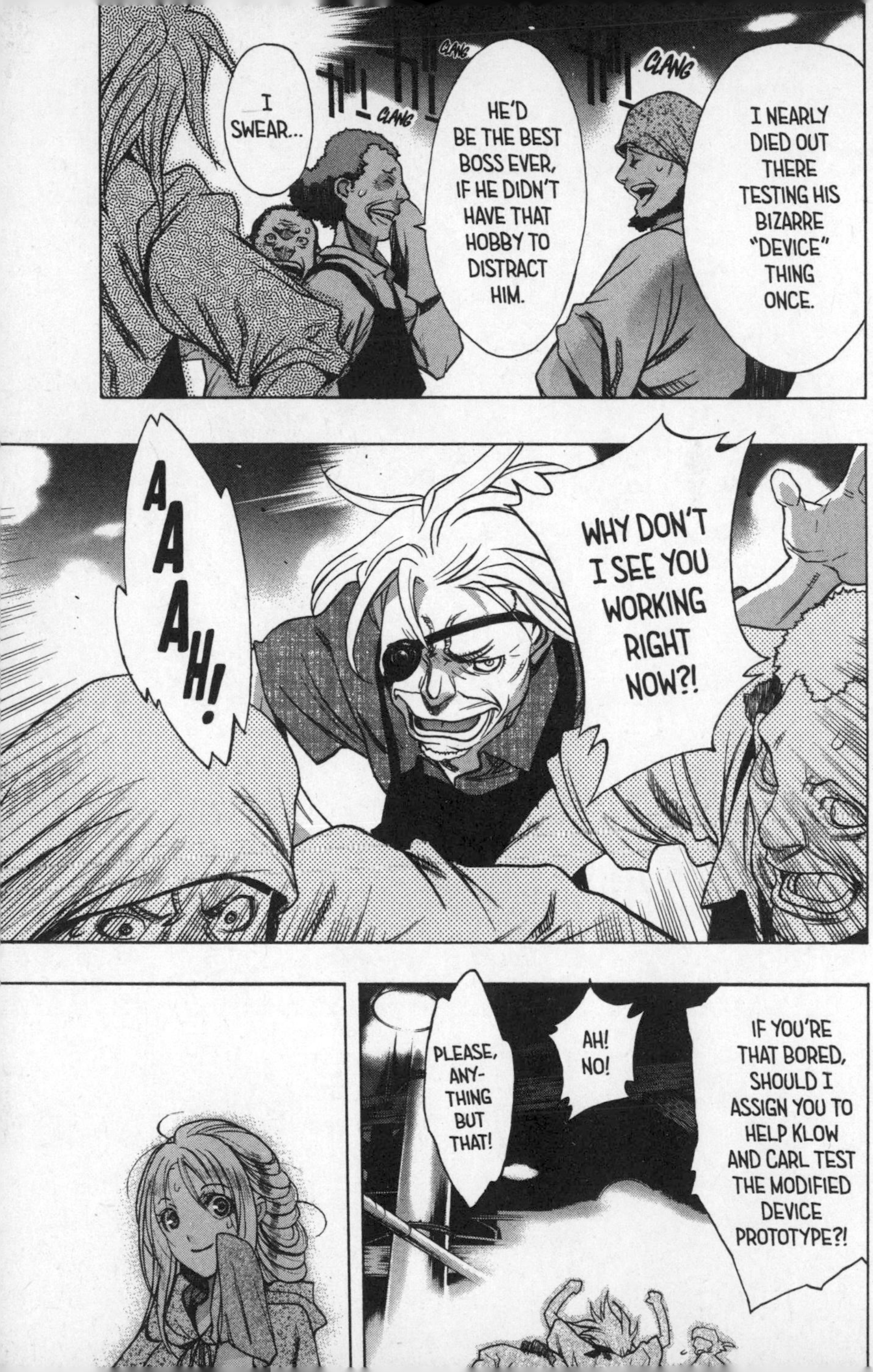
CLANG
I NEARLY DIED OUT THERE TESTING HIS BIZARRE "DEVICE" THING ONCE.
CLANG
HE'D BE THE BEST BOSS EVER, IF HE DIDN'T HAVE THAT HOBBY TO DISTRACT HIM.
CLANG
I SWEAR...
WHY DON'T I SEE YOU WORKING RIGHT NOW?!
AAAH!
IF YOU'RE THAT BORED, SHOULD I ASSIGN YOU TO HELP KLOW AND CARL TEST THE MODIFIED DEVICE PROTOTYPE?!
AH! NO!
PLEASE, ANY-THING BUT THAT!

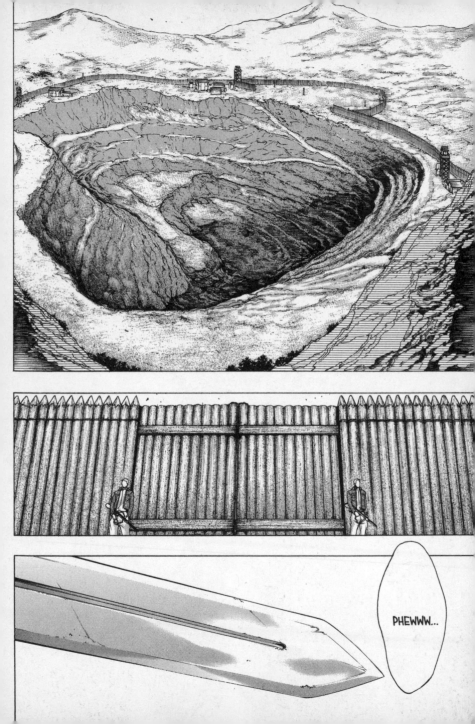

PHEWWW...

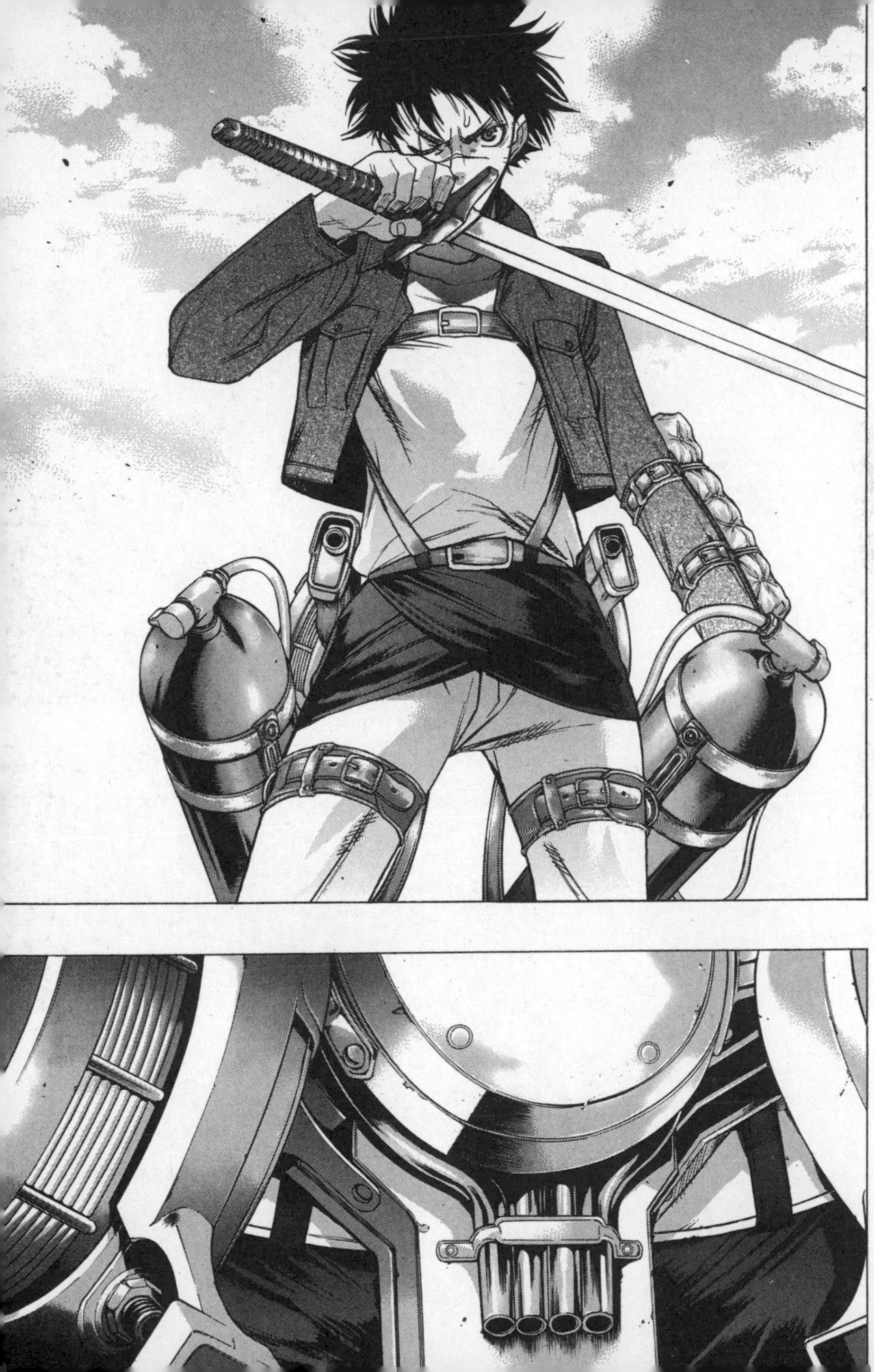

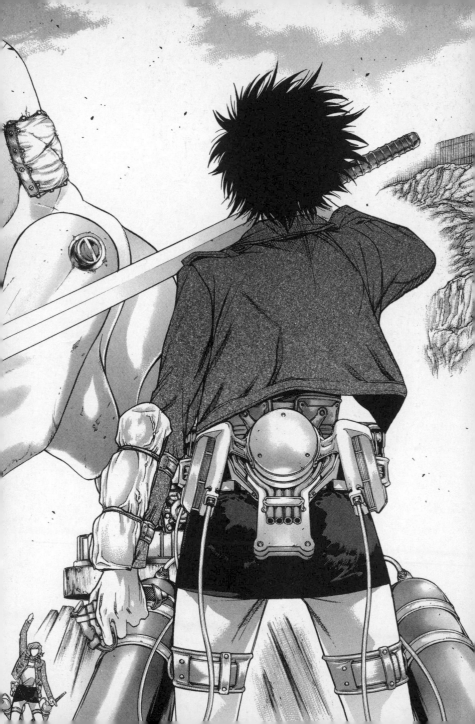

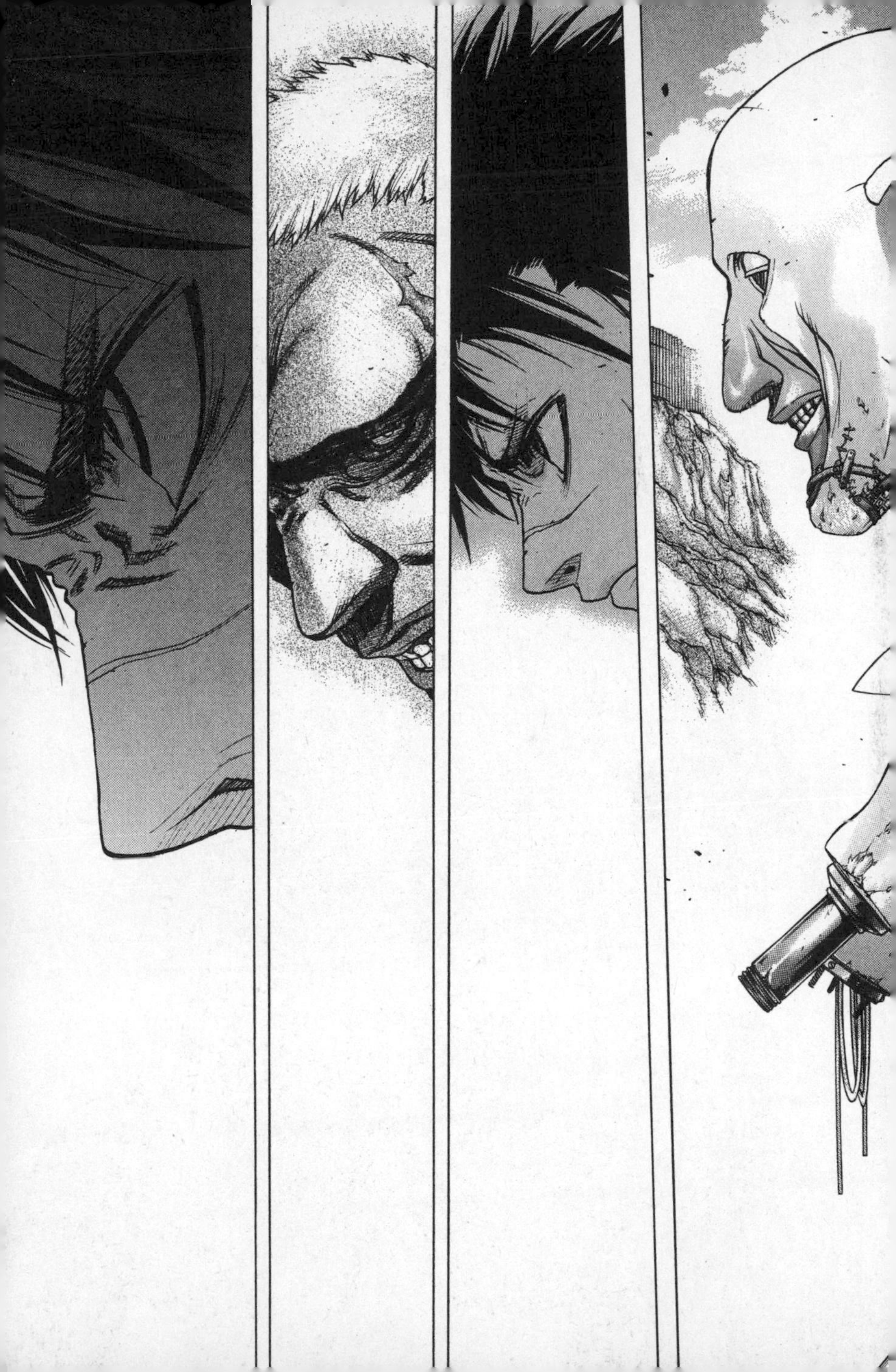

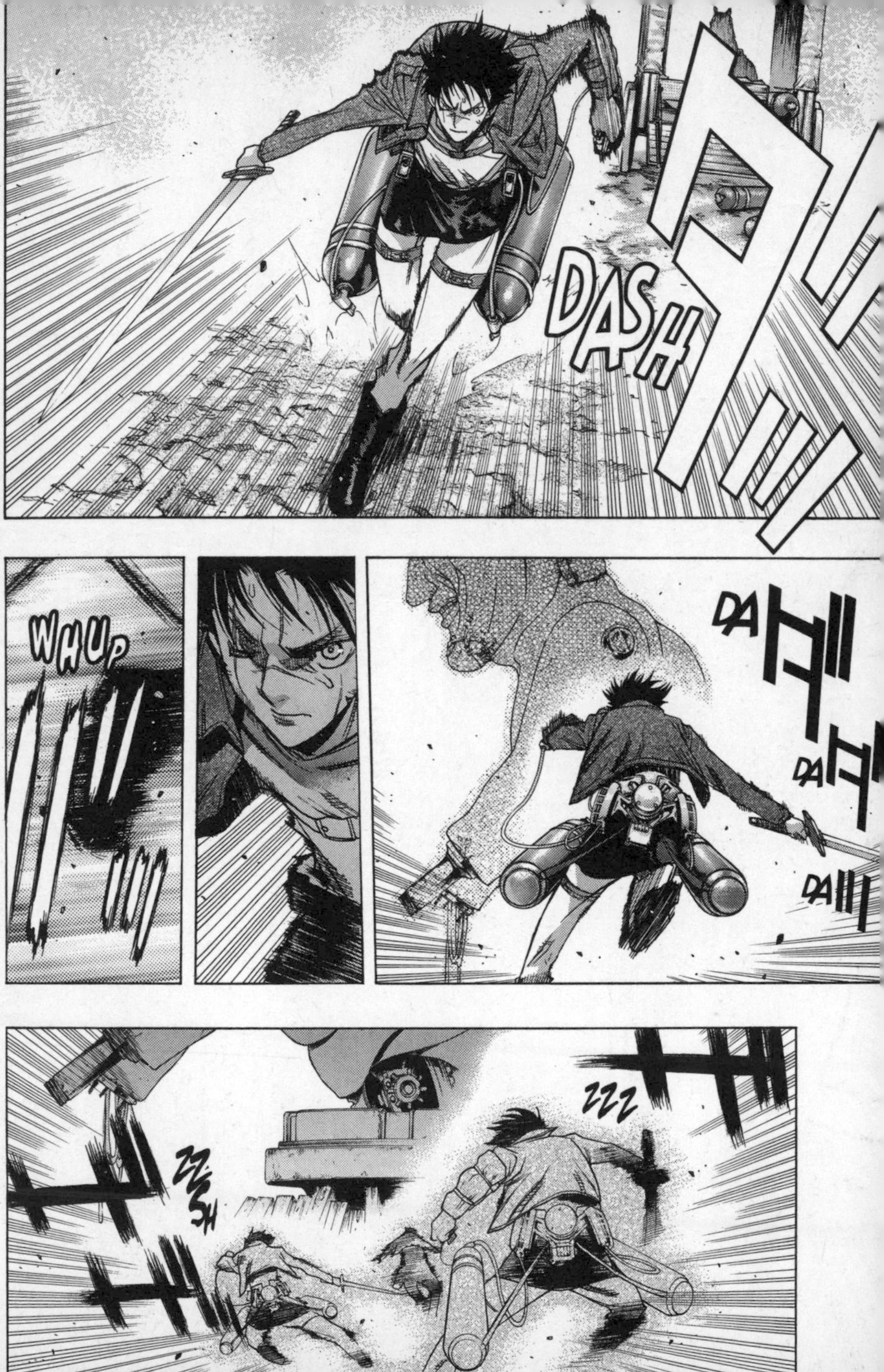
DASH
DA
DA
DA
WHUP
ZZZ
ZZNSH

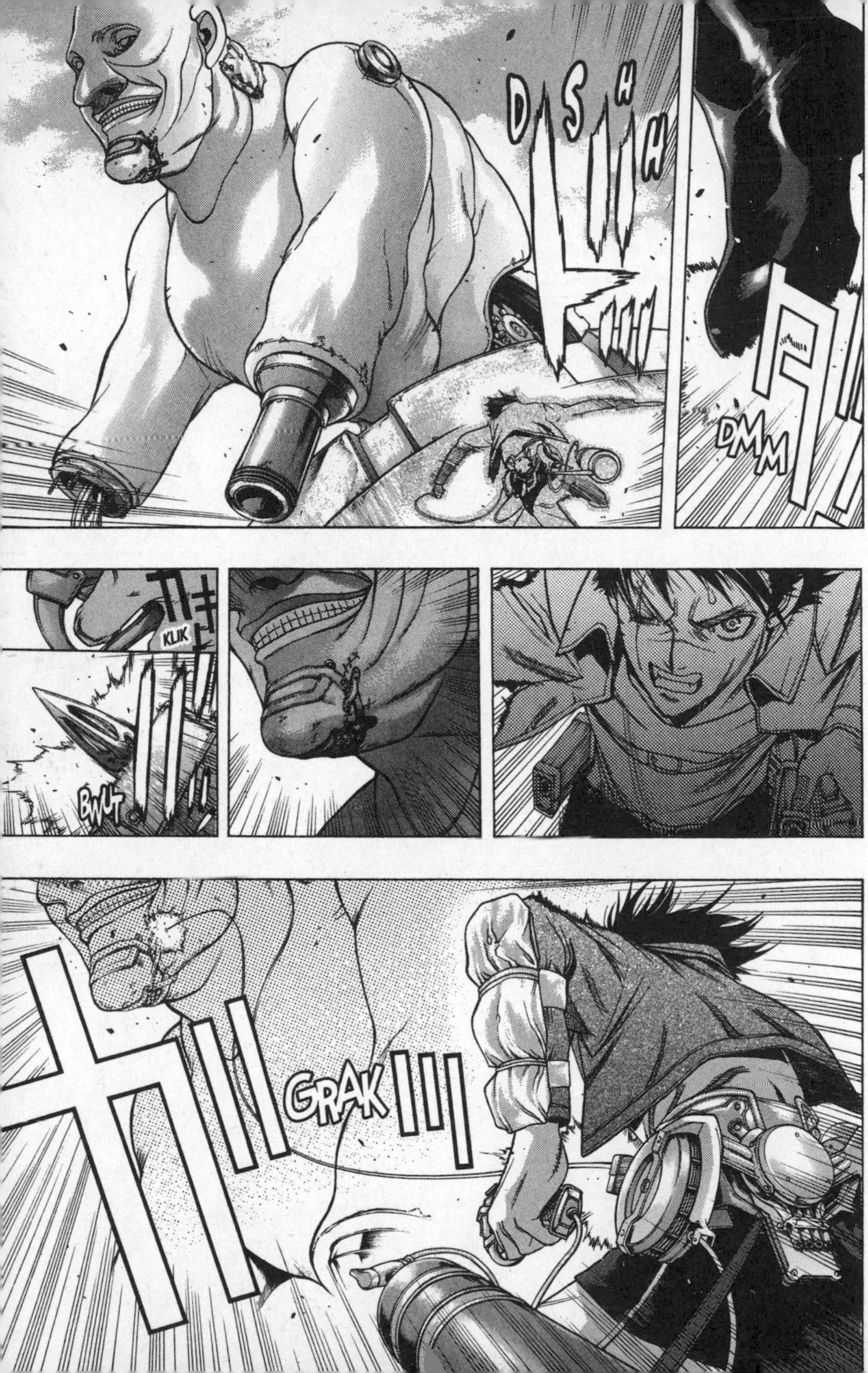
DMM
DSHH
KLIK
BWUT
GRAK

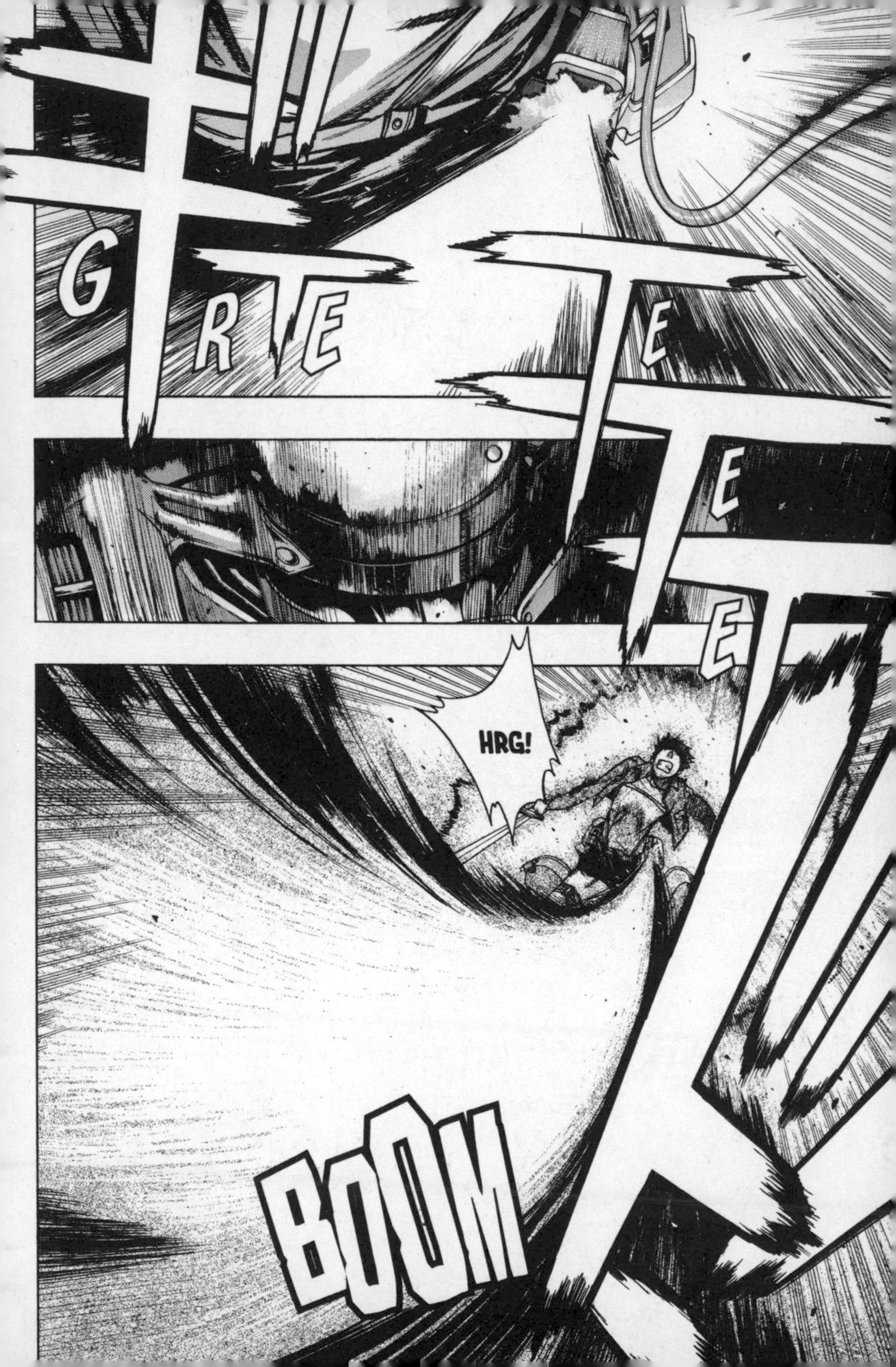
GREEEE
HRG!
BOOM

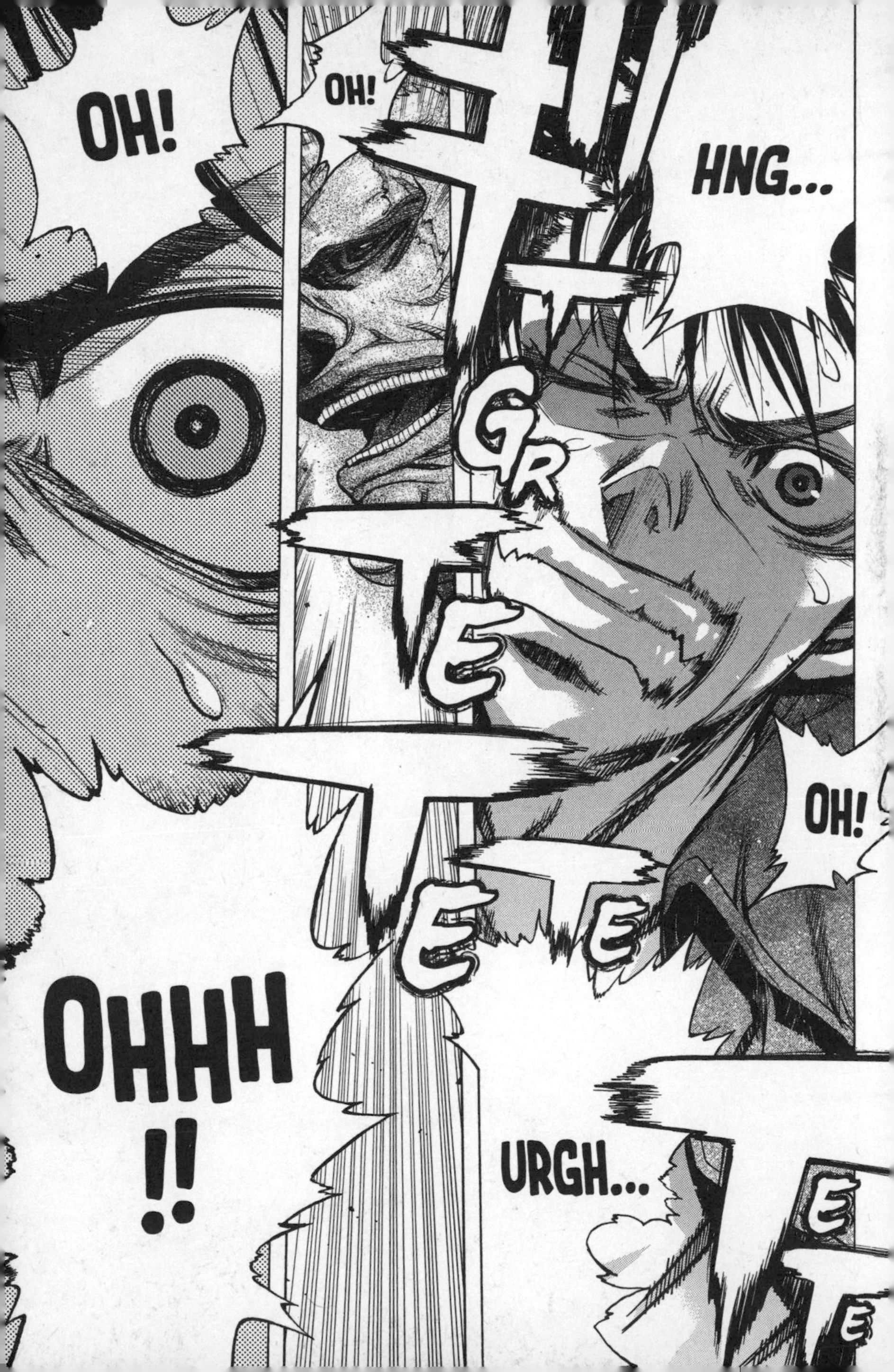
HNG...
OH!
URGH...
OH!
GRTETETE
TEE
OH!
OHHH !!

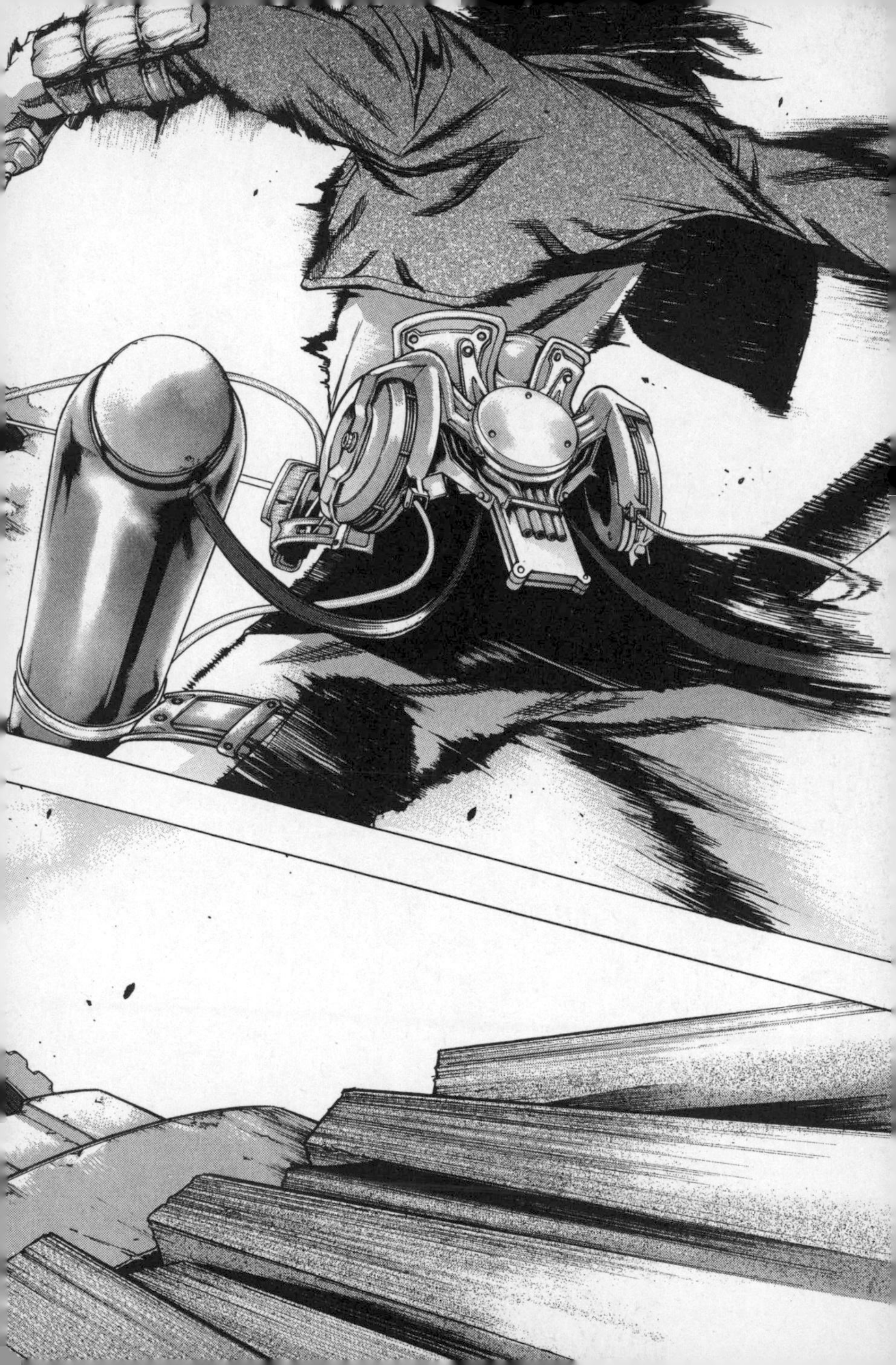

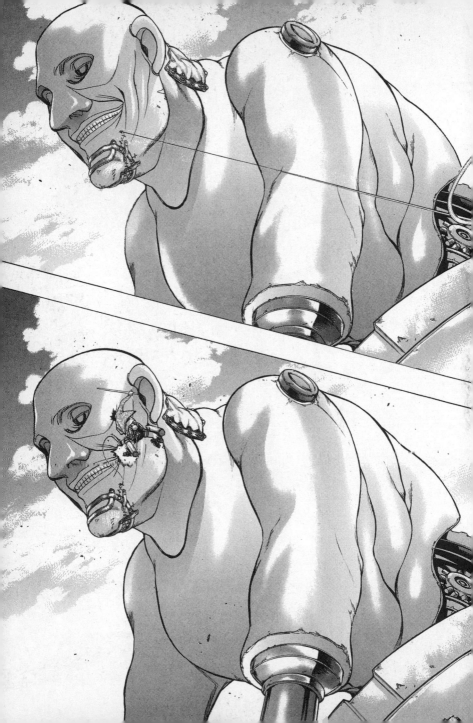

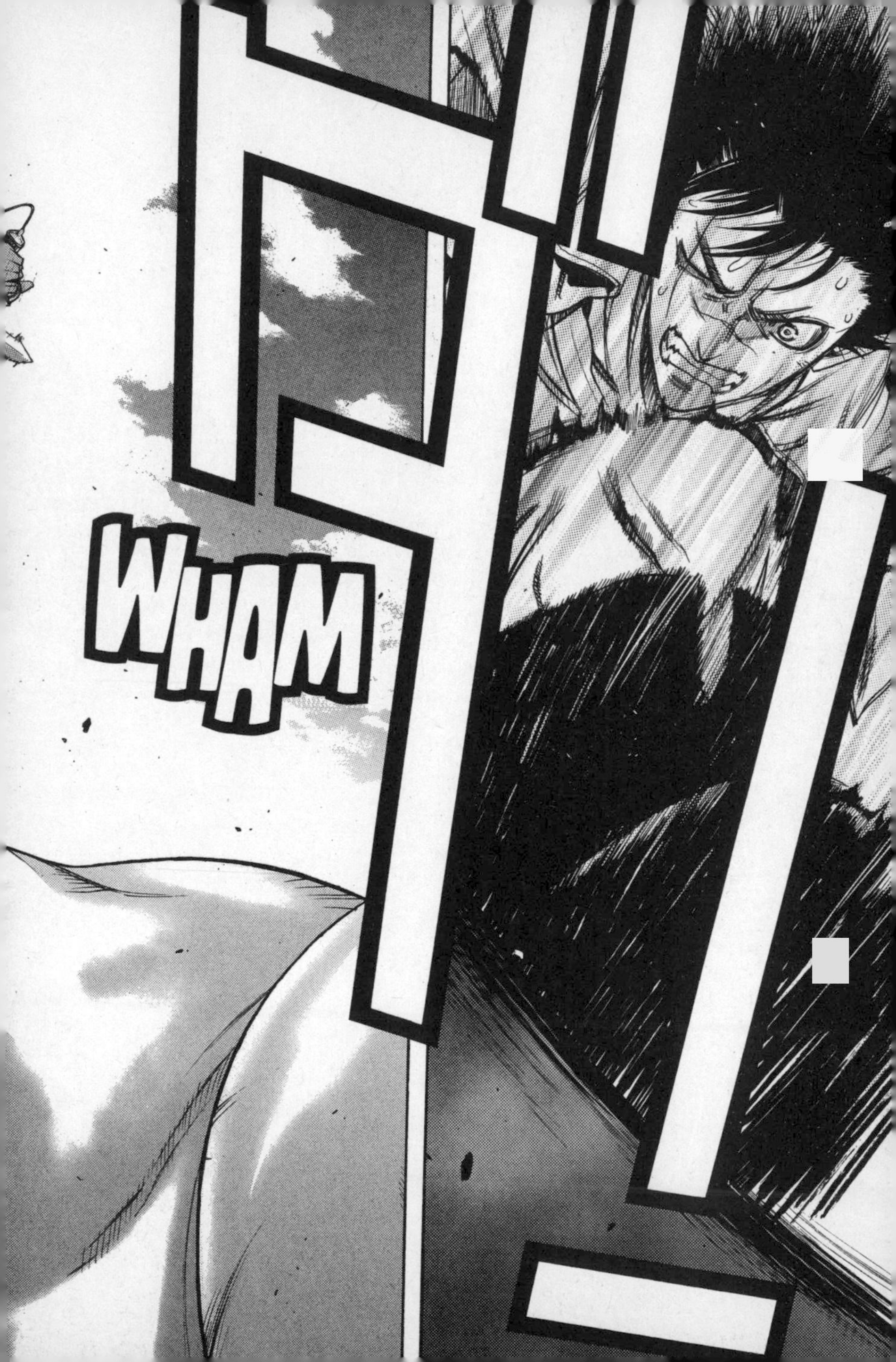
WHAM

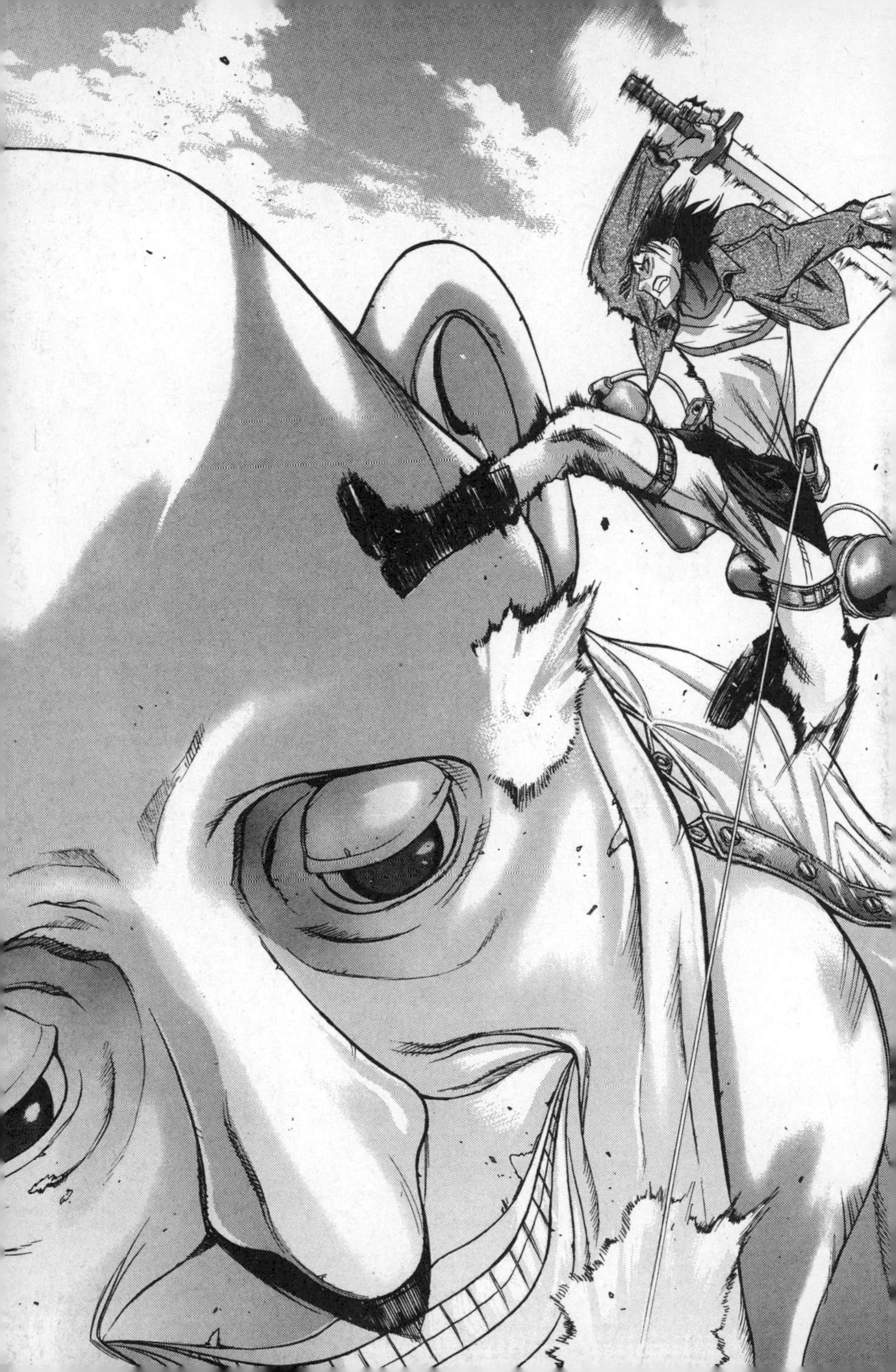

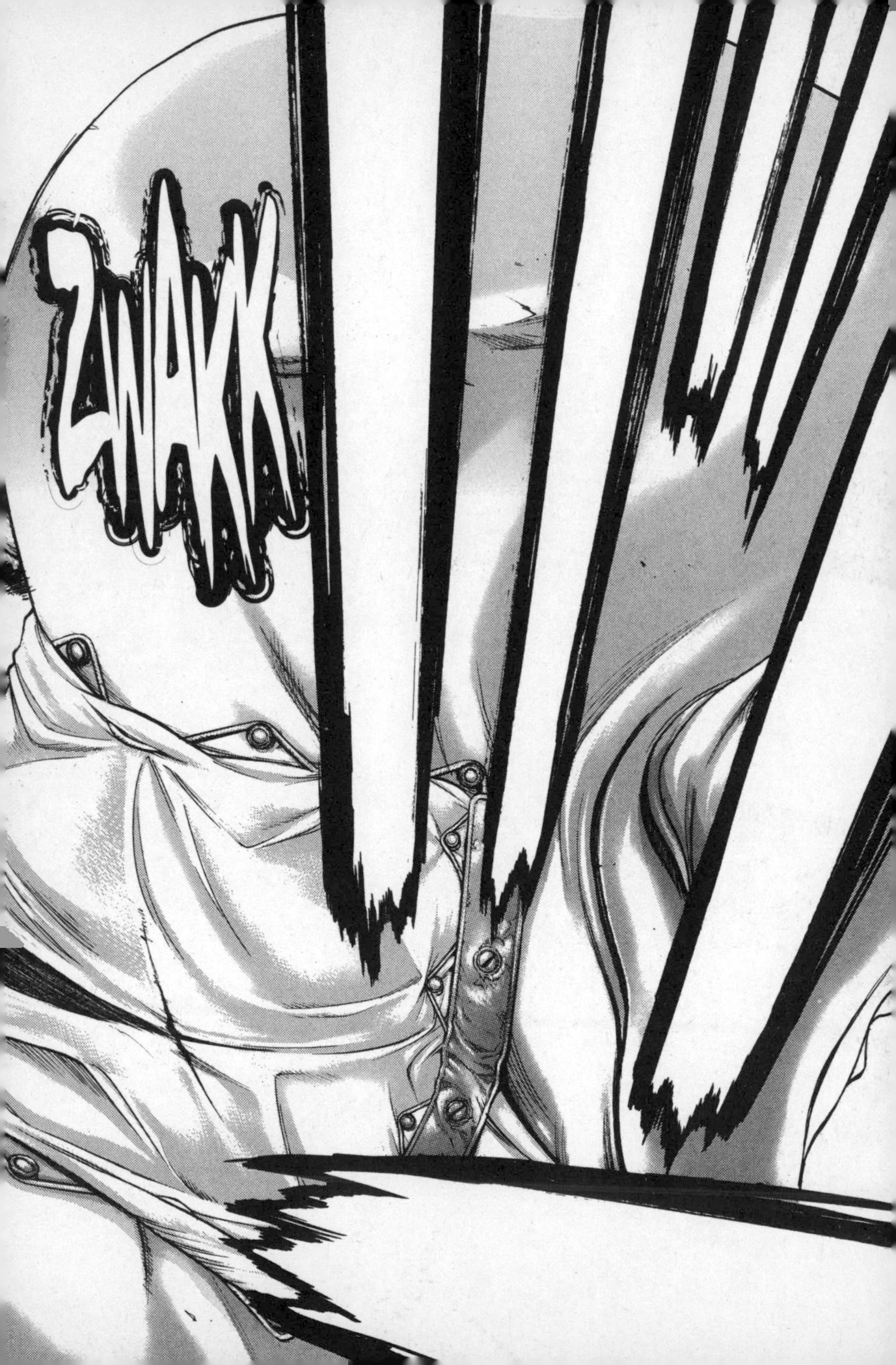
ZWAK

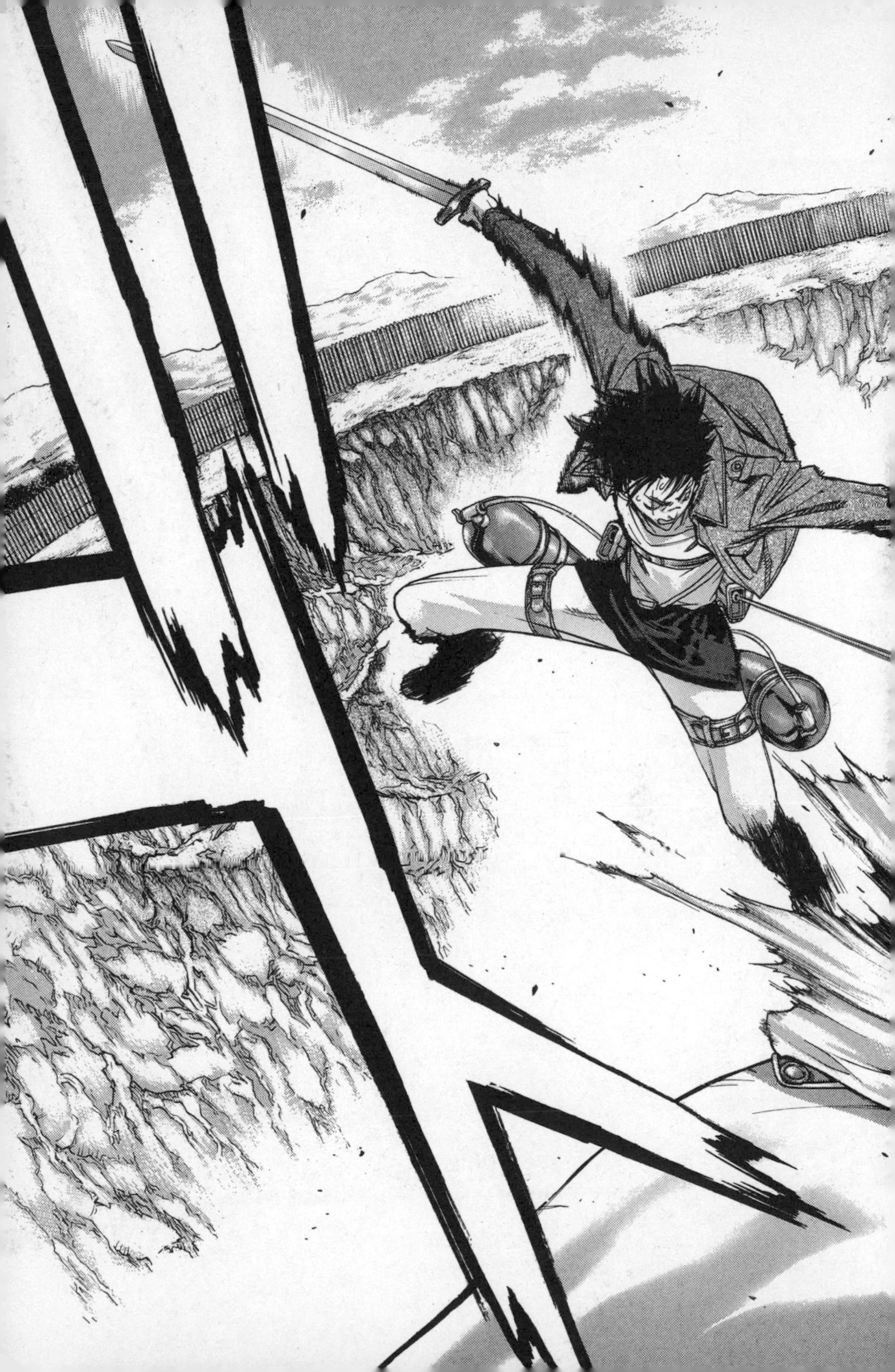

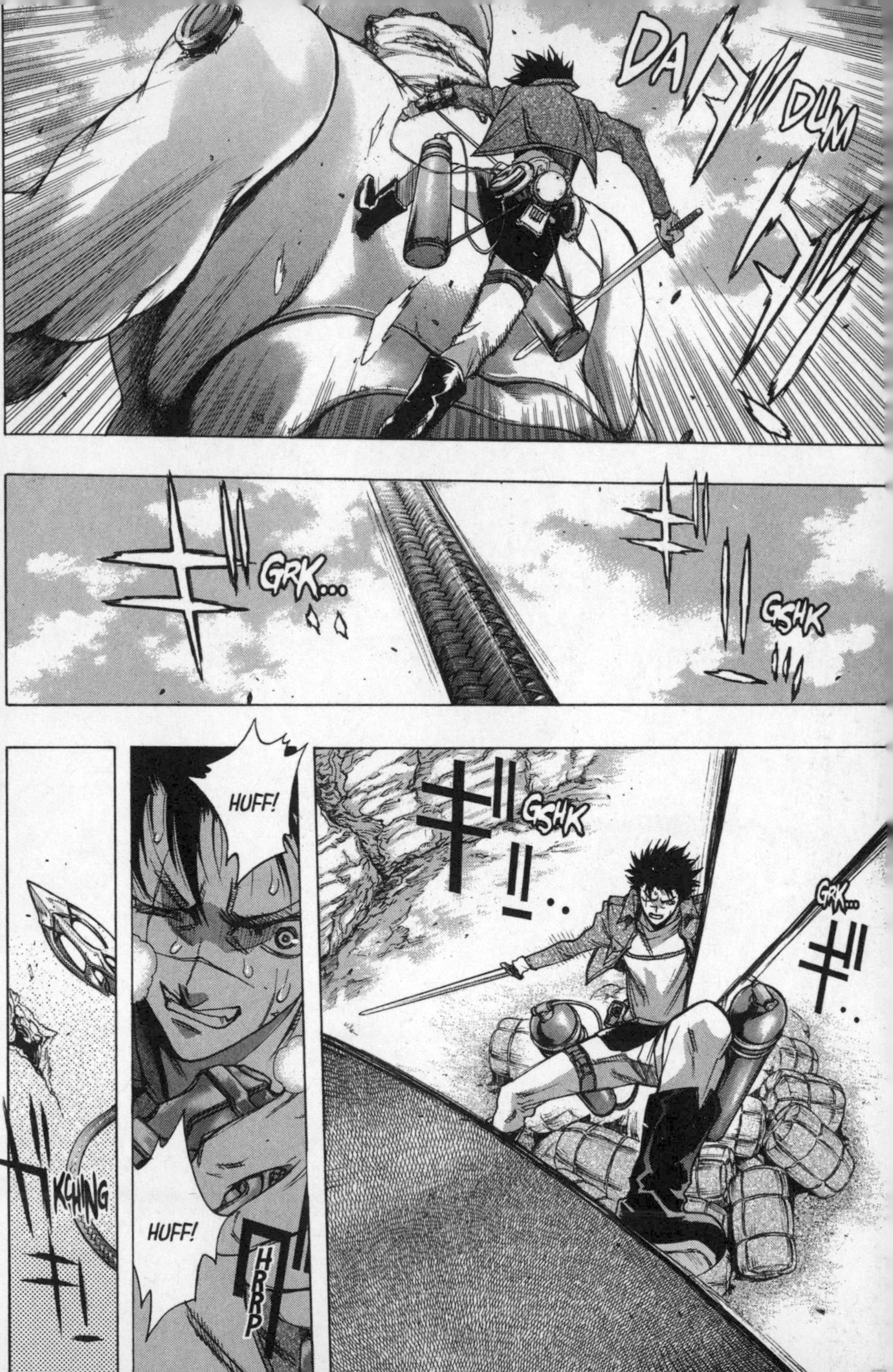

DA-DUM
GSHK
GRK...
GSHK
GRK...
HUFF!
HUFF!
HRRP
KCHING

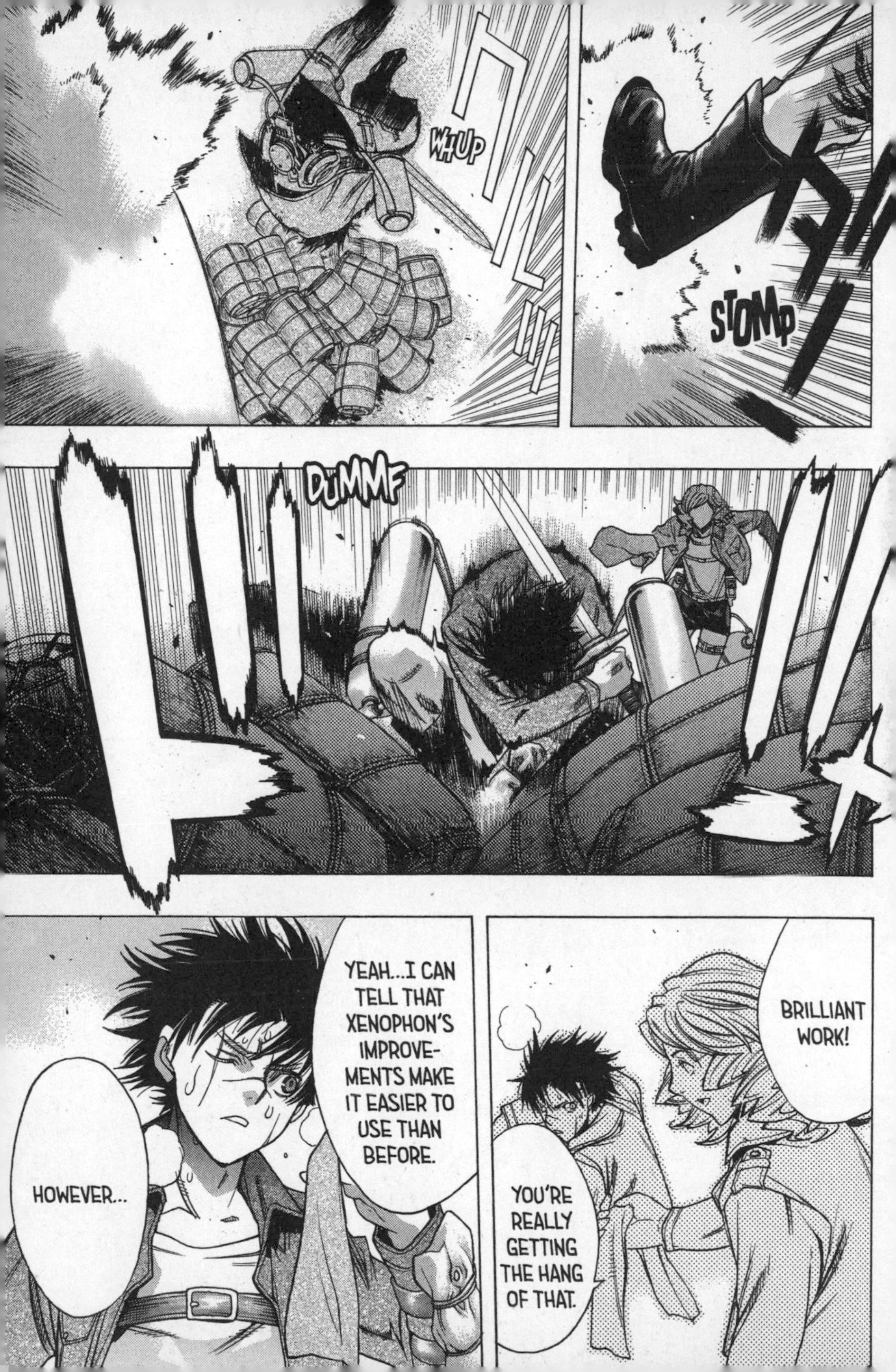
STOMP
WHUP
DUMMF
BRILLIANT WORK!
YOU'RE REALLY GETTING THE HANG OF THAT.
YEAH...I CAN TELL THAT XENOPHON'S IMPROVEMENTS MAKE IT EASIER TO USE THAN BEFORE.
HOWEVER...

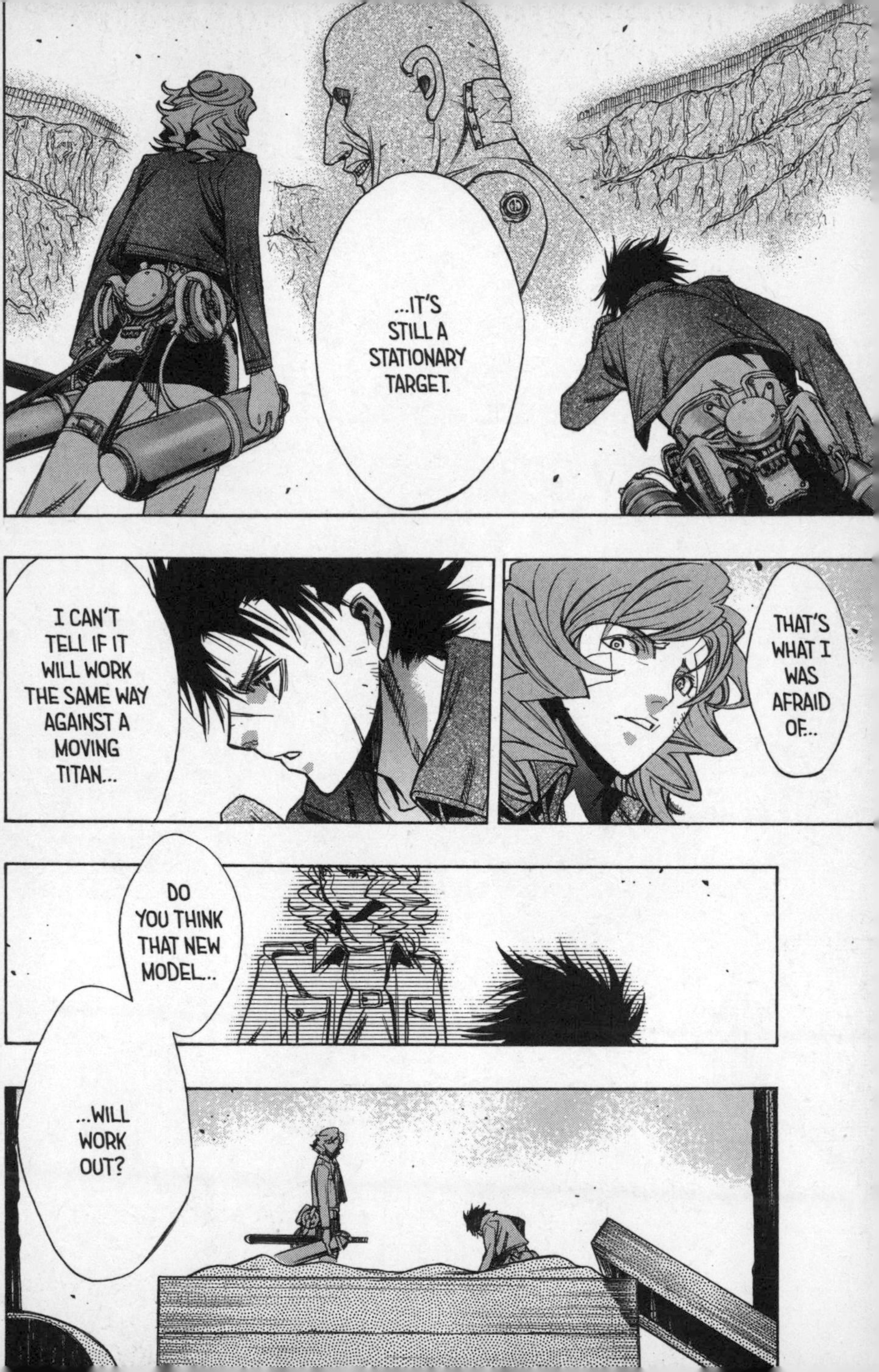
...IT'S STILL A STATIONARY TARGET.
THAT'S WHAT I WAS AFRAID OF...
I CAN'T TELL IF IT WILL WORK THE SAME WAY AGAINST A MOVING TITAN...
DO YOU THINK THAT NEW MODEL...
...WILL WORK OUT?

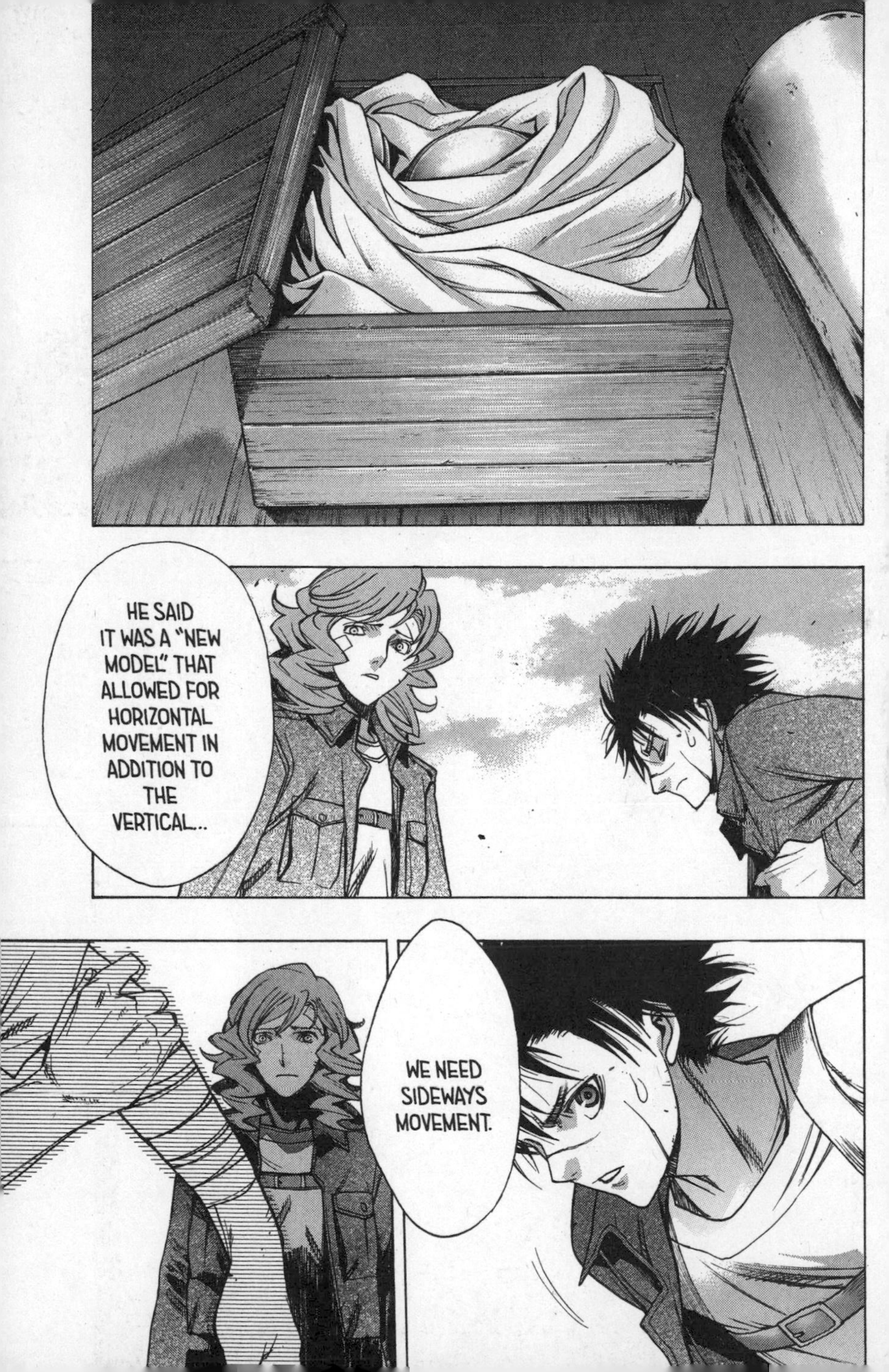
HE SAID IT WAS A "NEW MODEL" THAT ALLOWED FOR HORIZONTAL MOVEMENT IN ADDITION TO THE VERTICAL...
WE NEED SIDEWAYS MOVEMENT.

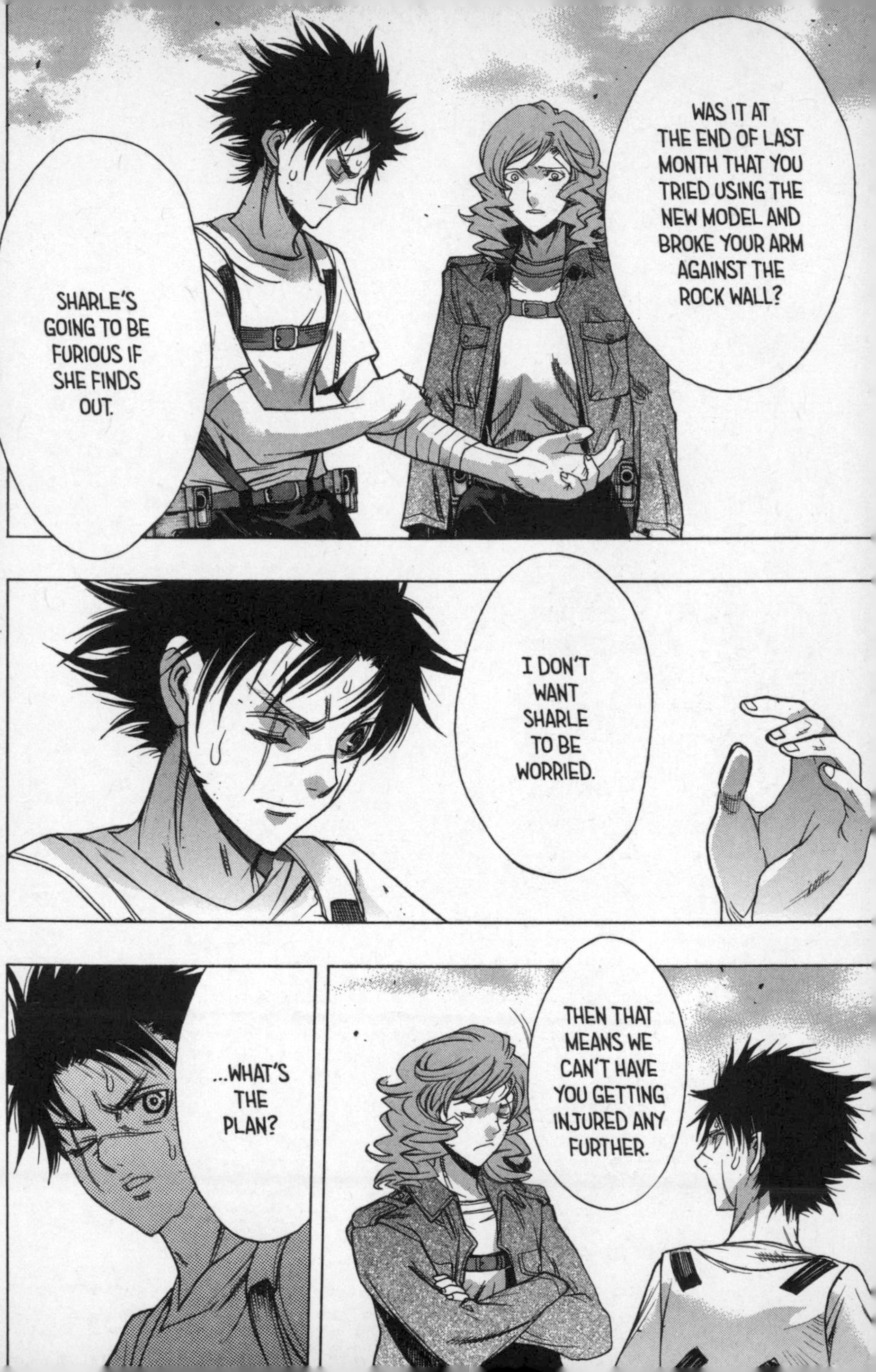
WAS IT AT THE END OF LAST MONTH THAT YOU TRIED USING THE NEW MODEL AND BROKE YOUR ARM AGAINST THE ROCK WALL?
SHARLE'S GOING TO BE FURIOUS IF SHE FINDS OUT.
I DON'T WANT SHARLE TO BE WORRIED.
THEN THAT MEANS WE CAN'T HAVE YOU GETTING INJURED ANY FURTHER.
...WHAT'S THE PLAN?

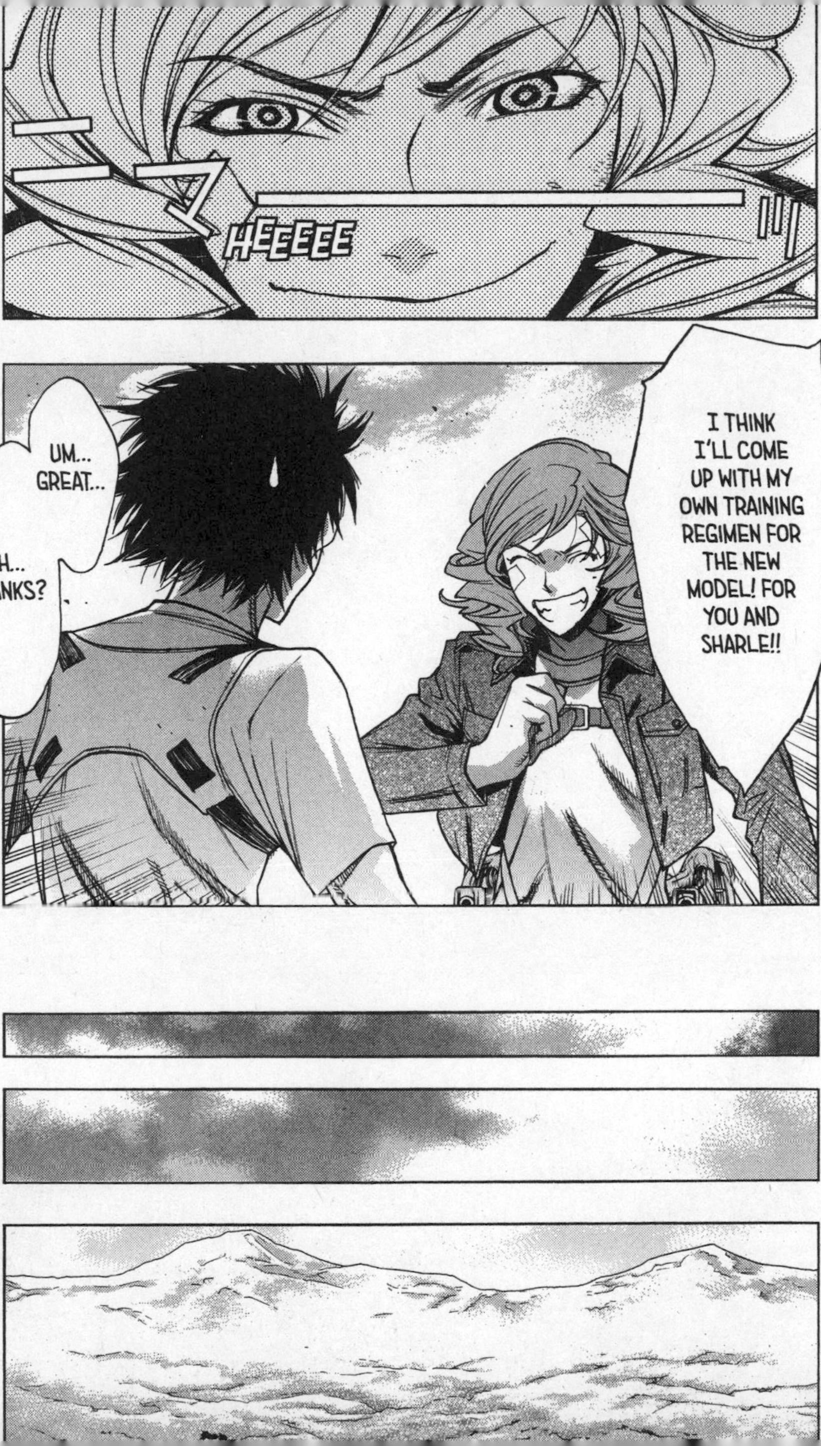
HEEEEE
I THINK I'LL COME UP WITH MY OWN TRAINING REGIMEN FOR THE NEW MODEL! FOR YOU AND SHARLE!!
UM... GREAT...
TH... THANKS?

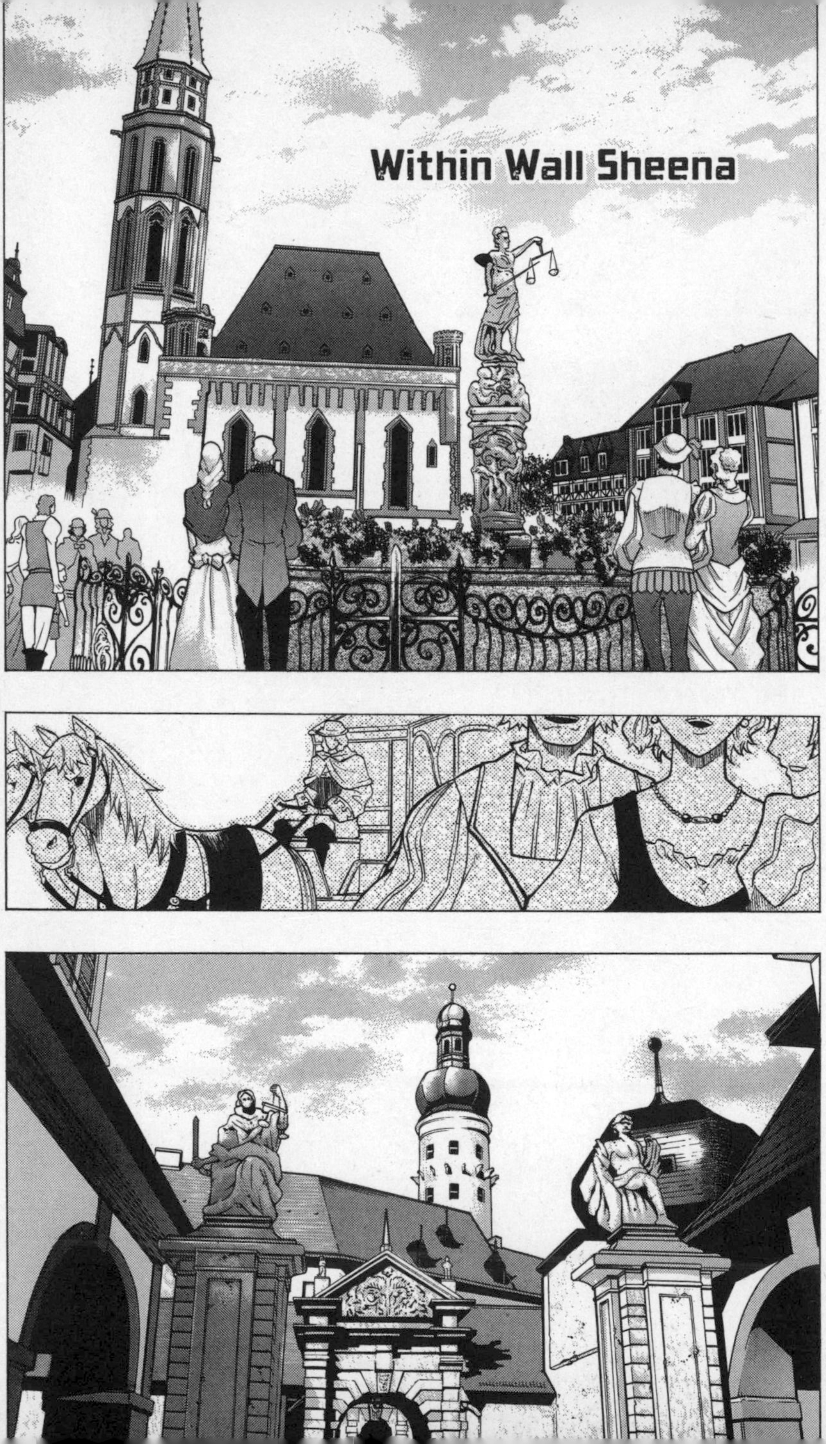
Within Wall Sheena

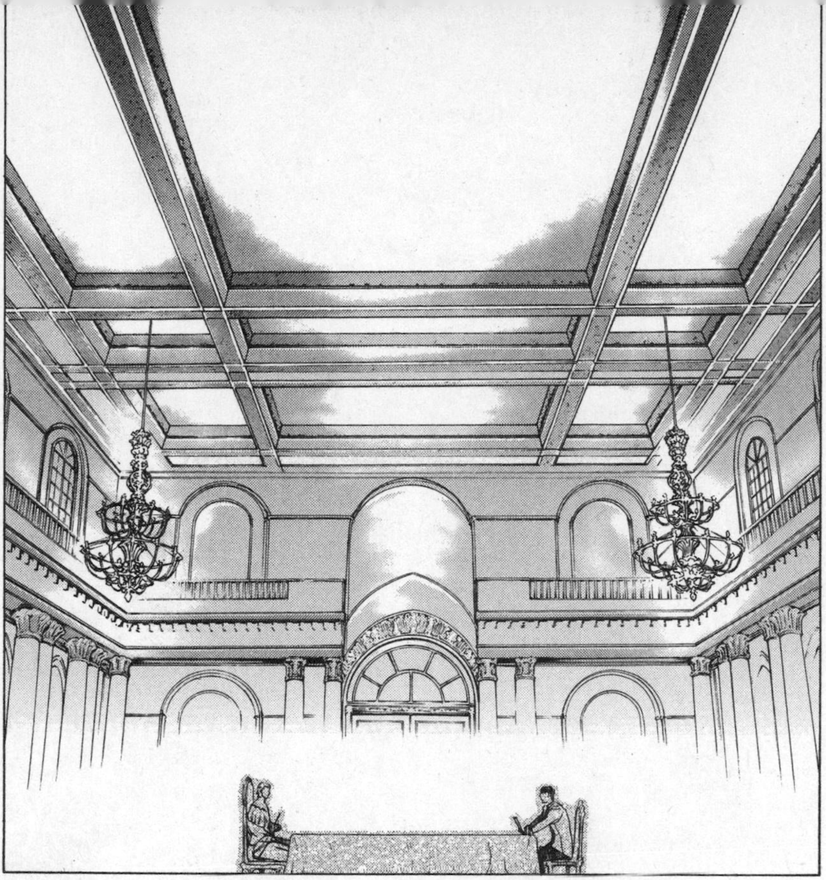
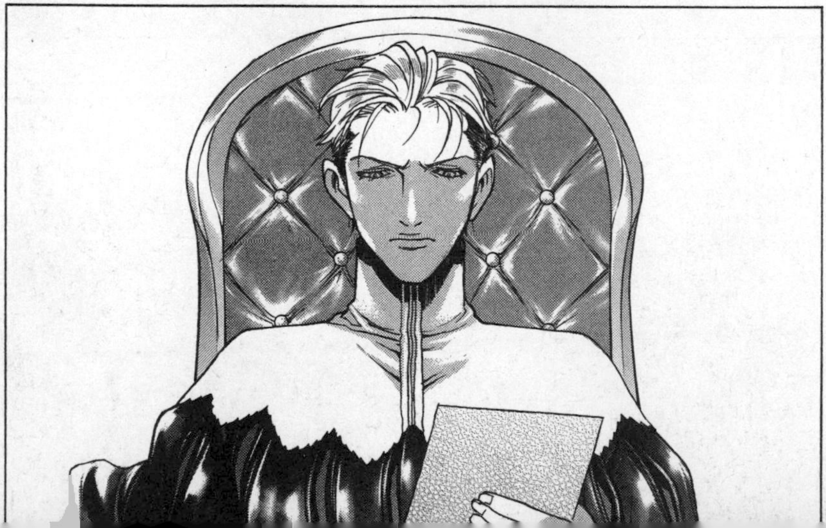

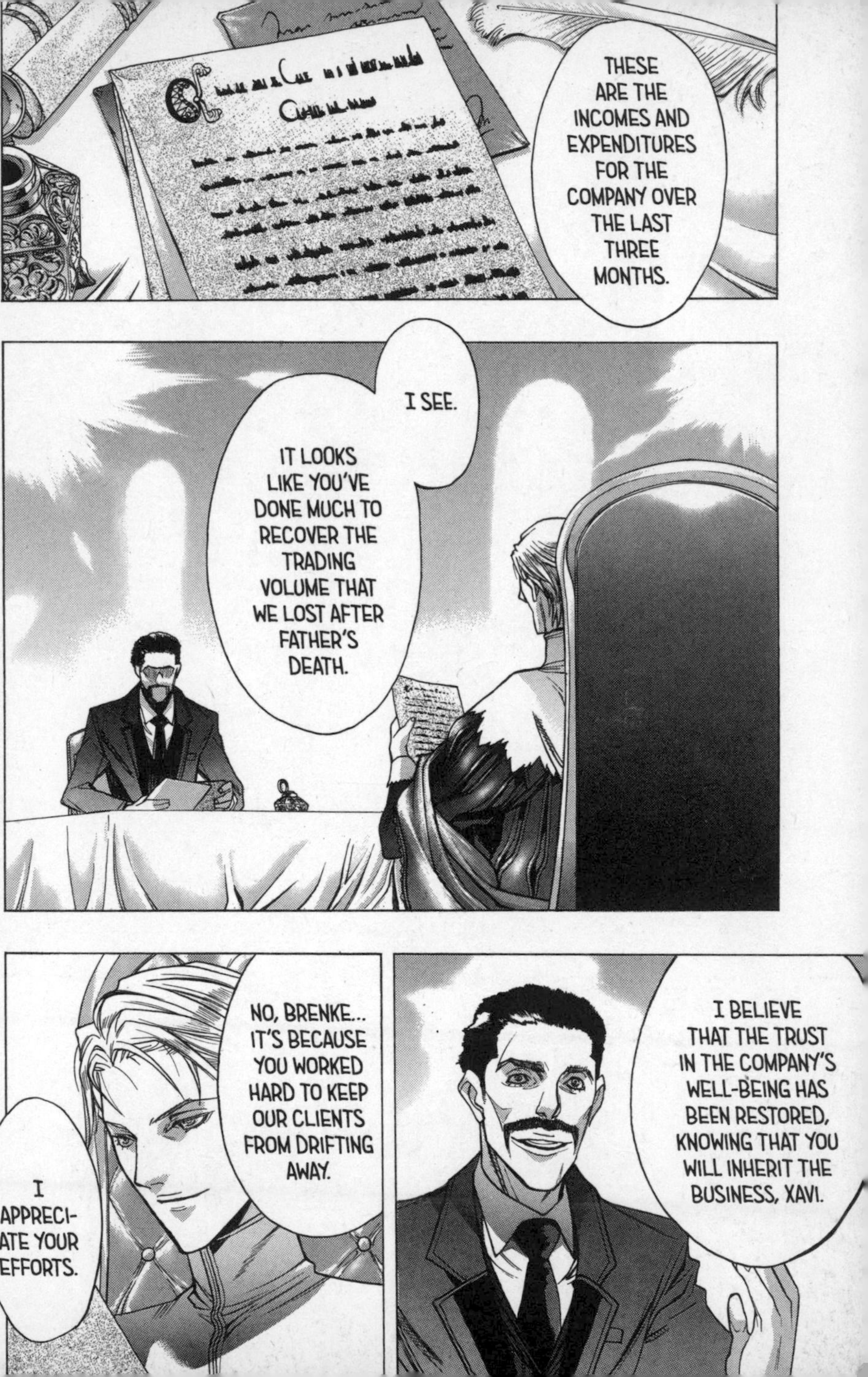
THESE ARE THE INCOMES AND EXPENDITURES FOR THE COMPANY OVER THE LAST THREE MONTHS.
I SEE.
IT LOOKS LIKE YOU'VE DONE MUCH TO RECOVER THE TRADING VOLUME THAT WE LOST AFTER FATHER'S DEATH.
I BELIEVE THAT THE TRUST IN THE COMPANY'S WELL-BEING HAS BEEN RESTORED, KNOWING THAT YOU WILL INHERIT THE BUSINESS, XAVI.
NO, BRENKE... IT'S BECAUSE YOU WORKED HARD TO KEEP OUR CLIENTS FROM DRIFTING AWAY.
I APPRECI-ATE YOUR EFFORTS.

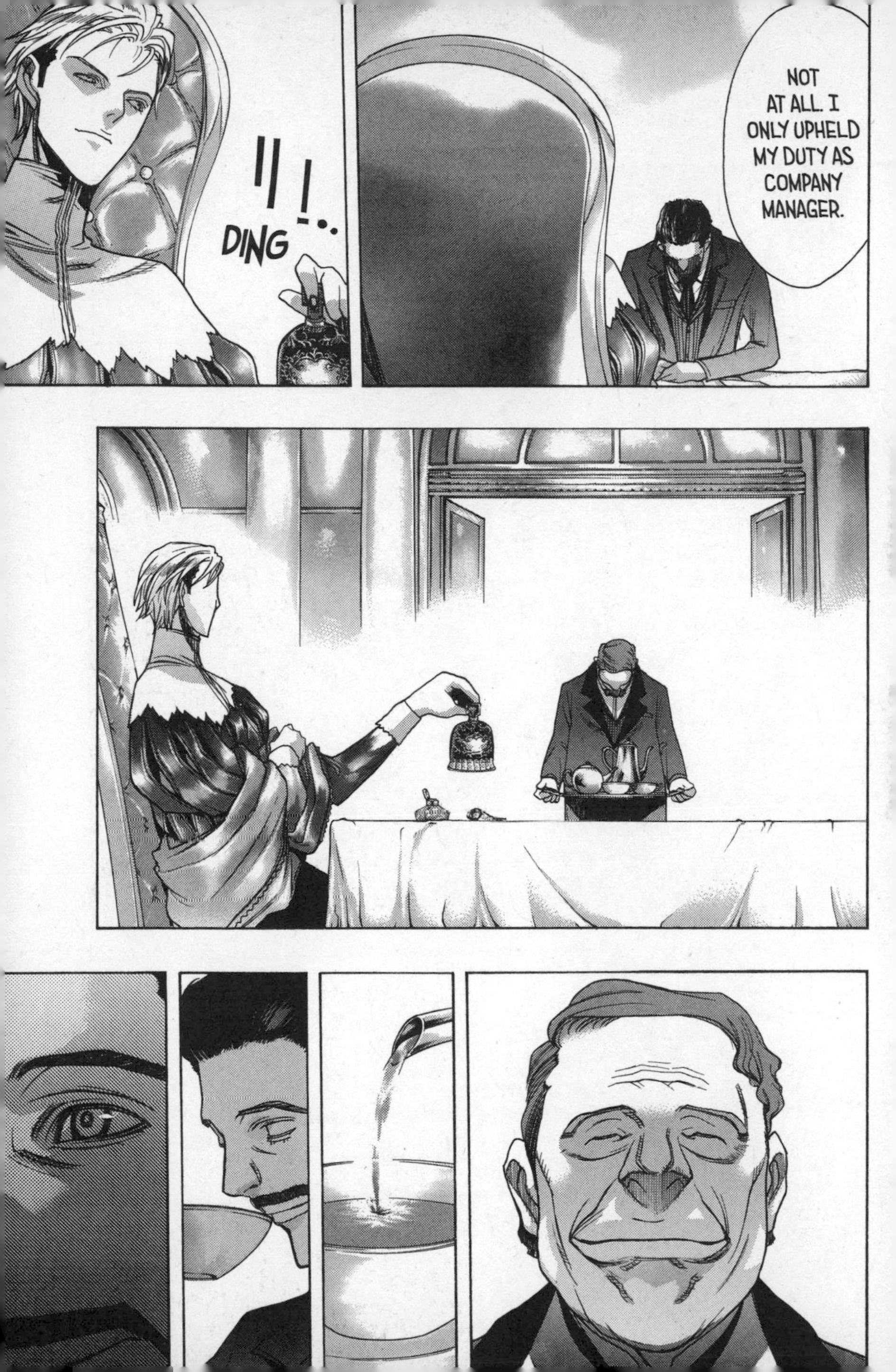
NOT AT ALL. I ONLY UPHELD MY DUTY AS COMPANY MANAGER.
DING

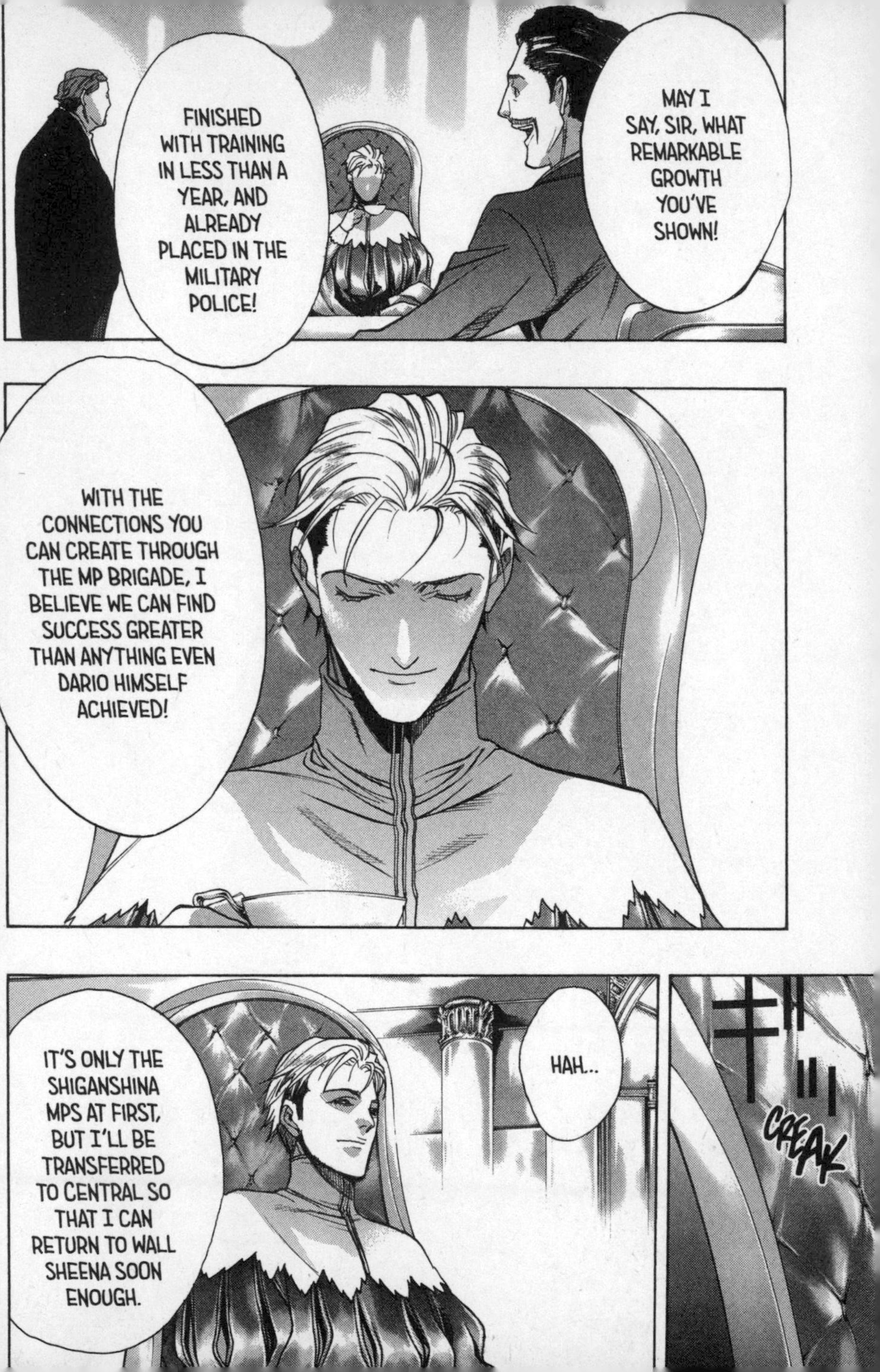
MAY I SAY, SIR, WHAT REMARKABLE GROWTH YOU'VE SHOWN!
FINISHED WITH TRAINING IN LESS THAN A YEAR, AND ALREADY PLACED IN THE MILITARY POLICE!
WITH THE CONNECTIONS YOU CAN CREATE THROUGH THE MP BRIGADE, I BELIEVE WE CAN FIND SUCCESS GREATER THAN ANYTHING EVEN DARIO HIMSELF ACHIEVED!
CREAK
HAH...
IT'S ONLY THE SHIGANSHINA MPS AT FIRST, BUT I'LL BE TRANSFERRED TO CENTRAL SO THAT I CAN RETURN TO WALL SHEENA SOON ENOUGH.

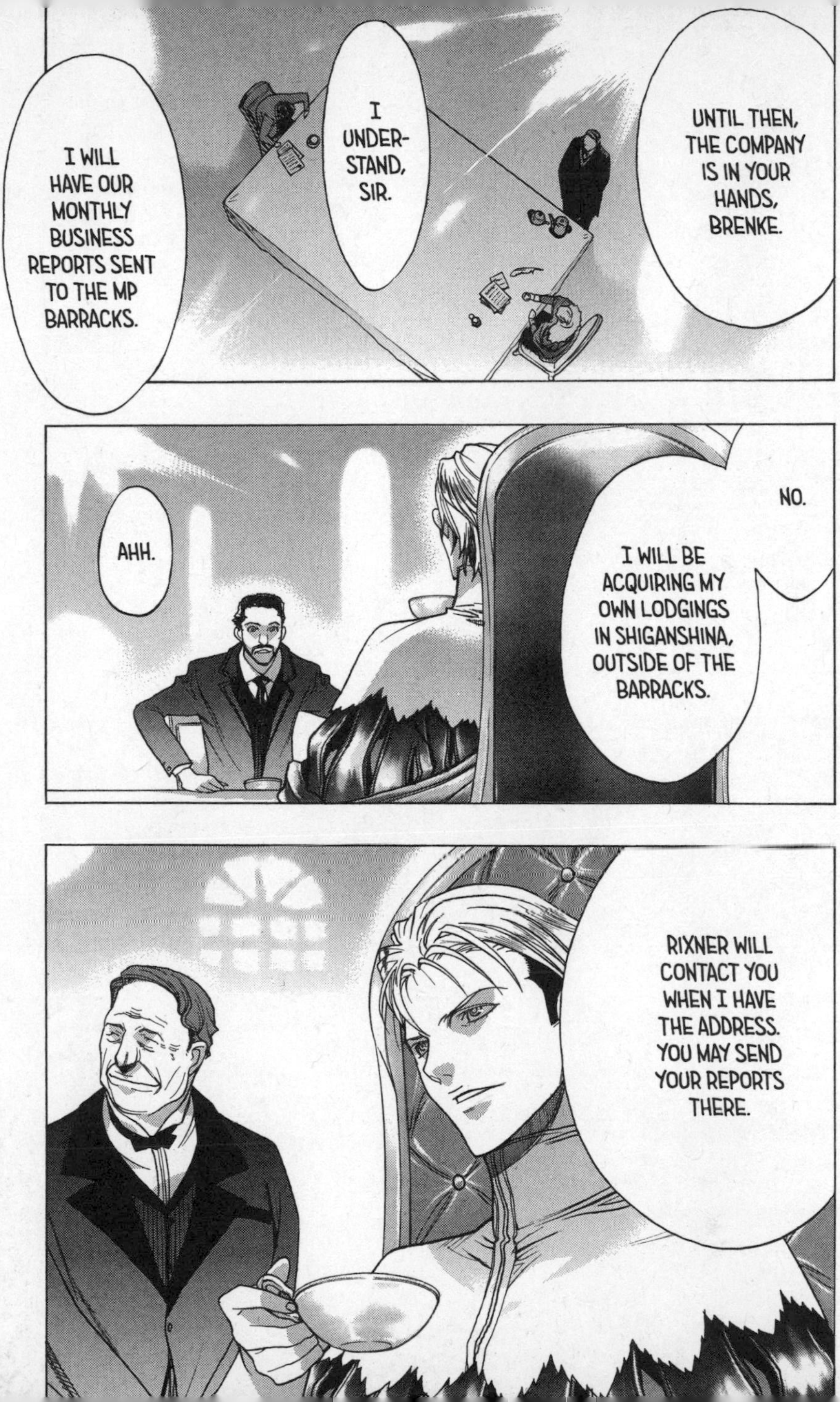
UNTIL THEN, THE COMPANY IS IN YOUR HANDS, BRENKE.
I UNDER-STAND, SIR.
I WILL HAVE OUR MONTHLY BUSINESS REPORTS SENT TO THE MP BARRACKS.
NO.
I WILL BE ACQUIRING MY OWN LODGINGS IN SHIGANSHINA, OUTSIDE OF THE BARRACKS.
AHH.
RIXNER WILL CONTACT YOU WHEN I HAVE THE ADDRESS. YOU MAY SEND YOUR REPORTS THERE.

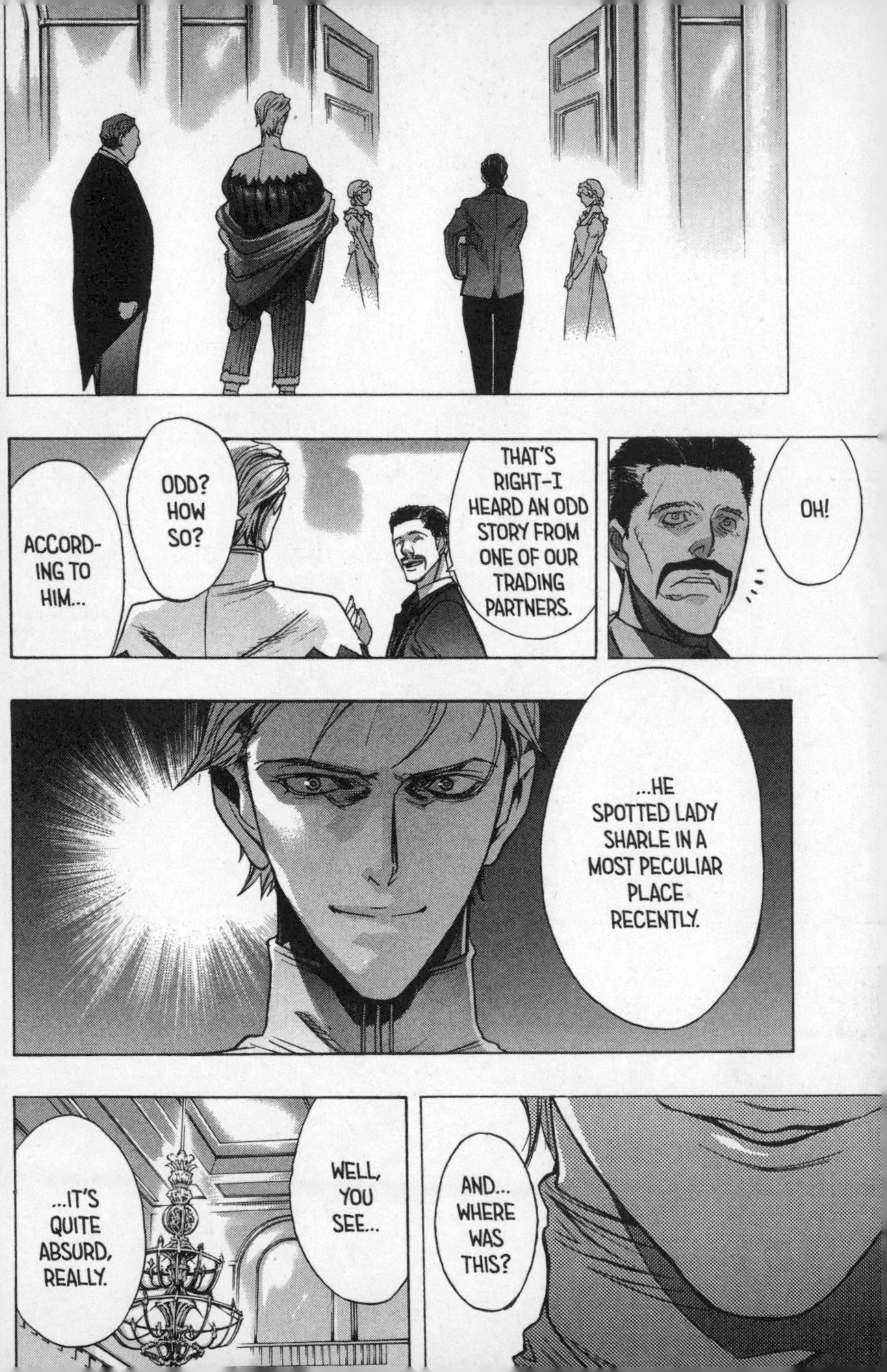
OH!
THAT'S RIGHT—I HEARD AN ODD STORY FROM ONE OF OUR TRADING PARTNERS.
ODD? HOW SO?
ACCORDING TO HIM...
...HE SPOTTED LADY SHARLE IN A MOST PECULIAR PLACE RECENTLY.
AND... WHERE WAS THIS?
WELL, YOU SEE...
...IT'S QUITE ABSURD, REALLY.

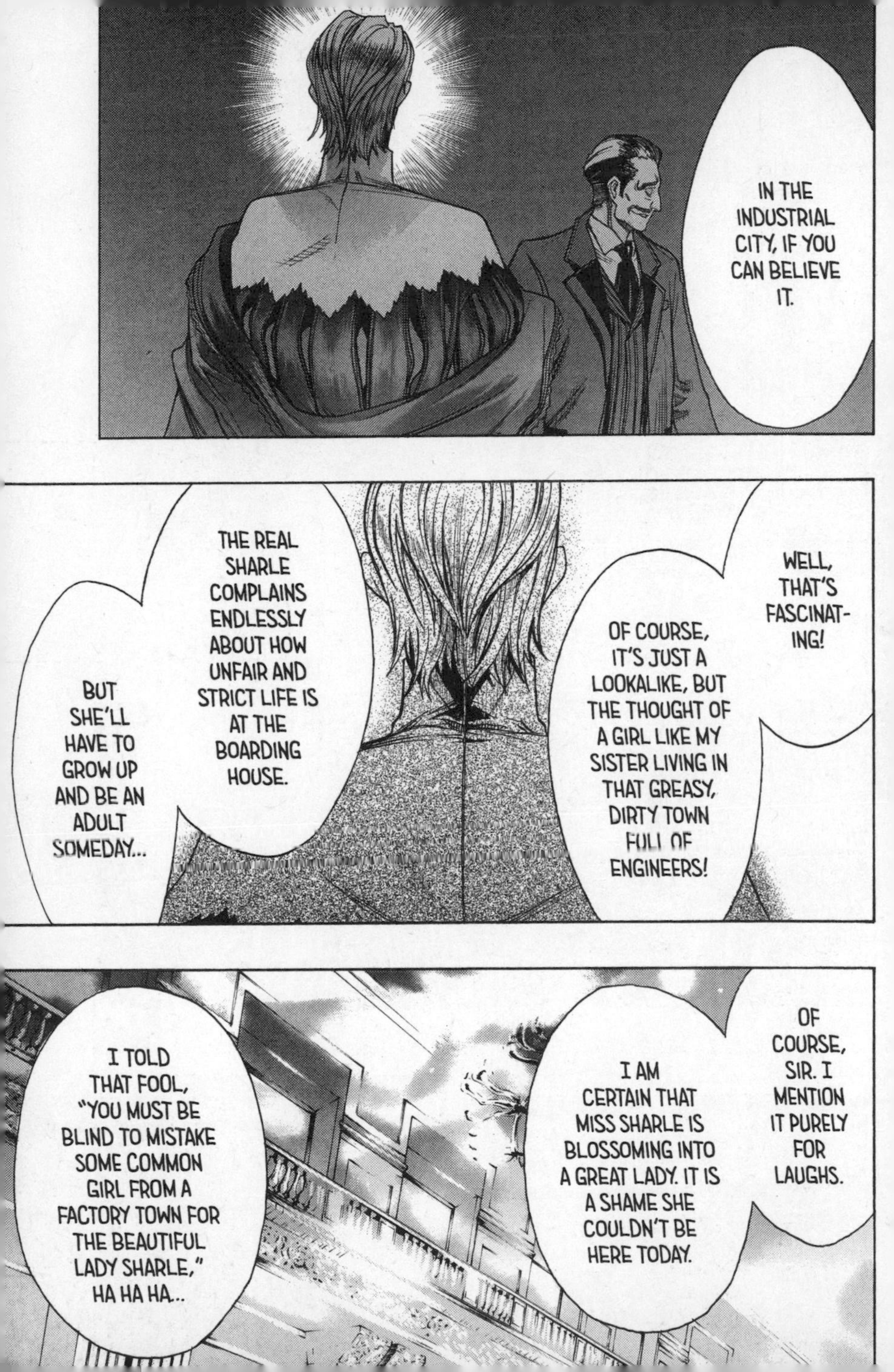
IN THE INDUSTRIAL CITY, IF YOU CAN BELIEVE IT.
WELL, THAT'S FASCINAT-ING!
OF COURSE, IT'S JUST A LOOKALIKE, BUT THE THOUGHT OF A GIRL LIKE MY SISTER LIVING IN THAT GREASY, DIRTY TOWN FULL OF ENGINEERS!
THE REAL SHARLE COMPLAINS ENDLESSLY ABOUT HOW UNFAIR AND STRICT LIFE IS AT THE BOARDING HOUSE.
BUT SHE'LL HAVE TO GROW UP AND BE AN ADULT SOMEDAY...
OF COURSE, SIR. I MENTION IT PURELY FOR LAUGHS.
I AM CERTAIN THAT MISS SHARLE IS BLOSSOMING INTO A GREAT LADY. IT IS A SHAME SHE COULDN'T BE HERE TODAY.
I TOLD THAT FOOL, "YOU MUST BE BLIND TO MISTAKE SOME COMMON GIRL FROM A FACTORY TOWN FOR THE BEAUTIFUL LADY SHARLE," HA HA HA...

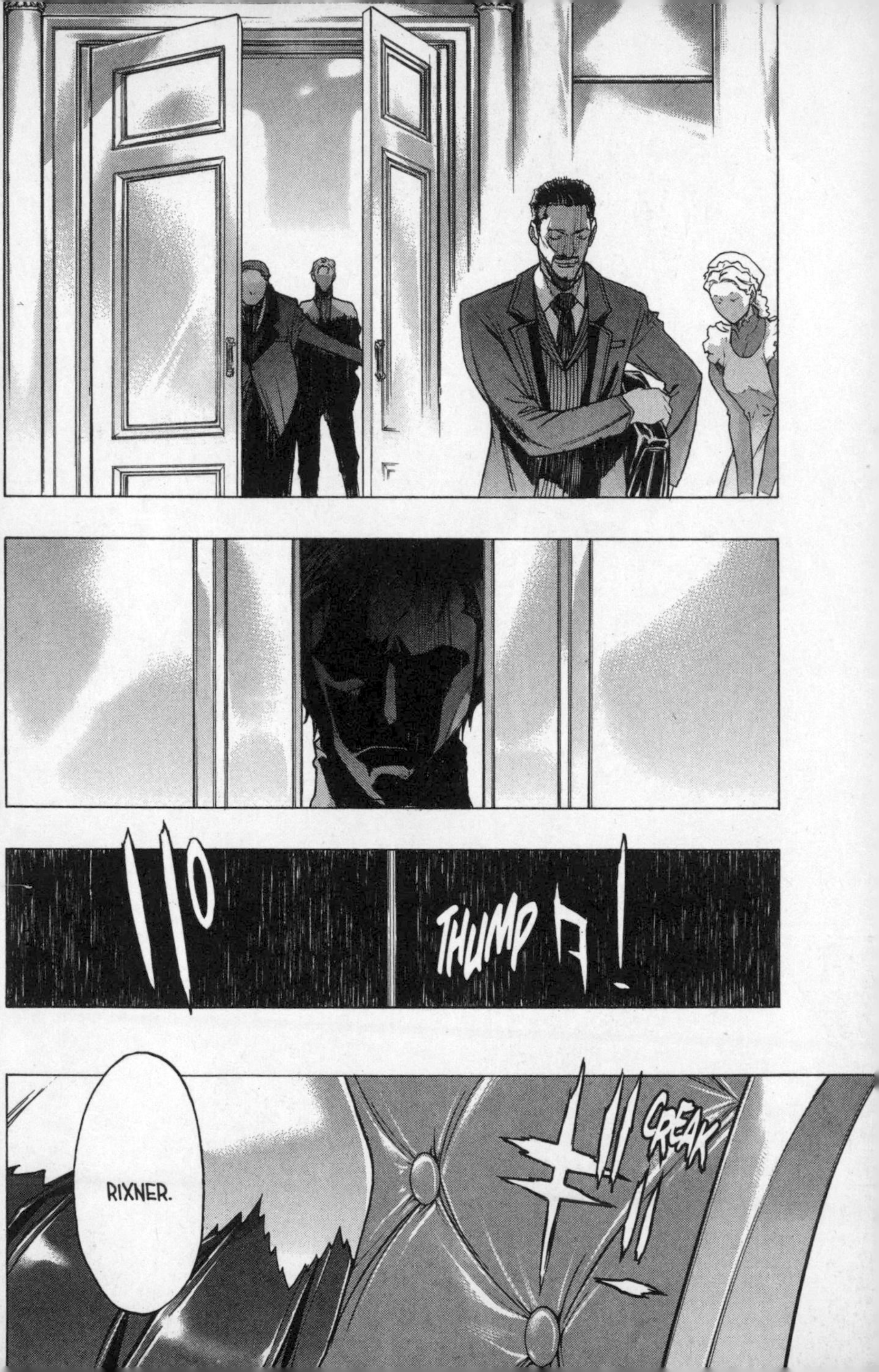
THUMP
CREAK
RIXNER.

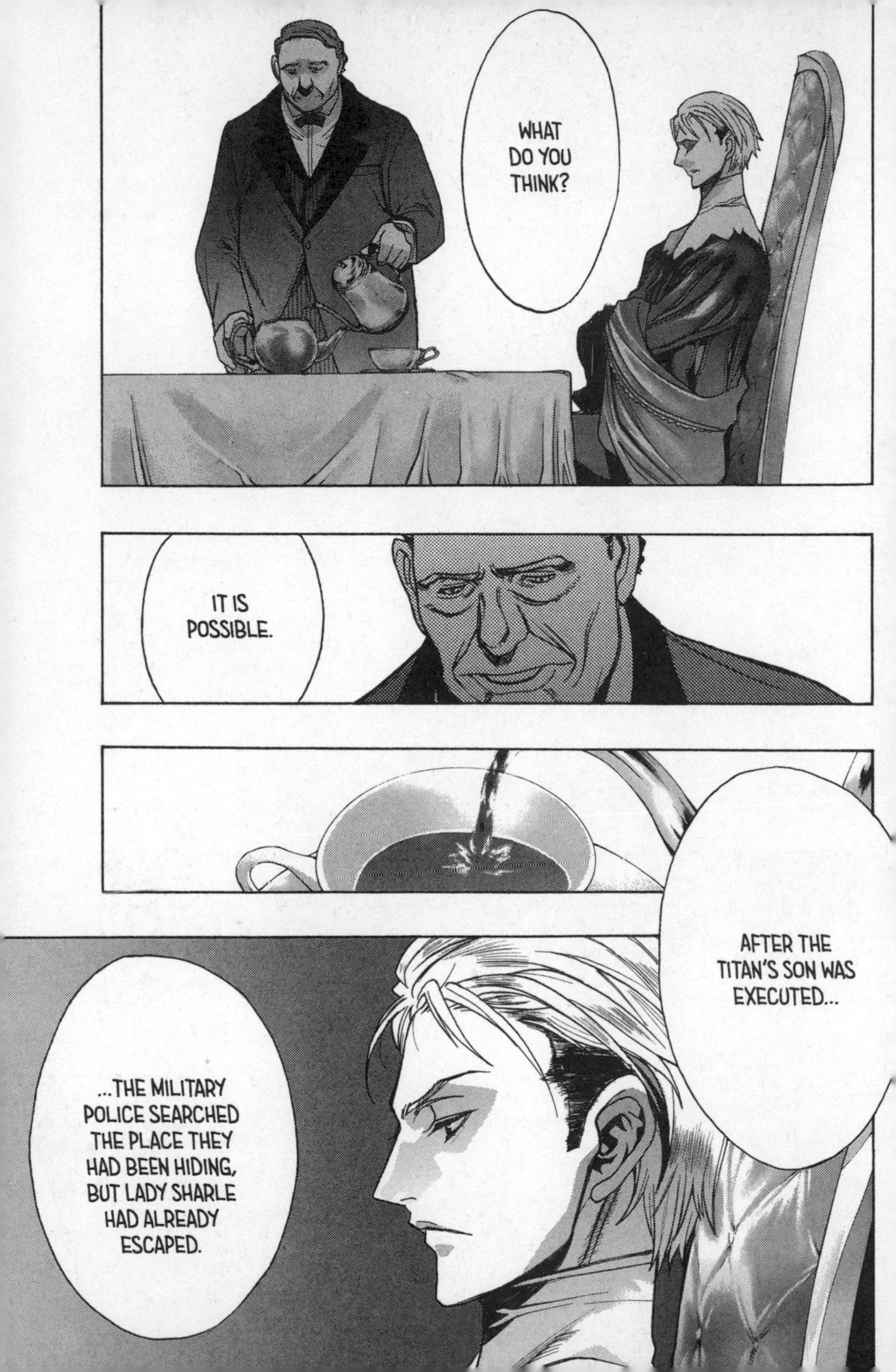
WHAT DO YOU THINK?
IT IS POSSIBLE.
AFTER THE TITAN'S SON WAS EXECUTED...
...THE MILITARY POLICE SEARCHED THE PLACE THEY HAD BEEN HIDING, BUT LADY SHARLE HAD ALREADY ESCAPED.

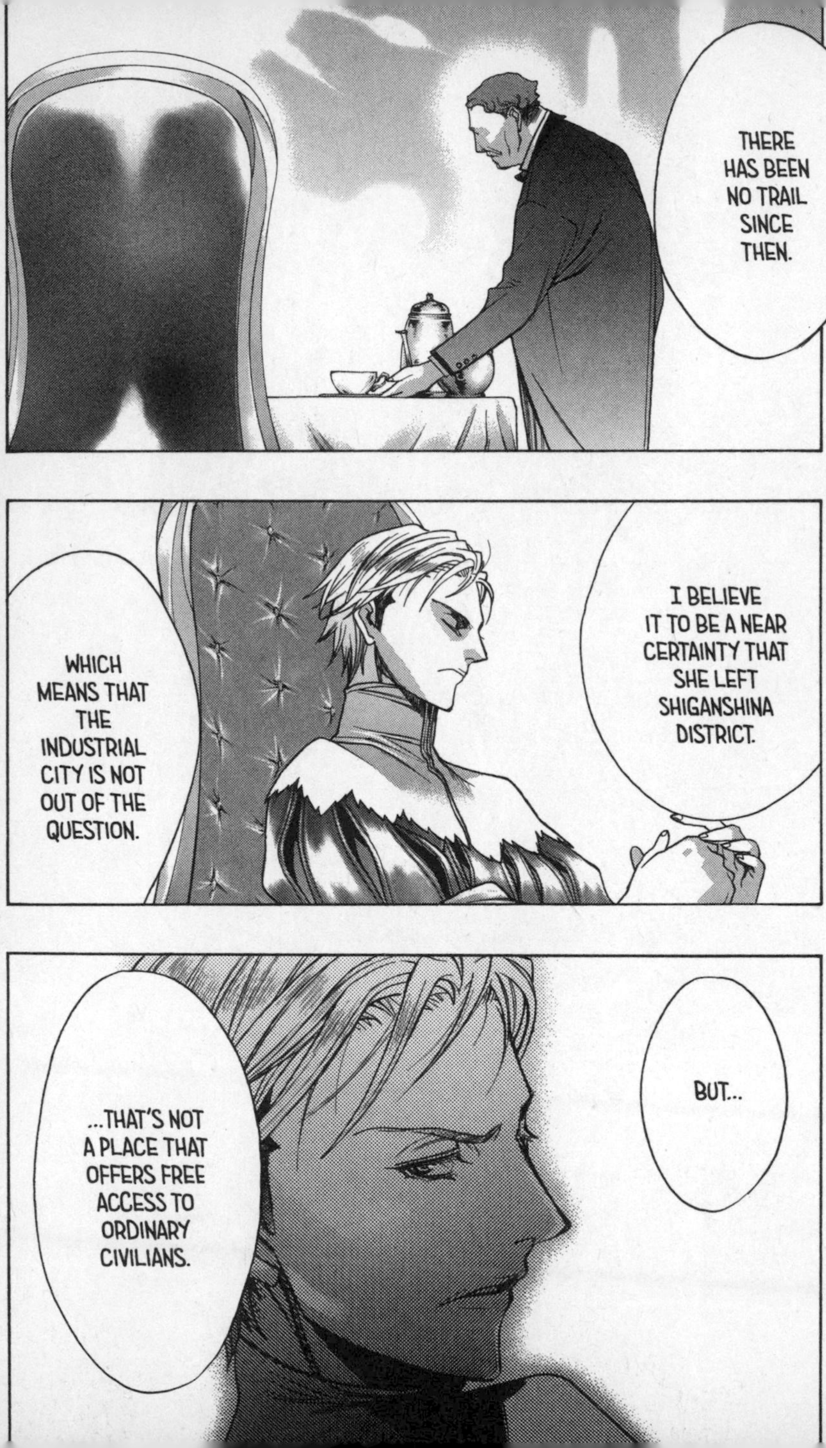
THERE HAS BEEN NO TRAIL SINCE THEN.
I BELIEVE IT TO BE A NEAR CERTAINTY THAT SHE LEFT SHIGANSHINA DISTRICT.
WHICH MEANS THAT THE INDUSTRIAL CITY IS NOT OUT OF THE QUESTION.
BUT...
...THAT'S NOT A PLACE THAT OFFERS FREE ACCESS TO ORDINARY CIVILIANS.

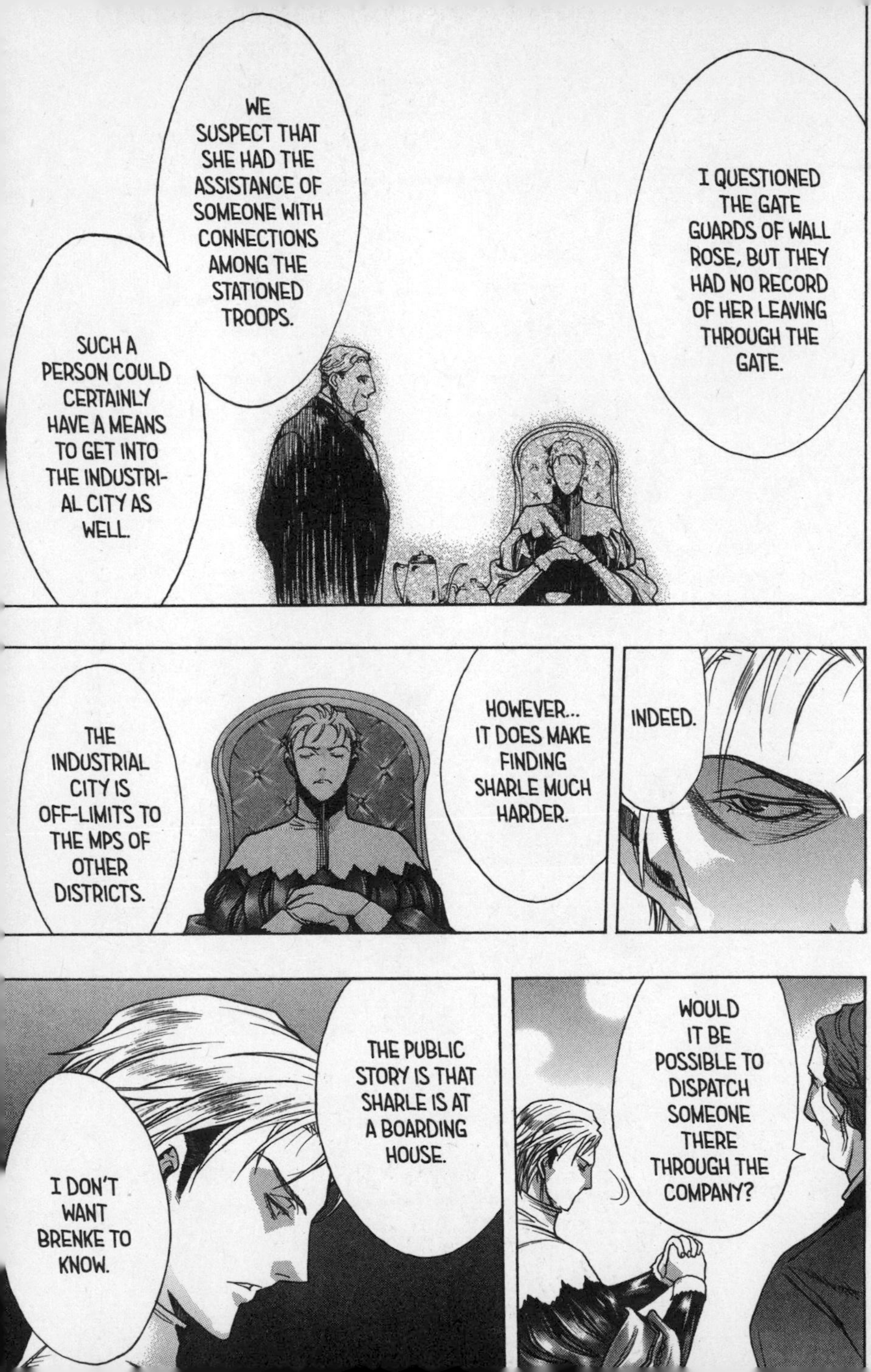
I QUESTIONED THE GATE GUARDS OF WALL ROSE, BUT THEY HAD NO RECORD OF HER LEAVING THROUGH THE GATE.
WE SUSPECT THAT SHE HAD THE ASSISTANCE OF SOMEONE WITH CONNECTIONS AMONG THE STATIONED TROOPS.
SUCH A PERSON COULD CERTAINLY HAVE A MEANS TO GET INTO THE INDUSTRIAL CITY AS WELL.
INDEED.
HOWEVER... IT DOES MAKE FINDING SHARLE MUCH HARDER.
THE INDUSTRIAL CITY IS OFF-LIMITS TO THE MPS OF OTHER DISTRICTS.
WOULD IT BE POSSIBLE TO DISPATCH SOMEONE THERE THROUGH THE COMPANY?
THE PUBLIC STORY IS THAT SHARLE IS AT A BOARDING HOUSE.
I DON'T WANT BRENKE TO KNOW.

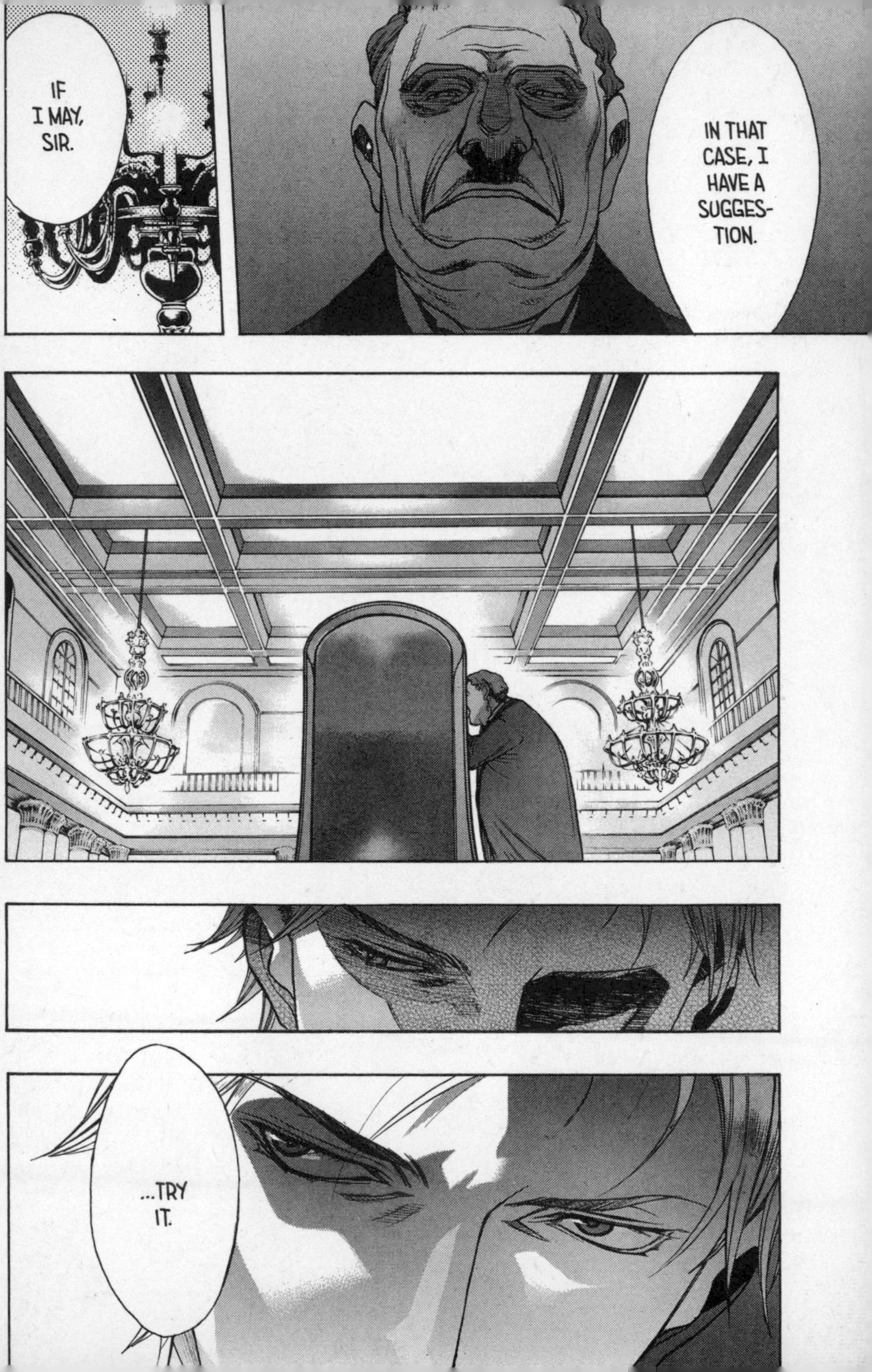
IN THAT CASE, I HAVE A SUGGES-TION.
IF I MAY, SIR.
...TRY IT.

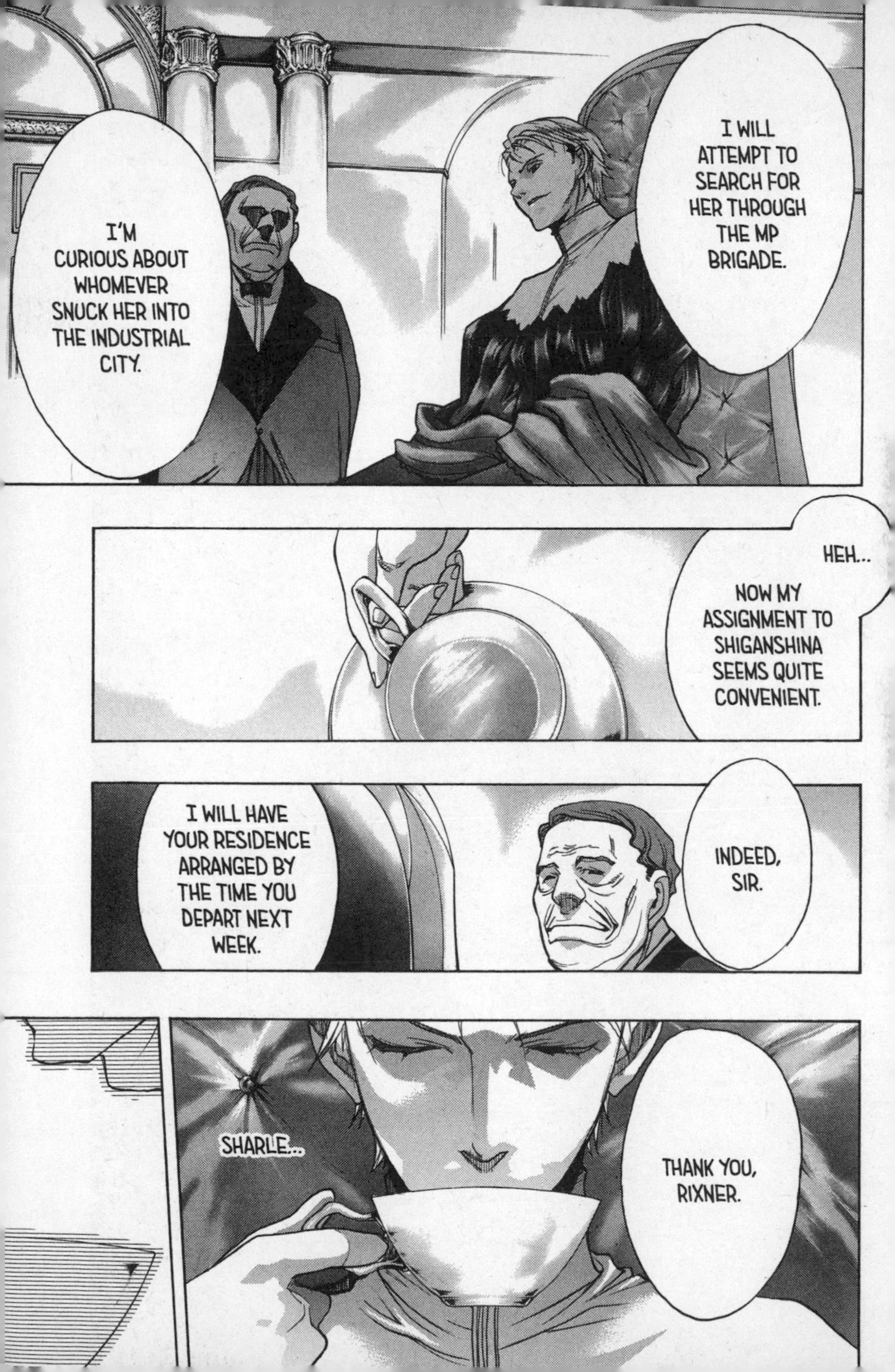
I WILL ATTEMPT TO SEARCH FOR HER THROUGH THE MP BRIGADE.
I'M CURIOUS ABOUT WHOMEVER SNUCK HER INTO THE INDUSTRIAL CITY.
HEH...
NOW MY ASSIGNMENT TO SHIGANSHINA SEEMS QUITE CONVENIENT.
INDEED, SIR.
I WILL HAVE YOUR RESIDENCE ARRANGED BY THE TIME YOU DEPART NEXT WEEK.
THANK YOU, RIXNER.
SHARLE...

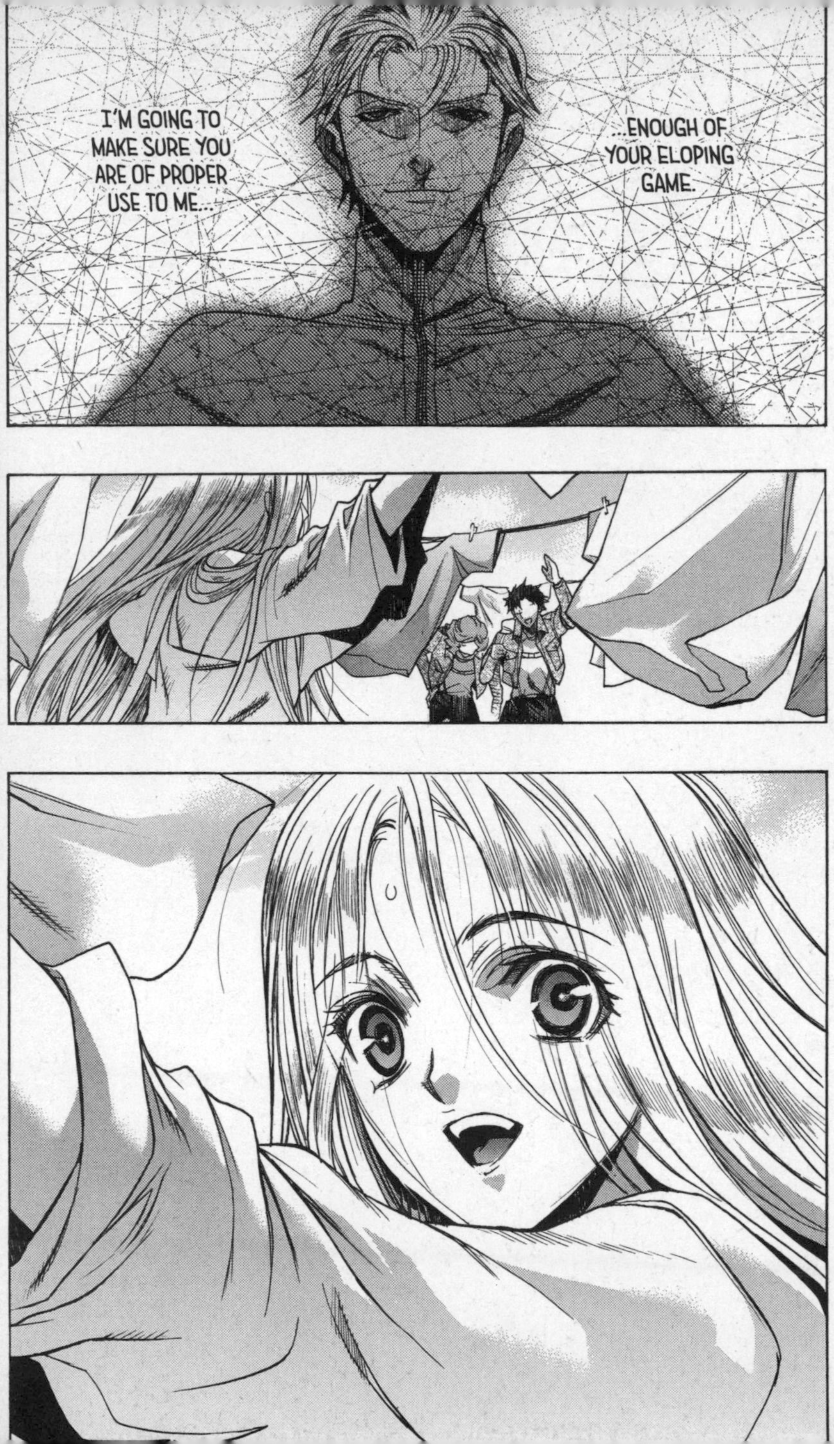
...ENOUGH OF YOUR ELOPING GAME.
I'M GOING TO MAKE SURE YOU ARE OF PROPER USE TO ME...

TO BE CONTINUED

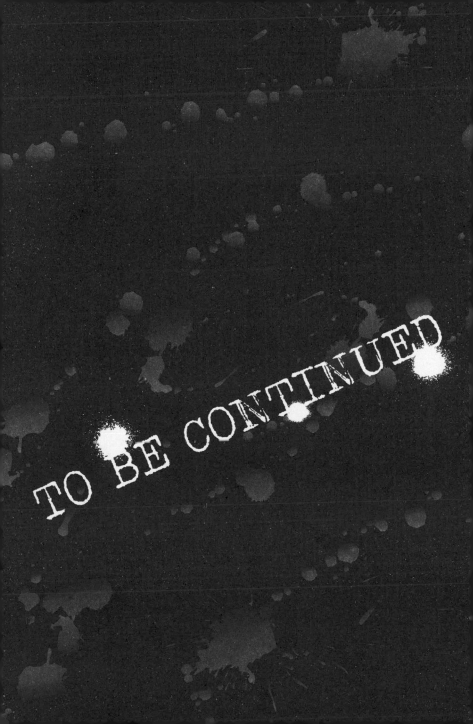

The Recruit's First Mission

A story from the viewpoint of a new military recruit charged with supporting the Survey Corps's retreat from atop Wall Maria, during the events of Chapter 9 in Volume 3.
Originally published: Bessatsu Shonen Magazine, January 2015 issue

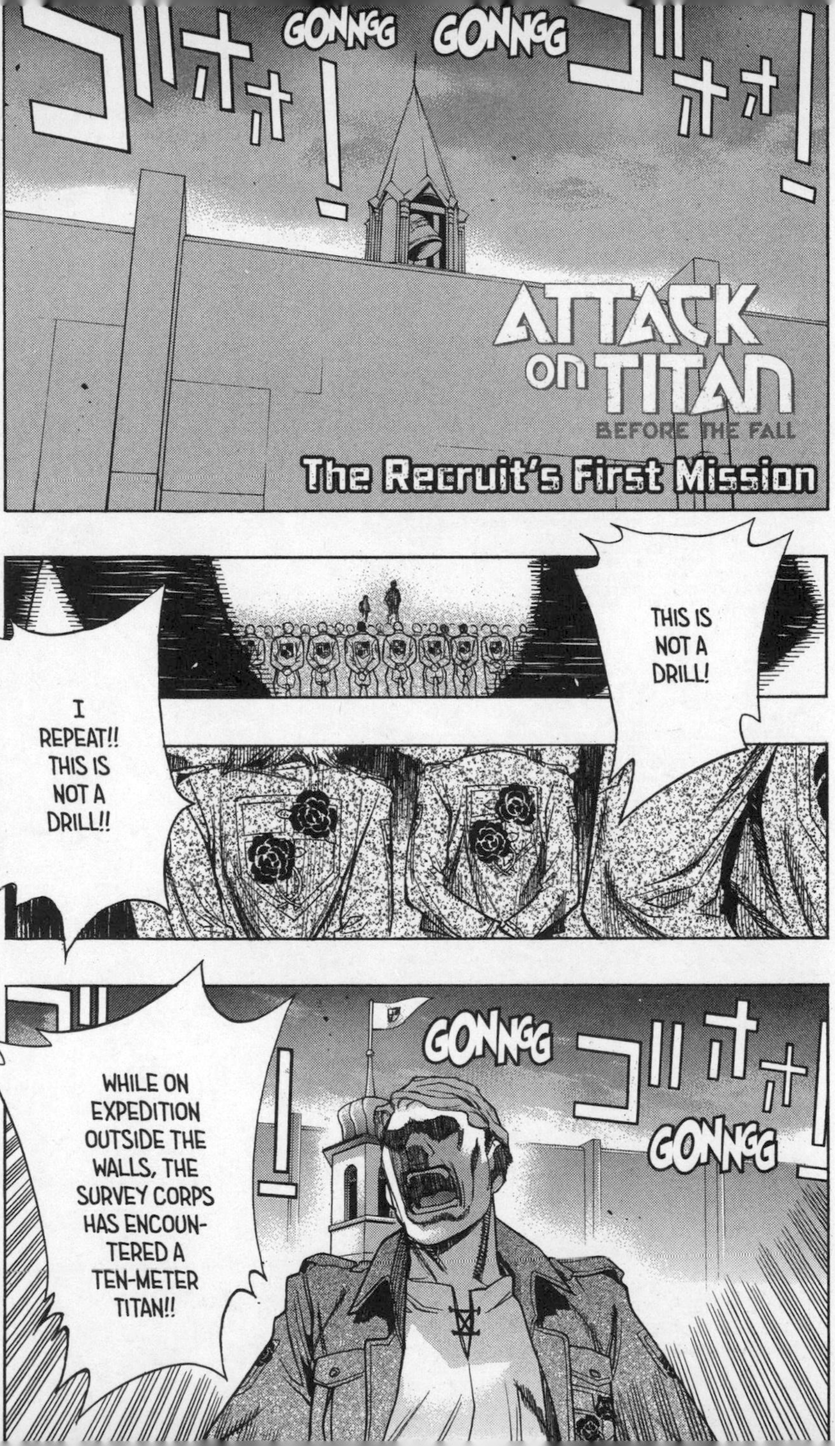
GONNGG
GONNGG
ATTACK on TITAN
BEFORE THE FALL
The Recruit's First Mission
THIS IS NOT A DRILL!
I REPEAT!! THIS IS NOT A DRILL!!
GONNGG
GONNGG
WHILE ON EXPEDITION OUTSIDE THE WALLS, THE SURVEY CORPS HAS ENCOUN-TERED A TEN-METER TITAN!!

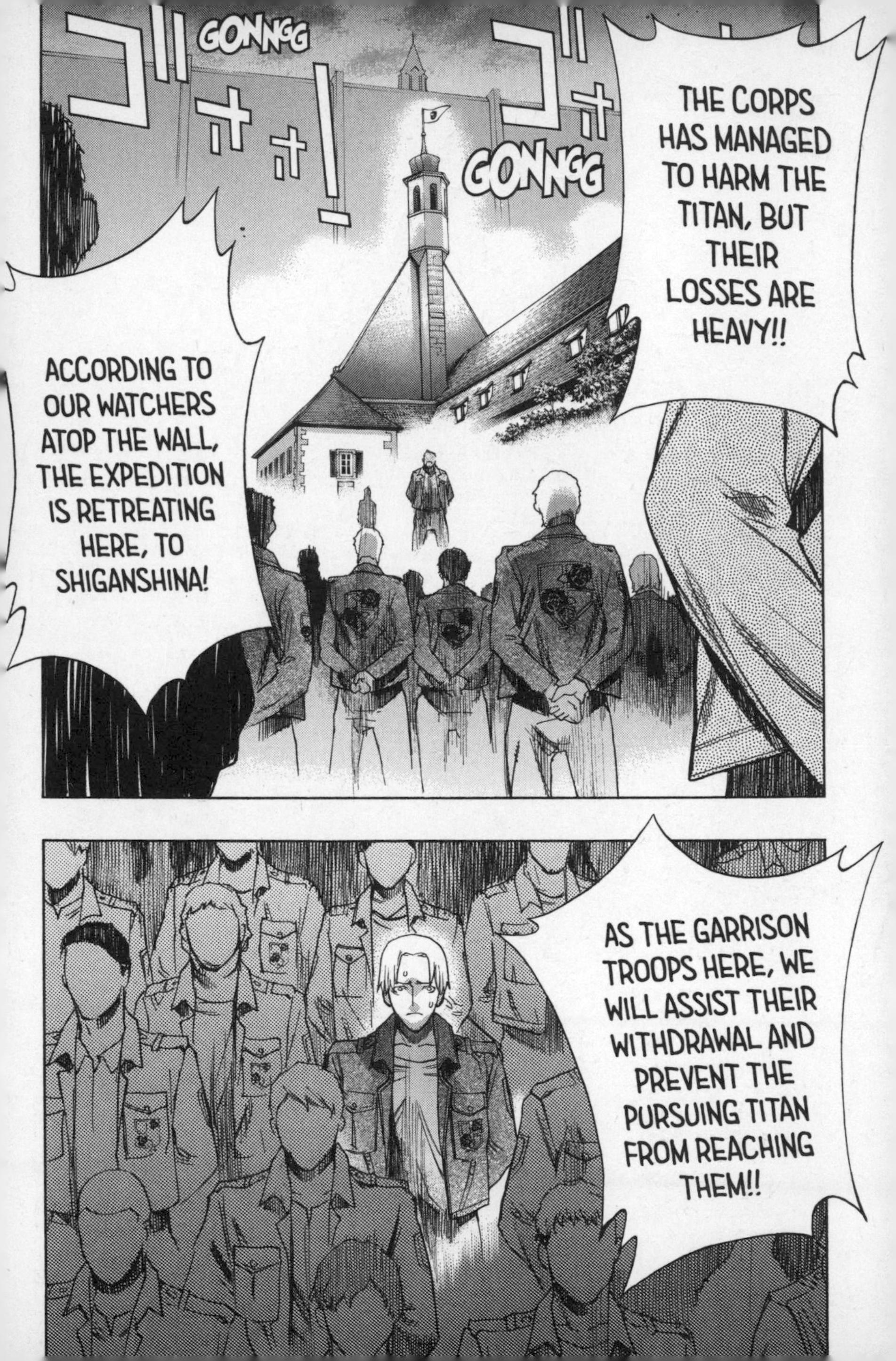
ゴォ
GONNGG
ゴォォ!
GONNGG
THE CORPS HAS MANAGED TO HARM THE TITAN, BUT THEIR LOSSES ARE HEAVY!!
ACCORDING TO OUR WATCHERS ATOP THE WALL, THE EXPEDITION IS RETREATING HERE, TO SHIGANSHINA!
AS THE GARRISON TROOPS HERE, WE WILL ASSIST THEIR WITHDRAWAL AND PREVENT THE PURSUING TITAN FROM REACHING THEM!!

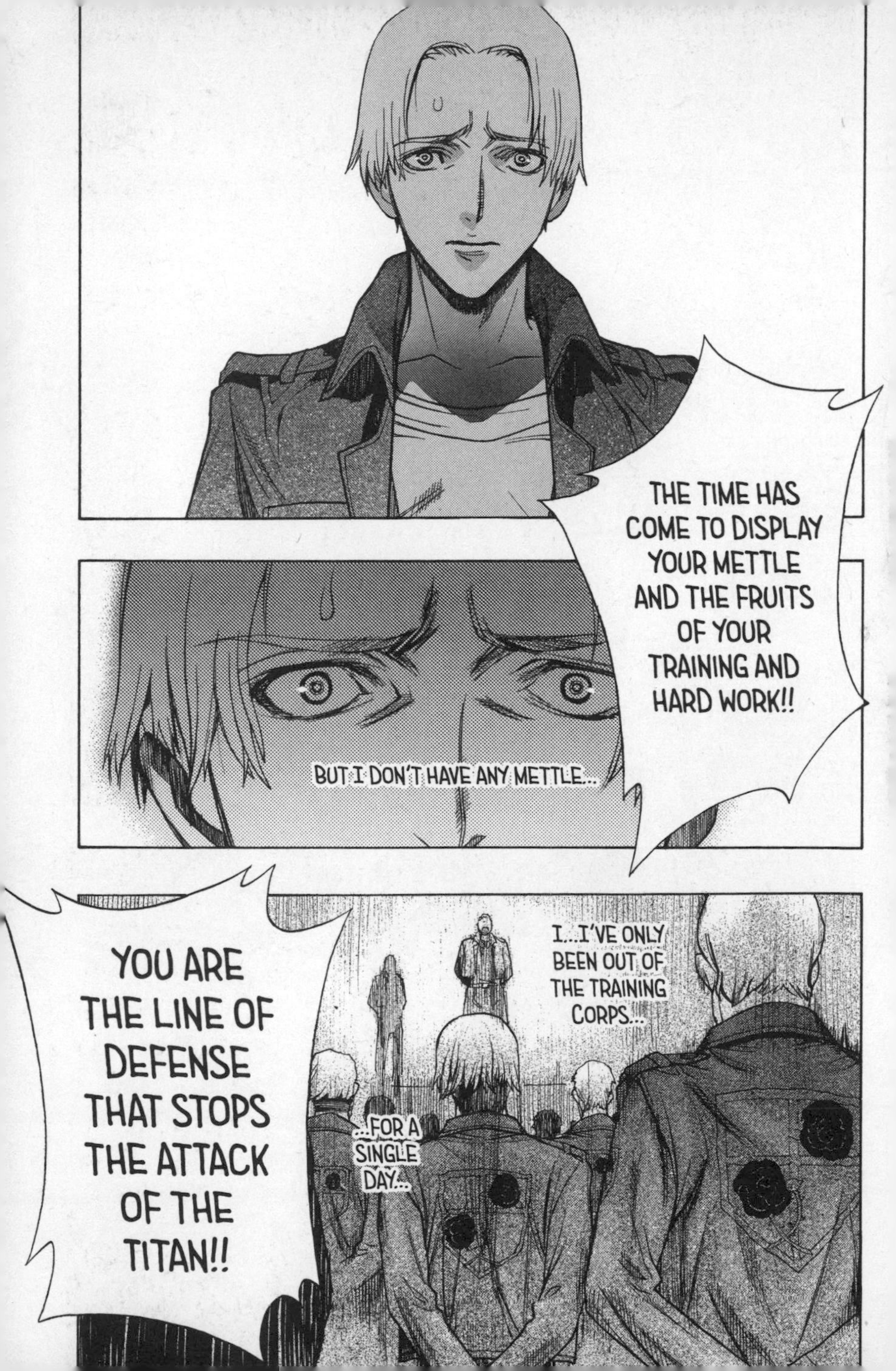
THE TIME HAS COME TO DISPLAY YOUR METTLE AND THE FRUITS OF YOUR TRAINING AND HARD WORK!!
BUT I DON'T HAVE ANY METTLE...
I...I'VE ONLY BEEN OUT OF THE TRAINING CORPS...
YOU ARE THE LINE OF DEFENSE THAT STOPS THE ATTACK OF THE TITAN!!
...FOR A SINGLE DAY...

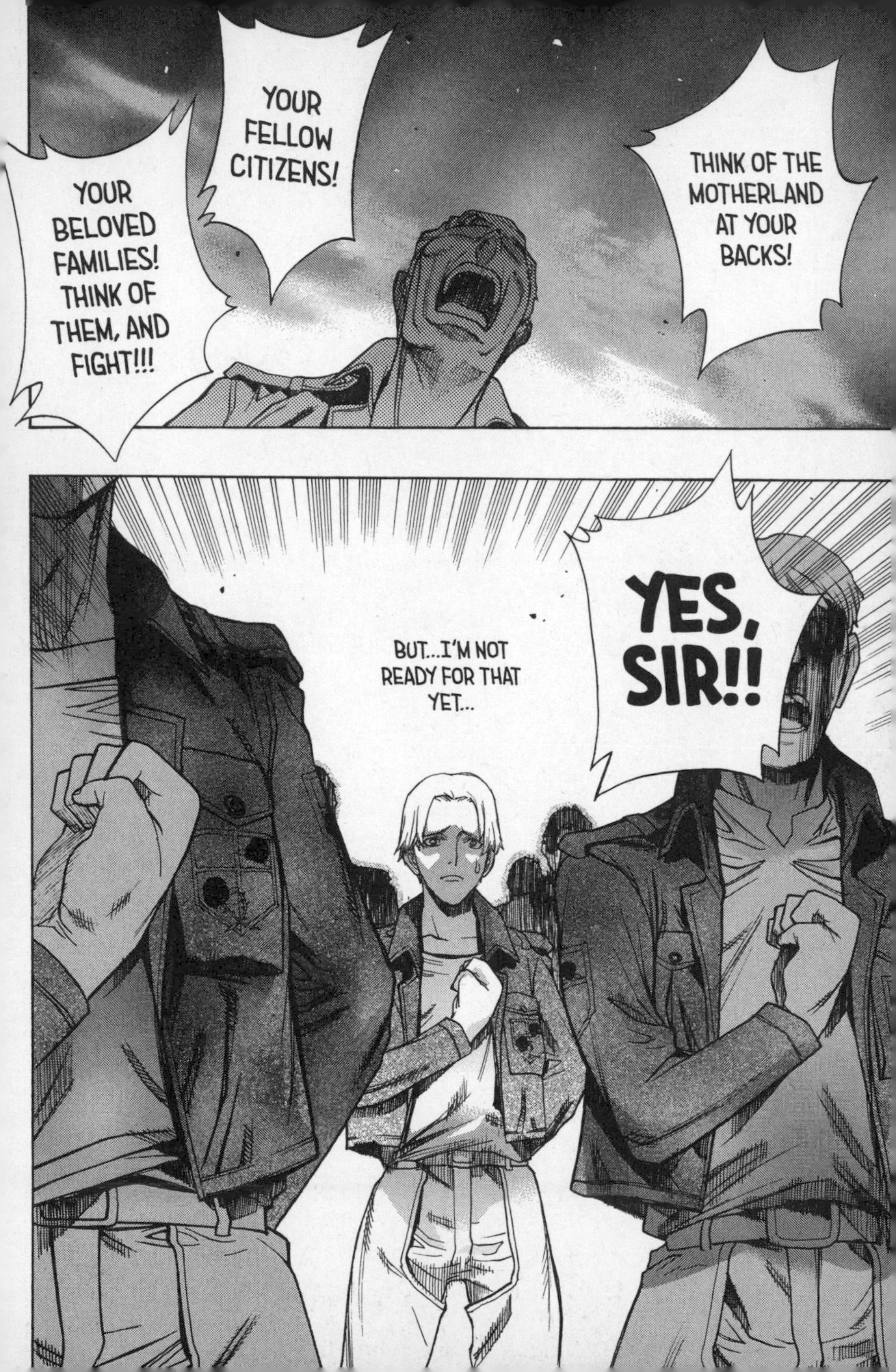
THINK OF THE MOTHERLAND AT YOUR BACKS!
YOUR FELLOW CITIZENS!
YOUR BELOVED FAMILIES! THINK OF THEM, AND FIGHT!!!
YES, SIR!!
BUT...I'M NOT READY FOR THAT YET...

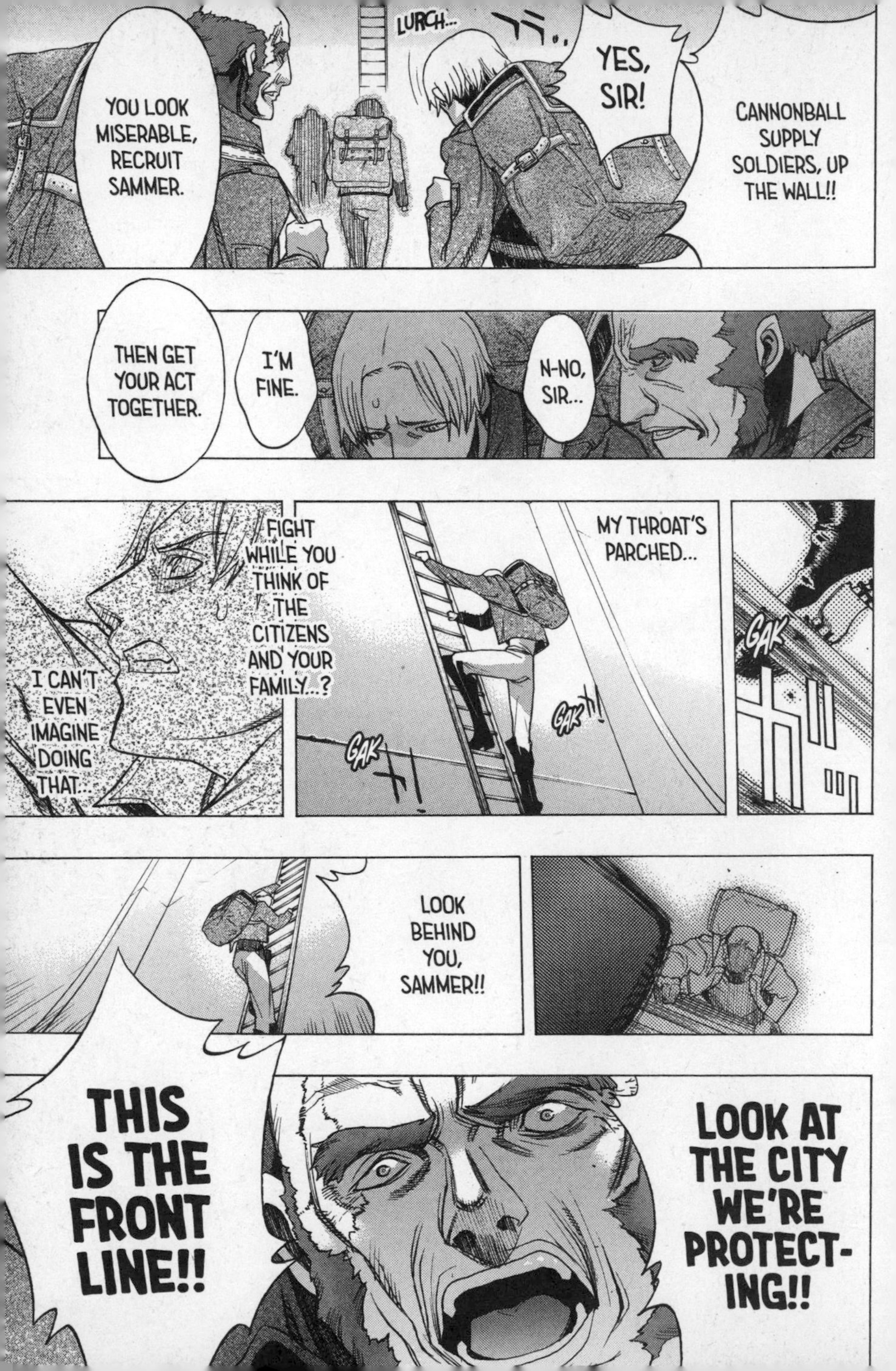
CANNONBALL SUPPLY SOLDIERS, UP THE WALL!!
YES, SIR!
LURCH...
YOU LOOK MISERABLE, RECRUIT SAMMER.
N-NO, SIR...
I'M FINE.
THEN GET YOUR ACT TOGETHER.
GAK
MY THROAT'S PARCHED...
GAK
GAK
FIGHT WHILE YOU THINK OF THE CITIZENS AND YOUR FAMILY...?
I CAN'T EVEN IMAGINE DOING THAT...
LOOK BEHIND YOU, SAMMER!!
LOOK AT THE CITY WE'RE PROTECTING!!
THIS IS THE FRONT LINE!!

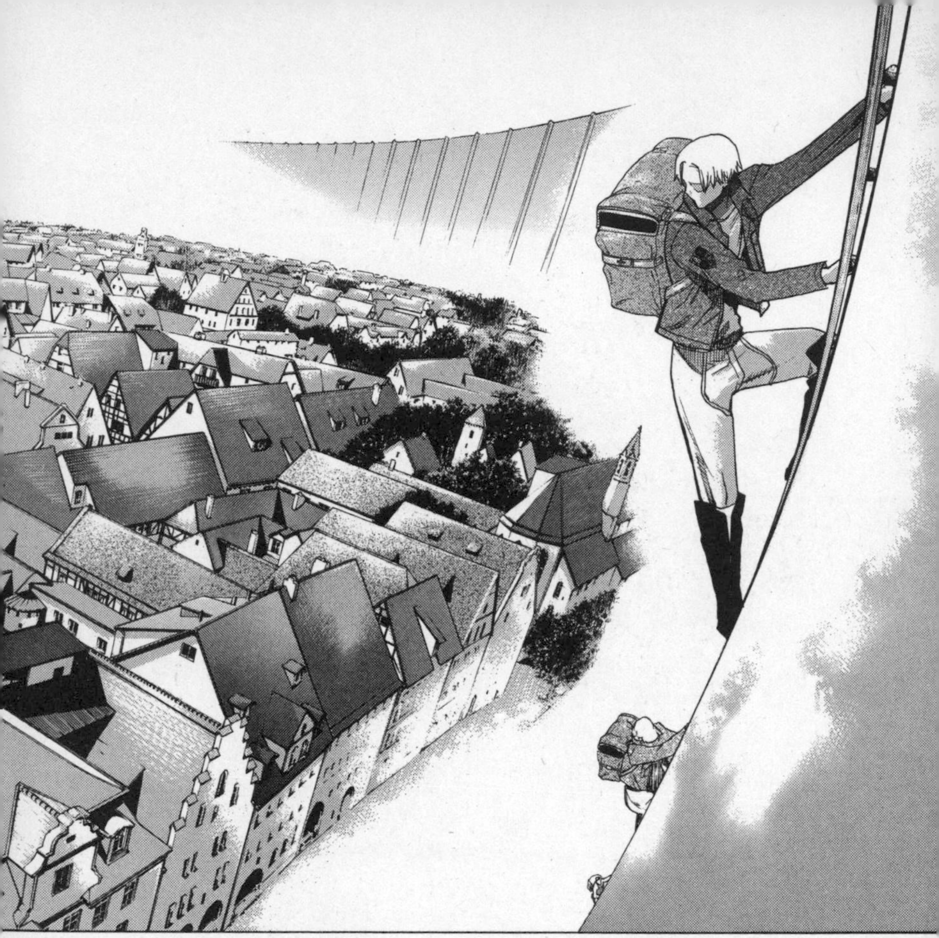
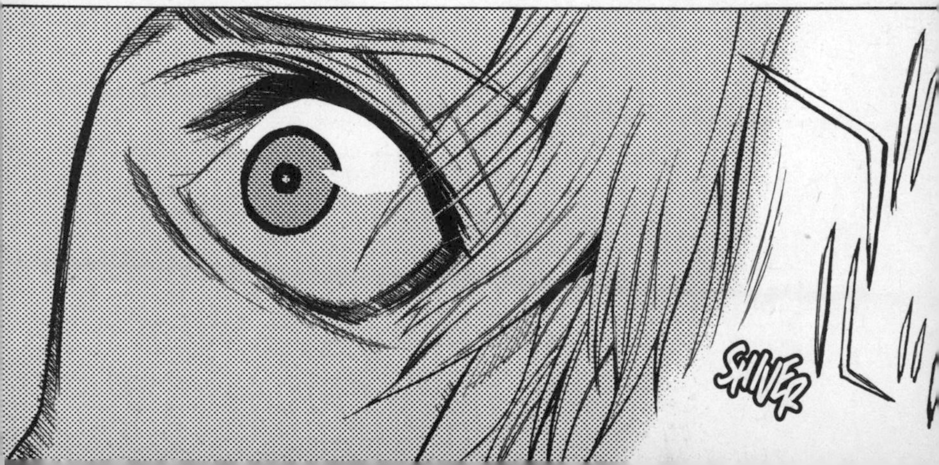
SHIVER

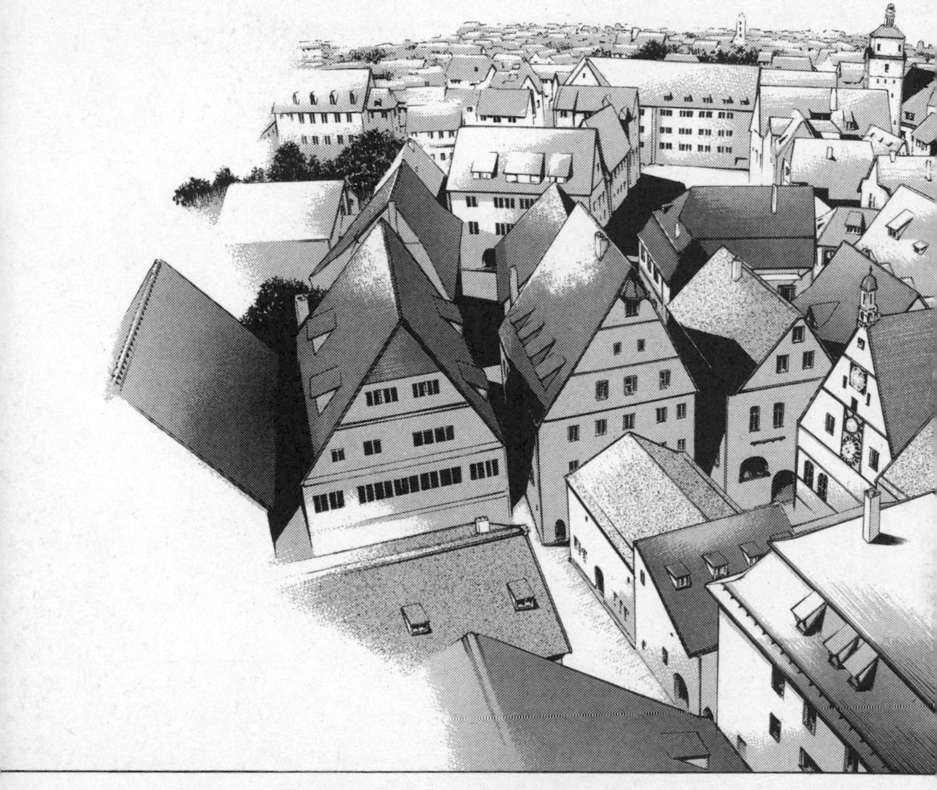
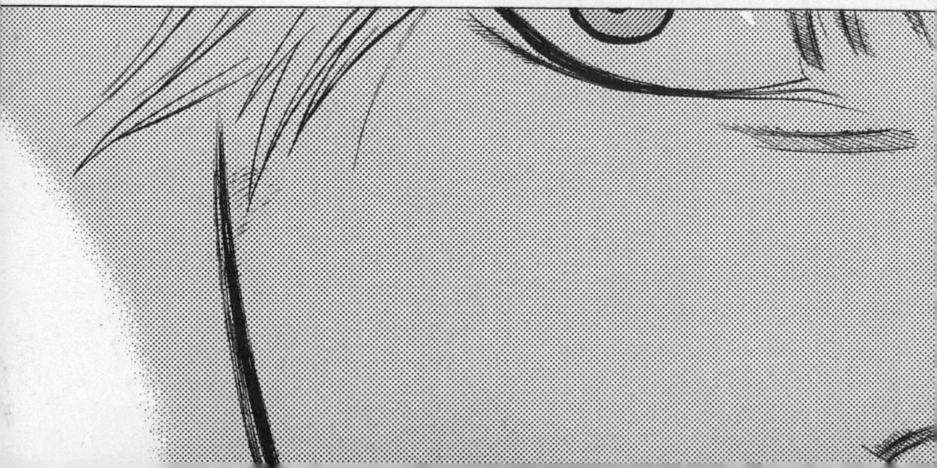

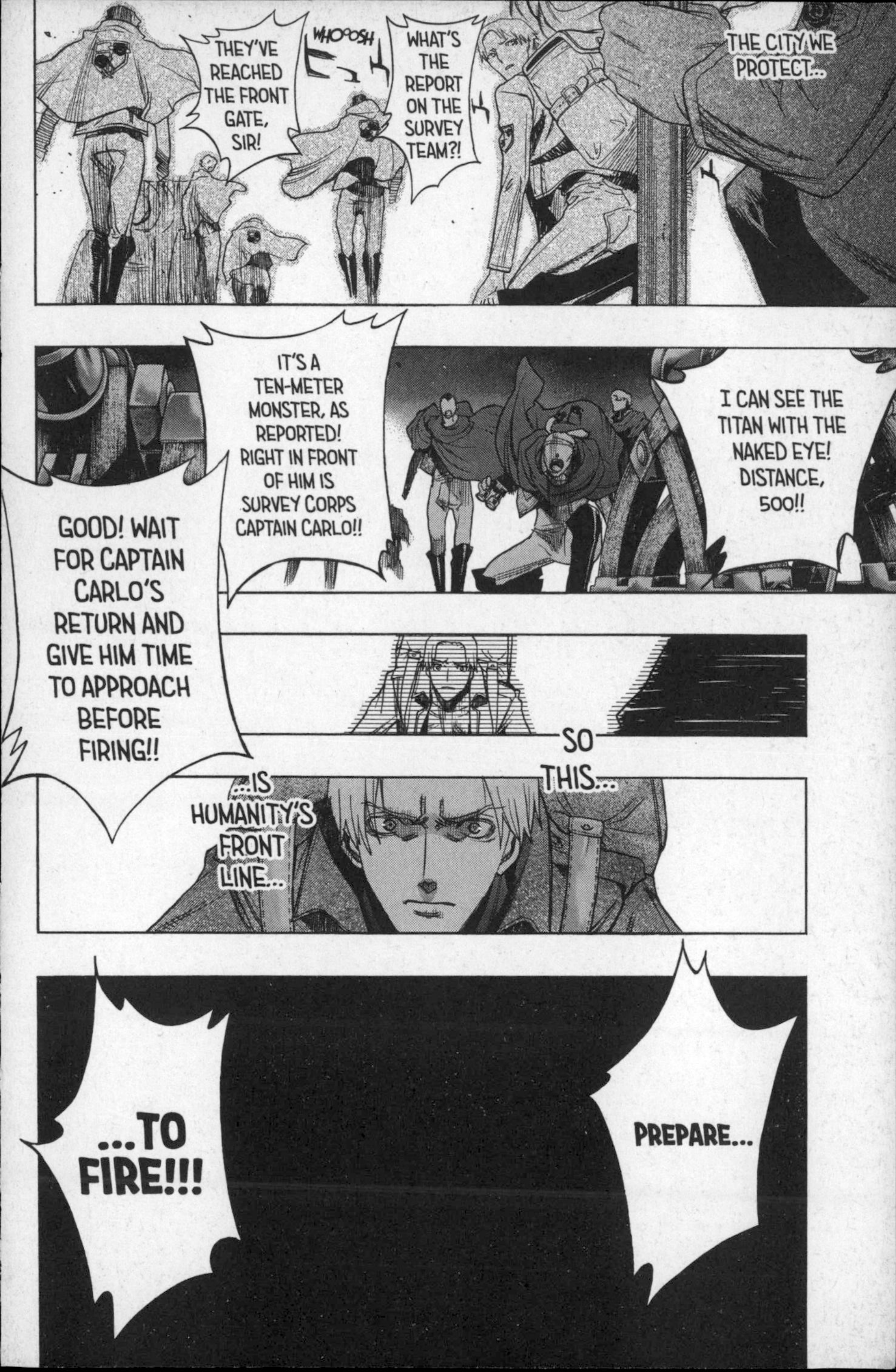
THE CITY WE PROTECT...
WHAT'S THE REPORT ON THE SURVEY TEAM?!
WHOOOSH
THEY'VE REACHED THE FRONT GATE, SIR!
I CAN SEE THE TITAN WITH THE NAKED EYE! DISTANCE, 500!!
IT'S A TEN-METER MONSTER, AS REPORTED! RIGHT IN FRONT OF HIM IS SURVEY CORPS CAPTAIN CARLO!!
GOOD! WAIT FOR CAPTAIN CARLO'S RETURN AND GIVE HIM TIME TO APPROACH BEFORE FIRING!!
SO THIS...
...IS HUMANITY'S FRONT LINE...
PREPARE...
...TO FIRE!!!

The Recruit's First Mission · End

The Girl Waiting in the Workshop

A story from the perspective of Sharle during the events of Volume 3, when she visited Captain Carlo of the Survey Corps and used his father Jorge's connections to reach Xenophon's workshop in the industrial city, where she waited for Kuklo's safe return.
Originally published: Bessatsu Shonen Magazine, May 2015 issue

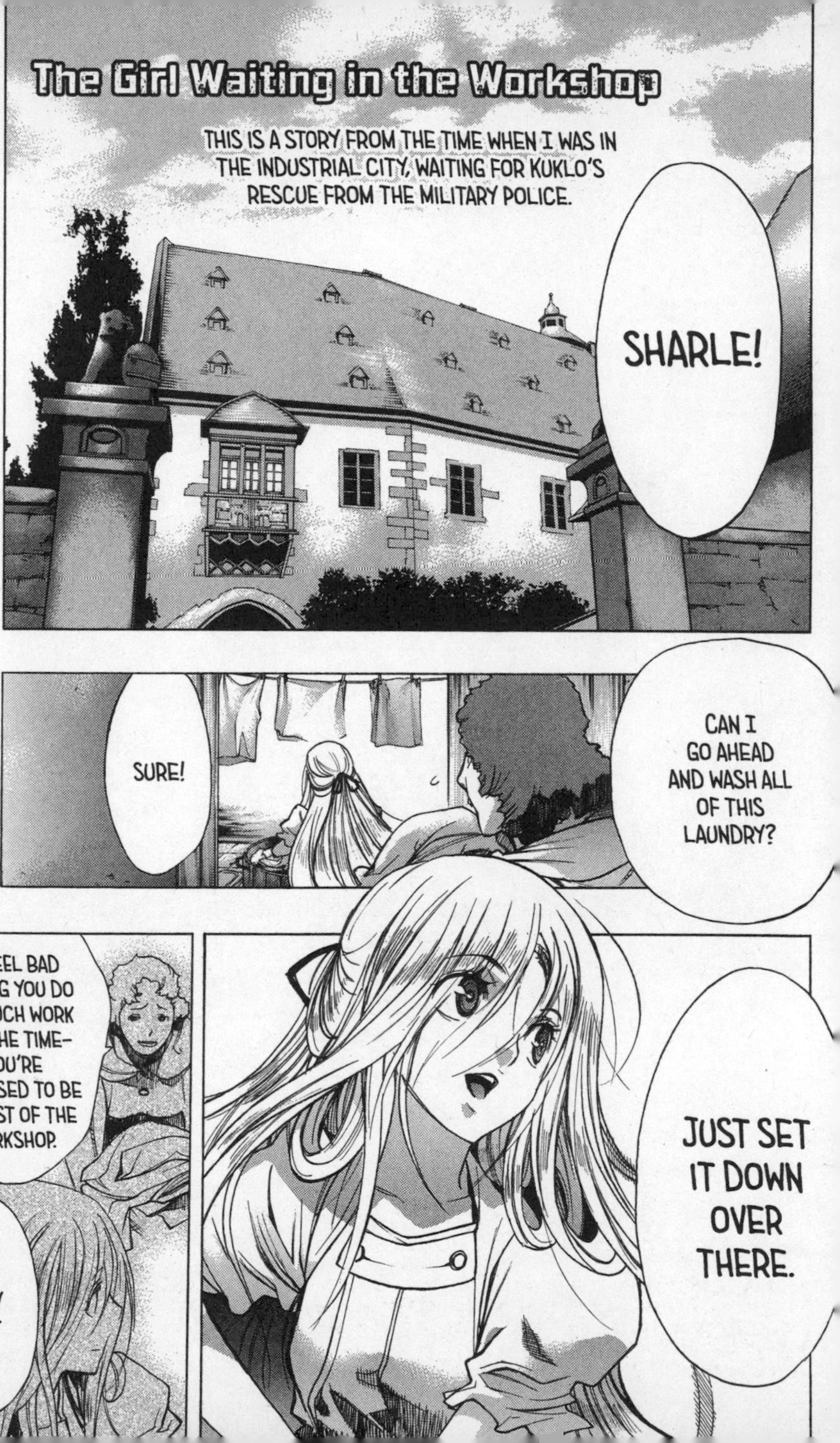
The Girl Waiting in the Workshop
THIS IS A STORY FROM THE TIME WHEN I WAS IN THE INDUSTRIAL CITY, WAITING FOR KUKLO'S RESCUE FROM THE MILITARY POLICE.
SHARLE!
CAN I GO AHEAD AND WASH ALL OF THIS LAUNDRY?
SURE!
JUST SET IT DOWN OVER THERE.
I FEEL BAD HAVING YOU DO SO MUCH WORK ALL THE TIME- YOU'RE SUPPOSED TO BE A GUEST OF THE WORKSHOP.
DON'T WORRY ABOUT IT.

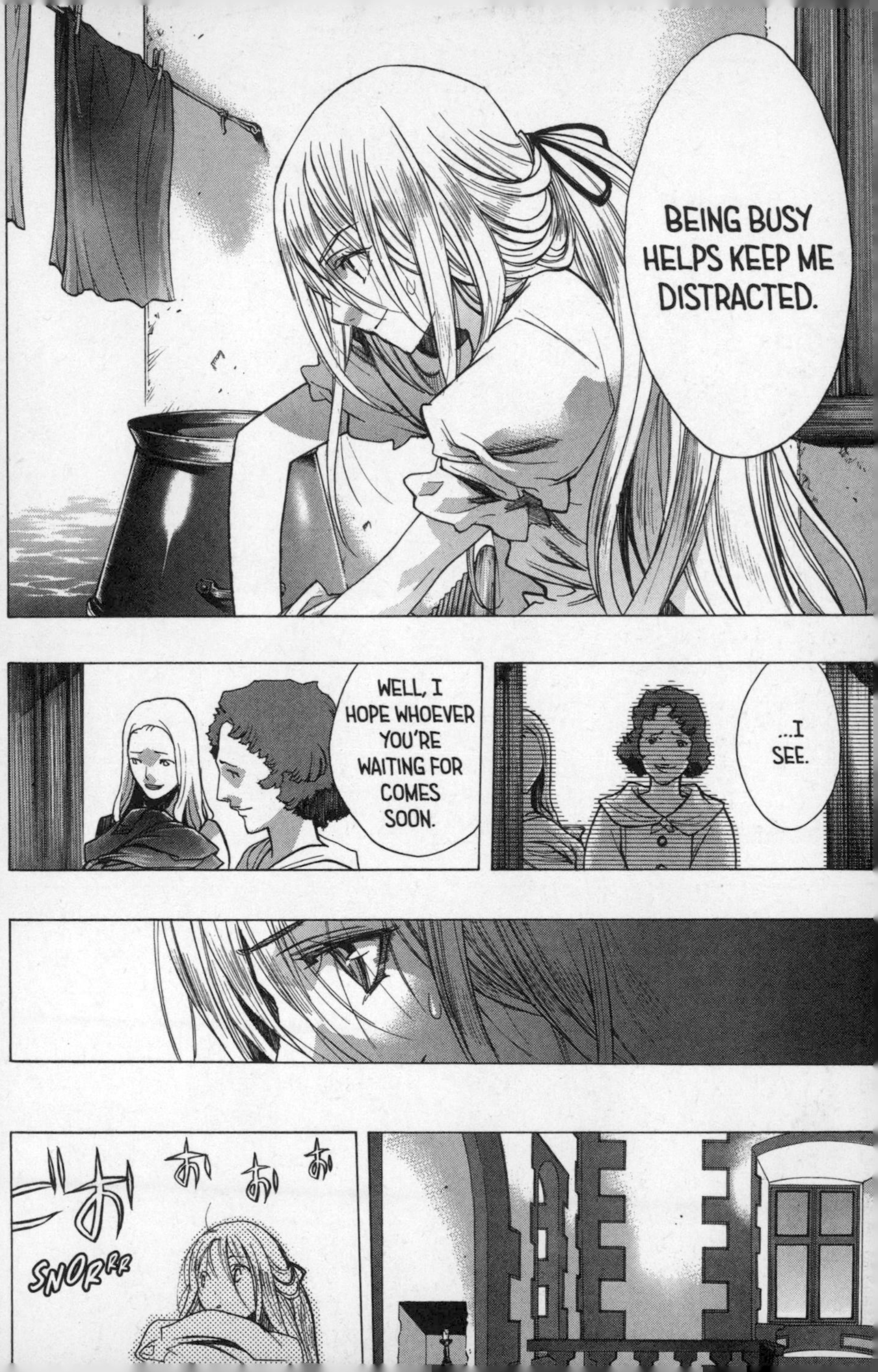
BEING BUSY HELPS KEEP ME DISTRACTED.
...I SEE.
WELL, I HOPE WHOEVER YOU'RE WAITING FOR COMES SOON.
ごおおおお
SNORRR

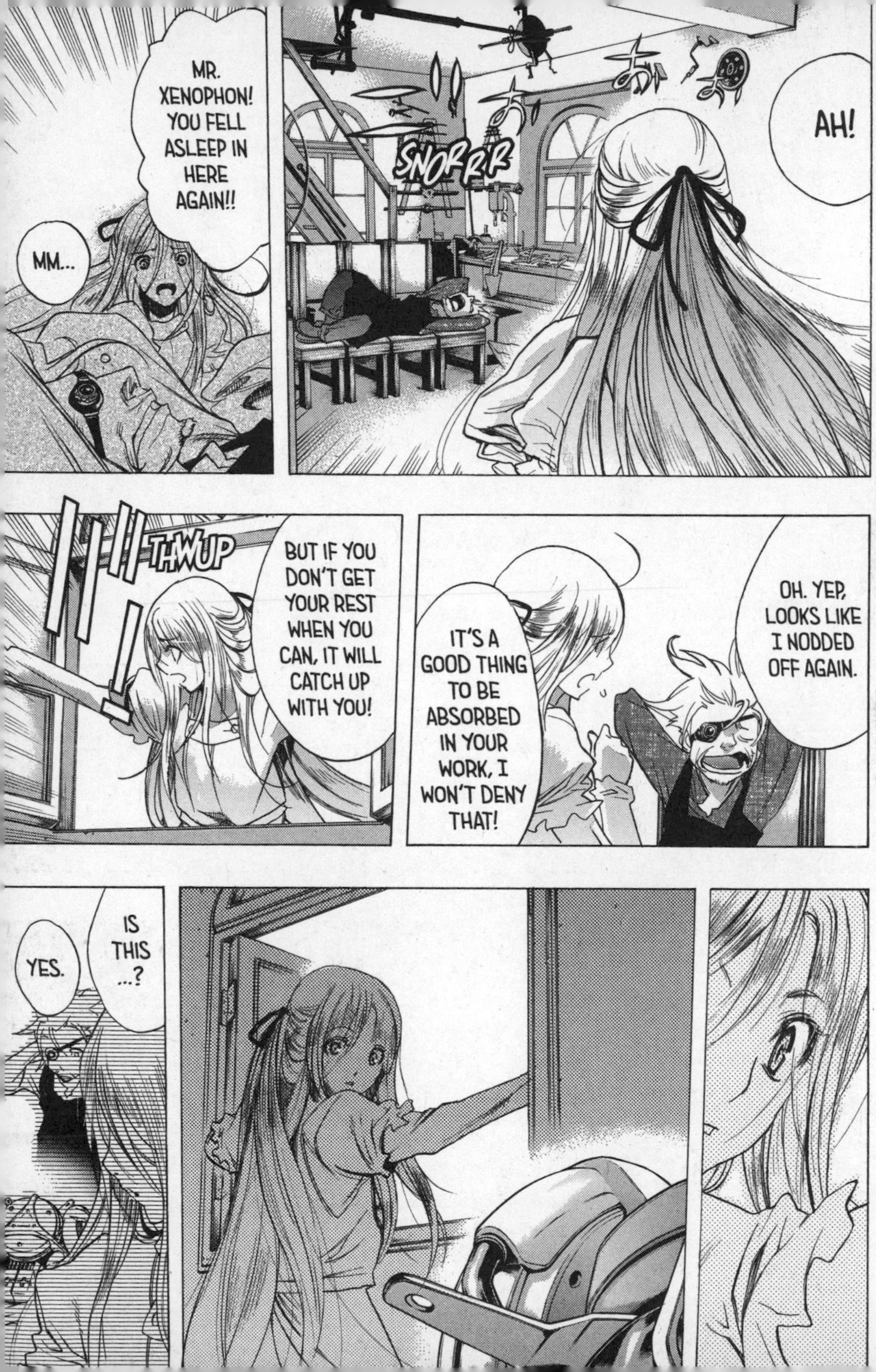
AH!
SNORRR
MR. XENOPHON! YOU FELL ASLEEP IN HERE AGAIN!!
MM...
OH. YEP, LOOKS LIKE I NODDED OFF AGAIN.
IT'S A GOOD THING TO BE ABSORBED IN YOUR WORK, I WON'T DENY THAT!
THWUP
BUT IF YOU DON'T GET YOUR REST WHEN YOU CAN, IT WILL CATCH UP WITH YOU!
IS THIS ...?
YES.

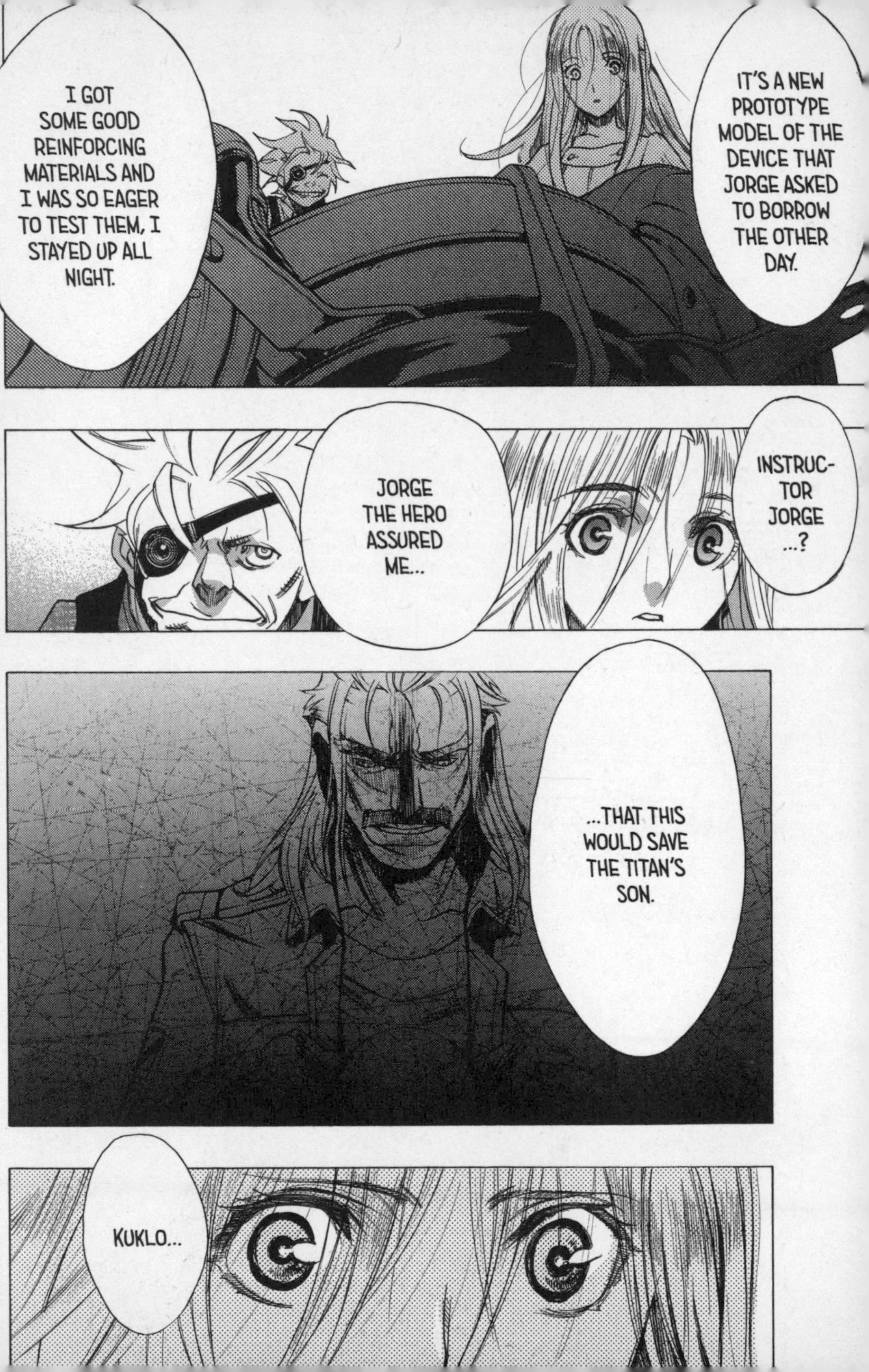
IT'S A NEW PROTOTYPE MODEL OF THE DEVICE THAT JORGE ASKED TO BORROW THE OTHER DAY.
I GOT SOME GOOD REINFORCING MATERIALS AND I WAS SO EAGER TO TEST THEM, I STAYED UP ALL NIGHT.
INSTRUC-TOR JORGE ...?
JORGE THE HERO ASSURED ME...
...THAT THIS WOULD SAVE THE TITAN'S SON.
KUKLO...

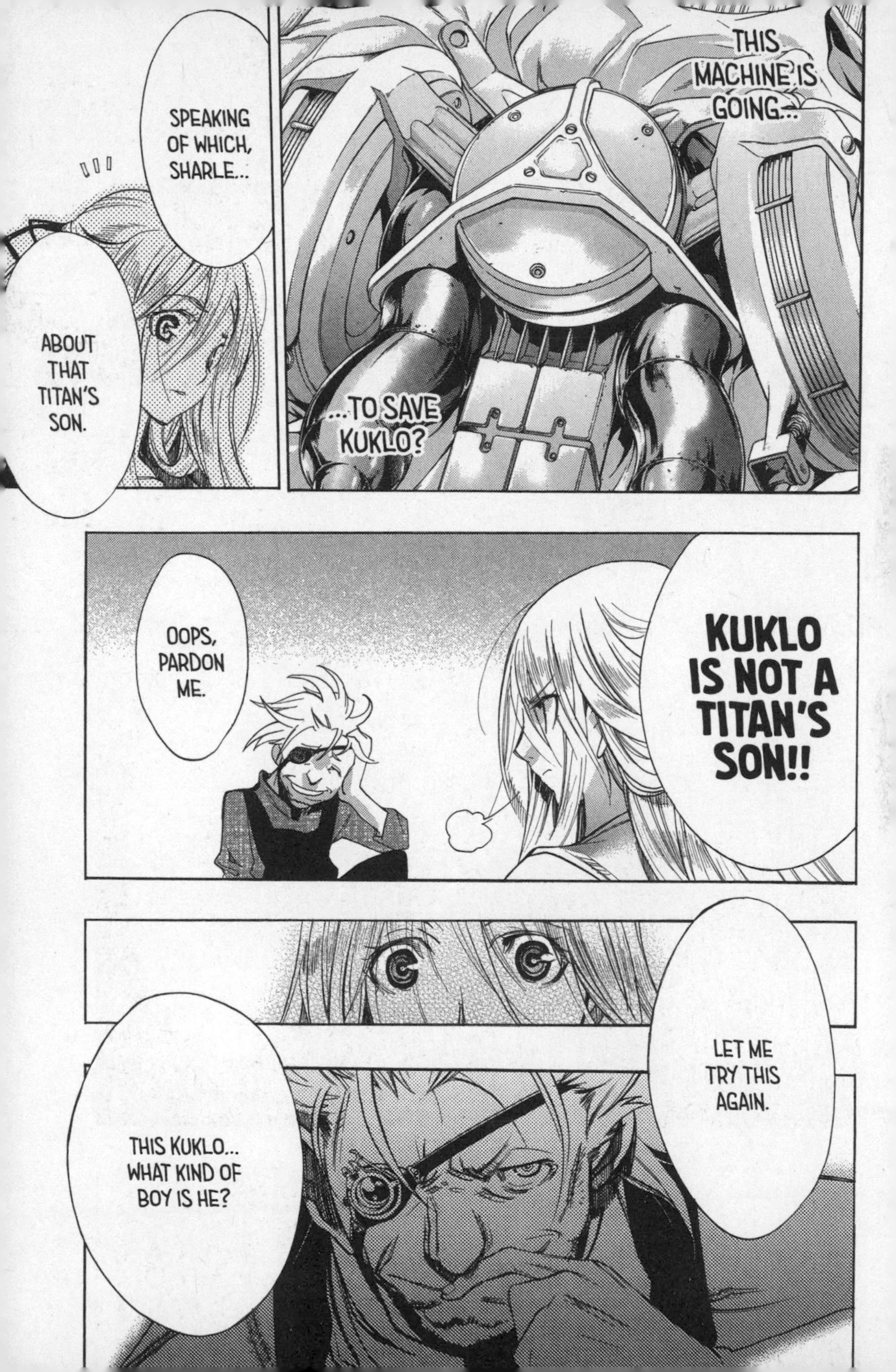
THIS MACHINE IS GOING...
...TO SAVE KUKLO?
SPEAKING OF WHICH, SHARLE...
ABOUT THAT TITAN'S SON.
KUKLO IS NOT A TITAN'S SON!!
OOPS, PARDON ME.
LET ME TRY THIS AGAIN.
THIS KUKLO... WHAT KIND OF BOY IS HE?

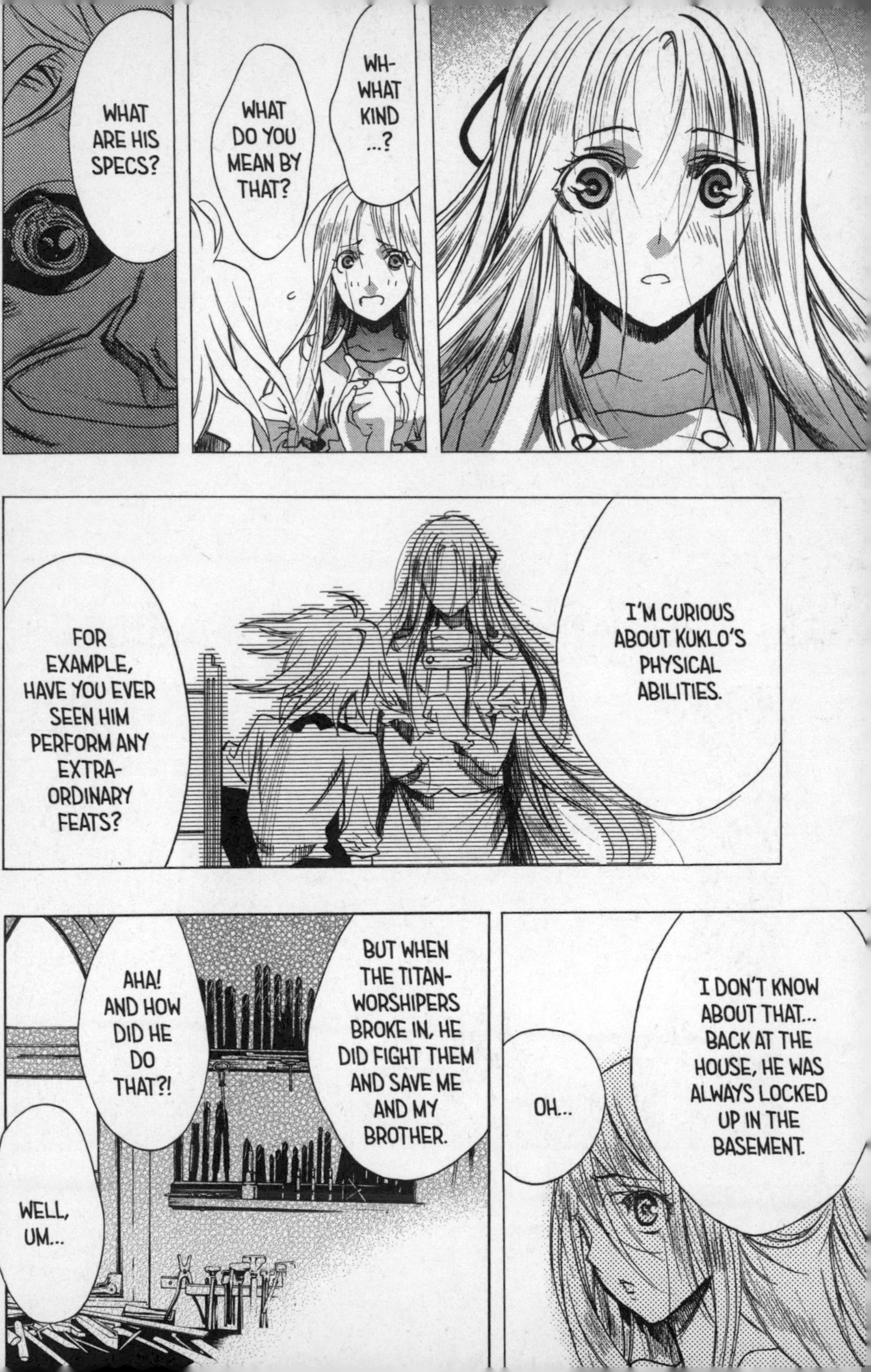
WH- WHAT KIND ...?
WHAT DO YOU MEAN BY THAT?
WHAT ARE HIS SPECS?
I'M CURIOUS ABOUT KUKLO'S PHYSICAL ABILITIES.
FOR EXAMPLE, HAVE YOU EVER SEEN HIM PERFORM ANY EXTRA-ORDINARY FEATS?
I DON'T KNOW ABOUT THAT... BACK AT THE HOUSE, HE WAS ALWAYS LOCKED UP IN THE BASEMENT.
OH...
BUT WHEN THE TITAN-WORSHIPERS BROKE IN, HE DID FIGHT THEM AND SAVE ME AND MY BROTHER.
AHA! AND HOW DID HE DO THAT?!
WELL, UM...

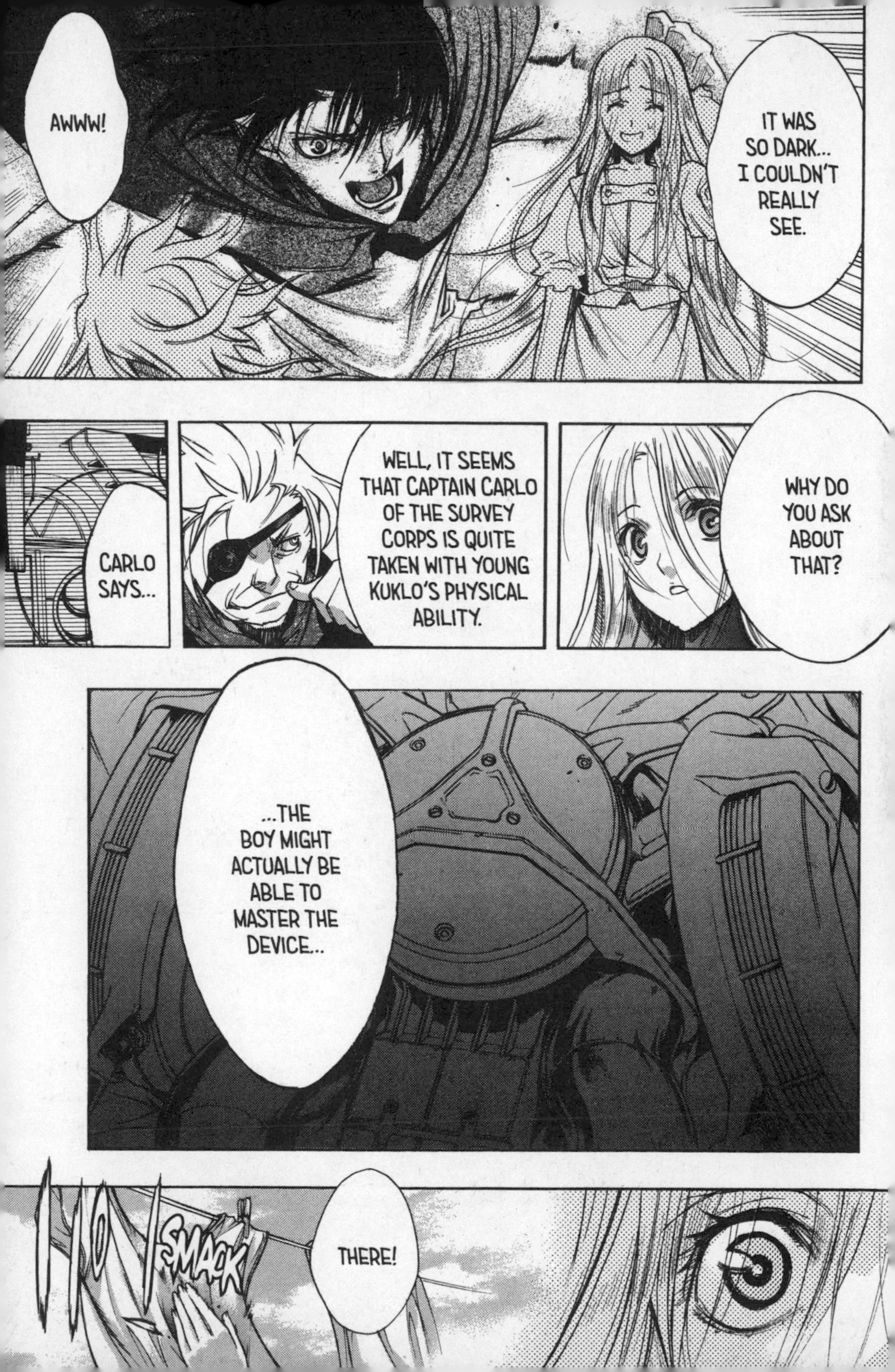
IT WAS SO DARK... I COULDN'T REALLY SEE.
AWWW!
WHY DO YOU ASK ABOUT THAT?
WELL, IT SEEMS THAT CAPTAIN CARLO OF THE SURVEY CORPS IS QUITE TAKEN WITH YOUNG KUKLO'S PHYSICAL ABILITY.
CARLO SAYS...
...THE BOY MIGHT ACTUALLY BE ABLE TO MASTER THE DEVICE...
THERE!
SMACK

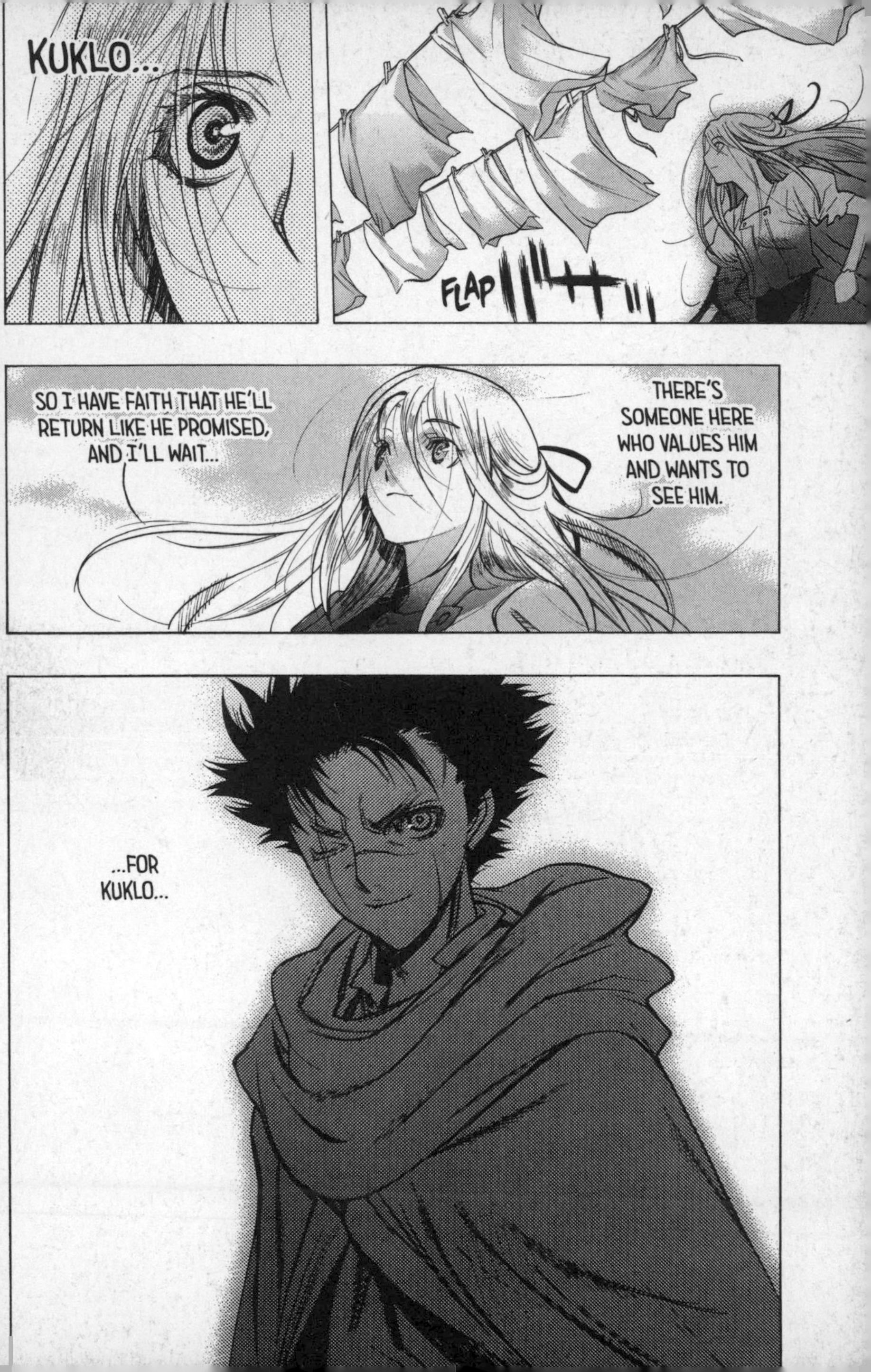
FLAP
KUKLO...
THERE'S SOMEONE HERE WHO VALUES HIM AND WANTS TO SEE HIM.
SO I HAVE FAITH THAT HE'LL RETURN LIKE HE PROMISED, AND I'LL WAIT...
...FOR KUKLO...

The Girl Waiting in the Workshop · End